URBAN HOUSING POLICY

URBAN HOUSING POLICY

William G. Grigsby
Department of City and Regional Planning
The University of Pennsylvania, Philadelphia

Louis Rosenburg
The Planning Exchange, Glasgow, Scotland

APS Publications, Inc., New York, N.Y.

**Center for Urban Policy Research -
Rutgers University**

APS Publications, Inc.
150 Fifth Avenue
New York, N.Y. 10011

Center for Urban Policy Research—Rutgers University
New Brunswick, N.J. 18903

Library of Congress Cataloging in Publication Data

Grigsby, William G.   1927–
    Urban housing policy.

    Includes bibliographical references and index.
    1. Housing—United States.   2. Housing –
Baltimore.   I. Rosenburg, Louis, joint author.
II. Title.
HD7293.G73   301.5'4   75-14296
ISBN 0-87988-012-0

Printed in the United States

Contents

Preface

This volume is the outgrowth of a larger inquiry financed by the Office of Economic Opportunity, with supplemental funding provided by the Life Insurance Association of America, through the Real Estate Research Program of the University of California, Los Angeles. Portions of this book were published in mimeograph form in 1971 under the title *Housing and Poverty*.* The earlier study, which focused exclusively on Baltimore, Maryland, sought to redirect prevailing approaches to housing problems by: (1) expanding the concept of a housing-deprived population to include several types of shelter problems that are usually ignored in policy discussions; (2) placing the exploration of housing problems within a larger policy framework, one which stresses the importance of multiple goals and conflicting interest groups; (3) demonstrating the need to shift public programs away from such heavy concentration on new-construction subsidies and toward more emphasis on preserving the existing stock; and (4) establishing the importance of a number of factors other than low income in explaining the decay of inner-city neighborhoods.

In the years subsequent to the publication of *Housing and Poverty* it has been gratifying to see many of our conclusions confirmed by later studies. Nevertheless, our original focus was too narrow to provide the policy guidance that is being sought today. In confining our attention exclusively to Baltimore, we failed to suggest differences between that city and newer and smaller communities. In addition, we dwelt too lightly on macro aspects of housing market dynamics. Also, of course, we had nothing at all to say about programs

*William G. Grigsby, Louis Rosenburg, Michael Stegman, and James Taylor, *Housing and Poverty,* Institute for Environmental Studies, University of Pennsylvania, April 1971.

and proposals which have come to the forefront since 1970, particularly housing allowances, revenue sharing, urban homesteading, and housing allocation plans.

The present volume tries to fill these gaps. Five new chapters have been added, two have been deleted, and the remaining ones have been extensively re-written. Still excluded from our examination of housing issues are several areas of widespread concern which have been extensively covered by others, most notably, the residential construction industry, land development controls, real estate taxation, the emergence of state housing agencies, and recent efforts to increase the efficiency of mortgage markets. We hope, nevertheless, that despite our lack of comprehensiveness, this volume will make some small contribution to the search for solutions to urban housing problems.

The study is the product of a group effort, and several persons besides the authors made important contributions which we should like to mention. Michael Stegman directed our survey of inner-city investors and drafted major portions of Chapter 9. James Taylor designed the survey of housing interest groups and drafted Chapter 14. Homer Favor and Morton Baratz provided over-all guidance, as well as many specific suggestions. Appendix A was written by Gordon Liechty, who together with Sue Moyerman and Barbara Rosenberg helped to design the questionnaires for the surveys of Baltimore households. Christy Emerson and Bernard Spector analyzed the performance of the Philadelphia Housing Development Corporation as it might relate to the situation in other cities. Spector also prepared extensive background memoranda for Chapter 13 and developed the initial version of our limited-partnership proposal. Milton Hollander and Joseph Azola developed the basic design for the survey of residential structures, and Hollander conducted most of the inspections in the inner city. Brenda Davies coordinated the survey and assisted with the inspections. William McNeill participated with Stegman and Grigsby in the interviews of inner-city investors and helped in the preparation of Chapter 9. The first household survey was conducted by Audits and Surveys, Inc. Valuable assistance in making the data from the survey usable was provided by Peter Kuner, William McDonnell, Patricia Hammond, Pao-Yu Chou, Warren Howze, and Steven Simkin. The second household survey was conducted by Sydney Hollander and Associates. Robert Pasternak, Marilee Considine, and Margaret Beatty from that organization were particularly helpful to us during this part of the study.

A number of persons contributed ideas and constructive criticism. We would like to mention in particular Margery Baker, Ernest M. Fisher, Oliver Jones, Morton Lustig, Katherine Martini, Chester Rapkin, Louis Singer, Stanely Sugar-man, and David Wallace.

Uncounted memoranda and rough drafts were typed and distributed by Judy Bergman, Laura Kessler, Patricia Schaefer, Doris Smith, and Florence Stone.

We save for the last our expression of gratitude to the many persons in Baltimore whose warmth and friendliness, advice and assistance, and unreserved cooperation made the study an unforgettable experience. Although we were strangers intruding on the time of individuals who had a much more intimate grasp of various parts of Baltimore's housing problem that we did, at no time were we turned away or made to feel unwelcome, however skeptically our efforts may have been viewed. It would be foolish to attempt to name everyone in the community who helped us. The list would be so long as to be meaningless. We would like to observe, though, that Baltimore is indeed the "No Mean City" that it has been characterized to be. It is that spirit which must be continuously nurtured if the problems of urban decay and poverty are ever to be solved.

CHAPTER 1

Introduction

For as long as statistics record and for an even longer time in the memory of man, housing conditions in the United States have been improving. More because of rising incomes than housing programs, American families have experienced a steady upgrading in the quality and quantity of shelter and associated services. Housing that only the rich once enjoyed is commonplace today; by today's standards, most of the population was ill housed at the turn of the century.

Midst this rise, inadequate living accommodations for a portion of the population have stubbornly persisted. In part, this is simply due to the fact that perceptions of what is adequate housing move apace with incomes, making substandard housing for some a perpetual inevitability. Elastic standards are an expression of our society's concern that increments to income and wealth be broadly distributed. In addition, however, many families endure housing deprivations which are severe even with respect to the norms of earlier years.

During the past decade, and especially in the last five years, significant changes in housing conditions, policies, and programs have occurred. These changes have reshaped large parts of the housing market and substantially altered traditional issues and concerns about shelter problems in urban areas. The most significant and unexpected break with the past has been the huge increase in subsidized housing production beginning in 1966. From the passage of the Housing Act of 1937 through the end of the first four years of the Kennedy-Johnson Administrations 28 years later, public housing and related subsidy programs never accounted for more than 5% of housing starts and were frequently in danger of annihilation by hostile Congresses. During President Johnson's second term in office, subsidized production gradually became more important, rising to 10% of total starts. Then during the first four years of the Nixon Administration, it really blossomed forth. Under programs inherited from the Democrats, federally assisted starts jumped to over one-quarter of total residential construction, and in less than four years equalled the aggregate production record of the previous 32. Even though there are now second thoughts about this achievement, resulting in sharp curtailment of activity, retrenchment to the position of earlier years is improbable.

Somewhat less sudden but no less dramatic has been the rise in mobile-home production. One-fifth of all housing starts, and the bulk of low-priced construction, are now accounted for by a type of dwelling unit that was not even recognized as permanent housing in 1960. In recent years, between 40% and 50% of starts have been in the form of mobile homes and subsidized conventional production. In a growing economy, the volume of unsubsidized conventional production has not increased for more than 20 years.

Yet another former tie has been severed by the Civil Rights Act of 1968 which, at least on paper, gives blacks and other minorities a degree of equality in the housing market that informed observers had previously thought would be years in coming. Despite inadequate funds for enforcement of the Act, erosion of discriminatory barriers seems to have been accelerating since the legislation came into being.

Along with the above changes, we have witnessed a gradual dismantling of exclusionary zoning barriers, increasing emphasis on planned large-scale residential development, and expansion of consumer rights in the real estate market. With all of this forward movement, one would expect housing problems to be rapidly diminishing. Not all of the movement, however, has been forward. Construction costs, land prices, and financing charges have risen so sharply that a smaller proportion of the population can afford newly built dwellings today than in 1965 (1). Just as disturbing, mounting evidence indicates that the long-term upward trend in housing conditions has leveled off and, in places, been reversed. The number of low-income families is no longer declining; the shelter problems of these families have either not improved or become worse, and their neighborhood environments are deteriorating. Non-low-income families residing in these same neighborhoods have suffered to an almost equal degree. Although the word "crisis" has been so overused and so inaptly used in describing various aspects of the urban condition that it no longer conveys its intended sense of urgency, it is a word which comes close to defining the present housing situation of the poor and the black in a number of cities (2). Such a situation, occurring as it has in the face of generally rising incomes and expanding federal social programs, is but one piece of evidence, albeit a dramatic one, that the relationship of housing efforts and objectives to the larger problems of poverty and urban development are not well understood.

Although the full impact of these various changes may not be felt for several years, one major effect is already apparent — a new conflict over goals and priorities. In particular, with much larger volumes of subsidized housing construction for which sites must be found, and with much greater public awareness and concern over the undiminishing concentrations of central-city poor, housing objectives relating to the locational distribution of the low-income population are for the first time challenging the preeminence of traditional objectives having to do with housing quality, space, and expense. The conflict over the relative importance of various housing deprivations is paralleled by disagreement as to the most effective means of dealing with any one of them. With experts divided into several opposing camps, those who must commit the public sector to one housing strategy or another can not be sure how best to proceed. The purpose of this study is to provide a partial basis for policy decisions by reexamining the housing needs of low-income families and exploring program interventions that might be both appropriate to current conditions and economically and politically feasible. Although, in confining its attention to the low-income sector, the study is forced to ignore certain important urban growth problems affecting the population generally, it does, hopefully, illuminate the most basic housing issues and dilemmas which cities face at this time.

RESEARCH QUESTIONS

This study addresses itself to five broad questions. First, exactly what is the low-income housing problem, how serious is it, and is it getting better or worse? Historically, the problem has been perceived as squalid shelter, high rents relative to income, and poor environment in almost equal proportions, with overcrowding an aggravating factor for some families. It appears, however, that one or two of these major dimensions of need are now much more severe than the others. Also, as outlined above, new dimensions have emerged. Further, it is not certain that the poor themselves view the problem in the same way as does the larger society. Indeed, from their perspective it may be inappropriate to define the problem purely in terms of housing.

Second, who are the families currently suffering from various housing deprivations and what are the populations most at risk? Numerous studies have related substandard housing conditions to such demographic variables as income, race, tenure, age and sex of head, and family size. While these variables are suggestive of policy directions, they do not pinpoint the incidence of the problem as precisely as would be desired. For example, there is scant

information on the housing situation of families on welfare and on the proportion of serious shelter problems that are accounted for by these households (3). Similarly, the causal relationships of housing deprivations to employment and health history of family members is a mystery. The apparent difficulties suffered by households that are upwardly mobile are not distinguished
from the problems of those who cannot seem to make it or are over the hill.
Overlapping deprivations have not been analyzed. More detailed client analysis
would seem vital to the establishment of priorities among deprived groups and
among alternative programs.

A third general question, which flows in part out of the two previous ones,
is to what extent can the present housing dilemma be explained by inadequate,
as opposed to inappropriate, remedial programs? Congress is continuously
chastised for not mounting housing programs that are commensurate to the
need. Yet estimates of the nature and extent of need do vary widely. And
legislators, with their ears permanently bent by predictions that seem to become gloomier in direct proportion to increases in appropriations, must be
forgiven if they pause to wonder if those who solicit huge additional sums for
housing fully comprehend the problem. This is not to assert by indirection
that the need is not great. It is to suggest that more accurate estimates of the
need-resources gap are badly needed if alternative interventions are to be
properly evaluated.

Fourth, to what extent does the way in which the real estate market functions, especially in the inner city, aggravate housing problems, and how can
public policy improve market efficiency? At present, the inner-city market
does not appear to be working in an orderly fashion, raising the cost and
lowering the quality of housing which low-income families occupy. Simultaneously, the income-related deprivations of these families tend to shape the
adverse market environment within which they must maneuver. Are sweeping
institutional reforms necessary if the market is to operate efficiently, or
would a number of minor structural modifications be sufficient?

Assuming that the four general questions described above can be
satisfactorily answered, the final set of issues is concerned with what should
and can be done. First, given all of the other deprivations of low-income
families and the limited resources that are available for solving social problems, which housing objectives should receive high priority and which can be
deferred? Second, are housing interventions the best way to achieve housing
goals, or would income and employment programs be more efficacious? Conversely, can housing strategies have a material impact on important nonhousing
problems? Third, are the policies which seem appropriate, politically acceptable? Given political and economic constraints, is any substantial reduction
in the low-income housing problem possible in the next decade or so? Research alone is incapable of definitively resolving conflicting policy positions.

It may, however, be able to define the problem in a way that is amenable to solution. It can also sometimes reduce areas of disagreement. Further, it can suggest policy directions that are consistent with opposing positions. Finally, it can determine what various groups are willing to do to solve the problem as they perceive it. These are the goals of the last section of the study.

Several recent housing studies of major importance and most current articles on the subject deal with the relevant issues on a national basis (4). There are enough common attributes of housing markets and shelter problems to validate such an approach. At the same time, many of the most valuable insights about racial discrimination in housing, residential financing, dynamics of the urban land market, and so forth, have been gleaned from examinations of local markets. While there are risks that findings from local studies cannot be generalized, even their uniqueness serves a purpose in demonstrating that federal policies likewise cannot be too broadly generalized. It is important to determine how federal programs must be recast to respond to the wide variation in local circumstances, and equally, what significant initiatives, if any, individual communities can take without assistance from higher levels of government. Our focus, therefore, is on a single city — Baltimore — which is large enough to have urban problems in all their complexity but small enough to be understood and managed. While no city is typical, Baltimore has enough of the old and the new, the North and the South, the black and the white, and the good and the bad to represent a sort of median along a number of urban dimensions. While Baltimore's situation is not completely representative of any other city, the record of its experiences, can, with appropriate adjustments, easily be transferred and related to other large urban areas. At least this was our assumption *ex ante* and remains our feeling *ex post*.

THE RELATIONSHIP OF HOUSING PROBLEMS TO POVERTY

The stress of most low-income housing studies is on the resource aspects of the problem. Low income and the high cost of housing are seen as the primary explanatory variables. Policy recommendations center on various ways of closing the dollar gap with housing programs. Without minimizing the importance of inadequate housing resources, it is clear that the problem today cannot be described so simply. Poor families suffer housing deprivations not because of low income alone, but because of the interacting network of negative variables which collectively constitute the state of poverty. To comprehend the present housing dilemma, then, it is useful to approach it as part of this larger problem. The reverse is also true. To some degree, poverty can only be understood as an intolerable condition of life of which housing deprivations are a most important element. It is the general relationship between housing and poverty which provides part of the context for the present study.

This relationship has been infrequently pursued. For example, during the relatively short history of the War on Poverty, the housing problems of low-income families have received only secondary attention. Proceeding from the assumption that the causes of poverty are much more to be found in the educational, employment, and political systems of the country and that inadequate shelter is basically a consequence rather than a cause of other deprivations, federal anti-poverty programs have done little more than brush against housing issues. This is in sharp, and perhaps realistic, contrast to the situation which existed 40 or 50 years ago when it was widely felt that good housing would make good people.

It may be, however, that the shift in emphasis has been too great, for severe housing deprivations and poverty are so closely intertwined that cause and effect cannot be simply assigned. Thus, although higher incomes might ultimately solve most of the shelter problems of the poor, the problems themselves are frequently both a direct and indirect barrier to the attainment of these incomes. In addition, if one looks at the standard of living which families experience and not just at their level of income, it is evident that being deprived with respect to housing is a large part of what it means to be poor.

Housing has a special relationship to poverty in several important ways. First of all, seriously substandard shelter creates other problems for the poor and magnifies some that already exist. There is a certain amount of evidence relating respiratory ailments to inadequately ventilated structures. The relationship of inadequate space to the splitting up of families has been documented. The dangers of living in firetraps and vermin-infested dwellings are well known. And there would appear to be some relationship between performance in school and the availability of suitable study and sleeping arrangements at home. Thus, bad housing may contribute to extra medical expenses, temporary or permanent loss of income, broken homes, and below-average educational attainment, to name a few significant poverty-related problems.

More subtle in its impact is the visual aspect of housing. Bad housing conditions are perhaps the most visible indicator of poverty. The original emergence of many housing programs, to the partial exclusion of other forms of assistance to low-income families, seems to stem from this very fact. The deficiencies of such programs were a result of the mistaken assumption that eradicating the visible signs of the problem would also eliminate the underlying causes. Yet the visible aspects are extremely important. The necessity to live in a slum environment, when one can see on all sides vastly superior housing accommodations which are available to most of the population, contributes to a feeling of being poor, or inadequate, or rejected, or part of an unfair social system. In fact, since even some of the bad housing in the United States is superior to average accommodations in many other countries, it may be the relative differences within this country that are most crucial because they suggest an inequitable distribution of income and wealth.

Equally important in their impact on poverty are the immobility of the housing product and institutional constraints, such as zoning and building codes, on the housing market. Because of these, low-income housing in large urban areas tends to be geographically concentrated rather than dispersed. It might be argued, therefore, that the so-called culture of poverty is in part caused and perpetuated by housing factors. Regardless of whether this argument is accepted, it is eminently clear that ghettoized housing contributes to unequal educational and employment opportunities across income groups (5). And for many of those who achieve such opportunities despite their confinement in the inner city, the stresses of having to live in a slum environment may make achievement more difficult.

Finally, as important as visibility and immobility, is the high cost of housing services. For low-income families, money spent for housing is a very large proportion of earnings, frequently one-third or more, and not uncommonly is the largest single item in their budget. Because it is also not a deferrable expense, except within narrow limits, other household necessities must be sacrificed, and involuntary moves may frequently occur. Equally, as incomes rise and most other needs can be satisfactorily met, the high cost of shelter forces many families to remain housing-poor. Aggravating this condition is the fact that the poor pay more, relative to quality and quantity of housing services received, than do other income groups.

Housing deprivations can, then, best be viewed as a fundamental aspect of the poverty syndrome — part cause, part consequence, and an important part of poverty itself.

FRAMEWORK FOR ANALYSIS

Approaching housing problems within a poverty framework enlarges some analytical horizons and contracts others. For the reader to appreciate both what is said and what is left unsaid in the chapters to follow, it may help to describe briefly the ways in which the poverty orientation has shaped the study.

Urban Systems Vs Housing Systems

The first consequence of using poverty as a basic parameter was a brief foray into systems analysis and just as hasty a retreat. Initially, in order to explore various possible policy mixes, an array of housing problems and clients were set within a matrix of potential causes and consequences, including employment, health, and other variables. This bit of self-education served only to expose our own naiveté, since as many analysts now realize, it is impossible with present knowledge to specify more than a few of the connections in such a matrix. A number of links from housing to health or from housing to education or vice versa can be established intuitively. But only by interjecting a large number of assumptions can they be specified in quantitive terms, and then only crudely. For this reason, the case for particular housing programs has to be made in part with respect to perceived housing benefits by the beneficiaries themselves, and not with reference to presumed preventive effects. Equally, the ability of nonhousing programs, other than massive income supplements or efforts that achieve quite substantial increases in earned income, to solve housing problems in the immediate future is just as doubtful. Just as better living accommodations will probably do little for education; by the same token, better schools will not correct malfunctions in the low-income housing market in the short run.

This is not to say that housing problems and programs can safely be examined in isolation. Paraphrasing Lewis Mumford, man has both a nesting instinct and a conquering instinct (6). Housing programs serve the one; programs to enhance employment, education, and political opportunities serve the other. Effectiveness of programs in either of the two arenas, however, is impaired if significant barriers in the other arena are allowed to exist. Worded differently, housing programs are necessary but insufficient to solve housing problems.

Those who argue for the holistic view and who purport to relate housing to everything else via various systems and planning techniques do not realize how little is known about the systems involved. Their tools become an inadequate substitute for needed knowledge, and have little to contribute when hard choices about housing programs must be made. The housing subsystem or any subsystem cannot be integrated analytically with other parts of the larger urban system until the dynamics of the subsystem itself are understood and until it is decided what internal rearrangements in that subsystem seem appropriate when viewed in isolation. Only at that point can connections to and substitutions across subsystems be intelligently explored. It seemed essentially correct, therefore, to define the housing problem initially in housing terms, even though it is obviously part of a larger social dilemma.

Intermediate-Term Vs Long-Term Analysis

The considerations just described lead directly to an intermediate-term policy focus of five to ten years, for in the long run, solutions to housing problems can come from a variety of directions. The emphasis here, then, is on what *can* be done to improve the situation now, not on what *might* be only started by 1980. While concentration on a middle-range time span may seem eminently reasonable, it is precisely this portion of the policy spectrum which receives little emphasis. Currently, efforts center primarily either on the day-to-day administrative details associated with existing activities or on planning programs that require long lead-times and huge infusions of public funds, such as major clearance, new towns, better education, and the opening of suburbia to low-income families. In a way, these foci, although necessary, represent a form of escapism. By laying the problem at education's door, persons in the housing field can excuse their own lack of progress. In calling for grand schemes, they can satisfy themselves that they have offered the commandments but that politicians are not intelligent enough or concerned enough to receive them. And resigned to the futility of it all, they can then bury themselves in day-to-day trivia.

If this judgment seems harsh, it is because in talking about the need for giant steps when it is patently clear that in the short-run actions will be small, housing advocates have unintentionally deceived the poor. They have painted futures which the poor will not live to see. Better it would be to explore what can reasonably be done *now*. If what seems politically realistic over the inter-mediate term is also unacceptable to the deprived or to other groups in society, then the issue is joined. But to go on promising what is acceptable but not deliverable in the near future is dishonest.

Limited Vs Unlimited Resources

As just implied, the relatively brief time period within which progress must be achieved almost automatically imposes a serious resource constraint. In the short-run, a large upward shift in housing subsidies is not to be expected.

This fact has several crucial interlocking implications. If a genuine attempt is made to upgrade the housing conditions of most of the low-income popula-tion in only a decade, the amount of subsidy and level of improvement per family can not be very great. This, in turn, means that most of the problem will have to be solved by using the existing inventory, for the subsidy per household required if each poor family were to be given a new unit costing anywhere from $20,000 to more than $30,000, depending on the area of the country, is politically out of sight. Although the nation has the resources for such an effort, it is not inclined to use them in this fashion, nor should it, given the fact that in every new home there is a measure of luxury which most of the poor would no doubt rather exchange for necessities. For the City of Baltimore, as an example, to try to house every low-income family in a new $25,000 home when the average value of dwellings in the private in-ventory is less than $10,000 would not make a great deal of sense. Recent national housing policy, however, has had this very thrust, though fortunately has not been supported by sufficient funds to permit implementation on a large scale. By allocating most of its limited housing subsidies to new construction and maximum rehabilitation for a few deprived families, the federal government effectively writes off the shelter problems of the bulk of the low-income population for at least a generation (7). Although such programs are a necessary component of any overall housing effort, whether they should effectively constitute that effort is open to serious question.

The implications of a middle-term policy horizon and limited resources do not end here. Not only must the problem be met within the existing stock, it must be met largely by using the now substandard units which are already occupied by low-income families. Were a city to try to intercept a large number of standard dwelling units as they came on the market and turn them over to low-income families, it would either seriously disrupt the housing market or be forced to stretch its rehousing program out over a very long period of time (8).

So it is an assumption of this study, not a finding, that in most cities rehabilitation must be a major component of any attempt to ameliorate the housing problems of a substantial portion of the low-income population within a time period that the poor themselves would feel is reasonable. This conclusion automatically removes suburbia from an important position in any solution, except in the long run (9).

Not only must the emphasis be on rehabilitation but, as already noted, the amount of upgrading per structure cannot be substantial, given the necessity to spread limited resources over a large number of units (10). If most of the substandard inventory in a particular city does not lend itself to such treatment and if the proportion of the inventory that is substandard is large, there is probably no solution to the low-income housing problem in that city within this decade. Certainly, there is no politically feasible *low-income* program that would meet the need. Conceivably, a large-scale construction program for middle-income families who would require only modest subsidies could, through the filtering process, free-up enough standard units for low-income families to solve the problem. There would, however, be the question of the political feasibility of such programs at the scale required. Also subsidies would still be necessary for low-income families just to support adequate maintenance. And additional funds would be needed to demolish and replace the structures vacated by these families.

Poverty Vs Low-Income

Operationally, poverty is usually defined as an income that is inadequate to purchase a specified minimum market-basket of goods and services. As already suggested, for the purposes of this study, poverty is conceived not as low income per se but as the collectivity of adverse living conditions which are associated with low-income, the precise adversities varying from family to family. This conception influenced this study in two ways. First, it expanded our view of housing deprivations to include twelve dimensions of housing need, most of them nonphysical: 1. substandard structures, equipment, and services; 2. insufficient indoor space; 3. unsatisfactory neighborhood environment; 4. excessive housing expense relative to income; 5. lack of choice of tenure; 6. racial discrimination in the ownership, rental, and home-financing markets; 7. inadequate furnishings; 8. restricted locational choice; 9. excessive housing expense relative to quality and size of dwelling; 10. lack of security of occupancy; 11. stigmatizing way in which housing services are delivered; and 12. housing-related problems stemming from illness or poor health. None of these dimensions represents a new discovery; each has been recognized somewhere in the existing housing literature. However, placing all of the dimensions side by side for simultaneous consideration permitted a more systematic review of priorities within housing and suggested additional lines of inquiry that might otherwise have been ignored.

The second way in which our conception of poverty guided the study was by forcing a reconsideration of causes and remedies. If poverty is not simply low income, then neither is the solution to poverty and to housing deprivations simply more resources efficiently spent. The nonresource aspects of the problem must be correctly defined. There is considerable evidence that they have not been. As a result, the technical capability to deal with the problem either does not exist or has not been mobilized and many programs are not effective in achieving stated objectives.

Political Vs Technical and Economic Feasibility

Although proposals for vastly improving housing conditions of low-income families frequently flounder because of serious disagreement over precisely what their impact will be, they more often fail to gain support for other reasons. Either they imply unacceptable shifts in power and influence, or seek goals which are not uniformly held, or conflict with broader city objectives, or appear to cost too much, or cannot be implemented by means that are consistent with prevailing social and political attitudes. It seemed at the outset of this study, therefore, that it would be fruitless to search with great care for the technically best solution without testing the results of the inquiry against the views of those who would be served and those who would implement the ideas. Indeed, where there are many conflicting needs of diverse client groups no solution which fails the political test in a politically equitable arena can be termed technically best. Equally, if this assumption is correct, it would be incorrect to infer from the political rejection of the presumably technically best solution that there is no solution at all; in other words, that there is no policy space within which conflicting groups can reach agreement.

Pursuing this line of reasoning, part of the study was devoted to testing the political realism of the apparent policy implications of the findings. If the suggested policies are unacceptable to decision-makers, or if the intended beneficiaries have other priorities, the solution obviously lies elsewhere. Although the political testing process was not fully structured, it does represent something of a departure from the current practice of postulating optimum housing futures for ghetto residents without, apparently, any input from the constituencies who are the most affected.

THE DATA BASE

Findings of the study are based on five primary sources of information: two household surveys; inspection of a sample of structures in which the families who were surveyed lived; interviews with a sample of the owners of the inspected structures; and meetings with groups who are directly concerned with housing issues.

First Household Survey

A major purpose of the overall study is to illuminate the distribution of housing deprivations across various demographic groups and to ascertain the overlap of housing and nonhousing problems within individual families. With this information, the nature and extent of housing problems can be specified more precisely than is now possible, and programs can be better tailored to need. To implement this purpose, interviews were conducted with a random, geographic sample of approximately 9,000 families throughout the city (11). Each interview lasted about 40 minutes and briefly touched upon housing, health, education, employment, consumption, and related matters.

The city-wide sample was necessary, because it was not known in advance how the problems would distribute themselves among households. However, because the focus of the research is on low-income families and because most of these families live near the center of Baltimore, the inner areas of the city were heavily oversampled. Of the 9,000 interviews, about 7,300 were in the inner ring, where the sampling rate was 7%, as compared with a rate of just under 1% in the rest of the city.

Second Household Survey

The first household survey provided a picture of the poverty problem in Baltimore that is somewhat more detailed than the sketches which can be drawn using national data. The survey did not, however, reveal respondents' own perceptions of conditions which outside observers label as problems. To gain these additional insights, a low-income subsample of the original 9,000 families was selected for further interviewing. Using first-survey information, the sample was stratified with respect to: age, race, and sex of head; participation in a selected number of economic opportunity programs; and self-perceived trend in the family's well-being (12). Approximately 900 families were interviewed for about two hours each. Questions covered not only housing but employment, education, and health as well. In addition to broadening and deepening our understanding of the poverty syndrome, the responses served as a useful, if uncomfortable check, to information obtained in the first survey.

Since one *a priori* assumption of this study was that program priorities in housing must be determined with reference to the wishes of the intended beneficiaries, a portion of the second survey was devoted to the task of eliciting housing preferences. The techniques used, however, were not sophisticated. Our conclusions regarding preferences, are, therefore, stated with great hesitancy. At a very general level, of course, it can safely be assumed that the poor want roughly the same things that more wealthy families already have. But this rather common observation is not particularly helpful. When families are deprived of a number of necessities all at once, and when these necessities cannot be supplied to them all at once, which ones they would prefer is the important question. It is a question which even they may be unable to answer. Perhaps it is not fair to ask it. Yet consumer preferences and attitudes with respect to home-ownership, neighborhood environment, and related matters cannot simply be ignored if remedial programs are to be successful. Regrettably, therefore, our preference data cannot be viewed as definitive.

Survey of Residential Structures

Most housing programs and many analyses of housing problems are based on extremely inadequate data concerning the quality of the residential inventory. Information which is gathered locally in connection with code enforcement and renewal programs is fragmentary, of doubtful accuracy, not regularly collected, and not susceptible to intercity, and sometimes even intra-city comparisons. Census statistics on housing quality have also been found to be of dubious validity, and in addition are fairly crude. The extent to which these data limitations have led to incorrect diagnoses and inappropriate policies can only be guessed.

For this study, accurate information on housing quality was felt to be crucial to the entire analysis. Consequently, census-type ratings which interviewers gave to each structure in the first household survey were supple-

mented by detailed inspections of a subsample of approximately 625 of these
structures (13). The inspections had four specific purposes: first, to calculate
the cost of upgrading the entire substandard housing stock in Baltimore to an
acceptable quality level; second, to validate or refute the census-type ratings
for the larger sample; third, to rank all of Baltimore's housing, both standard
and substandard, on a single fairly refined quality-condition scale that could
then be matched against rents, values, occupants' perceptions of housing
problems, and other variables; and fourth, to develop an inexpensive rating
scheme and inspection procedure which could be replicated periodically by
the city as part of a general program to monitor change.

Although the details of the survey are outlined in the Appendix, several
key features need to be mentioned here, since they bear directly on the findings which are presented later. Of most importance is the fact that the standards of adequacy against which deficiencies were compared and costed lies
somewhere between housing code specifications and FHA standards. It is
in no sense minimal. Second, since the team of inspectors was small, consist-
ing of only four persons, and since over two-fifths of the structures were inspected twice, and since one of the inspectors visited over four-fifths of the
dwellings at least once, whatever biases are reflected in the ratings are uniform
throughout the sample. Census ratings are seriously deficient in this respect.
Finally, all of the structures which seemed the least bit marginal when first
visited were inspected again by a professional builder/property manager with
over three decades of experience with inner-city residential real estate.

Survey of Investor-Owners

In many ways, the persons most intimately acquainted with the shelter
problems of low-income families, other than the families themselves, are
those who house them. Unfortunately, the counsel of landlords is seldom
sought when housing policies and programs are being formulated. And, with
the exception of code enforcement, the programs themselves seek to deal
existing landlords out of the game. The reasons for this situation are clear
enough. In the eyes of many of those who make policy, the inner-city landlord
represents the enemy. In failing to provide decent housing for those whom
society has brutalized and whom even public housing rejects, he becomes the
symbol of what society hates about itself. So he is to be chastized and avoided.

This attitude may not impede the formulation of effective long-term renewal policies, since these generally contemplate the creation of a completely
new group of owners. In the implementation of intermediate-term programs,
however, it is an expensive luxury, because these programs must work in
consonance with the existing market environment. The present investor-owner

cannot be avoided. Beyond that, landlords as a group represent an important management resource which public policy perhaps in some manner could utilize. Even if this were impossible, their intimate knowledge of the dynamics of inner-city markets is essential to the development of realistic intermediate-term policies. As individuals, many of them might not quite comprehend all the forces which affect their own situation. Collectively, however, they represent a fund of understanding and experience which government is not yet rich enough to ignore.

Pursing this assumption, interviews were conducted with the owners of a subsample of the rental structures that were inspected (14). In all, 92 investors, owning a total of 15,000 dwelling units in the inner city, were interviewed. Questions covered not only the inspected structures and their occupants but also the investors' real estate holdings throughout the inner city. The extent of cooperation received varied widely, as did the investors themselves. Much of the hard statistical data which had been hoped for did not materialize. Apparent contradictions were frequently encountered. Nevertheless, out of the interviews ultimately emerged a picture of the inner-city market that became a focal point for other parts of the study.

Meetings with Interest Groups

It has been widely observed that the inner city is oversurveyed and underserviced. New reports pile upon old reports but nothing happens. The present study may not alter that pattern. As mentioned earlier, however, it was decided at the outset of the research that the political feasibility of the study's recommendations should be determined. When the findings of the study were in hand, they were presented to and explored with groups having an interest in Baltimore's housing problems and who in one way or another help to shape local housing policy. In addition to producing factual information which had previously been overlooked, the meetings revealed an array of images about the housing problems that exist throughout the community. These images together with reactions to specific policy proposals were extremely helpful in assessing the probable reception to various types of programs.

CHAPTER ORGANIZATION

Development of housing policy requires a blending of technical data, theory, and political and ethical considerations. This study is organized, therefore, around what might be loosely termed a planning framework. Housing needs and objectives are specified; housing resources are identified; theories of the problem are explored; alternative strategies are reviewed; and one of several possible packages of programs is elaborated in detail. Particular emphasis is placed throughout on the multiplicity of housing and nonhousing goals and programs, and on the variety of client groups, which must be taken into consideration in trying to evolve an appropriate role for the public sector in this area of social concern.

The analysis begins in Chapter 2 with a quick sketch of Baltimore in order to set the context for the examination of local problems and policies. This chapter is intended for those who are already familiar with the city as well as those who are not.

Chapter 3 describes in conceptual terms the various dimensions of housing need, and reduces these concepts to measurable objectives where possible. The purpose of the chapter is both to enlarge our view of housing problems and to provide the basis for the subsequent empirical analysis of need.

In Chapters 4-7 an attempt is made to calculate housing need in Baltimore along six of the dimensions described in Chapter 3. Variations in the seriousness of need among demographic groups is analyzed. Special attention is given to overlapping problems.

Chapter 8 estimates the amount of resources going into low-income housing programs in Baltimore and compares this effort with the level of need as estimated in earlier chapters. The need-resources gap is measured not only in aggregate but also along specific dimensions of need.

Chapters 4-8 together present a static view of unmet need; they present it in macroanalytic terms, and they emphasize the resource aspects of the problem. Although the chapters are able, because of the richness of the underlying data, to furnish a number of new insights, their focus leaves a huge void in our understanding of the nature of the housing dilemma. In order to comprehend the forces which collectively produce the static picture and to appreciate how market processes might be manipulated by public policy, it is necessary to examine the functioning of the inner-city housing market. This means a stress on dynamics, and consideration of institutional as well as resource barriers. Chapters 9 and 10 aim in these directions. Chapter 9 studies the low-income market empirically from the perspective of the person whom poor families rely on for housing services – the so-called "slumlord." Chapter 10 explores several theories of slums, decay, and housing abandonment and tries to formulate a composite theory which can serve as a foundation for policy decisions.

The findings of Chapters 4 through 10 provide the basis for, but do not lead directly to, policy choices. Chapter 11 attempts to make this transition from problem to policy. It assesses housing interventions in terms of both their relationship to broader anti-poverty objectives and their probable efficaciousness in altering the market forces which produce part of the problem.

Chapter 11 concludes with a set of proposals that may for various reasons be completely impossible to implement on a large scale. Therefore, Chapters 12 and 13 explore technical aspects of the proposals in more detail, and Chapter 14, the concluding chapter, investigates their political feasibility.

After having gone through the above exercise for Baltimore, while casually observing conditions in newer and smaller communities out of the corner of our eye, we are convinced that placing primary emphasis on one or two national housing programs would not be the wise approach. Individual city differences are in fact too great. The federal government, can, however, through basic attacks on poverty, racial discrimination, and unstable and uneven flows of mortgage capital, create the environment within which local programs, whatever they may be, can succeed.

CHAPTER 2

The Market Environment: An Overview of Baltimore's Population and History

Most analyses of urban problems emphasize the common attributes of cities and, intuition to the contrary, proceed on the implicit assumption that commonalities are more significant than differences. The unique attributes of New York and Los Angeles are, of course, widely recognized, and a distinction is frequently made between large and small metropolitan areas. In general, however, urban America is treated as an undifferentiated mass.

This same preconception pervades federal urban programs. As Louis Winnick has observed, localities that participate in these programs are forced to march lockstep in time with a single set of rules and regulations (1). When asked to explain a particular policy direction which seems contrary to what would appear to be appropriate, municipal officials stress the necessity to capture federal funds. More subtly, in developing local programs, their thoughts are immediately channeled and constrained by what Washington allows. This may be good. It may be inevitable. It may also help to explain why progress across the country is so uneven, and why revenue-sharing came into being.

A major reason for confining this study to a single city was to determine whether joining federal programs to local situations is indeed a significant problem that should command more attention. It is important, therefore, to outline just what Baltimore's situation really is, and how it is different from and similar to other U.S. cities. A brief examination of its physical, social, and political environment provides the context for exploring specific housing problems and policies in later chapters.

THE CITY IN PERSPECTIVE

On the surface, Baltimore appears to be just another large, decaying, eastern city, experiencing population decline, outmigration of industry and commerce, an expanding black minority, a rise in social problems, and antagonism from suburban neighbors. With its predominance of row houses, proximity to a more dominant urban center, and diversified seaboard industrial base, it is not infrequently referred to as a smaller version of Philadelphia. This is where the confusion starts.

Perhaps because of its much smaller population — 906,000 in a metropolitan area of approximately 2,000,000 — and more interesting topography and architecture, it is, in a physical sense at least, more humane than its larger neighbor to the north. Though there are many blocks of bad housing, the miles and miles of depressing, treeless, litter-strewn slums which characterize Philadelphia and New York are proportionately less in evidence. The pleasantness of most of the city is heightened by the fact that the urban fringe is still a reasonable distance from downtown. And although the social environment still has not been entirely freed from its southern heritage of segregation, the presence of a leading, predominantly black college in the city has had some positive, if immeasurable, impact on attitudes and behavior.

One is led to believe, hopefully not naively, that unlike several of the other eastern cities, Baltimore can still solve its housing problems within a reasonable period of time without unduly straining public resources. Its urban mass and the mass of its slums are not yet unmanageable in size, though they may be becoming so. The urban area is growing and with it the inner ring of blight and decay. As later discussion will make clear, more and more of the signs read "Last Chance."

POPULATION

Although Baltimore lies at the edge of one of the most rapidly growing areas of the country, the Washington–Baltimore corridor, it has been experiencing a gradual but steady decline of population for almost 20 years. The city experienced a loss of 35,000 persons in the last decade, following on the heels of a prior decline of about 10,000 from 1950 to 1960 (2). In the inner ring of the city the 20-year loss exceeded 160,000 persons, reflecting a centrifugal population movement that began well before 1950 (3). In the outer reaches of the city, vacant land was able to absorb some of this flow, but with undeveloped acreage almost gone, the period of population growth anywhere in the city is virtually over.

These few statistics suggest several key problems and possibilities for Baltimore. First, the rapid growth of the Washington–Baltimore corridor provides the city with more than average opportunities to capture revenue-producing land uses which could help support social services and generally revivify the community. Second, the thinning out of the inner city, while it provides policy elbowroom which never before existed, cannot be viewed in housing terms alone. It reflects discontent with schools, fear of crime, and dissatisfaction with public facilities and services. Whether the inner city can be stabilized with the resource inputs which the city can be reasonably expected to mobilize is Baltimore's (and other cities') most significant policy question. Finally, now that expansion of moderately priced housing, which characterizes much of Baltimore's inventory, has bumped up against a hostile suburban wall, the elbowroom may soon disappear.

Racial Change

Like other major American cities, Baltimore has experienced a substantial rise in its black population and a more than corresponding decline among whites. During the decade just ended, the number of blacks rose by approximately 100,000 or 30%, while the number of whites dropped by about 130,000 or 20%. The two trends combined brought the black population to nearly half of the city total.

Only one-third of the black increase was the result of inmigration, which dropped to a very low level during the decade. Equally the loss of whites is probably explained to only a small degree by flight from Baltimore City to the suburbs. Rather, as part of *inter*-urban family movement, inmigrating whites have settled outside the city instead of replacing white families who leave Baltimore for other areas of the country.

The expansion of the black population in central cities is dutifully reported in countless publications and is now fairly common knowledge. The question is what is its significance with respect to housing problems and policies? Is the change only interesting, but irrelevant? The fact that it is so widely mentioned would seem to suggest its importance, but all inferences are usually left to the reader. Most inferences must be negative, because the transformation of cities from predominantly white to mostly black does not occur easily and without problems. There is much exploitation, a certain amount of violence, and considerable ill will on both sides. More important for the longer term, the stabilizing influences of social institutions frequently deteriorate during the transition period, so that blacks acquire homes but not a community. This situation is exaggerated when the change is rapid, as it has been in Baltimore, and when it involves succession by lower socioeconomic groups, as has also frequently been the case. It is also exaggerated by the fact that the transition is associated with a net shift from owner to rental occupancy, with ownership of the inventory continuing in the hands of white investors.

Clearly, the figures on racial change reflect trends which have profound implications for housing policy. Regrettably, preambles to housing policy statements are prone to recognize the trends while the policies themselves ignore them.

Shifts in Age and Sex of the Population

The impact of racial transition on housing needs in Baltimore (and other cities) is shaped to a very considerable degree by the significantly different age—sex profiles of the white and black populations in the city. A larger proportion of whites are over 45, almost two-fifths as compared with only one-fifth for blacks; and only one-third are under 21, as compared with a figure for blacks of almost one-half. Population changes since 1960 seem to have exaggerated these differences.

One interpretation of these figures is benign. Blacks are replacing whites, with a concomitant reduction in the average age of the population. The mix of problems shifts, but not the overall magnitude.

The figures, however, mask a shift of some importance to central-city housing. By 1970 there were 20,000 more black female-headed families than in 1960, an increase of 95% in only 10 years. Indeed 60% of the net gain in black households is accounted for by female heads, most of them in the 20—45 age group. Over one-third of the black households are now headed by females as against only 27% in 1960. By contrast, the number of female-headed white households rose by only 10% during the same period.

The figures are a depressing reminder of the continuing economic difficulties of much of the black population. Even more depressing with respect to hous-ing, families without a male head are the very group which responsible land-lords with good units seek to avoid. Much to be preferred are the elderly widows and spinsters who pose no rent collection or maintenance problems. Of all the trends in central-city populations since 1960, therefore, the huge increase in black, female-headed households is the most disquieting.

Income Change

While central-city populations have, as would be expected, experienced in-come gains in recent years, the figures on rising incomes do not necessarily measure progress. Of considerable importance to the issue of equal educa-tional opportunity, for example, is the question of whether there is a narrow-ing or widening gap between city and suburban incomes. Since a residential locational choice is also an educational choice for many families, this question bears directly on housing policy.

As would be expected, Baltimore has continued to lose ground relative to the surrounding counties. In 1949, it had virtual parity with the rest of the metropolitan area. By 1959, however, median family income in the city had dropped to well below 90% of income in the counties, and by 1969 it was down to around 75%. This relative disadvantage can be expected to become greater unless the city can increase its share of unsubsidized residential construction.

The Low-Income Population

Of most interest to this study are, of course, the housing and related living conditions of various sectors of the low-income population, somehow defined. Using a definition of low income which is very close to the Social Security Administration's (SSA) nonfarm near-poverty line (March 1967), we calculated that 65,000 families, or almost one-quarter of the city total, could be so classified (4). However, as Anthony Downs has noted, "the income which any household must attain to rent or buy adequate quality housing without spending too high a proportion of its total income on housing is significantly higher than the official 'poverty level' as defined by the Social Security Administration, which is based on the cost of an adequate diet rather than on costs of adequate housing. There are millions more 'housing poor' households in the United States than 'food poor' households." (5) For this reason, the low-income line used in this study was set arbitrarily at a level about 20% higher than the SSA near-poverty line, resulting in 85,000 households, or three-tenths of the city total being classified as low-income (Table 2.1)(6). Whether these families were also seriously deprived with respect to housing remained for our research to determine.

Table 2.1. Comparison of Baltimore Study Criteria For Defining Low-Income Population with Social Security Administration Nonfarm Poverty and Near-Poverty Indices

Number of Persons in Household	Baltimore Study[1] Low-Income Criteria	SSA Non-Farm Poverty	Indices, March 1967[2] Near Poverty
1	$0–2,499	$0–1,635	$1,636–1,985
2	0–3,499	0–2,115	2,116–2,855
3	0–3,999	0–2,600	2,601–3,425
4	0–4,999	0–3,335	3,336–4,345
5	0–5,999	0–3,930	3,931–5,080
6	0–6,999	0–4,410	4,411–5,700
7	0–7,999	0–5,010	5,011–6,500
8	0–8,999	0–5,610	5,611–7,300
9	0–8,999	0–6,210	6,211–8,100
10 or more	0–9,999	0–6,810	6,811–8,900

[1] Income received in 1967, as reported in First Household Survey.
[2] Mollie Orshanksy, The shape of poverty in 1966, *Social Security Bulletin,* March 1968, Table I, p. 4. Original table lists a single figure for households of 7 or more persons (poverty – $5,430; near poverty – $6,945). For greater comparability above 6 persons, increments of $600 for poverty and $800 for near poverty are assumed.

Mollie Orshansky has analyzed in considerable detail the risk which various population groups have of being poor. (7) Baltimore data generally confirm her national figures. Blacks constitute 60% of the low-income population, and the proportion of blacks who fall into this category is more than double that for whites.

Large families and female-headed households are much more likely to have inadequate income than are others. Over half of the families in each of these two groups are seriously deprived with respect to income. If they are black as well, the probability of their being in poverty rises even further. Only a handful of large, female-headed, black households are *not* in poverty. These figures serve to emphasize the seriousness of the increase, noted earlier, in this sector of the population.

In large measure, statistics on the black, fatherless household are simply proxies for data describing families receiving welfare payments under the Aid to Families With Dependent Children program. In Baltimore, this group doubled in size between 1960 and 1968, and accounted for almost half of all female-headed black households with at least one minor child in the latter year. By our measures, fully three-quarters of these families had inadequate incomes, despite their welfare payments. The welfare dollar, which supports so much of the low-income housing market, is an insufficient support at best.

Between 1959 and 1968, by our definition, Baltimore's low-income population diminished by approximately 10,000 households, or, in percentage terms, from 35% to 31% of the total population. Although data from national studies do not allow for precise comparison, it would appear that the rate of decline for the city has been appreciably less than that for the nation. (8)

In 1960, the aggregate "low-income gap," i.e., the number of dollars required in order to raise each low-income family to our minimum non-low-income line, amounted to $183 million (in 1968 dollars) or $1900 per low-income household. By 1968, the aggregate gap had fallen to $163 million, but the average gap per low-income household remained unchanged. This relationship would suggest that the $20 million aggregate reduction is the result of upward mobility on the part of certain household types rather than a more general increase in the living standard of low-income families.

HOUSING

It is the quality and condition of the housing stock which helps to set Baltimore apart from other large eastern cities. Despite a very small amount of new construction in recent years, most of the city's inventory is in surprisingly good repair and very attractive. (9) If desirable housing were the only concern of middle-class families, the preferences of such families for

Baltimore's suburbs would be substantially lower than it actually is, for there are many pleasant neighborhoods well within the city limits. Equally, at the other end of the quality spectrum very few of the city's dwelling units (under 5%) are dilapidated. As partial evidence of this situation, in our household survey, concern over neighborhood environment was expressed much more often than serious dissatisfaction with home, a fact which should be weighed in decisions regarding allocation of housing resources.

The predominant feature of Baltimore's residential landscape is the masonry row house, varying in size from the stately former mansion to the 12-foot-wide alley house. Less predominant but still in evidence are the famous, well-scrubbed, white marble steps. As one of the city's most significant physical features, the steps are being challenged by what is fast becoming another institution — form stone — a thin light-colored concrete block which is placed on top of the original brick siding to give the rowhouse a new look and hide defects. Literally thousands of homes have been refaced in this fashion in the past 15 years or so.

Starting at a radius of about two miles from downtown the rowhouses begin to give way to semidetached and detached units, many of which have wood or asbestos siding. Although nearly all of the substandard housing currently is concentrated in the inner city, there is considerable concern in some quarters over the wood and asbestos sectors of the outer-city inventory, since their age, incipient obsolescence, and maintenance costs make them ripe for decline. Some investors refer to these sectors as "soft" inventory, indicating that if they are not maintained the process of decay will proceed very rapidly.

Despite its large size, Baltimore is still very much a city of one- and two-family homes. Three-quarters of its occupied dwellings fall into this category. Another 5% are in three- and four-family structures, many of which were originally one-family units. Apartment buildings not only account for a small proportion of the inventory, but, since most are either public housing or recently constructed private projects, comprise an even lower proportion of the housing problem.

A city of homes does not necessarily mean a city of homeowners. Slightly less than half of Baltimore's families own their dwellings, and this figure represents a decline since 1960. Over 64,000 single-family homes are renter occupied. This situation is not due to high prices. Quite the contrary. The median price of a single-family structure in the city is less than $10,000, a figure that has not changed appreciably since 1960. Many houses in good condition can be found for as little as $5,000, and at prices well below their 1960 level. A more likely explanation for the decline in owner occupancy is that reasonable mortgage financing in the inner city is impossible to obtain. It is also true that many families who are seeking home ownership are not attracted to the types of homes and neighborhoods which are now predominantly renter occupied. But the home financing barrier is a principal culprit. It effectively thwarts the potential for an inner-city renaissance inherent in the inexpensive single-family structure.

In the rental sector, price levels and trends are quite different. On the average, rents rose over 30% between 1960 and 1970. Some of this increase can be attributed to new construction, nearly all of which came into the inventory at rental figures above the median. Much of the rise, however, reflects escalating operating costs which are difficult to control. At the time of our survey, median gross rent was $100 a month. Very few units rented for less than $60 a month, and most of these appear to be in poor condition. Whether rents in Baltimore are as reasonable as prices depends on one's point of view. Relative to quality received and occupant incomes, rents seem high in the inner city and modest elsewhere. With respect to rate of return by investors, just the reverse is true.

In both the rental and owner-occupied sectors of the stock, blacks are at a disadvantage. For reasons having much more to do with discrimination than low income, the bulk of them reside in predominantly black neighborhoods in the inner- and middle-rings of the city where the stock is oldest and most in need of repair. Along certain vectors from the central business district (CBD) they have managed to break out of the ghetto and spread to the city line. The iron curtain of discrimination along the remainder of the ghetto perimeter seems to be holding fast. As a consequence, they receive less for their housing dollar than do whites, More serious, the psychological effects of confinement do not facilitate neighborhood renewal.

THE INNER CITY

As suggested several times in the preceding discussion, the low-income housing problem in Baltimore and in most other cities is concentrated in an inner ring of older neighborhoods surrounding the CBD. It is this concentration which largely shapes the dynamic aspects of the problem and which, according to some observers, makes it so intractable. (10) In Baltimore, the inner ring that we defined for much of our statistical analysis includes just under two-fifths of the households in the city, but it contains three-fifths of all black and low-income households and only one-quarter of all white and non-low-income households (Fig. 2.1 and Table 2.2). (11) Half of its population is low income and two-thirds is black.

White households living in the inner city tend to be slightly younger, smaller in size, and more likely to be headed by a female than are outer-city households. The same differences hold within the black community, with the

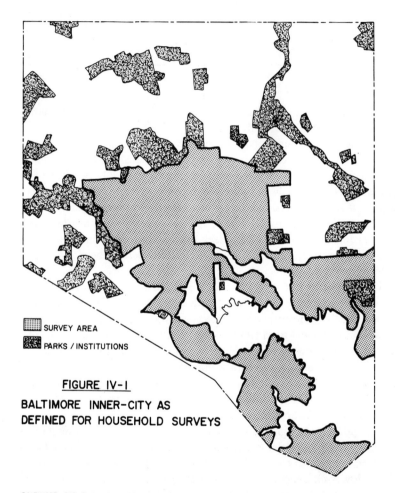

SURVEY AREA

PARKS / INSTITUTIONS

FIGURE IV-I

BALTIMORE INNER-CITY AS
DEFINED FOR HOUSEHOLD SURVEYS

BALTIMORE CAP EVALUATION STUDY, INSTITUTE FOR ENVIRONMENTAL STUDIES, UNIVERSITY OF PENNSYLVANIA
1968-1969

Fig. 2.1. Baltimore inner city as defined for household surveys. (Institute for
Environmental Studies, University of Pennsylvania, 1968–1969.)

Table 2.2 Number of Households by Race, Location of Residence, and Income Status, (Baltimore, Maryland, 1968[1])

Income Status	White		Black		Total	
	Inner City	Total	Inner City	Total	Inner City	Total
Low income	12,450	35,860	37,780	49,000	50,230	84,860
Non-low income	24,700	130,070	29,350	61,320	54,050	191,390
Total	37,150	165,930	67,130	110,320	104,280	276,250

[1] Source: First Household Survey. Criteria for low-income as per Table 2.1. Criteria for inner city as per Fig. 2.1.

important exception that black families in the outer city are, on the average, younger than those living in the inner city.

The pattern of tenure within the inner city differs significantly from that observed in outlying neighborhoods. Nearly three-quarters of the inner-city dwelling units are occupied on a rental basis as against only two fifths for the remaining areas of the city (Table 2.3). For whites living in the inner city, the rate of home ownership is more than one-third lower than the rate for white outer-city residents (41% vs 67%). The corresponding relationship for blacks is even more pronounced. Black households located in the inner city are one-half as likely (22% vs 44%) to be homeowners as their counterparts in the outer city.

As would be expected from the large amount of private abandonments as well as public demolition associated with urban renewal, the inner-city population declined significantly over the decade, with a loss of at least 15,000 households occurring from 1960 to 1968 alone (Table 2.4). Virtually all of this loss is accounted for by a reduction in the number of white owner-occupant households. Although the number of black inner-city households remained constant over the decade, the continued outward thrust of the black community is evidenced by the fact that the proportion of blacks living in the inner city declined from 85% to 61%.

Perhaps the most significant question with respect to the housing future of Baltimore and other cities is whether the inner-city inventory lends itself to long-term renewal of the city for all income groups or whether it is acceptable only to lower-socioeconomic sectors of the population who have little choice in the market. Some persons argue that row houses situated on square blocks with relatively little green space are an obsolescing architectural type which will be increasingly rejected as incomes rise. The structures are described as horizontal apartment houses with none of the attractions of an apartment and few of the features which families seek in a single-family home. The most desirable row houses from a structural standpoint are the large old homes which upper-income families rejected many years ago and which middle- and lower-

Table 2.3. Number of Households by Race, Location of Residence, and Tenure,
(Baltimore, Maryland, 1968[1])

Tenure	White		Black		Total	
	Inner City	Total	Inner City	Total	Inner City	Total
Owner-occupant	15,330	101,750	14,810	33,950	30,140	135,700
Renter[2]	21,820	64,180	52,320	76,370	74,140	140,550
Total	37,150	165,930	67,130	110,320	104,280	276,250

[1] Source: First Household Survey. Criteria for inner city as per Fig. 2.1.
[2] Including households acquiring homes under lease-purchase agreements and households occupying units without payment of rent in cash.

Table 2.4. Number of Households by Race and Location of Residence
(Baltimore, Maryland, 1960 and 1968)

	White		Black		Total	
	Inner City	Total	Inner City	Total	Inner City	Total
1960[1]	50,564	195,141	68,643	80,456	119,207	275,597
1968[2]	37,150	165,930	67,130	110,320	104,280	276,250

[1] 1960 figures derived from *1960 Census of Housing, City Blocks*, Table 2, using definition of inner city shown in Fig. 2.1.
[2] 1968 figures from First Household Survey, using definition of inner city shown in Fig. 2.1

income families cannot afford to maintain. Many of the other row structures offer even less hope, but for precisely the opposite reason. They are too tiny, and their obsolete heating and plumbing are expensive to replace properly (12).

If this reasoning is correct, there is a basic conflict between low-income housing goals and overall renewal objectives; that is, although the housing needs of the poor can be met by renovating the existing substandard stock, the residential preferences of other families whom the city seeks to attract cannot be. If such a conflict indeed exists, it will probably be resolved by a hold-the-line effort in the inner sections of the city until the existing inventory can be wiped out and new environments created which are more competitive with the suburbs.

The strongest arguments against this point of view are the vibrancy of a number of inner-city ethnic neighborhoods and the private renewal activities taking place in a few existing inner-city rowhouse areas that are well beyond walking distance of downtown. The strong demand for new attached homes in outlying lower density areas also suggests that rowhouse environments continue to appeal to a broad spectrum of the population. Moving on this hypothesis and working within the constraint of the existing street pattern, several architects in the Department of Planning have imaginatively designed out the undesirable features of present block configurations. While it is extremely difficult to forecast consumer preferences even a year in advance, the residental future that these persons are inventing for Baltimore does not seem to be unrealistic. Regardless of one's own preconceptions, it is to be hoped that they are correct, for the inner-city masonry row homes, even those in poor condition, represent an asset of inestimable potential value. Because most of them are of originally sound construction and not in very bad condition, they can be upgraded at a fraction of the expense required to replace dilapidated frame structures or crumbling masonry apartments in other cities. This point will be returned to in subsequent chapters.

THE CLIMATE FOR CHANGE

Although the rhetoric of local officials concerning the housing crisis has become nationally homogenized, cities do vary greatly in their willingness to cope with shelter problems. The City of Baltimore has long been a pioneer in the low-income housing field. It has a large subsidized housing effort, with approximately 4% of its occupied inventory in public ownership. Far more important, code enforcement, rehabilitation, tenant education, housing courts, and clean-block campaigns all owe some of their development to experience growing out of programs initiated in Baltimore. In addition to the direct effects which these programs have had on the city's housing stock, they have helped to create a large group of persons in both the public and private sectors who are exceptionally knowledgeable about housing.

During most of the 1960's, it appears that Baltimore either was resting on its laurels or had turned its pioneering spirit to other problems. Nothing much happened in housing either on an experimental or larger scale basis. Little use was made of new programs flowing out of Washington. By the end of the decade, however, the city had reorganized its housing agencies and is once again moving ahead with new programs.

CHAPTER 3

Housing Needs and Objectives: A Conceptual View

Low-income families are deprived with respect to housing in a number of different ways. Their homes are frequently in disrepair, as well as lacking in: space, privacy, and ventilation; cooking, bathing and heating facilities; basic furnishings; and protection from weather, fires, accidents, and vermin. Their neighborhoods are often crowded, strewn with trash, unsafe at night, interlarded with obnoxious uses, devoid of green space, and underserved by community and commercial facilities. To obtain even unsatisfactory living quarters, they are forced to pay such a high proportion of their income for housing that they have insufficient funds remaining for other necessities of life. Having secured a place to reside, not a few of them live in the knowledge that an interruption in income may suddenly force them to move. Were all this not enough, the poor find themselves discriminated against in the home ownership market by onerous financing terms, and prevented, by zoning restrictions and poor public transit facilities, from having access to housing, job, and educational opportunities at the urban fringe. Special groups among the poor suffer even further. Those with physical handicaps cannot find housing services to meet their special needs; blacks are daily reminded of their second-class status in the real estate market, and are frequently forced to pay more than whites for comparable dwellings. Finally, recipients of various forms of housing assistance may find that although their shelter problems are solved, they are stigmatized for accepting public aid. A similar fate befalls many of those who are forced to depend upon the benignity of private landlords for their survival.

These then are the 12 dimensions of the housing problem of the poor: lack of adequate housing space, quality, and furnishings; poor neighborhood environment; excessive housing costs relative to family income; lack of security of occupancy; restrictions upon choice of tenure; restricted locational choice; lack of special housing services for the physically handicapped; racial discrimination; excessive housing cost relative to quality and quantity of space received; and the stigma attached to receiving housing assistance.

These dimensions of housing need are but a small subset of the total array of deprivations which low-income families must endure. Such families are similarly disadvantaged with respect to health, education, employment, recreation, political participation, legal justice, and, in fact, nearly all aspects of their daily lives. Many of the housing and nonhousing deprivations are causally connected; reduction of one would ameliorate another, and vice versa. In addition, nearly all of them are intermediate in the sense that the purpose of their elimination is to achieve one or more higher level societal objectives such as physical comfort, good health, and safety and security, having to do with the overall physical and mental well-being of the general population. (1) These higher objectives are reflected in the hierarchy of deprivations presented in Figs. 3.1A and 3.1B. If the hierarchy in Fig. 3.1B were extended downward, it would link up with the 12 dimensions of housing need at numerous points, indicating that each of the 12 dimensions relates to one or more of the upper tier problems in Fig. 3.1A.

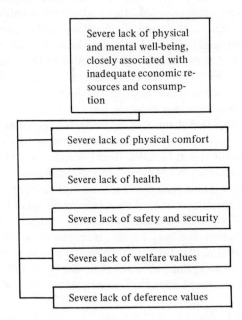

Figure 3.1A. Deprivations experienced by portions of the low-income population.

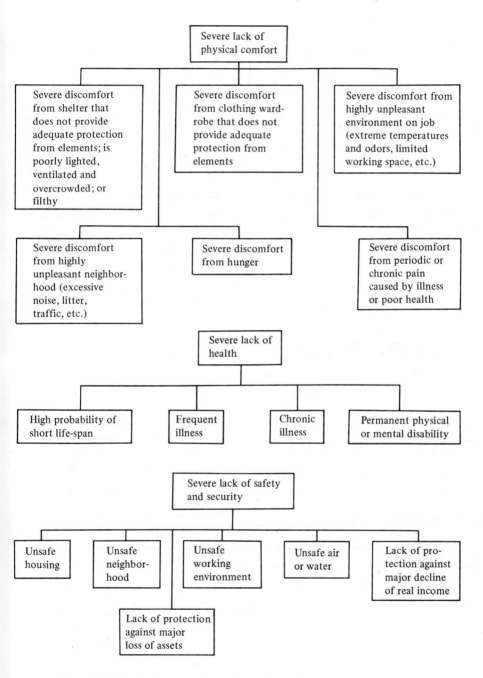

Figure 3.1B. Deprivations experienced by portions of the low-income population.

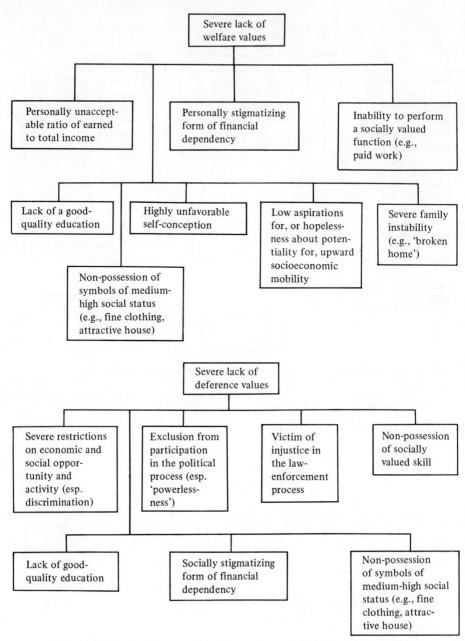

Figure 3.1B. Deprivations experienced by portions of the low-income population.

By positioning housing needs within a larger complex of interrelated deprivations, we are able to broaden the context within which housing policy is viewed. It is the existence of multiple, often conflicting goals each of which can be pursued by a variety of means for the benefit of any one of a number of different client groups that is at the heart of the policy problem. Using this general conceptual framework as a guide, our first policy-development task is the establishment of measurable housing objectives against which needs, resources, programs, and higher level goals can then be compared. This is the aim of the remainder of the present chapter. While the attempt to translate each dimension of need into a measurable objective is not completely successful, the exploration of needs and objectives in theoretical terms serves to set the framework for the empirical and policy discussions to follow later in the volume.

PURPOSES AND LIMITATIONS OF MEASURABLE OBJECTIVES

Before articulating the twelve elements of housing need and their related objectives in detail, it is necessary to explain the way in which the measurable objectives fit into the overall analysis. They perform a quite different role from that of high-level, nonmeasurable goal statements, e.g., that poverty should be eliminated, or that every family should be adequately housed. In contrast to such statements, around which agreement is usually sought, it is *not* expected, nor is it necessary, that consensus be reached on measurable objectives. Indeed, for all practical purposes, consensus is impossible. If diverse interest groups were brought around a table to pass judgment on the objectives presented here, for example, disagreement would inevitably arise over the desirability of at least a few of the objectives. Housing desegregation, for example, might be flatly rejected by certain groups and firmly espoused by others. Even, presuming, however, that everyone accepted all of the objectives as being worthwhile, some persons would want the specific targets, such as bringing every structure up to the housing code, set either higher or lower. And if these differences were resolved, conflict would emerge over priorities — desegregation vs better housing being an excellent real-life illustration.

Consensus is impossible primarily because a single set of values and goals is not held throughout society. In addition, the precise connections between a measurable objective (e.g., code-level housing) and higher-level immeasurable goals (say, comfort and well-being) toward which it is aimed are by definition immeasurable, hence an inherent source of disagreement. And finally, the ranking of objectives according to their priority is to a considerable degree a ranking of competing client groups. If this were not the case, decisions regarding priorities could usually be more appropriately made by the clients themselves. For all these reasons, conflict over measurable objectives is inevitable and irreconcilable. This being so, the search for consensus should be postponed until specific programs are being considered. It is necessary, though, in any statement of objectives that all aspects of the problem, as seen by various interest groups, are represented, and that none of the objectives are expressed in a way that would seem unreasonable to *all* of the groups involved. In brief, what is required is comprehensive coverage, not a set of recommendations.

Structured in this way a set of measurable objectives should be viewed as benchmarks against which progress, or lack thereof, can be measured; and more importantly, as a basis for analyzing program alternatives. For each objective there are obviously a number of such alternatives. Some of these will complement programs designed to achieve another objective; others may hinder that achievement. Choices among programs — which, again, is ultimately the point at which differences of opinion must be resolved — can be facilitated and improved if the implications of various programs for each objective are more clearly recognized and if the severity of each element of need is better known.

It should be pointed out that there is some disagreement as to whether measurable objectives should be specified at the initial stage of the planning process. It is argued that until the nature of particular problems is well understood, any attempt to translate goal statements into measurable terms runs the danger of focusing attention on the wrong issues. To avoid this possibility, the set of objectives presented here were defined, redefined, and redefined again as the research effort yielded new information.

Mention should also be made of the fact that in making objectives measurable, it is almost inevitable that there will be some distortion of the more general nonmeasurable goal which is being sought. At times, this distortion can be quite serious, causing entire organizations to pursue inappropriate programs. For example, high-school and college diplomas have become such important measures of educational attainment that many schools have relaxed their educational standards rather than deny students that coveted piece of paper. And the goal of a 3.5% rate of unemployment obscures the possibility that if unemployment were spread more evenly across the population so that everyone experienced this condition a little bit of the time, an overall rate as high as 6% or 7% might be perfectly acceptable. With this sort of pitfall in mind, we have tended to back away from precise definition of several objectives which seemed to require more study.

HOUSING NEEDS AND OBJECTIVES

With the general purposes and directions of the chapter now explained, it is possible to proceed to a conceptual exploration of the twelve dimensions of housing need that were listed at the outset and to work toward development of measurable objectives with respect to each. (2)

Conceptually, housing objectives could be classified according to whether they are intended to:

1. Improve the housing situation for most or all of the population;

2. Reduce differences among income and other groups by improving the housing situation of disadvantaged sectors; or

3. Create complete equality among income and other groups.

Because of the nature of this study, all of the twelve objectives discussed here fall into the latter two categories. It is possible, therefore, that in the short run, one or more of the objectives may be in conflict with other important national or local housing goals. (3)

It should also be kept in mind that, strictly speaking, the problem of formulating appropriate measurable objectives is distinct from that of actual measurement. However, the two are so intertwined, it is often not possible to discuss the one without the other. This is especially the case where the task of translating general goals into measurable objectives requires that certain complex concepts, e.g., "housing quality" and "discrimination," be appropriately defined. In instances such as these, it is useful to proceed partly by induction; that is, to test various possible measures with respect to whether they are adequately reflective of the concepts which the objective is intended to embody. In this trial and error fashion, the measurable objective is gradually developed. In several of the discussions which follow, our inductive reasoning is retraced for the reader. This results in an unevenness among the twelve sections that is unavoidable, but hopefully not disconcerting if the reasons for it are understood.

1. Housing Quality, Including Equipment and Services (4)

Although the goal of a decent home for every American family was adopted in federal housing legislation over 25 years ago and has been an objective of social reformers since the turn of the century, it is still surrounded by controversy. In various quarters it is held to be undesirable and unachievable. And there is a sharp division of opinion as to what standards are implied in the term "decent."

Reservations about the desirability of the goal are largely academic. It is argued simply that if an individual is able to exercise an informed choice in the matter and yet selects to live in a (legally defined) substandard dwelling, he or she should be allowed to do so, if this decision would not adversely affect innocent persons such as neighbors or children. Practically speaking, the universe of such situations is probably so limited as to make the point meaningless. There is a related argument, however, which is not meaningless. It might be described as analogous to the doctrine that enforced segregation of schools yields inherently inferior education to those against whom the practice is designed. In essence, the proposition as it applies to housing is that if discriminatory practices prevent certain groups in the population from having access to the more desirable sectors of the stock, their housing is inherently unsatisfactory even though it meets accepted standards of health and safety. Regardless of its physical quality, it cannot meet the minimum needs that a home should provide in a free society. In Stockholm, to illustrate the point in reverse, a considerable portion of the residential stock would fail to meet the plumbing and heating codes in many U.S. cities, yet it is regarded as perfectly acceptable, not because the Swedes have a lower standard of living than do Americans, but because much of the housing in question is occupied voluntarily by families who can afford better quarters. (5)

The question of whether the goal of a decent home is achievable also sounds academic, and also raises some substantive issues. It is argued by a few analysts that standards of decency will keep rising with the increasing affluence of the country. As a consequence, there will always be a segment of the inventory that is regarded as below acceptable norms, and the demand for more public attention to the nation's housing dilemma will never recede. There is some support in the record for this point of view. Standards have indeed risen over time, and it has usually taken a period of years to bring the inventory up to the new levels of acceptability. Eventually, however, outdoor plumbing does disappear, lead paint is removed, and electrical wiring is made safe. If, in the meantime, standards have risen again to include new community concerns, this fact should not deny the value of setting goals in the first place.

The most serious difficulty with elastic quality goals occurs not because achievement is impossible, but rather because rising standards permeate society quite gradually. Hence at any point in time there may be serious differences regarding what constitutes acceptable quality. This is currently the dilemma in most communities. The standards embodied in local housing codes, which are confined primarily to matters of physical health and safety, do not reflect, in the view of many policy-makers, the much higher aspirational levels of the average American family. If all the dwelling units in the United States were brought into compliance with any one of the good local codes, the unmet housing need as reflected in the goal statements of various advocates of better housing would still be enormous.

A gap between what is legally enforceable and what is regarded as minimally acceptable is not new either in housing or in other sectors of the economy. There is something new in the current relationship, however. For the first time in history, the better local housing codes do not seriously lag behind scientific knowledge in matters of health and safety, and even incorporate a few purely aesthetic items. It would be surprising, therefore, if these codes were upgraded significantly in the next decade or so. As a result, the gap between enforceable standards and generally accepted norms of housing consumers may become pronounced.

Because of the diversity and intensity of opinions about appropriate standards of housing quality and condition, a single set of standards, even if advanced only as a benchmark, runs the risk of being widely rejected as either too high or too low or both. Moreover, obtaining agreement on standards is only half the problem. In order to calculate the extent of need with respect to whatever quality objectives are deemed appropriate, the large number of disparate elements in each dwelling must be rated and the ratings somehow combined into a composite score. This is a problem that has engaged the attention of analysts for years, yet no completely satisfactory solution has been found. The most obvious common denominator is market value, or rent, but prices are influenced by a number of variables besides quality, including amount of indoor and outdoor space, landscaping, modernity, location, and racial discrimination. In the case of substandard units, a single index of quality can be created by weighting housing code violations either according to their presumed seriousness or by the amount of money required to abate them. This approach, while basically sound, excludes most dwellings of good quality. Moreover, it would give a lower ranking to expensive homes having a few violations than to accommodations that were far more modest but were in full compliance with the code.

Rather than risk becoming bogged down in serious arguments over quality standards, our study pursued three different types of ratings so that each could in a sense be tested against the others. The first of these was based on the criteria used in the 1960 Housing Census to classify structures as either sound, deteriorating, or dilapidated. Approximately 9,000 dwelling units were thus rated by the interviewers in our first household survey. Although the information obtained in this fashion was helpful in making tentative longitudinal and cross-sectional comparisons of housing quality, it was used quite gingerly, since the entire rating system has been found by the Bureau of the Census to lack reliability. The subjective judgments of the persons making the evaluations apparently cannot easily be reduced to an acceptable level. Even if the reliability of the data were not an issue, the ratings do not lend themselves to refined analysis. The three categories of quality are quite broad, with at least three-quarters of the inventory in most cities falling into a single class — "sound." And in order for relatively inexperienced persons to make the ratings, many ingredients of quality must be ignored. As a result, the relevance of the ratings to specific public policy questions is frequently open to serious question.

To overcome these various difficulties, as well as some of the problems mentioned earlier, the quality of a small subsample of the original 9,000 dwellings was evaluated much more carefully, using in effect one yardstick for the substandard inventory (cost of upgrading) and another for dwelling units of higher quality (estimated market value, excluding neighborhood factors). (6) Although the detailed evaluations represent a significant improvement over the census-type ratings, they are limited by their failure to include any input from housing users. The adequacy of housing is, after all, a function of the needs and desires of the occupants as well as of standards set by government. If low-income families were asked to express their complaints and desires in specific terms, it is conceivable that the minimum acceptable housing standards for public policy purposes would be either well above or below or quite different from those reflected in present housing codes. If all structures were brought up to standard, and serious complaints were still being voiced by occupants about housing quality, it might suggest not simply that the minimum standard was too low, but that the rating system itself was deficient. (7)

To obtain the perceptions of families regarding their housing, all 9,000 respondents in the first household survey were asked a general question about how they liked their home. A subsample was queried in detail about specific problems and was also asked to compare their present home with previous places of residence. Taken by themselves, these data must be interpreted cautiously. Low-income households may have high thresholds of pain and a low level of expectations. Some may be especially reluctant to criticize their own home, even if it is rented, because this would be tantamount to an admission of their inability to afford something better. To the degree, however, that their responses either corroborate objective measures or deviate from them in ways that can be explained by demographic or other variables, they enrich and support the quality ratings.

The subjective and objective measures just described leave one important aspect of the problem virtually untouched. The occupant of a residential structure, whether owner or renter, purchases in essence a stream of services, the quality of which is a function of the way in which the structure is managed as well as of the structure itself. For low-income families, the quality of management is increasingly being perceived as more critical than the quality of structure. The flow of heat is frequently interrupted; repairs are not made in a timely fashion; and so on. Some of these problems are covered by housing codes, but they cannot be measured by inspections, and records of complaints to public agencies probably grossly understate their prevalence.

Although what the measurable objective should be with respect to quality of services requires more thought, reliance would probably have to be placed on opinion surveys to identify the problem. Since a certain amount of dissatisfaction with management should be expected throughout the market, the proper objective would be a random distribution of discontent among income and ethnic groups, or perhaps a greater expression of discontent among the more advantaged sectors of the population. Given the possibility of systematic differences in levels of expectations, even this standard is not entirely satisfactory without an underlying base of objective measures.

One final note. Even if all dwelling units complied with the housing code and all residents were reasonably satisfied with their home or apartment, it could not necessarily be presumed that the residential inventory was of acceptable quality. Analysis of data on fires, accidents in the homes, and sickness and disease might reveal that portions of the stock were deficient in ways that had not previously been recognized. Such indicators do not, of course, necessarily measure housing deficiencies, so they cannot be used as measurable objectives, but they can serve as valuable signals of a possible need to adjust existing objectives.

2. Furnishings

A fact which is frequently overlooked in examinations of housing problems is that the stream of services which a family receives from its home is a function of the quality and quantity of furnishings as well as of the home itself. (8) Since shelter and furnishings are typically purchased in separate markets, a family could have too little of one and not the other, but usually the two types of deficiencies go hand in hand. The furnishings of a home, like the home itself, have both functional and symbolic value. The husband may find them comfortable while the wife is ashamed to have her friends in for a cup of coffee. (9) Many more low-income families are probably deprived with respect to the appearance of their furniture than with respect to its basic utility, yet initially it would seem sufficient to establish standards that relate only to the functional sufficiency of furnishings for normal family living. The two most severe deficiencies, for those households who lack them, are absence of an operating refrigerator and an inadequate number of beds. Inability to refrigerate food forces families to purchase in very small quantities at higher-than-average prices, and either restricts the range of their diet or increases the risk of their eating spoiled food, or both. The deprivation associated with too few beds need not be elaborated; nor is it necessary to discuss what would constitute an appropriate standard. What is less certain is why, given the rate at which Americans discard furniture, any family is lacking at least one bed per unmarried adult or adolescent, and one operating refrigerator.

In this study, no attempt was made to count the number of households who lacked even these minimum necessities. A somewhat higher but less precise standard was reflected in a rating by interviewers as to the adequacy of furnishings in the room in which the interview was conducted. One way to approximate the need for furnishings, if funds are unavailable for periodic surveys, might be through the records of local public-assistance agencies. If information were available from this source, it could be adjusted to reflect the likely need among low-income families not on welfare.

3. Indoor Space

Overcrowding is one of the oldest concerns of housing policy in the United States. It has been viewed as a factor in physical and mental illness and moral degradation. Although few could quarrel with the proposition that at some level overcrowding might indeed have these effects, what that level may be is far from certain. Much depends on whether the dwelling unit both can be and actually is adequately ventilated by the occupants; the amount of time spent in the dwelling; population density in the neighborhood as well as in the structure; the social mores of the culture; and resistance of the subject population to disease. In America, efforts to establish a relationship between overcrowding and various health and disorganization indicators have met with little success. (10) And populations in other countries somehow manage to live at much higher densities than do most Americans, with apparently no adverse physical, mental, or moral effects.

The case for various U.S. standards of overcrowding must, therefore, be made largely on grounds of comfort and equity, not health and safety. Stated as a goal, each low-income family should be able to acquire an amount of housing space that prevailing norms have established as sufficient for pleasant living.

Taking this as the general goal, the appropriate measurable objective must be specified. Implicit in most discussions of space standards is the notion that overcrowding must be eliminated, not simply reduced to a low level. As with substandard housing or racial discrimination, any evidence of offending situations is seen as intolerable. This view fails to recognize that a certain amount of overcrowding is inevitable, even among higher income families. The arrival of a new baby or a widowed relative or new in-laws may create a space squeeze for nearly any household for a short period until a satisfactory solution to the problem can be found. Thus at any point in time, some proportion of the families in nearly every sector of the population will be found to be overcrowded. The goal, therefore, should be to equalize these percentages across income and ethnic groups, or at minimum between middle- and low-income families, and between blacks and whites having similar incomes.

Stating the objective in these relative terms partially finesses the question of what constitutes an adequate amount of space per person, but it could conceivably complicate the measurement of progress. Presently-used data on persons per room understate differences among income groups, because on the average expensive dwellings have larger rooms and a greater number of baths and closets, both of which are excluded from room counts. Differences may also be obscured for quite another reason. Poor families with a large number of children are sometimes forced, because of overcrowding, to split up or to seek foster care for one or more of their youngsters. If greater equality in the distribution of housing space is to be the goal, these empirical subtleties should be recognized.

This does not mean that more refined information is absolutely essential at the present time. The traditional persons-per-room measure exposes the general magnitude of the problem, and can easily be supplemented by opinion data which might reveal some of the hidden differences just mentioned.

4. Neighborhood Environment

It has been frequently observed that it is not bad housing which makes a slum but rather the environment of filth and degradation both within the home itself and in the surrounding neighborhood. The neighborhood environment has both social and physical dimensions. Only the latter are discussed here. Social dimensions of the environment, such as crime, income and racial mix, and quality of schools, although frequently of greater importance to families than is the physical environment, and although intimately related to higher level societal goals, are reserved for exploration in later chapters. And since the problem of defining a neighborhood arises primarily in connection with social aspects of the environment, this historic concern of planners will be ignored here also.

Most of the physical environment of a neighborhood is created by the housing (including yards) itself. Hence, as residential structures are upgraded, the visual quality of the neighborhood will improve correspondingly. Also contributing to the quality of the surroundings, however, are the amount and character of traffic, condition of sidewalks and streets and alleys, amount of litter and junk in the streets, yards, alleys, and vacant lots; adequacy of street-lighting and signs; proximity of unpleasant land uses and abandoned buildings; noise levels; and the proportion of land devoted to open space and greenery. Although these aspects of the environment could be viewed as not within the province of housing policy, all of them are dealt with in various programs of the Department of Housing and Urban Development.

With respect to measurable objectives for these items, the standards in most cases would be the same for all neighborhoods, regardless of the income or ethnic composition of the occupants. (11) The standards themselves would have to vary with the density of development, but at any given density level, families at all income levels should enjoy approximately the same street illumination and paving, air quality, protection from traffic, etc. There might be some question as to what constitutes a noxious use or unpleasant or unsafe traffic condition, and it is not certain whether all families would perceive such situations approximately in the same way, but these conceptual problems are relatively minor.

There are two possible exceptions to the objective of environmental equality across demographic groups, The first has to do with neighborhood cleanliness. The objective here might better be stated in terms of inputs, not end results. The level of services provided by street and sanitation departments should clearly be equal (adjusted for population density), but it is perhaps too much to expect such a policy to yield neighborhoods of uniform cleanliness. Some blocks are spotless, because residents do part of the street cleaning and trash collection themselves. By contrast, in other areas where there is less community spirit, or different personal standards, families not only may be disinclined to make a special effort to keep yards and streets clean, but may actually contribute to the litter themselves. This variation in behavior may in turn induce a corresponding variation in the care with which street cleaners and trash collectors go about their work. The question is confused, however, by the fact that low-income neighborhoods tend to produce an extra large volume of certain kinds of junk — worn-out refrigerators, stoves, and automobiles — which sanitation departments are not equipped to handle and which the owners cannot afford to have trucked or towed away. Also, low-income families do not always have the resources to get rid of trash and junk in approved ways. Unless they are given adequate assistance in disposing of these items, the accumulation of debris in yards and alleys may quickly destroy normal incentives to keep an area clean. (12)

The second exception to environmental equality relates to population density and to the proportion of land that is covered by buildings. One of the most oppressive aspects of low-income neighborhoods in large cities is the unrelieved mass of buildings and humanity. In Baltimore, the prevailing sentiment is that both population density and land coverage in the inner city are too high. In the absence of a substantial reduction in the city's total population, however, it would be physically impossible to accommodate every low-income family at the same low density which prevails in the outer city. A certain amount of variation in population density across income groups seems inevitable, at least for a decade or two. It is possible, though, to create larger amounts of usable open space by redesigning blocks and shifting to different building types. Unfortunately, there are no agreed-upon standards of adequacy except what can be deduced from the expressed preferences of the population, and these are not very reliable indicators. Also the entire matter is highly relative in terms of time and place, with densities and land coverage that were considered satisfactory 50 years ago and which are still acceptable in very large urban areas probably being viewed as quite excessive in smaller communities. (13)

Several different types of measures of neighborhood environment were attempted in this study. In the first household survey, interviewers were asked to rate the cleanliness of the street front. As part of the detailed structural inspections, street fronts, along with alleys and yards, were again given a cleanliness score. In addition, the number of boarded-up buildings and the flow of traffic during nonpeak hours were noted. These objective measures were supplemented by the opinions which respondents in the first and second household surveys expressed concerning a number of elements of their immediate environment. Because of our uncertainty regarding exactly what the measurable objectives for neighborhood environment should be, all of this information was used only to indicate the probable general magnitude of various dimensions of the problem.

Taken together, the several indicators reveal expected differences in environment across income groups, but they fall short of providing one or a few easily replicable measures which could be used for establishing minimum standards and monitoring progress. If the objective of improving the housing environment and reducing environmental differences among urban populations is seriously pursued, much better measures will be required.

5. Locational Choice

The fact that inexpensive housing accommodations are not widely dispersed throughout urbanized areas, but instead tend to be geographically concentrated, creates several problems for low-income families and may aggravate others. Many analysts feel that these problems are of greater importance than those which are alleged to be created by substandard housing.

One frequently cited locational choice problem has to do with the transportation revolution in the U.S., which has widened the gap between the quality of living for the poor and those of more substantial means. The mobility of those who can afford an automobile has greatly increased, while the radius of activities for families who must rely on a steadily deteriorating public transportation system to reach increasingly remote job opportunities and community services has been reduced. The problem is particularly acute in larger metropolitan areas where desired trip destinations are most distant and where an auto-less family often cannot be helped by friends, because entire neighborhoods are dependent on buses and mass transit. The problem is felt most acutely by the family with no employed members, the disabled, and the job seeker. For the healthy job holder with not more than the average number of dependents and living anywhere except in the two or three largest metropolitan areas, automobile ownership is rarely an impossibility.

Although the problem can be defined as one of transportation and not housing, if the location of low-cost housing, employment opportunities, and community facilities were planned in a more coordinated fashion, the transportation requirements of many low-income persons would be reduced. Expressed differently, for part of the population there may be a housing approach to a transportation problem which to a limited degree has nontransportation origins.

A broader range of locational choices is important for reasons other than mobility. Low-income families, even those who own automobiles, lack access to good schools. If the findings of the Coleman report are correct, intermixing children from various income groups in the classroom would reduce inequality of educational attainment, thereby weakening one of the supports of rigid social strata. (14) Although the Coleman study has been challenged on various grounds, there does seem to be general agreement that social-class mixing in the schools increases educational equality to a modest degree. This mixing often cannot be achieved very effectively by busing, at least at the primary school level.

The measurable objective with respect to locational choice depends on what higher level goal is being sought. If it is improvement in employment opportunities, the objective might be creation in each minor civil division of a housing inventory that bore some correspondence to the job profile in that community. (15) If equal educational opportunity were the prime target, then each primary school district would have to contain a broad range of housing rents and values.

Objectives stated in these terms, however, partially deny the notion of choice, because all neighborhoods or communities would have to be heterogeneous. Also, the objectives as stated could be achieved only by programs that operated on the supply side of the market. It would be equally possible and preferable to express the objective in terms which would permit demand-side interventions to solve part of the problem of restricted choice. This approach would be particularly appropriate in cities where race and income are still causally intertwined. Defined somewhat imprecisely, the objective could stipulate that every family should be able to afford, through subsidies or otherwise, to buy or rent at least, say, 10% of the homes in, say, 70% of all neighborhoods (operationally defined) in the metropolitan area.

Since all of the surveys conducted as part of this study were confined to the City of Baltimore, no measures of this dimension of need were possible. With 1970 census data now available, this empirical gap can easily be closed.

6. Housing Expense Relative to Income

The fact that the high cost of shelter is a serious problem for low-income families is so widely accepted that it scarcely needs elaboration. Or does it? Almost by definition, the cost of everything which a poor family must purchase is excessively high in relation to total income. In this sense, the problem is not one of high housing expense but of low income. Housing, however, is frequently singled out for special attention for several reasons. First, it absorbs a very large proportion of the family budget, so on a percentage basis, progress in reducing housing costs could relieve pressure on other parts of the budget quite substantially. Second, with minor exceptions, housing costs cannot be deferred or reduced by low-income families, whereas other expenditures can be and are. As a result, households suffer from inadequate diet, clothing, and medical care, just to keep a roof over their heads. Third, low-income families do not get much housing for what they pay in rent, a matter to be discussed separately in Section 7 below.

If it is accepted that the problem is one of housing cost as well as income, a measurable objective with respect to what is an excessive expenditure relative to income must be established. A widely accepted objective in the U.S. is for no family to pay more than 20% to 25% of its income for housing, with a small adjustment for family size. However, both the figures themselves and the way in which they are derived seem open to question. The adjustments for family size have universally been inadequate, favoring small households over large ones by a substantial margin. More serious, the basic percentages are much too high for low-income families. Middle-income families, on the average, spend less than 20% of their earnings for housing. Using the reasoning that is implicit in any percentage standard, namely that housing expenses above a certain proportion of earnings will create serious hardship, poor families should be expected to allocate a *lower* proportion of their income to housing than do other families. Some poverty-stricken families should receive their living accommodations for only a nominal fee. The fact that they do not and are expected instead to spend up to one-fourth of their income for shelter, even in subsidized projects, is due to the limited amount of subsidies for housing, not the limited depth of the need.

One possible measurable objective, then, could be derived by matching family income against the total cost of an acceptable living standard, as reflected, for example, in one of the family budgets of the Bureau of Labor Statistics. The family's housing expenses should not be so great as to leave it with insufficient money to acquire the nonhousing necessities in any budget that is deemed appropriate. If housing expenses are found to be excessive in this respect, the problem still may not necessarily be one of low income. The excess could be due to discrimination or to the fact that the family is over-housed. The latter situation is not uncommon among the elderly.

Objection could be raised to the above standard on the grounds that it converts a housing problem entirely into one of income. Families in poverty automatically have the problem; others normally do not. The entire income deficiency may seem to stem from excessive housing expenditures when in fact it could just as logically be assigned to food, clothing, transportation, health care, or some other large item in the family budget. Moreover, if families were provided with funds sufficient to bring their housing expenses in line with their incomes, it seems probable that many of them, even some who were adequately housed, would move to more expensive accommodations and continue to appear to be in need.

To avoid these objections, one is forced back to using one or another rent–income ratio as a standard. The question then becomes whether any particular ratio, adjusted for family size and other relevant variables, is in some sense most reasonable and appropriate. Within limits the answer would seem to be no. Simply as an indication of the general dimension of the problem, however, it might be acceptable to use as a standard the median rent–income ratio of non-low-income families of the same household size. This benchmark would produce a substantially lower estimate of need than would the one described above. It would say, in effect, that low-income families should not be obliged to allocate a larger proportion of their incomes to housing than do other families, particularly when they do not obtain shelter of equal size and quality. Unfortunately, this standard implies that one-half of non-low-income families are also spending an unacceptable proportion of their income for housing.

In the absence of any adequate standard, this study accepted both of the two inadequate ones in order to produce a high and low estimate of need and thereby minimize later controversy. Regardless of which of the two is preferred, the information for the calculation of excess housing expense would have to come from field surveys. Without considerable probing by interviewers, the validity of such data may be questionable. Income is likely to be underreported and rent payments overreported, thus considerably exaggerating the extent of the problem. The reasons for the income bias are commonly known and need not be described. The bias in the typical rent figures stems from the widespread practice of rent forgiveness among landlords in the low-rent market.

In addition, rent–income ratios derived from annual income data hide the fact that the earnings of many families fluctuate widely from year to year with shifts in business and personal conditions. If ratios were based on a longer time span, the problem might be revealed to be much smaller, or larger, or different from what is suggested by conventional data.

7. Housing Expense Relative to Quality and Size of Dwelling

Through the years what has probably disturbed housing reformers most is not simply the condition of slum structures, bad as they are, nor the rents of slum quarters, high as they are, but the two in combination. Measured in terms of square feet per occupant, the cost of substandard housing is frequently found to be more expensive than much better residential accommodations. This phenomenon is not simply a function of overcrowding, for even ignoring the question of occupancy, low-quality units often do not command the cheapest rents. And even where rents for poor-quality housing are not as high as rents in dwellings which offer more amenities, they frequently are not appreciably lower. As a consequence, an apparently wide range of quality can be found at low rent levels.

Part of the comparative disadvantage of low-income households is illusory. The reason families who can afford, say, a rent of $100 per month receive so much more *apparent* quality than those who are able to pay only $90 is because most of the first $90 is needed for the barest essentials — safe structure, reasonable space, plus utilities and maintenance. It is only when rents rise above this marginal level that observable signs of quality can enter the picture. Hence, one cannot compare rent payments and quality without at minimum determining the proper allocation of these payments to each of the components of housing cost.

Nevertheless, even without this information it is possible to articulate a measurable goal. The minimum objective would be for all housing to command rents in proportion to the quality and quantity of the services which are provided. That objective, however, might still leave many low-income families residing in substandard structures and paying rents they could not afford. Therefore, achievement of the housing-quality objective and the income housing-expense objective, which have already been discussed, would actually supercede any objective relating quality and space to cost. In fact, if these other two goals were reached, low-income families would receive *more* quality and space for their dollar than would upper-income families.

A second reason for dropping this objective is that to some extent the relationship of housing quality to housing expense is a function of occupant behavior. Some tenants use more utilities, or are less careful in caring for their quarters, or move more often than the average family. These behavioral characteristics affect the rents that are paid relative to the quality of housing received. An objective which sought to make housing quality proportional to prices or to rents would have to be adjusted to reflect this fact, not an easy task. All this is not to say it is not useful to measure apparent quality/rent inequities in the housing market, however crudely, since these measures would be very helpful in identifying general upward or downward trends relative to a number of housing goals. It does not seem necessary, however, to establish a measurable quality/rent objective.

One final point. The problem of inadequate housing quality relative to cost should be viewed through time as well as cross-sectionally among income and ethnic groups. It would be expected that as real income rises, both the quality of housing and the relationship of quality to cost should improve also. This, of course, has been the case. By the standards of today, most of the nation's population in 1900 was ill housed. Since the improved quality which has been achieved was obtained without substantial increases in real per capita housing expenditures, it would be reasonable to infer that the quality/cost ratio rose as well. Recently, however, there have been signs of a reverse trend. Costs of new construction have outpaced upward movements in money income, and rising interest rates have compounded the problem. Meanwhile, quality of new and existing units seems to have improved more gradually. One would have to conclude tentatively on the basis of admittedly inadequate data that the quality/cost ratio is worse today than it was ten years ago.

8. Choice of Tenure

In low-income areas, financing for the acquisition of inexpensive, single-family homes by lower-income households is either onerous or virtually non-existent. Many families of modest means but with acceptable credit ratings find the dream of owning a home outside the realm of possibility. Yet their housing expense as renters is greater than it would be if they were owners. Not only do they suffer, but the inventory does as well, for the care of older rental structures is usually not as good as it is in comparable owner-occupied units.

Because homes in low-income neighborhoods are difficult to buy, they are also difficult to sell. Working-class homeowners who are moving up the economic ladder or who are retired and want less space find that they can dispose of their residence only at great financial sacrifice, if at all.

One possible objective, stated in nonmeasurable terms, would be to remove all financing barriers to home ownership by *moderate*-income families. If these families could find a house in their price range, they should not be denied the opportunity to purchase, because of high down-payments and interest rates or short amortization periods. A second objective would extend the same principle to low-income families who receive housing and income subsidies. If the subsidy put the family within reach of a home which the family would like to purchase, and if the family seemed capable of assuming the responsibilities of ownership, it should be allowed to do so. The achievement of these two objectives should have the effect also of significantly reducing the number of owners who cannot find buyers for their homes. If involuntary ownership persisted, however, it would have to be pursued as a separate problem.

The above objectives raise several issues, some having to do with what is desirable housing and others relating to the problem of measurement. With respect to the question of what is desirable, implicit in present mortgage-lending practices is the argument that the apparently onerous financing terms offered to families seeking lower-priced homes actually reflect extra risks associated with the borrower's financial situation, the neighborhood, or the structure. These are risks to which not only the financing institutions but also the borrower should not be unduly exposed. This argument could be taken more seriously if it were not for the fact that thousands of low- and moderate-income families do manage to become homeowners in older neighborhoods by circumventing institutional lending channels and resorting to land installment contracts and purchase-money mortgages, both of which devices impose heavy financial burdens on them. Since they survive the heavy costs of these forms of financing, surely they would be good risks for an ordinary mortgage loan. Restated, then, one homeownership objective for moderate-income families is simply to make high-cost financing mechanisms obsolete by equalizing access to the institutional mortgage market.

The argument against homeownership for more lower-income families also alleges that these families are not ready for this form of tenure because they cannot cope with the extra responsibilites associated with ownership. In addition, it is felt by some persons that ownership would make families less mobile in the labor market, with consequent income penalties. These arguments lose much of their validity in the context of condominium or cooperative ownership, and there is no reason why certain aspects of these ownership forms could not be applied to the ordinary owner-occupancy situation. Moreover, the opportunity for homeownership is already being extended to welfare families with reasonably favorable results, so the criteria as to which families are ready for ownership also needs rethinking. (16)

As with the other housing goals, the pursuit of policies to broaden ownership opportunities among moderate- and low-income families brings with it the need to measure the extent to which the objective is being met. The crudest measure would be a comparison of rates of ownership by income class, standardized for other demographic variables that affect preference for ownership. Such data could be obtained from the periodic sample surveys described earlier. A major deficiency with this measure is the assumption that preferences for ownership are constant across income groups, holding selected other factors constant.

Since this may not be the case, it would be better to determine preferences directly from families themselves. Such a procedure depends on the ability of survey instruments to elicit valid responses inexpensively, and in particular to distinguish the desire for ownership from preference for a single-family home or better neighborhood.

Even if valid responses were obtained, they might not accurately measure the extent of the problem, depending on exactly how the objective is stated. Many families who express a desire for ownership may indeed not be ready for it. They may handle credit poorly or lack even rudimentary home-management skills. Or they may want ownership of a single-family home where none

their price range, even with a reasonable subsidy. This raises the
to whether the objective of equalizing rates of ownership across
groups should be relaxed to reflect these problems. The answer varies
the type of problem. To the extent that the difficulty lies with the family,
inability to handle credit, it could be argued that even though choice of
tenure were being restricted, the appropriate objective would not be to expand
opportunity for ownership, but rather to solve the basic underlying problem.
To the extent, however, that the problem lies with the market, e.g., no construction of lower-priced homes because of zoning restrictions or because
moderate-income families cannot obtain financing to purchase them, then
the objective should not be modified.

Taking both the demand- and supply-side factors into consideration, the
measurable objective with respect to choice of tenure cannot be to equalize
completely either owner occupancy or satisfaction of preferences for owner
occupancy across income groups. As a consequence, although measures of inequality, carefully interpreted, would be helpful, we are left without any
firm guidelines as to how much inequality is acceptable. This fact suggests
that it might be better to state the objective in terms of opportunities rather
than outcomes. Approached this way, the objective would be to remove
barriers to more equal choice, and the measures would relate to the barriers
themselves rather than to the logical outcomes of their removal. If it could
be determined by periodic surveys that financing and other barriers were
falling, perhaps it could then be reasonably assumed that the objective was
being achieved.

9. Racial Equality in the Ownership, Rental, and Home-Financing Markets

Although the objectives here seem clear enough on the surface, when
attempts are made to translate them into measurable terms various difficulties
arise. This is due both to the numerous ways in which discrimination can
manifest itself in real estate markets and to the complex nature of the concept of discrimination itself.

Taking the conceptual aspects first, for analytical purposes, discrimination
can be described as either "direct" or "indirect" and as either "benign" or
"nonbenign." Indirect discrimination occurs when an individual or group seeks
to avoid another, but not in such a way as to consciously deny anyone else's
rights. The most common example of this is the flight of whites from racially
changing neighborhoods. Direct discrimination, by contrast, does infringe on
the legitimate freedoms of others, and hardly needs illustrating. The terms
benign and nonbenign attempt to reflect the thought behind the act. If a home-
buyer chooses a particular house because it is near a synagogue or a Catholic
church, this discrimination against gentile or Protestant areas bears no unpleasant connotations. If, however, he has no special preferences except to
avoid neighborhoods where certain ethnic groups reside, his feelings could not
be regarded so charitably. (17)

These distinctions among types of discrimination are not unimportant. As recently as four or five years ago, the predominant concern was to eradicate all categories of discrimination, implying a racially homogenized residential environment and a color-blind community. It was felt that every neighborhood should have a mixture of blacks and whites (where there were enough blacks to go around). More immediate importance was attached, however, to eliminating all-white neighborhoods than to integrating all-black ones. All-white neighborhoods, the argument went, forced white children to mature in a sterile environment — a predicament faced in earlier times by most white children, since prior to World War I there were too few blacks in most American communities to achieve the white liberal goal. Arguments to the effect that perhaps not all blacks desired this pattern of living were dismissed as ill-disguised bigotry, as they sometimes were.

Recently, positions have undergone drastic change. Emphasis has shifted to eliminating only direct, nonbenign discrimination, with ethnic clustering being viewed as a societal strength, so long as it is not preserved at the expense of freedom of choice. And the goal of uniform mixing is now seen to be benignly racist (18). It assumes blacks would be happy to be in the minority in white neighborhoods, but not the reverse; and its espousal of color-blindness is really an appeal for whites to be blind to the color black.

When mixing was the goal, the problem of establishing measurable objectives with respect to discriminatory practices was rather simple. As black families actually moved into more and more neighborhoods, it could be presumed that the reasons for landlords, brokers, and others to make racial distinctions would correspondingly diminish. Thus increasing intermixture in the spatial distribution of whites and blacks could be used as a proxy for progress in all facets of the market.

Now that freedom to choose, not a particular choice, is the goal, the measurable objective cannot be easily defined. The residential intermixture of blacks and whites is not relevant, unless the proportion of blacks who are desirous of various degrees of intermixture is known. In the absence of such knowledge, it is necessary to retreat to several individual measures of discrimination. Landlords, home sellers, home builders, mortgage lenders, real estate brokers, and even municipal governments all engage in subtle and blatant discriminatory acts. They either may deny blacks access to a particular sector of the market entirely or may exact an extra price of admission. Although it is relatively simple to define the objective as elimination of these practices, so many different actors are involved and the practices themselves are often so difficult to detect that measurement is both difficult and expensive.

The collective effects of all the discriminatory acts can be and have been measured with reference to data on house prices and rents, rates of home ownership, housing quality, and mortgage terms among comparable sectors of the black and white markets. However, since this information does not reveal the extent of various forms of discrimination, it cannot serve as the foundation upon which measurable objectives are constructed. Indeed, it cannot always be used with confidence to measure the extent of the problem. For, even in the face of discrimination, blacks may enjoy a comparative advantage over whites with respect to prices and rents, if they move into previously all-white areas at a pace which is slower than the desired outmigration rate of existing residents (19).

One of the best measures is provided by spot checks of the market by pairs of black and white "testers" to see whether sellers, brokers, and landlords treat the two races equally. Similar checks of mortgage-lending institutions are usually not feasible, unless the testers are genuine purchasers and can carry the test through to a tentative mortgage commitment on a specific house. Lenders can, however, be asked to disclose their basic lending policies to see whether these may inadvertently discriminate against black families or racially changing areas. To round out the picture, people's perceptions of racial barriers in the market must also be sought, because if blacks do not realize that barriers have fallen, it matters little that the barriers no longer exist.

10. Security of Occupancy

There is a high rate of mobility among low-income families, much of it involuntary. Involuntary mobility has several causes. In the public sector, urban renewal, code enforcement, and highway construction are major contributors (20). In both the public and private sectors court-ordered evictions for nonpayment of rent, abusive behavior, and poor housekeeping account for a large number of forced moves. Even more common are "constructive" evictions which include a variety of situations from rent increases, to "friendly" persuasion on the part of the landlord, to disappearance of the tenant when he is unable to keep up his rental payments. Finally, mortgage foreclosures strike a small number of families each year.

High mobility among a large part of the population in low-income neighborhoods creates a general feeling of rootlessness and works against the development of a sense of community which is generally thought to be so essential to the revitalization of these areas. Involuntary mobility exacerbates the problem, as reactions to urban redevelopment programs have amply demonstrated. Somehow or other, low-income families must be able to have the same sense of security about their tenure as do other households. And this goal must be accomplished without retarding the necessary business of public programs and without jeopardizing legitimate rights of landlords and mortgage lenders.

It is not possible to articulate a single objective regarding security of occupancy since each source of insecurity suggests its own goal. In the case of urban renewal, the involuntary aspects of dislocation are inherent but are exaggerated by fear of the unknown and by inadequate compensation and re-location services. If displaced families were overcompensated to reflect the involuntary nature of their move, many would look forward to the bulldozer, and this is perhaps as it should be. In many states, owners are already being overcompensated by renewal agencies for their fee interests. It is usually the leaseholders who suffer the most, however, and what they receive, when they are given anything at all, is frequently scarcely more than commiseration (21). How to measure when the scales are in balance is difficult to say. Perhaps attitudinal questions addressed periodically to families who had been dis-located would reveal whether negative aspects of the involuntary moves had been adequately compensated.

Turning to mortgage foreclosures, the objective of keeping foreclosures low can be achieved quite easily by pursuing conservative lending practices, and this is exactly what has happened. In the process, low-income families have been heavily burdened in other ways, as pointed out in Section 8 above. Any ob-jective with respect to foreclosures, therefore, must be tied to the goal of more equal access to mortgage capital. Within this constraint, mortgage foreclosures should be equalized across income groups. Mortgage foreclosure data by in-come class and over time would provide a reasonably valid measure of the problem, although it must be recognized that there are constructive fore-closures just as there are constructive evictions.

With respect to court-ordered and constructive evictions, the measurement problem is perhaps even more difficult. Since most evictions are constructive and thus not recorded, the number of involuntary moves can not be determined except by quite sensitive field interviewing. Beyond that, the number of those moves is not synonymous with lack of security of occupancy, because many are occasioned by negative tenant behavior. In the inner-city market where really good tenants do not exist in profusion, most landlords will not evict an otherwise satisfactory tenant who misses an occasional rent payment. Usually, only a longer interruption in payments or an interruption associated with negative behavior or negative behavior by itself causes an eviction. If a tenant creates his own lack of security, his constructive or actual eviction can hardly be considered part of the problem (22). This conclusion leaves us for the moment with no completely satisfactory measurable objective, but only several crude indices which possibly could be refined with more experience.

A partial substitute for an objective that measures results is one that focuses on some of the processes that yield the results. In this case, if the eviction process were weighted heavily in favor of the landlord, as it is in some juris-dictions, revision of the rules of the game might eliminate a certain number of unnecessary evictions. It might also, though, shift some evictions to the constructive category where they would be hidden from view.

11. Stigma

A common complaint about welfare programs is that they are demeaning
to recipients. Housing programs for low-income families have not escaped
this criticism, though the charge is difficult to prove. Anecdotal evidence is in
abundance, but such stories may illustrate the exceptions rather than the rule.

The element of stigma attaches as much to the situation as to the parties
concerned, but given the donor/recipient context, it is difficult for both
parties not to fall into expected forms of behavior. Perhaps for this reason, the
problem extends as well into the private sector where landlord and low-income
tenant do not bargain from equal positions and do not have equal social status.
Over time many poor families slide into a dependency situation, vis â vis their
landlord, which may be just as demeaning as any relationship between public
agency and welfare client.

While the objective with respect to stigma is clear, the appropriate measures
are not, mainly because the individuals who are most affected gradually become
either inured to the condition or unaware of what has happened to them.
What others would renounce, to them is a way of life. If the problem is, for all
practical purposes, immeasurable, it is necessary again to shift from an output
objective to process objectives; that is, to create policies, programs, and
procedures which reduce the likelihood of stigmatizing situations developing
in the first place. The most obvious programs would be ones which enabled
low-income families to bargain more effectively in the market, including efforts
designed to raise incomes, reduce discrimination, sensitize management, expand
the role of tenants in certain kinds of landlord decisions, and, where applicable,
improve grievance procedures in both public and private housing.

12.   Housing Services for Persons Who are Ill or in Poor Health

An increasing number of individuals, particularly the aging, find themselves
in a position of being too healthy to require hospital care, but not well enough
to cook their meals or get up and down stairs or use normal bath facilities.
Well-to-do individuals can cope with the problem by purchasing special equipment, hiring practical nurses, or moving to quarters more suited to their special
needs. Many persons are assisted by relatives or friends. A large number are also
serviced by volunteer agencies. A growing proportion are moving to homes for
the aged. It is probably still true, however, that adequate care for most
partially disabled persons does not exist, and they suffer silently.

The objective of eliminating this situation can fairly easily be put in
measurable terms, even though agreement as to means probably could not be
as readily obtained. The measure of need would have to be obtained from a
sample survey of the disabled themselves and those who care for them. Some
judgment would have to be exercised in interpreting the seriousness of the
expressed needs, but this is the case with all of the objectives.

SOME SUMMARY OBSERVATIONS

Now that we have expanded the traditional list of low-income housing objectives, placed them within a larger hierarchy of societal goals, and expressed
a number of them in measurable terms, the question again arises, as it did at
the beginning of the chapter, as to what this approach to housing issues contributes to policy formation. The answer to this question will come in bits and
pieces as the study progresses. Two points merit brief comment here, however.

First, the multiplicity of housing objectives, the difficulties which surround
efforts to cast them in measurable terms, and the maze of possible links among
objectives in any hierarchy of community goals provide a partial explanation
of why conflicts concerning housing policies and programs are so widespread.
Differences of opinion arise not only over which strategies are likely to be
most efficient in achieving particular objectives but also over which objectives
should be sought. For example, "fair-share" plans differ sharply from proposed
housing allowance programs with respect to both the housing objectives which
they favor and the relationships which they assume to exist between housing
and other societal goals (23). Ultimately, therefore, the decision as to which
of these two strategies should receive greater public support is likely to be
made not on the basis of which one is most cost effective, but rather according
to which set of intended outcomes is preferred.

Second, regardless of whether one chooses to accept or reject the goal
statements which are presented here, it is discouragingly clear that the nation
is wedded to and vigorously pursuing a totally inadequate and, to some extent,
inappropriate set of housing objectives. At the highest level, the immeasurable
uncontestable goal of "a decent home and suitable living environment" provides no policy guidance. At a much lower level on the goal hierarchy, the
national production target of 26 million new and rehabilitated dwelling units
in ten years (1969—1978) (24) and local fair-share quotas, while precisely
measurable, are analogous to the educational standard of a certain number of
pupils per teacher, and suffer for the same reason — they bear no necessary
relationship to a prescribed set of desired higher-level housing outcomes. It is
this set of outcomes, which would explicitly link "decent home and suitable
living environment" to specific production and other programmatic targets,
that the present discussion has attempted to provide and that form the framework for the exploration of housing needs in the next few chapters.

CHAPTER 4
Housing Quality, Space, and Costs

In recent years, at all levels of government, increasing amounts of attention have been directed toward assessing the size and nature of the low-income housing problem. Several Presidential task forces have undertaken comprehensive studies of national housing needs and programs (1). Huge experiments are under way in an attempt to resolve basic issues of implementation. Many state and local governments have shown rising interest in the development of their own housing programs. Despite these efforts, few cities are in a position, for lack of requisite data, to resolve two questions which are of fundamental importance in policy deliberations: what are the overall dimensions of the problem, and are they becoming more or less severe?

Consideration of these two general relationships should take precedence over the many other questions which have relevance for housing policy; indeed, even over those aimed at specifying the forces which are generating the problem. Prior to understanding causes, it is essential to determine whether, in resource terms, the housing problem is manageable or whether it is really insoluble, at least in the short run, without dramatic shifts in the allocation of public funds. If housing needs were judged to be small, programs could safely be held at their current level and public attention shifted to other issues. If the situation, though serious, were improving and a direct causal link with existing housing programs could be established, this might suggest continuing along present paths with increased funding. Conversely, if needs were becoming more pronounced, revision of present programs and new approaches might seem necessary.

In this chapter and the four that follow, Baltimore's low-income housing problem is analyzed at the macro-level within a need—resources framework.

Taken together, the chapters represent an attempt to establish the basic parameters of the city's problem. To the extent that various empirical issues are resolved, the findings provide the context for examination in subsequent chapters of both underlying causal relationships and viable policy alternatives.

The need—resources analysis seeks to do more than simply add to the growing body of data on the subject. First of all, by focusing in detail on a single city, the analysis attempts to highlight the importance of developing solutions which are sensitive to local configurations of housing need. Too often, the housing problem is viewed at a national scale, presumably on the assumption that programs which appear relevant at that level will have general utility in any given community. Nation-wide statistics on housing quality, rents, and other relevant variables, however, blur out critical differences among localities and regions, with consequent adverse effects upon the potential impact of federal policies.

Second, the problem is examined not only in aggregate but also with respect to its distribution along various dimensions of housing need and among particular subgroups within the population. Currently, a major barrier to a better understanding of the nature of the problem and hence to the establishment of effective programs is sheer lack of knowledge as to what types of families suffer from what combinations of housing deprivations, as perceived both in their own terms and by external standards. Frequent attempts have been made to overcome this barrier, but data limitations have effectively thwarted in-depth analysis. The Baltimore data, while applicable to only one city, do illuminate a number of important dimensions of the housing problem which studies usually must bypass.

Finally, the analysis seeks to make a formal connection between needs and resources, both theoretically and empirically, in such a way that the contribution of a particular program to a particular need of a particular group can be readily identified. In this way, the differential benefits among and within client groups can be subjected to analysis. Equally important, a determination can be made as to whether eliminating the need with respect to a given client group requires a modest or major increase in resources presently being devoted to the problem.

The need—resources analysis, then, is intended to develop a sense of both the magnitude and the character of the tasks ahead. The discussion is divided into five chapters covering six of the twelve dimensions of housing need which were outlined conceptually in Chapter 3. This chapter looks at the following: inadequate housing quality, including equipment and services; insufficient private indoor space; and excessive housing costs relative to income. The next three chapters examine: poor neighborhood environment; lack of choice of tenure; and lack of locational choice.

Chapter 8 examines the resource requirements which would be necessary in order to eliminate in the short run just the first three of these six dimen-

sions of housing need, and compares that scale of effort with the level of
accomplishment of housing programs in Baltimore during the 1960's. Taken
together, Chapters 4–8 provide a macroscopic context for detailed considerations of policy options.

HOUSING QUALITY

Because the quality and condition of the residential inventory is central
to the entire housing problem and because there are wide differences of
opinion as to the adequacy of the stock, a major focus of our research effort
was directed toward establishing a comprehensive picture of this dimension
of need. A number of independent measures were undertaken in order to gain
an accurate view of the level of housing quality. In analyzing these data, four
research questions were of primary importance:

(a)   What is the overall magnitude of the substandard housing problem;
upon what sectors of the stock does it impinge; and what types of treatment
seem most viable for purposes of upgrading the existing inventory in the
near term?

(b)   What has been the trend in the level of housing quality over the
past decade, i.e., have conditions in general been improving or declining?

(c)   What types of households currently occupy substandard housing?

(d)   How do the occupants of substandard housing perceive their
accommodations?

The analysis of housing quality presented below is organized around the questions just outlined. Although the data reflecting upon these questions in
certain instances are crude and are subject to varying interpretations, the
major findings which emerge from the analysis, when taken together, do in
our view have serious implications for the direction of housing policy.

Magnitude of the Substandard Housing Problem

In mid-1969, 65,000 occupied dwelling units, or nearly one-quarter of the
entire occupied stock in Baltimore, were found to be at a quality level below
what is regarded as minimally acceptable in the city's housing code (Table 4.1)
(2). A significant number of additional substandard units were either vacant
or withdrawn from the market. Thus, the total number of units for which
some form of remedial treatment — either rehabilitation or demolition — was
necessary at that point in time in order to achieve a minimum level of adequacy throughout the inventory was probably at least 75,000.

As would be expected, the bulk of the occupied substandard stock, over

Table 4.1. Physical Quality of Occupied Housing Stock by Structure Type and Tenure[1,2] (Baltimore, Maryland, 1969)

Dwelling Units With:	Number of Dwelling Units in:				
	1-Family Structures	2 to 4- Family Structures	5 to 9- Family Structures	10 or More Family Structures	Total
Major physical deficiences	6,970	1,160	–	–	8,130
Owner occupied	380	–	–	–	380
Renter occupied	6,590	1,160	–	–	7,750
Intermediate physical deficiencies	10,460	2,240	150	–	12,850
Owner occupied	1,100	100	–	–	1,200
Renter occupied	9,360	2,140	150	–	11,650
Minor physical deficiencies	24,440	9,990	5,000	4,420	43,850
Owner occupied	8,730	310	60	20	9,120
Renter occupied	15,710	9,680	4,940	4,400	34,730
No physical deficiencies	146,060	36,280	8,960	20,020	211,320
Owner occupied	110,830	9,840	240	600	121,510
Renter occupied	35,230	26,440	8,720	19,420	89,810
Total	187,930	49,670	14,110	24,440	276,150
Owner occupied	121,040	10,250	300	620	132,210
Renter occupied	66,890	39,420	13,810	23,820	143,940
All substandard	41,870	13,390	5,150	4,420	64,830
Owner occupied	10,210	410	60	20	10,700
Renter occupied	31,660	12,980	5,090	4,400	54,130

[1] Rental units include those being acquired under lease–purchase agreements and those occupied without payment of rent in cash.

[2] Source: Survey of Residential Structures.

55,000 units, are concentrated near the urban core. Whereas in the outer city only 1 unit in 20 is below the minimum standard, the corresponding relationship for the inner city is 1 unit in 2.

Historically, in virtually every urban area, units of low quality have tended to be occupied on a rental basis. Not surprisingly, therefore, in Baltimore over four-fifths of all substandard units are renter-occupied. And whereas for the city as a whole nearly two-fifths of the rental units are substandard, the figure for the owner-occupied sector is less than one-tenth. The interaction of geography and tenure yields a particularly bleak picture for inner-city rental units, three-fifths of which fail to meet a minimum level of adequacy.

Given these findings, there can be no denying that the substandard housing problem is a depressing one, in the sense that a significant portion of the city's housing stock is below a minimum standard of decency. The picture brightens somewhat, however, when consideration is given to the intensity of the problem, that is, the degree to which the substandard inventory falls below acceptable norms.

Of the 65,000 occupied substandard units, only 8,000, or one-eighth of the total number, are seriously deficient. These units, most of which are located in the inner city, occupied on a rental basis, and situated in one-family structures of inferior original construction, would require rehabilitation costing at least $3,500 including overhead costs (1969 dollars). For one-half of this group, the only viable treatments are either maximum rehabilitation, i.e., gutting and reconstruction, or demolition and subsequent replacement at a cost of approximately $20,000 per dwelling including overhead.

Another 13,000 units, or one-fifth of the substandard stock, have intermediate-level physical deficiencies which would require investments in the range of $1500–$3499 per dwelling in order to raise them to at least housing code standards. The remaining 44,000 units, including 7,700 in the outer city, have only minor physical deficiencies needing treatment ranging in cost from $300 to $1499 per dwelling. Nearly 20,000 of the units in this category appear to require investments that in a healthy market would be forthcoming annually as a matter of course.

Thus, when degree of deficiency is taken into account, the housing problem, at least in physical terms, seems less formidable and the prospects for its solution more encouraging. A minimum level of adequacy could be achieved through a relatively small injection of funds. Baltimore is by no means unique in this respect. Similar estimates have been made for Boston and New York. And the housing stocks in nearly all midwestern and western cities are in even better condition. But this optimistic assessment lacks the perspective of time, for it is not clear from what has been stated so far whether conditions in the lower quality sectors of the stock have been improving, declining, or stable. The question of the dynamics of the current problem is taken up next.

Trends in Housing Quality, 1960–1969

It is difficult from any single source of information to make judgments about trends in housing quality within the city. The only historical data are the condition ratings obtained in the 1960 Census of Housing, and these have been judged by the Bureau of the Census to be somewhat unreliable. We were forced, therefore, to take several independent soundings in order to be certain that our assessment of the situation was correct.

First, all dwelling units that were visited in the course of the first household survey were evaluated according to criteria used in the 1960 Census and assigned a rating of sound, deteriorating, or dilapidated. Second, a subsample of 600 structures was rated with respect to cost of upgrading to code level. Each of these measures produced approximately the same aggregate estimate of substandard housing, and each estimate was greater than the corresponding figure for 1960 (3). Responses to questions in the second household survey about neighborhood trends as well as opinions of persons who have been watching the local housing market corroborated these figures.

Although the trend in quality over the decade appears to be negative, it is necessary to go beyond this general finding and identify the extent of the decline in various sectors of the market. To do this, we chose just one of our 1969 rating systems — the one based on estimated cost of improvement — and used it to make comparisons with the 1960 Census ratings. In making these comparisons, the following relationships between elements in each of the two systems were assumed: (a) our rating "Standard" was taken as equivalent to the census category "Sound With All Plumbing Facilities"; (b) our rating "Moderately Substandard" was matched against the sum of the census categories "Sound But Lacking Some Or All Plumbing Facilities," "Deteriorating With All Plumbing Facilities," and "Deteriorating But Lacking Some Or All Plumbing Facilities"; and (c) our rating "Seriously Substandard" was related to the census category "Dilapidated." Although it might have been preferable to use the 1969 Census-type ratings to measure change, we wished to use our best set of 1969 ratings throughout all our analyses. Moreover, the assumed equivalencies just mentioned were arrived at only after careful comparison of the several sets of 1969 ratings.

Based on the assumptions just listed, between 1960 and 1969 the number of substandard units increased by 22,000, from 43,000 units to 65,000 units, or from 16% to 24% of the inventory (Table 4.2). In terms of intensity of decay, a relatively clear trend emerges. The number of seriously substandard accommodations is virtually unchanged since 1960, despite a significant level of demolition undertaken in conjunction with urban renewal, code enforcement, and highway construction efforts. The increase of 22,000 substandard units, therefore, is accounted for by dwellings in less advanced stages of decay.

A definite pattern of deterioration emerges also with respect to spatial distribution and tenure of substandard units. Regardless of location within the city the rate of decay for owner-occupied units appears to be relatively slight. The net increase of 1,100 substandard owner-occupied units constitutes only 1% of the current owner-occupied sector and could be accounted for by sampling error. The same cannot be said for the rental inventory, particularly in the inner-city market where a dramatic decline in quality has occurred. The inner-city rental market accounted for 18,000, or four-fifths, of the 22,000 units which were added to the substandard portion of the stock during the period.

As might be surmised, the brunt of this unfavorable trend in quality within the city has fallen upon blacks. Whereas the proportion of white

Table 4.2. Number of Occupied Dwelling Units, by Condition
(Baltimore, Maryland, 1960 and 1969)

U.S. Bureau of the Census, Condition Rating	Dwelling Units, 1960	Survey of Residential Structures, Quality Rating	Dwelling Units, 1969
Sound with all Plumbing facilities	232,302 (84.3)	Standard (i.e., with no physical deficiencies)	211,320 (76.5)
Sound, but lacking some or All facilities		Moderately substandard (i.e., with minor and	56,700 (20.6)
Deteriorating with all plumbing facilities	35,496 (12.9)	intermediate physical deficiencies)	
Deteriorating, but lacking some or all facilities			
Dilapidated	7,799 (2.8)	Seriously substandard (i.e., with major physical deficiencies)	8,120 (2.9)
Total Occupied	275,597	Total occupied	276,150
	(100.0)		(100.0)

families living in substandard dwellings remained virtually constant (at 10%) over the decade, the proportion of black families who were residing in deficient accommodations increased substantially from 32% in 1960 to 43% in 1969 (4). Taking into account possible improvements in the housing of black families in the surrounding counties does not alter the picture for blacks very much. Even if one assumes unrealistically that all black suburban households are now living in standard housing, the black community region-wide is still worse off, on the average, than it was in 1960 (5). Indeed, the Baltimore region as a whole appears to be worse off. The magnitude of decay in the central city has been such that even if there were a one-third reduction in the number of substandard units located in the suburbs, the overall picture at the regional level would still be comparable to 1960. Whether the Baltimore metropolitan area is atypical in this regard cannot, unfortunately, even be surmised from any of the 1970 Census data.

On the whole, then, the indicators of change appear rather foreboding. Despite both a decade of unparalleled economic prosperity and significant innovations in housing policy, housing conditions in the region do not appear to be greatly improving. Moreover, signals such as increased abandonment of relatively good structures in the inner city indicate that decay is continuing. Although the inner-city rental market has evidenced by far the most pervasive deterioration, the inlying portions of the outer-city rental stock are increasingly affected. The continued basic soundness and potential salvageability of the inventory offers a somewhat redeeming note, but time is surely of the essence. If the present trend is not arrested and reversed in the near future, the opportunity for less intensive forms of remedial treatment will diminish and the magnitude of Baltimore's housing problem will become more than proportionately larger.

Respondent Perceptions of Trends in Housing Quality. Our firm conclusion, based on two field inspections and conversations with landlords and city officials, that a larger portion of Baltimore's housing inventory is substandard today than in 1960, does not appear to be concurred in by the persons who should know best, the residents themselves. They seem to feel the stock is improving. The first hint of this sense of an upward trend is contained in response to a question put to families in our second household survey. "What is the best house you ever lived in?" Almost half of the renters and two-thirds of the owner occupants said their present home was best. And of this group, slightly more than half said their home was *much* better than any of their previous dewellings.

By themselves, these responses are not inconsistent with an actual downward trend in housing quality within the city, since many of the interviewees were no doubt comparing their Baltimore accommodations with prior residences in other communities. We, therefore, probed further, asking how their present housing situation compared to that of five years ago (1964). Taking only renters, who from the previous question appeared to exhibit the least amount of upward residential mobility, it turns out that fully 40% viewed their housing situation as improving, 20% felt there had been no change, and slightly over 30% were still in the same dwelling unit. An insignificant 9% said their housing was getting worse. These figures, moreover, understate the extent of perceived improvement, because they exclude households who had moved up and out of our low-income category during the five years prior to the interviews, while including those who had crossed over the line in the opposite direction.

The contradiction between our independent measures of changing quality and the collective perceptions of the respondents can be resolved if we make five assumptions: (a) The number of Baltimore families whom we would define as "low income" increased between 1960 and 1969; (b) On balance, the housing of the non-low-income sector has been deteriorating; (c) Most of the respondents who said their housing situation was improving had already been living in standard dwellings in 1964; (d) A substantial number of the families who had not changed residence during the five-year period were occupying units that were not being properly maintained; (e) The recent inmigrants whom we interviewed had moved into housing that was declining in quality but was still superior to the accommodations in which they resided before coming to Baltimore. The first three of these assumptions seem unreasonable, and the latter two would not by themselves tip the balance in favor of deterioration. Thus, we must search elsewhere for an explanation of the difference.

If we accept respondent perceptions as essentially correct, it could be reasoned that, on the average, the dwelling units which are deteriorating today are of higher basic quality than those which were slipping downhill five to ten years ago. Fewer of them have space heaters; their kitchens are somewhat better; and they are slightly more spacious relative to number of occupants. It seems possible too that as demolition near the core pushes the ring of blight outward, the appearance of growing deterioration of the stock as a whole is greatly exaggerated. However, even if appearances are misleading and even if basic housing quality is improving, the real increase in number of deteriorating units which we measured should be a cause for concern.

Occupants of Substandard Housing

It has often been argued that lack of income is the prime force generating the problem of substandard housing. This view is given support by the finding in Baltimore that two-thirds of the 65,000 families in need of a standard quality unit were classified as low income (Table 4.3) (6). There are significant differences, however, between the ill-housed and low-income populations. Fully one-third of the households occupying inadequate accommodations were not in the low-income group. Conversely, almost half of all low-income households were occupying standard units. The relationship between housing quality and income level, therefore, requires closer scrutiny.

The interaction of race and income sharply increases the risk of experiencing a housing quality problem. Two-thirds of low-income black households occupy deficient accommodations as compared with only three-tenths of low-income whites and one-quarter of non-low-income blacks. Proportionately, almost as many non-low-income blacks are in bad housing as are low-income whites. All told, over 90% of the families that lack a physically adequate dwelling are either nonwhite or low-income, or both.

Virtually all of the 8,000 households occupying seriously substandard housing are black renters, four-fifths of whom are disadvantaged with respect to income as well. More important, perhaps, is the fact that nearly all of them are either receiving public assistance, or headed by a female, or comprised of at least six persons (Table 4.4) (7). The likelihood of an AFDC family living in a structure that is in serious disrepair is particularly high. Among this group, one family in five occupies such a unit.

Curiously, the proportion of elderly who occupy seriously substandard housing is conspicuously low; indeed, even lower than the figure for the general population (Table 4.5). This finding appears to confirm statements

Table 4.3. Housing Quality by Race, Tenure, and Income Level of Occupants[1] (Baltimore, Maryland, 1969)

Household Characteristic	Seriously Substandard	Moderately Substandard	Total Substandard	Standard	Total Occupied Dwelling Units
Low income	7,120	37,020	44,140	40,660	84,800
White owner	–	3,700	3,700	15,680	19,380
White renter	90	7,130	7,220	9,560	16,780
Non white owner	370	2,870	3,240	7,110	10,350
Non white renter	6,660	23,320	29,980	8,310	38,290
Non low income	1,010	19,680	20,690	170,660	191,350
White owner	–	1,780	1,780	76,520	78,300
White renter	110	3,850	3,960	46,280	50,240
Non white owner	–	1,980	1,980	22,200	24,180
Non white renter	900	12,070	12,970	25,660	38,630
Total household	8,130	56,700	64,830	211,320	276,150
White owner	–	5,480	5,480	92,200	97,680
White renter	200	10,980	11,180	55,840	67,020
Non white owner	370	4,850	5,220	29,310	34,530
Non white renter	7,560	35,390	42,950	33,970	76,920

[1] Source: First Household Survey and Survey of Residential Structures.

made often in the course of our interviews with investor-owners to the effect that older persons are viewed as a desirable tenantry and are highly sought after.

The nature of the process whereby many of the large, female-headed or welfare families gravitate to the worst dwellings is not apparent from the data at hand. In each case, only a minority of the households with one or more of these characteristics actually live in a seriously substandard unit (8). One possible explanation may be that families who pose problems for landlords because they are poor housekeepers or destructive of property are excluded from better accommodations. However, this hypothesis is substantially undermined by our finding that only 15% of the families in seriously substandard dwelling units were rated by our interviewers as apparently poor housekeepers.

In the less deficient sectors of the substandard inventory, the quality deprivations are spread across a broader spectrum of the population. Low-income black renters are still the largest and most disadvantaged category among race/tenure/income groupings; however, they constitute only two-fifths

Table 4.4. Housing Quality by Source of Income, Sex of Household Head, Size of Household, and Income Level of Occupants[1] (Baltimore, Maryland, 1969)

Household Characteristic	Quality of Dwelling Unit:				Total Occupied Dwelling Units
	Seriously Substandard	Moderately Substandard	Total Substandard	Standard	
Households either receiving public assistance, headed by a female, or large in size	7,450	36,140	43,590	59,640	103,230
Receiving AFDC	2,960	8,700	11,660	3,570	15,230
Receiving other welfare	1,130	7,270	8,400	7,720	16,120
Non welfare, female head	760	14,210	14,970	22,500	37,470
Non welfare, male head, 6 or more persons	2,600	5,960	8,560	25,850	34,410
Other households, low income	450	9,520	9,970	12,730	22,700
Non welfare, males head, 1 to 5 persons	450	8,190	8,640	12,710	21,350
Non welfare, sex of head/size of household unknown	–	1,330	1,330	20	1,350
Other households, non low income	230	11,040	11,270	138,950	150,220
Non welfare, male head, 1 to 5 pers.	220	10,950	11,170	118,830	130,000
Non welfare, sex of head/size of household unknown	10	90	100	20,120	20,220
Total households	8,130	56,700	64,830	211,320	276,150

[1] Source: First Household Survey and Survey of Residential Structures.

of households living in moderately substandard housing (Table 4.3). One-third of the families in this sector of the stock had incomes which exceeded our criteria for low income. The proportion of white families (one-third) is significantly greater than it is in the seriously substandard sector. Likewise, the proportion who are owner occupants (one-fifth) shows a marked increase.

Additional evidence of the more generalized nature of the problem in the moderately substandard portions of the stock is revealed by the finding that approximately one-fifth of the households headed by an elderly person were

Table 4.5. Housing Quality by Selected Household Characteristics[1,2]
(Baltimore, Maryland, 1969)

| Household Characteristic | Quality of Dwelling Unit: | | All Occupied Dwelling Units |
	Seriously Substandard	All Substandard	
Black	7,930. (7.1) (97.5)	48,180 (43.2) (74.3)	111,450 (100.0) (40.4)
White	200 (0.1) (2.5)	16,660 (10.1) (25.7)	164,700 (100.0) (59.6)
Female head[3]	3,250 (5.5) (40.0)	27,420 (46.7) (42.3)	58,750 (100.0) (21.3)
Male head[3]	4,880, (2.4) (60.0)	37,410 (18.4) 57.7)	203,400 (100.0) (73.7)
Small size (1 to 5 persons)	4,090 (1.8) (50.3)	50,760 (22.0) (78.3)	230,870 (100.0) (83.6)
Large size (6 or more persons)	4,040 (8.9) (49.7)	14,070 (31.1) (21.7)	45,280 (100.0) (16.4)
Elderly head[3]	470 (1.1) (5.8)	9,060 (21.0) (14.0)	43,240 (100.0) (15.7)
Non elderly head[3]	7,660 (3.5) (94.2)	55,770 (25.5) (86.0)	218,910 (100.0) (79.3)
AFDC	2,960 (19.4) (36.4)	11,660 (76.6) (18.0)	15,230 (100.0) (5.5)
Other welfare (OAA, AB, APTD, GA)	1,130 (7.0) (13.9)	8,400 (52.1) (12.9)	16,120 (100.0) (5.8)
Non welfare	4,040 (1.7) (49.7)	44,770 (18.3) (69.1)	244,800 (100.0) (88.7)
Head employed[3]	4,230 (2.3) (52.0)	38,170 (20.3) (58.9)	187,600 (100.0) (67.9)
Head not employed[3]	3,900 (5.2) (48.0)	26,660 (35.8) (41.1)	74,550 (100.0) (27.0)
All households	8,130 (2.9) (100.0)	64,830 (23.5) (100.0)	276,150 (100.0) (100.0)

[1] Source: First Household Survey and Survey of Residential Structures.
[2] This table is designed to show the risk of occupying substandard housing for various subgroups in the population. Strictly speaking, neither the rows nor the columns are additive,
although certain subsets of rows (e.g., low income and non-low income, black and white)
add up to the total population. The figures shown in parentheses are percentages. The percentage to the right of each entry is the result of dividing the entry by the number of all
households in that row, e.g., for the first entry in the table, 8.4 is the percentage of all
low-income households that are living in seriously substandard dwellings (7,120/84,800).
The percentage below each entry is the result of dividing the entry by the number for all
dwellings in that column, e.g., for the first entry in the table, 87.6 is the percentage of
all seriously substandard dwellings which are occupied by low-income households. This
general format is used in many of the tables throughout the study.
[3] The figure shown for the total number of households having this characteristic does *not*
include approximately 6,000–8,000 middle- and upper-income white households living in
high-rise apartments constructed since 1960. Since all of these dwelling units are well
above the minimum standard, the row percentages for this group are somewhat inflated
and the column percentage for the "All Occupied Dwelling Units" column is somewhat
deflated.

living in dwellings of this quality (Table 4.5). These units, many of which are owner occupied, constitute one-sixth of the moderately substandard sector.

As would be expected, however, the special plight of large, welfare, and female-headed families persists at this quality level. All told, nearly three-fifths of families receiving AFDC, for example, are housed in this sector of the inventory. What appears clear, though, is that the deterioration of the inner-city rental inventory affects many families who would generally not be regarded as the most deprived groups within the population.

Housing Quality as Perceived by Respondents

Despite general agreement as to the inherently judgmental nature of housing standards, attempts to measure residential quality have rarely, if ever, taken into account attitudes and opinions of consumers. Yet, the question of what constitutes adequate housing cannot be divorced from the perceived needs and desires of occupants. In the course of conducting the field surveys, therefore, an effort was made to determine how respondents felt about their dwellings and to compare their opinions with our independent ratings of housing quality. Two types of attitudinal questions were posed to respondents: (1) those directed toward obtaining a general assessment of the level of satisfaction with the dwelling unit, and (2) those directed toward determining whether specific aspects of structural condition and performance of equipment were creating serious problems in the occupants' daily lives (9). In various ways, the answers received were both reassuring and discomforting.

When the first household survey respondents were asked how they liked their homes, 9 of 10 expressed no dissatisfaction (Table 4.6). Of the 27,000 whose attitudes were negative, the vast majority were only moderately discontented; fewer than 5,000 persons seriously disliked their present dwellings.

Table 4.6. Housing Quality Rating by Respondent's Attitude Toward Dwelling Unit[1] (Baltimore, Maryland, 1969)

Respondent's Attitude Toward Dwelling Unit	Quality of Dwelling Unit:				Total Occupied Dwelling Units
	Seriously Sub-standard	Moderately Sub-standard	Total Sub-standard	Standard	
Very bad	370	1,870	2,240	1,080	3,320
Somewhat unsatisfactory	3,400	4,770	8,170	15,550	23,720
Total dissatisfied	3,770	6,640	10,410	16,630	27,040
Satisfactory	2,830	24,960	27,790	54,240	82,030
Like very much	1,520	23,570	25,090	123,650	148,740
Attitude unknown	10	1,530	1,540	16,800	18,340
Total households	8,130	56,700	64,830	211,320	276,150

[1] Sources: Survey of Residential Structures and First Household Survey.

In other words, using the general attitudinal question as a cross-reference, families gave their homes a higher rating, on the average, than did either the interviewers or the inspectors.

Given that so few persons disliked their dwelling units, a weak relationship between occupants' general attitudinal responses and the independent ratings of housing quality is to be expected. With only 27,000 discontented respondents and 65,000 dwelling units rated substandard, even if the overlap were complete, only two-fifths of the families occupying substandard dwellings would have been counted among the discontented. In fact, the correspondence between the two variables is lower still, and by a considerable margin. Only 1 of 6 households living in substandard housing stated that the dwelling unit was either somewhat unsatisfactory or very bad. The corresponding rate of discontent among the 8,000 occupants of seriously substandard units was less than 1 in 2, and only 5% of this group were intensely dissatisfied. Conversely, three-fifths of the dissatisfied respondents were occupying units which, upon inspection, received a rating of standard. Among respondents expressing serious disaffection, one-third were living in standard units.

As would be expected, negative attitudes were held, in the main, by blacks and renters. Indeed, three-quarters of those who were dissatisfied with their dwelling units were blacks, and a comparable number were renter-occupants. The proportion of families that were dissatisfied was four times higher among blacks than among whites, and three times higher among renters than among owners.

In contrast, differentials with respect to level of income and location of residence were less pronounced than might be anticipated. The proportion of families that were dissatisfied was only 50% higher among low-income families than among non-low-income families, while virtually no difference was observed, on the average, between inner- and outer-city residents (Table 4.7). Those who were extremely discontented, however, tended to be heavily concentrated among low-income families living in the inner city.

The findings presented to this point concerning general attitudes toward the dwelling unit provide only a partial description of the perceptions of occupants and, additionally, may tend to understate the level of dissatisfaction. Although relatively few families replied negatively when asked how they liked their homes, there is some evidence that a significantly greater number of respondents, particularly among renters, did feel that specific aspects of the dwelling unit were posing serious problems for them. In the inner city, for example, whereas only 1 low-income renter in 7 expressed general dissatisfaction with the home, more than two-thirds mentioned at least one serious problem with it. Inner-city renters who voiced serious dissatisfaction with some particular feature of their residence mentioned as many as 4 individual problems, on the average.

Table 4.7. Respondent's Attitude Toward Dwelling Unit, by Location of Residence and Income Level[1] (Baltimore, Maryland, 1969)

Income Level of Household/ Location of Residence	Attitude Toward Dwelling Unit:						
	Very Bad	Somewhat Unsatis-factory	Total Unsatis-factory	Satis-factory	Like Very Much	Attitude Unknown	Total House-holds
Low income	2,260	8,080	10,340	33,250	38,820	2,390	84,800
Inner city	2,260	4,230	6,490	20,800	21,810	1,850	50,950
Outer city	–	3,850	3,850	12,450	17,010	540	33,850
Non low income	1,060	15,640	16,700	48,780	109,920	15,950	191,350
Inner city	440	3,080	3,520	15,060	31,590	3,860	54,030
Outer city	620	12,560	13,180	33,720	78,330	12,090	137,320
Total households	3,320	23,720	27,040	82,030	148,740	18,340	276,150
Subtotal, inner city	2,700	7,310	10,010	35,860	53,400	5,710	104,980
Subtotal, outer city	620	16,410	17,030	46,170	95,340	12,630	171,170

[1] Source: First Household Survey.

Perhaps the most striking finding concerning the perceptions of specific dwelling-unit deficiencies is that the problems which were cited most frequently as being serious are not traditionally associated with structural condition. For example, of the 5 problems identified by more than 20% of the low-income renters living in the inner city – roaches (42%), drafts (37%), rats (22%), loose and falling plaster or paint (22%), and heat in summer (21%) – only one relates directly to physicial dilapidation. Other deficiencies which bear a more direct relationship to structural quality – weak or broken floors; defective windows or doors; leaking or clogged bathroom sink, shower, toilet, or tub; and bad stairs or railings – were mentioned much less frequently. The pattern of specific serious complaints would appear to be consistent with the major conclusion regarding physical quality of the inventory mentioned earlier, namely, that only a small segment of the inventory has declined to a state of extreme decay. On the other hand, the pattern of perceptions raises some question as to whether the standard of physical quality which we have used, is totally appropriate, since it excludes pest and temperature control.

The question arises as to why the frequency of specific dissatisfactions is higher than the level of general discontent described earlier. The answer may lie in the nature of the interview. During the second household interview, respondents were initially asked how they liked their homes, and subsequently were asked whether they considered various aspects of the dwelling unit to be a big problem. If the order of the questions had been reversed so as to afford the respondent an opportunity to reflect upon specific problems before offering a general assessment of the dwelling, perhaps the results would have been more consistent.

The lack of correspondence between our single independent standard of quality and the hundreds of subjective views of respondents cannot be explained away quite so readily. Certainly a degree of difference is to be expected, yet it is troublesome that, among families living in seriously substandard accommodations, 50% were not dissatisfied with their housing. Either these persons must have more pressing problems on their minds, or the questionnaire was deficient in some yet unidentified respect.

PRIVATE INDOOR SPACE

Data on this dimension of housing need are not very satisfactory. A completely acceptable measure of overcrowding would relate floor area and ventilation to the number, age, and sex of the occupants. And, furthermore, a proper interpretation of indices of overcrowding would require knowledge as to the length of time families had been experiencing the situation. Since there is a continual flow of families into and out of an overcrowded status, as their household composition changes and as moves are made, cross-sectional data on crowding overstate the problem.

This study was not able to pursue the refined measures that would have been desirable. Some general notions of the magnitude of the problem may be ascertained, however, from the crude data that were gathered on persons per room. Even these figures may seem more precise than they really are, because of the likelihood of obtaining inaccurate room counts from many respondents.

In contrast with the physical quality aspect of the housing problem, which is increasing in magnitude, deprivation with respect to indoor space appears to be diminishing over time. At the taking of the initial household survey, 22,000 households, or only 8% of the city total, were occupying quarters which provided less than one room per person (Table 4.8). Of this number, approximately 4,000 households were experiencing severe overcrowding, i.e., had more than 1.5 persons per room.

Since roughly two-thirds of the households lacking adequate indoor space are poor, and almost the same proportion are black, one might argue generally that the problem is a manifestation of low income and limited choice due to racial discrimination. A closer look at the data, however, suggests a somewhat different, but not unexpected, interpretation which focuses upon the special concentration of the problem among large households. Families of six or more persons account for four-fifths of those living in crowded conditions, and the probability of such a household being overcrowded exceeds by a substantial margin the corresponding figures for black or low-income families generally. Whereas only one-fifth of low-income blacks and one-eighth of low-

Table 4.8. Adequacy of Space, by Race, Tenure, and Income Level of Occupants[1]
(Baltimore, Maryland, 1969)

Income Level/ Tenure/ Race of Occupant	Adequacy of Indoor Space:			
	Serious Overcrowding (PPR > 1.50)	Moderate Overcrowding (PPR 1.01–1.50)	Total Overcrowding (PPR > 1.00)	Total Households
Low income	2,720	12,370	15,090	84,850
White owner	400	1,450	1,850	21,100
White renter	430	2,350	2,780	14,760
Black owner	140	1,580	1,720	10,610
Black renter	1,750	6,990	8,740	38,380
Non low income	1,160	5,270	6,430	191,400
White owner	280	1,630	1,910	80,660
White renter	570	600	1,170	49,420
Black owner	30	1,270	1,300	23,330
Black renter	280	1,770	2,050	37,990
Total households	3,880	17,640	21,520	276,250
White owner	680	3,080	3,760	101,760
White renter	1,000	2,950	3,950	64,180
Black owner	170	2,850	3,020	33,940
Black renter	2,030	8,760	10,790	76,370

[1] Source: First Household Survey

income whites had less than 1 room per person, the corresponding figure for
all households of 6 or more persons was nearly 1 in 2. The larger the household the greater the risk; three-quarters of all 8-or-more-person families failed
to achieve this standard of adequacy despite the large number of under-utilized
three-story row houses in the inner city.

Although blacks are 3 times as likely as whites to be overcrowded, much
of the difference results from the fact that black households are larger, on the
average, than are white households. When size of household is held constant,
the experience of both groups falls rather closely into line. In addition to large
households generally, overcrowding is particularly prevalent among families
receiving AFDC payments. Nearly two-fifths of this group have less than 1
room per person. AFDC households, however, account for less than one-
quarter of the problem.

Since 1960, the number of families living in crowded conditions appears
to have declined by about 6,000 or 20% of the total at the start of the decade
(10). The proportion of blacks who are overcrowded declined appreciably over
the period, from 1 household in 5 in 1960 to 1 in 8 in 1969 (Table 4.9).
Most of the reduction in overcrowding occurred in the rental sector where
the proportion of households in need dropped from 1 in 8 in 1960 to 1 in 10
in 1969. The rate of overcrowding among owner occupants remained virtually
constant at 1 in 20.

Table 4.9. Number of Households Occupying Dwelling Units Which Provide Less than One Room Per Person, by Race   (Baltimore, Maryland, 1960, 1969)

	White		Black		All Households	
	PPR > 1.00	Total	PPR > 1.00	Total	PPR > 1.00	Total
1960[1]	11,090	195,141	16,286	80,456	27,376	275,597
1969[2]	' 7,710	165,940	13,810	110,310	21,520	276,250

[1] Source: 1960 figures from 1960 Census of Housing.
[2] Source: 1969 figures from First Household Survey.

As was pointed out at the start of this discussion, standards based upon persons-per-room ratios provide only a crude approximation of the level of space deprivations. It is likely, therefore, that there will be some discrepancy between the households who perceive themselves as lacking enough space and those who are judged independently to be overcrowded. Undoubtedly, some families who are below the stipulated minimum level will be content, while others whose situations are deemed adequate may feel that they have too little space. Ideally, however, if the standard in question is to serve as a cornerstone for policy decisions, these mismatches should be fairly uncommon.

Unfortunately, the results of the field surveys do not follow this pre-scribed pattern. During the second household interview, respondents were asked a question regarding the adequacy of space provided by their present dwellings ("How do you feel about the size of this place?") Although, in aggregate, the number of families who perceived themselves as crowded was virtually equal to the number having less than one room per person, only a bare majority (53%) of the respondents who considered their dwellings too small actually had too few rooms by our standard; and conversely among the families with less than one room per person, those who complained that their homes were too small were a minority (43%). Given this pattern of re-sults, caution is warranted in assessing the distribution of space deprivations in Baltimore. Clearly, the data on perceptions of crowding indicate that efforts to obtain more sensitive measures of this dimension of housing need are in order.

Within this frame of reference, we may now summarize the findings per-taining to inadequate indoor space, and assess their implications for policy. Relative to the housing quality situation, the problem of overcrowding appears both less formidable and decidedly more favorable with respect to current trends. For all practical purposes, the figure of 22,000 households with less than one room per person tends to overstate the problem for two reasons. First, it includes 6,500 non-low-income families who are over-crowded but who can without too much difficulty relieve the pressure of limited space by moving to larger quarters of at least equal quality. Second, with the possible exception of AFDC families, the rate of overcrowding among small, low-income households is only slightly higher than the minimum dis-equilibrium which is inevitable at any point in time.

There is, then, a residuum of, perhaps, 10,000 to 12,000 large, low-income families who face particular difficulty in obtaining adequate space under current market conditions. Virtually all of them are renter occupants and in most cases their accommodations are not only too small but also substandard. Although, when described in these terms, the overcrowding problem would appear to be manageable in scale, its elimination will require the explicit attention of public policy. If a modicum of progress in meeting the space needs of large families has been made over the past decade, it has not been the direct result of public programs. For example, in Baltimore, as in other cities around the country, maximum cost limitations imposed on the construction of public housing have made it virtually impossible to extend the program in directions which meet the needs of families requiring four or more bedrooms. If space deprivations are to be eliminated in the short run, not only must these constraints be removed, but additional ways of dealing directly with over-crowding problems must also be found.

HOUSING COSTS RELATIVE TO INCOME

In recent years, as the nation has attempted to combat both poverty and inflation, the special burden which housing expense poses for low-income families has received growing attention in policy debates. Despite this heightened awareness, as well as renewed interest in demand-side interventions as a means to solving housing problems, significant gaps in knowledge regarding the over-all magnitude of excessive housing expense persist. The Baltimore data reflect the enormity of this dimension of the housing problem and, in all likelihood, typify the situation which exists in most cities.

On the average, Baltimoreans spend about 20% of their incomes for hous-ing (Table 4.10) (11). As would be expected, the proportion of income which families allocate to housing decreases as income increases (12). For example, whereas more than two-fifths of all low-income families pay more than 40% of income for shelter and utilities, the same is true for only a handful (1%) of non-low-income families. And, at the opposite end of the scale, fewer than one-sixth of the low-income families as against more than two-thirds of non-low-income families are paying 20% or less of income for shelter and utilities.

These figures are suggestive of the difficulties which many low-income families encounter in obtaining accommodations which they can afford. They do not, however, measure the incidence and severity of the problem. To pursue this question, it is necessary to discard arbitrary rent—income ratios and specify what constitutes an excessive amount of housing expense relative to income for various household types.

Two methods were employed for purposes of estimating how many families are burdened by excessive housing expenditures. The initial method compared family income with the total cost of an acceptable living standard, as reflected in the "lower budget" of the Bureau of Labor Statistics (BLS). Using this approach, it was assumed that the family's housing expenses should not be so great as to leave it with insufficient money to acquire nonhousing necessities. If this situation obtained, then by definition the family would be paying more than it should for shelter.

In 1968, the "lower budget" totaled $5,820 for a four-person family living in Baltimore (13). Several steps were involved in determining whether and to what extent a given household was spending an excessive amount for housing with respect to this budget. First, the amount required for nonhousing expenses under the BLS standard was determined for households of various sizes. Then, for the individual household, the appropriate figure for nonhousing need was compared with household income. If income was less than or equal to nonhousing need, it was assumed that the household could not afford to spend anything at all for housing. If income exceeded nonhousing need by an amount which was less than current housing expense, the household's current allocation was taken as excessive. The subsidy requirements estimated in this manner, therefore, were based solely upon what the family was spending for housing at the time of interview. Additional amounts which would be required in order to eliminate other dimensions of housing need, e.g., resources for upgrading a substandard unit or for relocation of crowded families to larger units, were not taken into consideration at this point in the analysis.

According to the criteria just outlined, 85,000 households, or nearly one-third of the population of Baltimore, are bearing costs for housing which may be considered excessive relative to income. The group in need includes virtually the entire low-income population, as defined herein. It also includes a small number (3,000) of non-low-income households who could presumably reduce their housing expenses by moving to more modest but still adequate accommodations.

Table 4.10. Annual Housing Expense as a Percentage of Income, by Income Status, Race, and Tenure¹ (Baltimore, Maryland, 1969)

Income Status/ Tenure/Race of Occupant	Annual Housing Expense As a Percentage of Household Income:							
	Over 40%	31–40%	26–30%	21–25%	16–20%	15% or Less	Total Known	Total Households
Low income	28,370	12,230	9,260	7,820	5,720	3,530	66,930	84,850
White owner	8,080	2,350	2,310	2,560	1,440	720	17,460	21,100
Black owner	2,370	2,080	690	530	1,080	1,010	7,760	10,610
White renter	5,430	3,290	1,620	1,120	600	370	12,430	14,750
Black renter	12,490	4,510	4,640	3,610	2,600	1,430	29,280	38,390
Non low income	1,910	6,020	10,080	24,150	46,050	55,620	143,830	191,400
White owner	720	2,360	3,710	10,820	20,000	24,060	61,670	80,660
Black owner	470	400	790	1,600	5,740	7,200	16,200	23,330
White renter	510	1,680	3,230	7,010	11,830	11,840	36,100	49,420
Black renter	210	1,580	2,350	4,720	8,480	12,520	29,860	37,990
Total households	30,280	18,250	19,340	31,970	51,770	59,150	210,760	276,250
Subtotal owner	11,640	7,190	7,500	15,510	28,260	32,990	103,090	135,700
Subtotal renter	18,640	11,060	11,840	16,460	23,510	26,160	107,670	140,550

¹ Source: First Household Survey

As will be explained in greater depth in Chapter 8, the majority of families requiring subsidies to eliminate burdensome expenses are not currently benefiting directly from any housing program. Over two-thirds of them, for example, are not receiving public assistance (Table 4.11). Also, surprisingly, as many as two families in five are headed by a person who is working at a full-time job.

On the surface, these findings suggest that the excessive expense dimension of the housing problem is more extensive than the physical quality dimension. However, not all of the 82,000 low-income households are making real sacrifices of other consumer items in order to obtain adequate housing. A certain number of them have, no doubt, underreported their incomes. Others, particularly the elderly, maintain a decent home by living off assets accumulated over the years. Still others rely on parental resources. If these factors could be taken into account, the number of families having excessive housing expenditures would probably range somewhere between 60,000 and 65,000, still a substantial number (14).

With respect to severity of the problem, the findings are even more dramatic. Of the 82,000 low-income households incurring excessive costs for shelter relative to their income, nearly three-quarters — including most of those persons currently receiving public assistance — can afford to spend absolutely nothing for housing and would require complete subsidization of their shelter costs (Table 4.12). Of the remaining 20,000 families, the majority could afford to put up at least one-half of the total housing outlay from their own pockets.

The aggregate subsidy required to eliminate excessive expense under this definition of need is obviously quite large, since it would imply public support for almost the entire bill for housing the low-income population. The total cost would be roughly $75 million (in 1969 dollars) annually, with the vast majority of families receiving between $600 and $1,500 per year (Table 4.13). If arbitrary adjustments are made for underreporting of income, etc., the aggregate amount is about $60 million. The national equivalent to this figure would be about $14 billion, an amount that exceeds some estimates of the cost of a guaranteed annual income program. Quite a bit more remains to be said about the magnitude of these figures relative to ongoing efforts in housing; however, that discussion is more appropriately taken up in Chapter 8.

Objection could be raised to the standard used in the above calculations on the grounds that it is too liberal and that it converts a housing problem entirely into one of income deficiency. The $5,820 budget is higher than our low-income line. And families with low incomes automatically have the problem, while others normally do not. The entire income gap may seem to stem from excessive housing expenditures, when, in fact, it could just as

Table 4.11. Number of Households Requiring Subsidy to Relieve Housing Expense Burdens, by Selected Household Characteristics[1,2] (Baltimore, Maryland, 1969)

Household Characteristic	Full Amount of Current Housing Expense	Part of Current Housing Expense	Total Requiring Housing Subsidy	Total Households
	Households Requiring			
Low income	62,300 (73.4) (100.0)	20,010 (23.6) (86.9)	82,310 (97.0) (96.5)	84,850 (100.0) (30.7)
Black	39,050 (35.4) (62.7)	9,830 (8.9) (42.7)	48,880 (44.3) (57.3)	110,310 (100.0) (39.9)
AFDC	11,370 (86.7) (18.3)	680 (5.2) (3.0)	12,050 (91.9) (14.1)	13,120 (100.0) (4.7)
Other welfare (OAA, AB, ATD, GA)	10,020 (54.3) (16.1)	2,260 (12.3) (9.8)	12,280 (66.6) (14.4)	18,430 (100.0) (6.7)
Elderly head (65 years or more)	14,800 (29.1) (23.8)	7,950 (15.6) (34.5)	22,750 (44.7) (26.7)	50,880 (100.0) (18.4)
Female head	28,120 (41.1) (45.1)	8,220 (12.0) (35.7)	36,340 (53.1) (42.6)	68,360 (100.0) (24.7)
Large size (6 persons or more)	18,330 (47.3) (29.4)	2,760 (7.1) (12.0)	21,090 (54.4) (24.7)	38,780 (100.0) (14.0)
Head not employed	33,610 (43.9) (53.9)	10,770 (14.1 (46.8)	44,380 (58.0) (52.0)	76,580 (100.0) (27.7)
Renter occupant	43,160 (30.7) (69.3)	9,990 (7.1) (43.4)	53,150 (37.8) (62.3)	140,540 (100.0) (50.9)
Non low income	-- (0.0) (0.0)	3,010 (1.6) (13.1)	3,010 (1.6) (3.5)	191,400 (100.0) (69.3)
White	23,240 (14.0) (37.3)	13,200 (8.0) (57.3)	36,440 (22.0) (42.7)	165,940 (100.0) (60.1)
Non welfare	40,910 (16.7) (65.7)	20,080 (8.2) (87.2)	60,990 (24.9) (71.5)	244,700 (100.0) (88.6)
Non elderly head	45,820 (20.8) (73.5)	14,990 (6.8) (65.1)	60,810 (27.6) (71.3)	220,610 (100.0) (79.9)
Male head	32,880 (16.1) (52.8)	14,590 (7.2) (63.4)	47,470 (23.3) (55.6)	203,770,(100.0) (73.8)
Small size (1 to 5 persons)	42,410 (18.1) (68.1)	20,240 (8.6) (87.9)	62,650 (26.7) (73.4)	234,870 (100.0) (85.0)
Head employed full time	23,320 (13.0) (37.4)	10,700 (6.0) (46.5)	34,020 (19.0) (39.9)	179,100 (100.0) (64.8)
Owner occupant	19,130 (14.1) (30.7)	13,030 (9.6) (56.6)	32,160 (23.7) (37.7)	135,700 (100.0) (49.1)
Total households	62,300 (22.6) (100.0)	23,020 (8.3) (100.0)	85,320 (30.9) (100.0)	276,250 (100.0) (100.0)

[1] With no adjustment made for possible underreporting of income, gifts, etc.
[2] Source: First Household Survey.

Table 4.12. Number of Households Requiring Subsidy Under "Nonhousing Need" Criteria by Income Status of Recipient and Subsidy as a Percentage of Current Housing Expense[1,2] (Baltimore, Maryland, 1969)

Percent of Housing Expense Requiring Subsidy	Low Income	Non-Low Income	Total
1 to 24%	3,060 (3.7)	2,050 (68.1)	5,110 (6.0
25 to 49%	8,650 (10.5)	960 (31.9)	9,610 (11.3)
50 to 74%	7,590 (9.2)	– (0.0)	7,590 (8.9)
75 to 99%	710 (0.9)	– (0.0)	710 (0.8)
100%	62,300 (75.7)	– (0.0)	62,300 (73.0)
Total requiring subsidy	82,310 (100.0) (97.0)	3,010 (100.) (1.6)	85,320 (100.0) (30.0)
Total households	84,850 (100.0)	191,400 (100.0)	276,250 (100.0)

[1] With no adjustment made for possible underreporting of income, gifts, etc.
[2] Source: First Household Survey.

Table 4.13. Aggregate Subsidy Requirements Under "Nonhousing Need" Criteria[1,2] (Baltimore, Maryland, 1969)

Amount of Subsidy	Average Subsidy	Number of Households	Aggregate Subsidy
1– 199	$ 100	3,210 (3.8)	$ 321,000 (0.4)
200– 399	300	7,330 (8.6)	2,199,000 (2.9)
400– 599	500	8,360 (9.8)	4,180,000 (5.5)
600– 799	700	20,280 (23.8)	14,196,000 (18.6)
800– 999	900	12,960 (15.2)	11,664,000 (15.3)
1,000–1,499	1,175	23,660 (27.7)	27,800,500 (36.5)
1,500–1,999	1,625	8,990 (10.5)	14,608,000 (19.2)
2,000 or more	2,250	530 (0.6)	1,192,500 (1.6)
Total		85,320 (100.0)	76,161,000 (100.0)

[1] With no adjustment for possible underreporting of income, gifts, etc.
[2] Source: First Household Survey.

logically be assigned to food, clothing, transportation, health care, or some other large item in the family budget. Moreover, if families were provided with funds sufficient to bring their housing expenses into line with their incomes, it seems probable that many of them, even some who were living in adequate accommodations, would move to more expensive units and continue to appear to be in need.

Because of these objections, a second calculation was made using a more conservative standard. In this case, the determination as to whether low-income families are spending excessive amounts of income for housing is based on the goal of parity in expenditure patterns vis-à-vis non-low-income households rather than upon a comparison of total family needs with total family income. According to this standard, low-income households would be expected to pay a proportion of income for housing which is no greater than the proportion being paid, on the average, by non-low-income families of the same number of persons (15). Philosophically, the standard implies that low-income families should not be obliged to allocate a higher proportion of their incomes to housing than do other families when they obtain shelter of much lower quality.

Unfortunately, the second standard also has a number of defects. In reality, it is simply a nontraditional variation on the general method of employing an arbitrary rent—income ratio to determine whether housing expense is burdensome. Hopefully, the standard embodies more realistic assumptions than are usually applied in ongoing programs regarding what is a reasonable housing outlay for low-income families. A problem arises, however, in that should the criteria be judged as fair, by implication one-half of all non-low-income families would also be spending an unacceptable proportion of their income for housing.

Using the second method, the number of low-income families experiencing burdensome housing expense is reduced only marginally to 80,000. This relationship results from the fact that nearly all low-income families are currently allocating proportionately more for housing than does the average non-low-income family.

The aggregate subsidy requirement, however, drops substantially to $47 million per year. Allowing for underreporting of income, use of measured rather than permanent income in the calculations, and similar factors, the true figure is probably about $40 million ($9 billion nationally). With the exception of 1,000 households who reported zero income, each family in need would make an out-of-pocket contribution in order to achieve parity with non-low-income families. Collectively, these contributions would total almost $30 million and would serve to cut the average individual subsidy requirement from $800 per year under the first calculation to $500 per year.

During the course of the second household survey, an effort was made to ascertain whether low-income occupants perceived their housing costs as burdensome. In general, these results raise some question about the validity of both of the two methods of estimation just described. For example, when asked if high housing expense was creating a problem for them, only 21,000 households, or one low-income household in four, gave a positive reply (16). Another 19,000 did not acknowledge having specific difficulties meeting housing costs, but did feel that their income was inadequate. Thus, from the

occupant perspective, just under one-half of all low-income households in
Baltimore perceived either a housing expense or an income deficiency problem.

Certain types of households within the low-income population complained
more than others about excessive housing expense. Particularly sensitive to
this dimension of need were AFDC families (35%), households that identified
themselves as downwardly mobile (32%), and families of six or more persons
(32%). In contrast, the pattern of response which obtained for households
that were receiving forms of public assistance other than AFDC (17%), public
housing occupants (14%), and the elderly (12%) indicate that these subgroups
were less likely on the average to perceive the cost of housing, per se, as
a problem.

Ordinarily, one might expect that the families who felt burdened by the
high cost of housing would be those who were paying large amounts for their
accommodations, either in absolute dollar terms or in relation to income. In
point of fact, however, perceived excessive expense is virtually uncorrelated
with the ratio of gross housing cost to income, and is only weakly associated
with the actual level of housing outlays. Given these rather puzzling findings,
it is extremely difficult to know how to interpret the respondents' perceptions of excessive housing expense. On the whole, the number of low-income
households who regarded high housing expense or income deprivation as a
problem is substantially lower than the number who were judged to be in
need under either of the independent criteria discussed earlier. This difference
cannot be rationalized with any degree of confidence; however, it suggests
that some care in avoiding overstatement would appear warranted.

Turning now to the dynamic aspects of this dimension of need, one might
expect that several decades of rising real incomes should have brought with
them gradually declining rent—income ratios and a reduction in the number
of families burdened by excessive housing expenditures. Since 1960, however,
despite the War on Poverty and related domestic programs, there is a broadly
held view that the housing expense—income problem may have become worse
for many low-income households. Their failure to share in national income
gains together with the escalation of housing costs are believed to have imposed
special hardship upon them.

The Baltimore figures, however, suggest a general easing of the situation.
For example, over the decade, the proportion of families paying 35% of income or more for housing was reduced one-quarter for black renters (from
39% to 28%) and by one-fifth for white renters (from 22% to 17%) (17). Data
from the 1960 and 1970 housing censuses indicate a similar trend nationally.

While these figures are encouraging, they do not deal explicitly with the
contention that housing expense burdens of *poor* families have been worsening. Unfortunately, it is not possible to make a rigorous analysis of this

question from the data at hand. Nevertheless, it can be said with certainty that some low-income families did experience falling real incomes over the decade, and unless they have managed somehow to cut back on housing costs accordingly, their expense burdens have intensified.

MULTIPLE DEPRIVATIONS WITH RESPECT TO PHYSICAL QUALITY, INDOOR SPACE, AND EXCESSIVE HOUSING EXPENSE

Thus far in the chapter, three dimensions of housing need — lack of adequate housing quality, lack of adequate private indoor space, and excessive housing expense relative to income — have been analyzed separately. A question of considerable importance for housing policy is the amount of overlap among these problems. This section, therefore, analyzes the extent to which households in Baltimore have been experiencing multiple housing deprivations with respect to quality, space, and expense.

The reasons for seeking this additional perspective are twofold. First, in housing, as in other areas of social policy, the goal of providing flexible programs which may be adapted to the specific needs and aspirations of intended beneficiaries has received growing attention in recent years. If sensitivity toward the particular situations of individual clients is to be realized, there must be greater appreciation than in the past of the linkages among dimensions of housing need. Second, knowledge of the distribution of need profiles has relevance for more general issues of program planning and innovation. Such data furnish insight into how much of the total problem might be solved by a given type of intervention. For example, if the client population for a proposed program of housing allowances were to include all families who spend excessive amounts for shelter relative to income, a relevant question is how many families occupying substandard or overcrowded quarters would benefit directly from the program. Conversely, if priority were given to efforts aimed primarily at upgrading the inventory, how many families experiencing overcrowding would be reached? In short, analyzing the overlap among deprivations will help distinguish those instances where multifaceted interventions are required in order to solve several dimensions of need from situations where one-dimensional interventions might effectively do so. With these observations in mind, we may turn now to the findings from the various field surveys which pertain to the amount of overlap among quality, space and expense problems.

Based upon the independent standards of need utilized in earlier sections of the chapter (19), fully 115,000 households, or two-fifths of the total number in Baltimore at the close of the decade, either lived in a substandard dwelling, or lacked sufficient indoor space, or were spending excessive amounts of income for housing, or were experiencing more than one of these three problems (Table 4.14). Virtually the entire low-income population as well as one-seventh (29,000) of the non-low-income population encountered at least one of the three dimensions of housing need. As will be explained in Chapter 8, only 94,000 of these families would require financial assistance in order to eliminate whichever of the problems they were experiencing. The number of families who were judged to be experiencing some combination of quality, space, and expense problems is substantial. Approximately 50,000 of the 115,000 households were faced with multiple housing deprivations. The vast majority of these 50,000 households had two problems to contend with; only 7,000 familes were deprived in all three areas simultaneously.

Families living in crowded quarters — in the main large, low-income black households — were most likely to be experiencing other dimensions of housing need as well. Of the 22,000 families who had less than one room per person, three-fourths had at least one additional problem. The next highest degree of overlap was found among occupants of substandard housing. Of the 65,000 living in physically deficient accommodations, two-thirds, or 44,000, were experiencing additional dimensions of need. The overlap between space and quality deprivations, however, is less extensive than might be expected; only 9,000 of the 44,000 families were occupying units which provided less than one room per person. The principal area of overlapping needs is moderate physical deficiency and excessive housing expense. Households experiencing this combination of needs (including both minor and intermediate physical deficiencies) totaled 30,000 in number, or three-fifths of the entire group faced with multiple housing deprivations. These families also occupy over one-half of the moderately substandard inventory. Since, by definition, they cannot bear additional housing costs, upgrading most of the marginally deficient sectors of the stock cannot be financed out of increased rents.

While the degree of overlap among the three dimensions of need is substantial, it is far from complete. If, for example, a program of housing allowances were created to provide financial assistance to only those households currently burdened with excessive housing costs, one-third of the 77,000 families that were experiencing either quality or space problems would not receive direct benefits. Equally relevant to housing policy, over two-fifths of those who did receive an allowance would already be living in uncrowded standard accommodations. This latter fact stems in part from the liberal criteria we have used in defining excess expense.

From the standpoint of coverage, a program directed toward families occupying physically deficient housing would reach a smaller proportion of the total number of families having one or more of the three dimensions of

Table 4.14. Composite Need Profiles With Respect to Physical Quality, Space, and Housing Expense by Number of Housing Problems Experienced[1] (Baltimore, Maryland, 1969)

	Number of Households	% of All Households
No housing problems (with respect to quality, space, and expense)	162,440	58.8
One housing problem	63,030	22.8
Excessive expense only	36,560	13.2
Inadequate space only	5,320	1.9
Minor physical deficiency only	17,640	6.4
Intermediate physical deficiency only	2,340	0.9
Major physical deficiency only	1,170	0.4
Two housing problems	43,700	15.8
Inadequate space – excessive expense	7,100	2.6
Minor physical deficiency – excessive expense	20,920	7.6
Minor physical deficiency – inadequate space	1,760	0.6
Intermediate physical deficiency – excessive expense	8,990	3.2
Intermediate physical deficiency – inadequate space	260	0.1
Major physical deficiency – excessive expense	4,670	1.7
Major physical deficiency – inadequate space	0	0.0
Three housing problems	7,080	2.6
Minor physical deficiency – inadequate space – excessive expense	3,520	1.3
Intermediate physical deficiency – inadequate space – excessive expense	1,270	0.5
Major physical deficiency – inadequate space – excessive expense	2,290	0.8
One or more housing problems	113,810	41.2
Total households	276,250	100.0

[1] Sources: First Household Survey and Survey of Residential Structures.

need than would the expense-oriented effort just described. It would miss slightly over half of the families who are deprived with respect to either space or expense. Coverage, however, is but one criterion for evaluating alternative intervention strategies. Whether the amount of assistance would be sufficient to eliminate excessive housing expense and whether resources channeled through the demand-side of the market would in turn generate the desired level of upgrading in the short run are among the additional factors which must be weighed in choosing among policy alternatives.

CHAPTER 5
The Neighborhood Environment

The crucial importance of the neighborhood environment in the attainment of decent housing for urban families has long been recognized. Since the closing decades of the 19th century, local housing codes have prescribed official standards pertaining to both the structure and its immediate surrounding. At the national level, more than a half-century later, the Housing Act of 1949 formally proclaimed the provision of a suitable residential environment to be a primary objective of federal housing policy. Although long acknowledged as important, the tremendous difficulties involved in realizing this goal are only just becoming widely appreciated. If the experiences of the 1950's pointed up the limitations of large scale, high-density projects as the solution to the substandard housing problem, then the main lesson of the 1960's has been that small scale, decentralized efforts in the inner city which provide a handful of isolated new or rehabilitated units, but leave the larger residential environment unchanged, are not the answer either.

Rectifying mistakes of the past decade is more than a matter either of proper coordination with nonhousing efforts or of simply expanding present approaches so that a greater impact is achieved. It is a question of acquiring a better understanding of the elements of an adequate neighborhood, assessing which aspects of the present environment warrant change, and determining whether and how these changes may be effectuated through housing policy decisions.

Mere definition of the neighborhood environment is difficult because of the numerous facets of residential life which must be taken into account. The residential environment may be defined broadly to include all factors, other than physical quality of the dwelling unit itself, which directly affect the level of consumer satisfaction realized from occupancy of that dwelling unit. So defined, the residential environment embraces both social and physical elements. Many of the physical elements are closely related to the housing inventory and might therefore be considered for programmatic purposes as extensions of the stock itself. They would include at least the following:

> Quality of yard or other private outdoor space associated with the given structure and with surrounding structures;
>
> Quality of sidewalks, alleys, and streets in the immediate vicinity;
>
> Quality of other structures in the immediate vicinity;
>
> Cleanliness of streets, yards, sidewalks, and alleys;
>
> Quality of physical services such as sewerage and street lighting;
>
> Quality of public, residentially related open space;
>
> Presence or absence of nonconforming uses, traffic, abandoned structures, abandoned cars, littered vacant lots, air and noise pollutants, etc.;
>
> Density of development;
>
> Availability of parking space;
>
> Presence or absence of natural amenity;
>
> Presence or absence of rodents.

Social aspects of the residential environment are equally numerous yet fundamentally different in nature. They include the various personal relationships that a resident is either casually exposed to or that he (she) develops with individuals, groups, and organizations as a direct consequence of living in a particular dwelling unit. The level of satisfaction that an occupant derives from a given residence is, to some degree, a function of the pattern and content of social interaction which that residence affords. The qualitative aspects of the following forms of social interaction contribute either positively or negatively to residential satisfaction:

> Relations between tenants and landlords or other persons directly involved in the delivery of housing services;
>
> Relations among residents of the same or adjacent neighborhoods which may involve interaction across racial, class, religious, ethnic, or generational lines, and which, in turn, will affect the extent of (a) community solidarity or personal anonymity that a given location affords, and (b) victimization or exposure to various forms of criminal or other acts which threaten personal safety or property damage;
>
> Relations between residents and various public officials operating at the neighborhood level such as police, fire fighters, housing inspectors, etc.;

Relations between residents and neighboring educational, religious, commercial, financial, political, cultural, recreational, and service organizations (not quality of physical facilities or propinquity, but personal relations with those involved in the ongoing activities of these organizations).

Few of the social and physical elements of neighborhood environment have
ever been systematically measured, partly because "neighborhood" itself is
difficult to define operationally and, in fact, has different definitions depending on the particular spatial variables being examined (1). For this reason, in
our field surveys the measurement of environmental quality was approached
in an exploratory fashion and from several different directions with no a priori
notion as to which measures would be most helpful. First, several elements of
the physical environment immediately surrounding each respondent's home
were rated. Second, respondents were asked about problems in their neighborhood that were of serious concern to them. In this area of questioning, neighborhood was self-defined and boundaries were not recorded by the interviewer.
Third, to establish the relative importance of neighborhood in the housing
choices of low-income families, recent and expected moves of respondents
were probed. And finally, in order to determine what types of neighborhood
are seen as offering a suitable environment, we asked families where they
would like to live. In this chapter, the results of these inquiries are analyzed
and some tentative conclusions are drawn regarding implications for housing
policy.

Ratings of the Immediate Physical Environment

In conjunction with the survey of residential structures, condition and
cleanliness ratings were given to rear yards, alleys, sidewalks, and streets. The
overall exterior condition of other structures on the street front was also
recorded, using a 5-category scale of "very good," "good," "fair," "poor,"
and "terrible." In addition, a count was made of boarded-up structures and
abandoned cars on the street front, and traffic volume and noxious uses
were noted.

Unlike the ratings of dwelling unit quality described in Chapter 4, the environmental ratings cannot be translated readily into resource requirements.
They do suggest, however, that several types of environmental problems are
more prevalent than are major deficiencies in housing quality. Most frequently cited by inspectors as serious environmental problems were heavy
traffic flows, noxious uses, and rear yards and alleys that were either unclean
or in poor condition (Table 5.1). For the city as a whole, each of these problems directly affected more than 10% of the population, and were therefore

Table 5.1. Percentage of Occupied Dwelling Units with Selected Environmental
Deficiencies, by Location[1] (Baltimore, Maryland, 1969)

Type of Environmental Deficiency	Percentage Dwelling Units With Problem		
	Inner City	Outer City	Total City
Rear yard unclean or in poor condition	26.0	2.1	11.2
Alley unclean or in poor condition	12.3	9.2	10.4
Sidewalk in poor condition	8.1	1.2	3.8
Street in poor condition	4.4	0.4	1.9
More than minimal amount of trash/ garbage on sidewalk or street	10.4	3.2	5.9
At least one boarded-up structure on street front	19.5	0.4	7.7
At least one abandoned car on street front	3.0	0.0	1.1
Heavy off peak hour traffic flow or noxious uses on block	18.5	7.2	11.5
Occupied dwelling units in need of major improvements, i.e., with serious/intermediate structural deficiencies	17.4	1.6	7.6

[1] Source: Survey of Residential Structures.

more prevalent than major deficiencies in housing quality, which directly
affected only 8%. In general, interior areas of blocks were in much worse
shape than street fronts. Sidewalks and streets were fairly clean and in good
repair, and the number of abandoned cars was minimal.

As would be expected, environmental problems were heavily concentrated
in the inner city. Indeed, except for some bad alleys and heavy traffic, the
outer city was virtually free of major deficiencies. By comparison, in the inner
city, rear yards that were unclean or in poor condition directly affected one-
fourth of the households, while boarded-up structures, heavy traffic flows,
and noxious uses on the street front were experienced by approximately one
family in five. Within the inner city, environmental deficiencies were noted
much more often in black neighborhoods than in white, and non-low-income
families were much more likely than low-income families to have well-main-
tained surroundings. Nevertheless, for whites, owner occupants, and non-low-
income families in the inner city, the immediate physical environment was,
on the average, in worse condition than the dwelling unit. Blacks, renters, and
low-income households, in contrast, tended to live on blocks where quality of

housing and quality of environment were about the same. Perhaps most interesting was the finding that fully one-fourth of the 50,000 standard dwellings
in the inner city were situated on poorly maintained blocks, where, on the
average, over one-fifth of the housing units were substandard and more than
5% required major repairs.

Respondents' Perceptions of the Neighborhood Environment

Frequently, in efforts to improve residential areas, resource limitations
dictate that choices be made between housing expenditures and investment
in other aspects of the neighborhood environment. With relatively little
information at hand regarding levels of need for various services and facilities,
these decisions are usually made intuitively or in response to the demands of
community groups or larger political forces. As a result, the feelings of individual residents about priorities among types of improvements rarely enter the
picture in a direct and structured way.

During the course of the household interviews, respondents were asked to
comment upon numerous aspects of life in their neighborhoods. While the
answers cannot be translated into precise measures of need, they do provide
some indication as to which types of neighborhood problems are considered
by residents to be most pressing. They do not, unfortunately, give a balanced
picture of feelings about neighborhood, since favorable comments were not
solicited. This asymmetry is partially corrected by other data presented in
succeeding sections of the chapter.

The most striking finding concerning attitudes toward the residential
environment is that consistently throughout the first and second household
surveys, the number of respondents who expressed serious dissatisfaction
with the quality of their neighborhood exceeded the number who expressed
similar feelings about the quality of their dwelling units. In the initial household survey, this differential was suggested by respondents' perceptions of
neighborhood safety as compared with their attitudes toward the home.
Whereas only one respondent in ten expressed any discontent with his (her)
dwelling unit, one in four considered the neighborhood unsafe (Table 5.2).
Within the inner city, the corresponding relationship was slightly more pronounced; 13% of the residents were dissatisfied with their homes, as against
35% who viewed their immediate areas as unsafe.

Data from the second survey show that while low-income households, regardless of location and tenure of residence, were more likely to express negative feelings about the environment than about the dwelling unit, the tendency
is particularly marked in the case of owner occupants (2). Whereas, for renters,

Table 5.2. Respondents' Perceptions of Neighborhood Safety, by Location of Residence, Race of Head, and Tenure[1] (Baltimore, Maryland, 1969)

Location of Residence/Race/ Tenure	Neighborhood Unsafe	Neighborhood Reasonably Safe	Don't Know	Total Households
Inner City	37,130 (35.2%)	58,640 (55.7%)	9,620 (9.1%)	105,390
White owner	2,690 (17.5)	12,250 (79.9)	400 (2.6)	15,340
White renter	5,770 (26.4)	12,950 (59.4)	3,100 (14.2)	21,820
Black owner	6,680 (44.4)	7,300 (48.5)	1,070 (7.1)	15,050
Black renter	21,990 (41.3)	26,140 (49.2)	5,050 (9.5)	53,180
Outer City	34,680 (20.3)	126,680 (74.1)	9,500 (5.6)	170,860
White owner	14,950 (17.3)	70,790 (81.9)	680 (0.8)	86,420
White renter	7,970 (18.8)	27,550 (65.0)	6,840 (16.2)	42,360
Black owner	3,600 (19.0)	14,690 (77.8)	600 (3.2)	18,890
Black renter	8,160 (35.2)	13,650 (58.9)	1,380 (5.9)	23,190
Total Households	71,810 (26.0)	185,320 (67.1)	19,120 (6.9)	276,250
Subtotal, white households	31,380 (18.9)	123,540 (74.5)	11,020 (6.6)	165,940
Subtotal, black households	40,430 (36.7)	61,780 (56.0)	8,100 (7.3)	110,310
Subtotal, owner	27,920 (20.6)	105,030 (77.4)	2,750 (2.0)	135,700
Subtotal, renter	43,890 (31.2)	80,290 (57.1)	16,370 (11.7)	140,550

[1] Source: First Household Survey.

Table 5.3. Comparison of Attitudes of Low-Income Households Toward Dwelling Unit and Neighborhood Environment, by Tenure[1] (Baltimore, Maryland, 1969)

	Dwelling Unit	Neighborhood
Owner Occupants Percentage of households who mentioned at least one serious problem	34.4	75.1
Average number of problems mentioned	1.8	3.2
Renter Occupants Percentage of households who mentioned at least one serious problem	61.8	64.9
Average number of problems mentioned	4.1	3.9

[1] Source: Second Household Survey.

the number of families who mentioned at least one serious neighborhood problem was about the same as the number who mentioned at least one serious dwelling-unit problem (65% vs 62%), for owners, the former outnumbered the latter by more than a two-to-one margin (75% vs 34%) (Table 5.3).

The results of the second survey point up not only the comparatively greater disenchantment with the environment than with the dwelling, but also how widespread are negative attitudes toward quality of neighborhood among residents of low-income areas of the city. Within the low-income population, seven persons in ten cited at least one serious problem in their immediate areas. Outer-city low-income residents were almost as critical of neighborhood quality as were those living in the inner city. Whereas three-quarters of inner-city respondents noted one or more serious problems, the corresponding figure for families located in the outer city was almost two-thirds. The complaints which the two groups registered most frequently, however, were quite different, as we shall discuss. In the inner city, three aspects of the residential environment — lack of play areas for small children (not necessarily tot-lots), noise, and robberies and other crimes — were regarded as major problems by three respondents in ten (Table 5.4). Six additional aspects of neighborhood quality — condition of other housing on the block, street cleaning, neighborhood shopping, traffic, police protection, and abandoned housing and littered lots — were perceived as seriously inadequate by from one-sixth to one-fifth of the low-income households located in the inner city. Surprisingly, schools were considered a big problem by fewer than one low-income person in ten (3).

In terms of both the types of problems that were viewed as most pressing and the proportion of respondents expressing negative attitudes, the findings just described appear quite consistent with an earlier study undertaken in the initial stages of the Community Action Program (4). The relationship between residents' perceptions and independent ratings of neighborhood quality is also reassuring. For most aspects of the environment where both a rating and an attitudinal response were obtained, aggregate estimates of need yielded by the two types of measurement were quite similar. Individual ratings, however, agreed with corresponding attitudinal responses in only a minority of cases. For example, among low-income households in the inner city, only two-fifths of the respondents who were living on streets regarded as dirty by inspectors felt street cleaning was a major problem, while only three-fifths of those who perceived street cleaning as a major problem were located on streets which received an unsatisfactory rating.

The configuration of attitudes is quite different in the outer city. For nine out of the ten most frequently mentioned neighborhood problems, the percentage of low-income outer-city families who were seriously concerned bore

Table 5.4 Dimensions of Neighborhood Environment Most Often Cited as Serious
Problems, by Location of Residence[1] (Baltimore, Maryland, 1969)

Dimension of Neighborhood Environment	Percentage of Households who Perceived the Dimension as a Big Problem in Their Neighborhood	
	Inner City	Outer City
Play areas for small children	30.7	19.4
Noise	29.0	20.7
Street cleaning	21.1	23.1
Robberies or other crime	28.2	9.7
Parking spaces	11.6	23.8
Condition of other housing on block	22.8	5.5
Police protection	17.6	10.0
Traffic	17.6	9.6
Street lighting	10.3	20.1
Neighborhood shopping	17.7	5.5
Abandoned housing and littered lots	16.9	2.3
Smells	13.8	9.4
Bars and taverns	10.9	11.2
Public transportation	9.1	9.5
Schools	7.4	7.5
Neighbors	6.6	2.8
Abandoned cars	5.0	1.8
Fire protection	2.9	3.7

[1] Source: Second Housing Survey.

no resemblance to the corresponding figure for inner-city households. The
dimensions of neighborhood quality which were most often viewed critically
in the outer city include availability of parking spaces, street cleaning, noise,
street lighting, and play areas for small children (5).

Respondents' Perceptions of Neighborhood Trends

Although it is useful for planning purposes to identify aspects of the
neighborhood environment which families currently find most unpleasant, in
the case of inner-city residents, perceptions of changes over time may be more
important. If residents feel their neighborhoods are improving, this may
indicate that renewal efforts are either effective or need not be applied. If, on
the other hand, pessimism is prevalent, further decay and abandonment can be
expected.

As part of the second household survey, low-income families were asked
whether their neighborhoods were improving, staying about the same, or

Table 5.5. Percentage Distribution of Low-Income Respondents' Perceptions of Neighborhood Trends, Within Tenure, Race, and Location Categories[1] (Baltimore, Maryland, 1969)

Location/Tenure/Race	Improving	Neighborhood Has Been: Staying About the Same	Going Downhill	Don't Know
Inner city	16.7	36.8	39.2	7.3
White owner	25.6	32.7	34.7	7.0
Black owner	5.4	35.4	58.7	0.5
White renter	18.6	36.8	36.7	7.9
Black renter	16.7	37.8	37.1	8.4
Outer city	16.0	56.4	27.6	–
White owner	14.8	52.1	33.1	–
Black owner	37.8	62.2	–	–
White renter	–	95.0	5.0	–
Black renter	21.9	10.8	67.3	–
All low-income households	16.4	44.7	34.5	4.4
All white households	14.0	55.3	28.0	2.7
All black households	18.2	36.9	39.3	5.6
All owner occupants	18.6	47.4	32.7	1.3
All renter occupants	15.1	43.1	35.6	6.2

[1] Source: Second Household Survey.

going down hill. A large proportion (one-third) of them said the general trend in the quality of their immediate residential environment was worsening (Table 5.5). Although this attitude was more prevalent among inner-city residents, it was still shared by a significant minority of households living in outlying areas. Interestingly, the two groups among whom pessimism was most common — inner-city black owners and outer-city black renters — appear to be the same ones whose concern over neighborhood safety was also most widespread (Table 5.2) (6).

These gloomy figures should not be allowed to obscure totally the positive side of the picture. One-sixth of respondents in both the inner and outer city thought trends in their areas were upward. Among two groups — outer-city black owners and white renters — there were practically no negative forecasts at all. And, strangely enough, there was almost a balance of positive and negative opinion among inner-city white owners.

The various responses just described must be interpreted with great caution. Since some persons are either inveterate optimists or pessimists, a range of answers is to be expected regardless of the actual facts. Also, respondents would be expected to vary in their retrospective time horizons, depending on how long they had lived in their neighborhood. Further, they would be expected to differ with respect to dimensions of the environment with which they would be most concerned. Finally, since the data are highly aggregated, the responses reflect actual differences among neighborhoods. If we had subdivided the inner and outer city into smaller areas, it is likely that within each neighborhood either positive or negative responses would have been more clearly dominant. And were the survey to be repeated periodically, changes in the relative proportion of optimistic and pessimistic answers might suggest a different pattern of trends throughout the city.

Neighborhood Quality and Residential Mobility

The future of neighborhoods is determined ultimately by the change over time in the number and characteristics of a set of families not now living in the neighborhoods — the in-migrants. For this reason, inferences which can be drawn from cross-sectional data on the concerns of current residents are limited. Information on recent and expected moves of these residents, however, is a partial substitute for a longitudinal study, and thus is of some help in further delineating the size and nature of neighborhood problems. With this thought in mind, we devoted part of the second household survey to the question of residential mobility.

The decision to move and the selection of a new place of residence are generally acknowledged as complex processes; usually, the household in question weighs numerous factors before settling upon a definite course of action. In previous studies of residential mobility, when recent movers have been asked what factors impelled them to leave their previous dwellings and what features of their newly occupied homes particularly attracted them, they have tended to stress attributes of the dwelling unit rather than aspects of the neighborhood environment. Since residential mobility is often viewed as the spatial expression of vertical social mobility as well as a process of adjustment to changing shelter needs over the life cycle, it is somewhat surprising that neighborhood characteristics such as high prestige, locational advantage, and good community facilities have, on the whole, been articulated as primary reasons for moves relatively infrequently. Much more common are responses relating to condition and design of dwelling, amount and arrangement of indoor and outdoor private space, and cost of occupancy.

In many but not all respects, the data on moving decisions of low-income households in Baltimore support the findings of other studies (7). As noted earlier, dissatisfaction with the neighborhood environment is widespread throughout the low-income population, regardless of race, tenure, or location of household. Despite this high level of disenchantment, when asked to give their principal reasons for either recent or intended moves, respondents still stressed factors relating to the dwelling unit itself. For example, nearly three-fourths of the 16,000 low-income renters who moved voluntarily in the past three years mentioned as their primary reason for leaving their previous residence either size (32%), condition (32%), or cost (8%) of dwelling unit. In contrast, only one-sixth of the recent movers said things which might be interpreted as neighborhood dissatisfaction. Most of these respondents were whites who claimed they did not like their neighbors. Moreover, the majority of secondary reasons for leaving the previous residence were still directed toward attributes of the dwelling unit. Neighborhood factors accounted for only one-fourth of the secondary reasons, with dislike of neighbors, poor accessibility, and lack of safety each falling in the 6 to 8% range.

By and large, when the same group of recent movers were asked why they selected their present homes, a similar preponderance of dwelling unit factors was obtained. Again, three-fourths of the respondents mentioned either size (35%), condition (18%), or cost (22%). For both whites and blacks, neighborhood factors were regarded as of primary importance by only one-tenth of the respondents. Curiously, virtually all of those who said they were concerned with neighborhood factors in selecting their current residence had relocated in the inner city. Among this group, whites pointed most often to satisfaction with neighbors as the main reason for their choice, while blacks were more likely to mention improved accessibility.

Shifting now to prospective moves, dwelling unit factors are once again seen to dominate the overall pattern of results. Among the 13,000 low-income renters who had decided voluntarily to move within the next year, nearly three-quarters mentioned either inadequate space (42%) or poor condition of unit (30%) as the primary reason. Again, neighborhood factors accounted for only 10% of the primary reasons for relocation. Generally speaking, inner-city residents were more likely than outer-city households to mention dissatisfaction with aspects of the neighborhood environment (14% vs. 1%), as were whites relative to black families (15% vs 8%). Why so many respondents stressed dwelling unit factors cannot be determined from the data at hand. Conceivably, finding more suitable accommodations in locations which differ only marginally and which in the main are undesirable may be the best that they hope to accomplish under current market conditions. If this is so, respondents' descriptions of the calculus of their moving decisions would be accurate.

Locational Preferences

To many housing analysts, data on the locational preferences of low-income families are somewhat beside the point. In their view, it is virtually impossible to create a suitable living environment in the inner city as long as so many low-income deprived families are there. "Suitable" implies dispersion of the poor. "Gilding the ghetto" perpetuates an inherently undesirable spatial distribution of the population. Although we will address this argument in detail in Chapter 7, it is useful here to consider the attitudes of poor families themselves in this regard. Their locational preferences have immediate relevance for policies directed either at dispersal or at revival of the core.

In the course of administering the second household survey, the principal respondent for each household was asked the following question regarding his or her locational preference: "If you had an opportunity to live anywhere in the Baltimore area, in a house or apartment that cost about the same as this one, where would you like to live?" The question was intended primarily to determine where the respondent would prefer to live, in a "pure" sense, regardless of present economic constraints which might be operating to prevent the family from realizing that choice. A second purpose was to find out whether families would be likely to move from their present neighborhoods if they obtained additional resources which could be spent on housing; and if so, where.

Surprisingly, more than one-half of the low-income respondents in the inner city stated that they would choose to live in their present neighborhood or in another section of the inner city, even if opportunities were available throughout the Baltimore metropolitan area (Table 5.6) (8). Locational preferences of inner-city residents varied somewhat by type of tenure of respondent with well over three-fifths of owner-occupant households wishing to remain in or near their present neighborhoods. In terms of socioeconomic characteristics other than race and tenure, AFDC recipients, female-headed households, and large families tended to be less attached to their present neighborhood. Two-thirds would choose another neighborhood. As might be expected, the elderly were most desirous of staying on. Two-thirds would stay where they are.

Of families who would choose to leave the inner city, 70% mentioned various locations in the outer city. The remaining responses were divided among the surrounding counties. For the most part, the areas mentioned in the suburbs were ones which already contain significant numbers of low-income families, such as Catonsville, Dundalk, Turner's Station, and Essex. The preferences of blacks and whites who would choose to leave the inner city appear to differ radically. Four-fifths of the black families mentioned a neighborhood within the outer city, usually areas where middle-income blacks already predominate. By way of contrast, seven white respondents in ten wished to live in areas beyond the boundaries of the city.

In the outer city, the pattern of responses was, in certain respects, quite similar. For example, slightly more than half of the low-income households stated a preference for either their present or a nearby neighborhood. Of the

Table 5.6. Locational Preferences of Low-Income Households Living in the Inner City, by Race and Tenure[1] (Baltimore, Maryland, 1969)

Locational Preference/ Type of Household	Present or Nearby Neighborhood in Inner City	Distant Section of Inner City	Outer City	Outside Balt. City, Inside SMSA	Suburbs/ Country	No Preference or Don't Know	Total Households
White owners	3,400 (61.4)[2] (13.4)	140 (2.5) (9.4)	640 (11.5) (5.4)	790 (14.3) (22.0)	410 (7.4) (26.0)	160 (2.9) (2.2)	5,540 (100) (10.9)
Black owners	3,630 (64.3) (14.3)	– (0.0) (0.0)	890 (15.8) (7.6)	170 (3.0) (4.7)	240 (4.3) (15.2)	710 (12.6) (9.9)	5,640 (100) (11.0)
White renters	3,880 (54.8) (15.3)	220 (3.1) (14.9)	690 (9.8) (5.9)	1,670 (23.6) (46.4)	100 (1.4) (6.3)	520 (7.3) (7.3)	7,080 (100) (13.9)
Black renters	14,490 (44.2) (57.0)	1,120 (3.4) (75.7)	9,560 (29.2) (81.1)	970 (3.0) (26.9)	830 (2.5) (52.5)	5,790 (15.3) (80.6)	32,760 (100) (64.2)
Total, low-income inner-city households	25,400 (49.8) (100)	1,480 (2.9) (100)	11,780 (23.1) (100)	3,600 (7.0) (100)	1,580 (3.1) (100)	7,180 (12.6) (100)	51,020 (100) (100)
Subtotal, owner occupants	7,030 (62.9) (27.7)	140 (1.2) (9.4)	1,530 (13.7) (13.0)	960 (8.6) (26.7)	650 (5.8) (41.2)	870 (7.8) (12.1)	11,180 (100) (21.9)
Subtotal, renter occupants	18,370 (46.1) (72.3)	1,340 (3.4) (90.6)	10,250 (25.7) (87.0)	2,640 (6.6) (73.3)	930 (2.4) (58.8)	6,310 (15.8) (87.9)	39,840 (100) (78.1)
Subtotal, white households	7,280 (57.7) (28.7)	360 (2.9) (24.3)	1,330 (10.5) (11.3)	2,460 (19.5) (68.4)	510 (4.0) (32.3)	680 (5.4) (9.5)	12,620 (100) (24.8)
Subtotal, black households	18,120 (47.2) (71.3)	1,120 (2.9) (75.7)	10,450 (27.2) (88.7)	1,140 (3.0) (31.6)	1,070 (2.8) (67.7)	6,500 (16.9) (90.5)	38,400 (100) (75.2)

[1] Source: Second Household Survey.
[2] Figures in parentheses are percentages.

remainder, two-thirds said they would choose a distant section of the outer city and one-third wanted to leave Baltimore City for one of the surrounding counties. All but a handful of the latter families were white.

In general, therefore, the proportion of families who are more or less satisfied in locational terms is virtually identical in both sections of the city. It is important to point out, however, that while many inner-city households wish to move to outlying neighborhoods, the reverse is not true — none of the outer-city households want to return to the inner city.

Implications for Housing Policy

Having reviewed the survey results which bear most directly upon quality of the residential environment, we may now assess the implications of the findings for housing policy. Let us consider first the most prevalent environmental problems as perceived either by independent evaluators or by the residents themselves. For discussion purposes, prevalent problems are taken arbitrarily to include those which were mentioned as being serious by at least one-sixth of the low-income respondents. According to the results presented in Tables 5.1 and 5.4, ten aspects of neighborhood amenity meet this criterion — play areas for small children, noise, crime, condition of other housing on block, neighborhood shopping, traffic, police protection, condition of rear yards, and abandoned housing and littered lots.

Taking the problems in random order, the concern over nearby housing, streets, alleys, and vacant lots could be addressed through modest expansion of existing programs. Play areas would be inexpensive to create and would contribute to longer-term reconstruction of the inner city, but they also would burden an already burdened city operating budget. Traffic patterns are more intractable. Improvement of neighborhood shopping facilities also must be viewed as a fairly difficult task if the experience in a number of cities around the country is any guide. The problem of noise may or may not be susceptible of solution, depending on whether the primary sources are traffic, nonconforming uses, or simply high population density. Crime and police protection are largely outside the province of housing policy, although in the case of crime it has often been pointed out that the mere presence of vacant and abandoned structures invites vandalism and provides a potential haven for drug addicts.

Given the importance which respondents attach to these neighborhood problems, strategies to eliminate the problems should not be given ancillary status in policy decisions. They should receive a level of priority in the housing effort which is equal to that given other dimensions of need. Precise estimates of what it would cost to achieve various standards of quality and service are beyond the scope of our study. There is reason to expect, however, that with respect to most of the problems the necessary public outlays would not be prohibitive.

The data on locational preferences of the low-income population also have relevance for policy decisions. Perhaps most important is the finding that over one-half of the low-income families in the inner city prefer their present neighborhoods. This fact, coupled with the probability that many other families who desire outlying locations will be unable to obtain them in the short run and the fact that thousands of non-low-income families also have personal and financial ties in the inner city, argues strongly for continued emphasis upon inner-city upgrading efforts. Surely, it would be a mistake to neglect the less deteriorated, but declining sections of the core neighborhoods on the grounds that decline seems inevitable. At the same time, our findings indicate clearly that unless the inner city can be improved, it is going to attract fewer families each year as normal turnover of dwellings occurs and incomes rise. Most of this loss will take place among non-low-income households thus increasing the very concentration of poor that new thrusts in housing policy are seeking to eliminate.

Also of considerable importance is the evidence that the vast majority of low-income families who prefer to leave the inner city would like to locate somewhere else within Baltimore. Equally, most low-income families who are already living in the outer city are likely to remain within the city limits for some time to come. The number of poor households, especially blacks, who currently would choose to reside in the surrounding counties is certainly not large enough to justify a "suburban solution" to the low-income housing problem on the grounds of locational preferences. Still the number who would prefer the suburbs is more than token and in all probability exceeds the level of available opportunities by a considerable margin. This is particularly likely given the sizeable group of poor families already living in the suburbs who by virtue of current proximity and better familiarity with local housing efforts would undoubtedly be the first to take advantage of new suburban subsidy programs. All told, this potential demand is sufficient to warrant consideration of limited provision of low-income accommodations in the suburbs. But in light of existing preferences and large individual subsidy requirements, these efforts should not be thought of as a way to solve a major portion of the housing problem (9).

CHAPTER 6
Choice of Tenure

In recent decades, general economic prosperity and liberal mortgage financing have enabled the vast majority of white, middle-class families in this country to realize the American dream of having a home of their own. By and large, the same opportunities for home ownership have not been extended to black and poor families. In virtually all cities, a majority of such families occupy rental accommodations. The situation in Baltimore provides a good illustration of these differences in tenure patterns with respect to race and income (Table 6.1). In 1970, whites living within the city were twice as likely as blacks to be owner occupants (60% vs 30%). Since blacks, on the average, are younger than whites, their lower rate of ownership is to some extent the result of differences in age distribution. Accounting for age reduces the white/black ratio to 1.8:1; however, within the low-income population, the age adjusted white/black differential was 2.2:1.

The variation in ownership rates across income groups, while somewhat less pronounced, was nevertheless still substantial. Non-low-income families were 1.5 times as likely as low-income households to own a residence (54% vs 37%). Exclusion of the elderly population greatly increases this imbalance because of the very high ownership propensity among older, low-income white households. Inclusion of suburban families would no doubt also widen the gap.

Much of this difference in tenure patterns is usually attributed to imperfections in the private real estate market and in public programs rather than simply to low income or to variations in preferences for home ownership or to a dearth of modestly priced structures that are suitable for owner occupancy. Two specific imperfections have frequently been suggested. The first relates to mortgage financing. Institutional lenders will not put money into

Table 6.1. Proportion of Owner Occupant to Total Households, by Race and Age of Head and Income Status of Household[1] (Baltimore, Maryland, 1968)

Race of Head/ Income Status	Age of Household Head				
	Under 30	30– 44	45– 64	65 or more	All Households
Black households	.079	.262	.402	.483	.308
Low income	.054	.166	.265	.439	.217
Non-low income	.097	.327	.501	.680	.381
White households	.259	.622	.700	.681	.613
Low income	.183	.404	.633	.782	.588
Non-low income	.273	.678	.712	.623	.620
Total households	.175	.447	.591	.626	.491
Low income	.094	.250	.409	.618	.374
Non-low income	.207	.532	.653	.633	.543

[1] Source: First Household Survey.

the types of neighborhoods where housing that low-income families can afford is ordinarily available, and they regard most of the families as poor credit risks. Regulations of the Federal Housing Administration and Federal Home Loan Bank Board, it is alleged, support these policies. The second imperfection is embodied in the federal low-income housing programs which until recently were structured to exclude the possibility of owner occupancy.

To begin to rectify this situation, federal subsidy programs were initiated which provide opportunities for low- and moderate-income families to own rather than rent decent accommodations. This effort began in 1965 under the provisions of FHA Section 221 and was extended significantly under the FHA Section 235 and Public Housing Turnkey III programs. Justification for these program innovations has been made on various grounds. The traditional arguments in favor of home ownership are well known — that owning a home promotes self-reliance, affords greater privacy and control over one's immediate environment, gives the family a stake in community affairs, and reduces certain out-of-pocket expenses. In addition, several less obvious disadvantages of renting have been cited. To the extent that black and poor families are denied opportunities to own their homes, they are also denied the most viable hedge against inflation that is open to white and middle-income households, and are precluded from participating in an important method of capital accumulation (1). All of these arguments view home ownership as an instrumental goal the achievement of which would facilitate attainment of other presumably more basic objectives. The point is sometimes made, however, that in a society where home ownership is such an integral part of the dominant culture, inability to own one's residence constitutes a basic deprivation in and of itself.

Many housing analysts have raised doubts as to the wisdom of expanding home-ownership opportunities for the poor. The contentions of these critics extend beyond the notion that owner occupancy per se is no panacea for solving housing problems, a point with which advocates of owner occupancy would agree. The argument is made that home ownership would saddle poor families with responsibilities that they either do not want or are ill-prepared to assume. Moreover, if such opportunities are provided mainly in those sectors of the stock which are already occupied by low-income households, the privilege of ownership may be more bane than blessing, since capital appreciation is unlikely and older units are more expensive to maintain. Also, as Peter Marcuse has pointed out, through creative design of leasehold arrangements it should be possible to combine those features of renter and owner occupancy which are most appropriate for low- and moderate-income families (2). The high rate of foreclosure under Section 235 is offered as evidence to bolster the case of the anti-ownership protagonists.

While debate continues, prevailing opinion has it that poor families have roughly the same housing preferences as do middle- and upper-income households and that given the opportunity, a large proportion of them would indeed opt for a home of their own. Although this supposition may be correct, it is not based on knowledge of either the attitudes of the poor toward owner occupancy or their actual experiences in the housing market. Such information would seem important in order to determine how much emphasis should be given to subsidized home-ownership programs.

In conjunction with our second household survey, an attempt was made to determine how many low-income families in Baltimore are deprived with respect to choice of tenure as well as how intensively they feel about this dimension of housing need. Unfortunately, there is no easy or straightforward means of answering these questions. Without elaborating upon all of the methodological pitfalls, our basic approach may be described as an analysis of the difference between stated preferences and constrained market choices of recent and intended movers. There is one overriding problem with this approach. In many cities there is little similarity between the physical characteristics of the renter- and owner-occupied stock. If a family wishes to live in a single-family structure located in a low-density neighborhood, it almost always must purchase such a home, regardless of its preferences for owning or renting. The task of establishing whether home ownership is perceived as a separate goal is therefore a perplexing one. The characteristics of the Baltimore inventory, however, facilitate matters somewhat. In many sections of the city, medium-density single-family row housing is both predominant and available on either a renter- or owner-occupancy basis. Families seeking this type of housing should be in a position to make a genuine choice of tenure if financing for purchase can be readily obtained. Equally, if asked whether they prefer home ownership to renting, they should be unlikely to confuse owner occupancy with the type of living environment which this form of tenure often implies.

TENURE PREFERENCES OF RECENT MOVERS

In recent years, relatively few poor families in Baltimore have purchased homes. Of 32,000 low-income owner-occupant households in the city, only 2,000 or 6% had obtained their homes within three years of the time of being interviewed. About one-half of these households were buying homes under land installment contracts but did not yet have title (3). This low rate of acquisition, as compared with a much higher rate of ownership for low-income families overall, reflects the fact that most poor families acquired their homes when their incomes were higher.

By themselves the above figures do not reveal whether latent ownership preferences are being repressed or are simply not very widespread. To ascertain which of these possibilities is more likely, we must look at those who did *not* buy. Among recent movers who chose to rent, only 1,500, or fewer than one in ten, had given consideration to ownership when looking for a new place of residence. When asked why a home was not purchased, the majority (60%) of the 1,500 families said they were not able to find an acceptable home within their price range. The remainder either were unable to obtain financing or could not produce the required down payment. These data might seem to indicate that inexpensive homes are simply not available, but as suggested in Chapter 2, quite the contrary is the case. So it is more reasonable to infer that most of the thwarted buyers searched for homes in sections of the city where values are higher than average. Data on housing preferences of intended movers, presented in the next section, support this conclusion.

Comparing the 2,000 low-income families who were successful in their home-buying efforts with the 1,500 who were not, it would appear that not many low-income families in Baltimore are being denied the tenure arrangement which they feel is best for them under present circumstances. There are indications, however, that the relative infrequency of consideration given to home ownership by renter households is due primarily to financial constraints rather than to widespread preference for rental occupancy. For example, among the 90% of recent movers who gave no thought to purchase of a home, two-thirds stated simply that they could not afford it. Only one-third claimed that owner occupancy would be a poor choice for them — 14%

felt that they were too old to buy a home, 12% thought home ownership involved too much responsibility, 3% said a single-family house exceeded their
space needs, 2% mentioned that they moved too often to own, and 1%
wanted to avoid burdensome debt.

TENURE PREFERENCES OF INTENDED MOVERS

In many respects, the findings pertaining to tenure preferences of intended
movers are similar to those just described for recent movers. Only one-fourth
of the 13,000 low-income renter households who were thinking about moving
in the next year were actually in the market to purchase a home. Nearly three-
fourths of the remaining 10,000, however, would like to own a home some
day. And even among the families who were not interested in home ownership, a significant number of younger respondents indicated that they would
consider purchasing a home if the costs involved were equal to or less than
their present level of housing expense. On the whole, virtually all nonelderly
intended movers who were occupying rental units expressed at least conditional interest in owning a home at some point in the future.

It should be emphasized that none of these findings for either recent or
intended movers indicates that low-income families feel *seriously* deprived
because their efforts to buy a home are being thwarted. In fact, several inner-
city real estate investors whom we interviewed are convinced that desire for
home ownership among the poor is minimal. They claim that good single-
family properties which are located in stable neighborhoods and which, therefore, can be rented with ease are difficult to sell at reasonable prices even with
100% financing. On the other hand, the large number of lower income families
who purchase homes on relatively unattractive terms under land installment
contracts would seem to be evidence of intense desire to escape renter status.
Regrettably, our survey did not probe preferences for owner occupancy in
sufficient depth to resolve this issue.

TENURE VS RELATED PREFERENCES

The widespread potential interest in home ownership on the part of renters
who intended to move must be interpreted with caution because, as noted
earlier, it is especially difficult to determine whether the positive response
toward owning a home reflects a desire for owner occupancy, per se, or for a
single-family home, or for a lower residential density, or for a better neighborhood environment. If low-income families who express an interest in owner-

ship really want these other things, the arguments for expanded owner occupancy, especially in the inner city, are considerably weakened. Although our data are inconclusive on this point, certain insights may be gained from an analysis of the various aspects of residential preferences of inner-city renters who were planning to relocate within a year of the time of interview.

Let us consider first the inner-city renters who were planning to buy. Among this group of households, over two-thirds were already occupying single-family units, virtually all of which were row homes. Less than two-fifths of these households were seeking the lower density environment of detached or semidetached dwellings. The majority were looking for another row house in a different location.

On the other hand, virtually none of the families who were planning to buy a home preferred to remain in the inner city — two-thirds desired an outer-city neighborhood, and the remainder said they would move to another section of the city but had not yet decided upon a specific location. At first glance, this finding would seem to support the notion that home ownership is simply a means to the realization of locational preferences. However, one half of intended renters also favored outlying neighborhoods. Thus, although intended buyers appear more prone than intended renters to leave core neighborhoods, the desire to move outward is hardly synonymous with preference for owner occupancy. In fact, fully two-thirds of the inner-city respondents who said they would move to outer-city or suburban neighborhoods in the near future were seeking other rental accommodations.

CONCLUSIONS

On balance, the above evidence would seem to suggest that home ownership is indeed perceived by most low-income households as a distinct goal. The potential demand for home ownership among low-income households, even in the short run, surpasses by a considerable margin the number of opportunities which are currently being supplied through public programs and the mainstream of the private market. Moreover, as already mentioned, there is an ample supply of suitable housing which these families could easily afford if reasonable financing were available to them. Although it would be foolish, given the income-related problems of many low-income families, to attempt to raise their rate of home ownership to that of non-low-income families (an effort which would require shifting about 15,000 of them out of rental status), mechanisms should possibly be created to facilitate the purchasing efforts of those among them who seriously want to be owners and who could benefit by becoming ones. Without such mechanisms, these families will either be forced to use land installment contracts, with all of the extra costs which these contracts impose, or forego ownership entirely. Non-low-income families who would like to live in red-lined areas of the inner city will also be adversely affected.

Despite the large potential demand for ownership, it should be stressed that the number of families who wish to purchase homes in the inner city, where transfers of single-family rental units could most readily materialize in the near term, is presently quite small, a fact which has obvious policy implications. Unless a program to expand opportunities for home ownership were accompanied by substantial improvement in the inner-city environment, it would serve simply to accelerate out-migration and the downward spiral of decay.

CHAPTER 7
Locational Choice

Until quite recently, major low-income housing battles in the United States focused primarily on a single objective for poor families — safe and sanitary shelter. Perhaps because of the enormity of the substandard housing problem, little attention was given to the question of where low-income families should be able to live. When public housing was launched, it seemed only natural that projects should be placed either in existing low-income areas or on open land in marginal locations. Later, the "suitable living environment" mandate of Congress led to attempts to scatter public housing units in middle-income neighborhoods, but when these efforts failed, few persons were greatly disappointed. And hardly anyone at all argued that the housing should be dispersed beyond the borders of central cities into the newer suburbs. The suburban housing arguments revolved at that time around exclusionary zoning, not subsidized housing.

Suddenly, this entire perspective has changed. The severity and seeming intractability of social problems in low-income neighborhoods, the fiscal crises of cities, the realization that from now on nearly all of the net growth in population and employment will occur in the suburbs, the publication of the Coleman report on equality of educational opportunity (1), the sharp rise in subsidized housing production, and concern over the increasing spatial separation of blacks and whites have brought locational issues into the fore-front of concern. Deconcentration of the poor, not primarily for the purpose of improving their housing conditions but rather in order to achieve a variety of essentially nonhousing objectives, has become an article of faith among many persons in the housing field. Suburban barriers to low- and moderate-income families are fought with moral arguments; one being that suburban

113

communities should accept their "fair share" of subsidized construction. Programs designed to enable low-income families to reside in new suburban complexes are accepted without question as being good (2). And filtering, even to the extent that it can be made to "work," is rejected as a solution to the housing problem, because it will not reduce the existing concentration of low-income families in inner-city areas.

Yet neither the costs and benefits nor the equity and allocational efficiency of programs that would substantially expand residential location opportunities for low-income families have been evaluated. As a consequence, policy-makers lack the information they need to determine how much emphasis should be placed on the locational-choice objective relative to other housing goals which are competing for the same resources. It is the purpose of this chapter, therefore, to explain as briefly and in as neutral terms as possible, the key issues involved. In the process we hope to lay part of the foundations for the program options introduced in Chapter 11.

The issues are addressed mainly at the city/suburban scale, because it is here where the bulk of the controversy lies. Nearly all low-income housing programs expand residential opportunities to some degree. But all save a few of them — even including housing allowances which are advocated, in part, precisely because they do increase consumer sovereignty among beneficiary families — generally serve to confine recipients to fairly narrowly proscribed sectors of the market. Either the subsidies attach to dwelling units that are situated in low-rent neighborhoods or, as in the case of housing allowances, they are not large enough to enable families to move very far up the housing ladder. In order to achieve the stated objective of substantially expanded choice, a large proportion of recipients would have to be given subsidies of sufficient size to permit them to move into newly built structures or units of comparable value in the standing stock. This is exactly the level of choice which "fair-share" plans contemplate; and it is at this level, because of the large per-family subsidies involved, that basic policy dilemmas arise.

Eight arguments for and one against a locational-choice emphasis in housing policy are presented. The individual analyses proceed virtually without data from Baltimore itself. This is because, with few exceptions, the issue of whether lack of locational choice is a serious problem for low-income families is still more theoretical than empirical in nature (3).

Discussions of locational choice frequently make no distinction between the low- and moderate-income sectors of the population, even though most of the relevant arguments do not apply with equal force to both groups. Our focus here is primarily on low-income families, whom we define as those who cannot afford a *decent* home. They are the ones who are supposed to be served by public housing, rent supplements, and housing allowances. Moderate-income families by contrast can afford decent accommodations but not a *new* home. The Section 235-236 programs have been directed at their needs. There is a third group of families, perhaps best described as middle-income, who can afford a new home, but who are nevertheless denied access to many suburban communities because of exclusionary zoning. Subsidies are not required to meet the needs of these families, and none of the arguments to follow should be interpreted as applying to them.

ARGUMENTS IN FAVOR OF PROGRAMS TO EXPAND LOCATIONAL CHOICE

Promote Equal Educational Opportunity

Evidence of great inequalities in educational opportunity, not simply educational outcomes, exists in abundance. The deplorable situation in many inner-city schools is just one example. Just as depressing is the fact that over eighty percent of the children of upper-income families go on to college, whereas only sixteen percent of the children from low-income families do so (4). It is generally felt that little of this difference is genetically determined.

Numerous remedies have been suggested to solve the educational problems of inner-city schools: new plant and equipment; Headstart; improved teacher training; different curricula; more involvement of parents; remedial courses; better diets for the children; smaller classes; removal of trouble-makers; desegregation through busing or other means; different teachers; and local control of hiring, firing, and budget allocations. All of these devices may be necessary to varying degrees; collectively, however, they have not yet resulted in widespread substantial improvement in student performance. One device that does appear to hold promise is greater socio-economic mixing in the classroom. Several studies of educational achievement have concluded that low-income youngsters who are in classes with middle- and upper-income pupils perform better than do their counterparts in predominantly low-income schools even where per pupil expenditures are the same (5). From this finding many persons have concluded that to promote the American ideal, or perhaps myth, of equal opportunity much more income mixing in primary and secondary schools is necessary.

Much more than mixing would be required to close the inequality gap completely. Low-income kids would have to be properly counseled, not shunted off to inadequate vocational education programs, and so forth. But if the various studies are to be believed, mixing would close about ¼ of the gap. To achieve mixing, only two strategies are possible — busing and provision of more low- and moderate-income housing in each school district. Busing, especially reverse busing across district lines, to achieve educational equality is anathema to nearly all suburban parents. Even Hubert Humphrey has deplored the fact that "Parents put the kids on the bus and say good-bye. The parents never see the schools or the teachers" (6). The busing itself has in many cases been mistakenly aimed at de facto racial segregation rather than income segregation. And the results of the busing have been quite mixed (partly because some of the schools to which children have been transported have used tracking systems to resegregate the youngsters at the classroom level).

This leaves the mixing of income groups residentially as a possible approach to increasing equality of educational opportunity (7). In the short-term, this approach would have very little impact, because most of the current crop of children would have grown up and left school before a significant amount of mixing could be financed and arranged. Over the longer term, however, a program that began now might have a substantial impact on existing segregated patterns.

Equally, though, if subsidized housing represents a long-term route to educational equality, there may be more cost-effective strategies. The $2,000 or so per family per year that would be required to provide subsidized housing in upper-income areas is much greater than the cost of other remedial approaches which educators have proposed (8). Even within the housing sphere, progress toward educational equality could be achieved much more inexpensively and quickly if low-income families were provided subsidies that enabled them to move into older middle-income neighborhoods rather than into the new suburbs. Not surprisingly, this suggestion has not been greeted with much enthusiasm either.

It is worth noting too that if educational equality is to be viewed as a primary purpose of subsidized housing in the suburbs, then the emphasis on moderate-income families in existing subsidy programs should be drastically altered. As a group, these families would derive fewer educational benefits than their lower-income counterparts by a move to the suburbs, and their out-migration would increase the concentration of low-income children in central-city classrooms.

Reduce the Problems of the Poor through Dispersal of Poor Families

This argument states that when the poor are gathered together their problems are compounded for several reasons: individuals in any group tend to adopt each other's modes of behavior; poor families who do try to cope with their hostile environment eventually see that it is useless to do so and give up trying; and low-income neighborhoods get the short end of the stick in the distribution of public services, which means that their environment is additionally unpleasant (9). Thus, no matter where the poor are grouped together, there will be group distherapy. If they were dispersed, they would gradually conform to the prevailing social norms in their new neighborhoods, and they would receive the same level of services as the rest of the population (10).

The dispersal argument does not, obviously, apply to moderate-income families (though, curiously, in view of much of the current rhetoric about concentration, over 80% of subsidized housing starts in recent years have been for this group). Their norms are firmly middle class. The argument really does not apply to most low-income families either. Although newspapers are filled with accounts of antisocial behavior in low-income areas generally and in public housing projects in particular, the persons who commit these acts account for a small percentage of the total low-income population. Through careful screening of families, there is no reason why the problem types should wind up in better neighborhoods (11).

But if all of this is so, it undermines a great deal of the foundation for deconcentration in the first place. If only a tiny fraction of low- and moderate-income families present problems, and if they would be unlikely to move anyway, the presumed therapeutic aspects of dispersal would not apply. In fact, if problems are compounded by concentration, then creaming off the stable low- and moderate-income families would only tend to exaggerate the difficulties of those who were left behind.

Our reservations do not end here. Arguments for deconcentration emphasize low-income families moving to the suburbs. In all cities, however, there are neighborhoods which are comparable in size to so-called "exclusive" suburbs but which have higher average incomes and less subsidized housing than do these suburbs. Beyond that, provision of low-income housing in the suburbs would not materially reduce the concentration of low-income families in the city. Baltimore, for example, has about 85,000 such families. Roughly 15,000 of these families are already housed in subsidized dwellings. Subsidized construction for the remaining 70,000 families proceeds at a rate of a few thousand units a year. Even if this rate were doubled, it would take over three decades to house the families, whether it be in the city or the suburbs. Assuming realistically that the rate is not going to be doubled and that a large proportion of low-income families want to be and will be provided housing in the city, Baltimore is going to have the bulk of the area's low-income population in the year 2000 regardless of any emphasis on suburbanization of poor families. This fact highlights the importance of determining exactly which types of families should be encouraged to deconcentrate and how many must exercise their opportunity to disperse in order for specific objectives to be achieved.

Finally, the positive benefits to the poor of being suburbanized have never been adequately demonstrated. Even though suburban life has been roundly criticized by many analysts (some of the same ones who want to suburbanize the poor), we intuitively feel that benefits would ensue. We have discussed an important one in the preceding section on equal educational opportunity. These benefits come at an extra cost, however, which the proponents of suburbanization may not have adequately considered. If the housing problems of low-income families are treated in the city, the existing stock can be utilized. Relatively inexpensive units in standard condition are available, and most of the substandard structures can be upgraded for well under $10,000 each. By contrast, a suburban solution requires new construction at more than $20,000 a unit. As a result, the housing subsidy required to provide shelter for a low-income family in the suburbs is about three times what it would cost in the city. This obviously means that in the city either three times as many poor families can be served with a given amount of money or the problem can be solved three times as fast. Or, and this may be more to the point, it means that a city solution releases substantial monies to help the families in other ways than housing, whereas the suburban solution does not. Some persons have even argued that many low-income families would almost automatically get fewer nonhousing services in the suburbs because they would be less visible and because suburban communities are not geared to deal with them. And, isolated from public transportation, their problems might increase. In any event, the costs and benefits of the city and suburban alternatives do need much more study, and the types of low-income families who would be better or worse off in each of the two situations should be identified.

Enable Persons to Live and Work in the Same Community

If a person works in a community, surely he should have the opportunity to live there. If he is a solid worker, it stands to reason he would be a solid citizen. It is not right to ask him to work in one town and force him to live in another. More important, social and political processes are strengthened if people's lives are not segmented in this fashion.

The initial intuitive appeal of these statements diminishes upon closer examination. Strictly speaking, the notion that people should be able to live and work in the same community should apply not just to low- and moderate-income families and not just to the suburbs, but to upper-income families and to the cities as well. That is, high-income persons who work in the city should have the same opportunity to live there as lower-income families have to live in the suburbs. For all practical purposes, however, most of them do not; for to provide an environment acceptable to them would require public subsidies and the displacement of lower-income families. In fact, urban renewal projects for upper-income families in the cities are being fought just as strongly as are subsidized housing projects for low-income families in the suburbs. Exclusion clearly works both ways. Perhaps it should not work either way. But the fact that it does suggests that the social and political benefits of enabling persons to live and work in the same political subsection of a metropolitan area are not perceived to be compelling enough to warrant the costs of providing these opportunities.

A second reason for questioning the idea is that it seems somewhat artificial in today's metropolitan environment. For better or worse, many persons in large metropolitan areas voluntarily choose not to work and live in the same minor civil division. The proportion who do not varies inversely with the size of the jurisdiction. Thus, if governmental functions that are now performed at the township and borough level were consolidated at the county level, many persons would suddenly be living and working in the same community. And if central cities reverted to the separate political units they once were, most of their residents would find themselves living and working in separate communities. But would their lives have changed materially? Almost certainly not. The price of decentralized political power in a metropolis is that a large number of wage earners will not be living in the same community in which they work, and it does not seem too heavy a price to pay.

But, it will be argued, there should at least be the opportunity for persons to make the choice. If it could be shown that most persons would exercise the choice, hence demonstrating that it was important to them, the argument would be more persuasive. Casual evidence, however, suggests that even where reasonable choices are available, they are exercised by only a minority of those who have the opportunity to do so. Moreover, in metropolitan areas with a large number of minor civil divisions, a policy requiring balance might badly distort and impede healthful business expansion and relocation. It would be the same as requiring each subsection of any large city to have a balance of jobs and housing.

Let us take the most extreme case of two communities, A and B, where all of the residents of A work in B and vice versa. The A workers *will not* live in B, because it is a lower-class community. The B workers *cannot* live in A because there is no housing available for them. If this situation is considered to be a political-process problem, then the simple solution is consolidation. Then the A workers can continue to live in A and the B workers in B, and everyone will presumably be much happier. If it is considered to be a social-process problem, then either the A workers should be provided heavy subsidies to move to B, or the B workers should be given large grants to move to A. It would be well to know more precisely, though, what social goals would be furthered by such moves and whether they could be achieved more inexpensively in some other fashion.

Increase Housing Opportunities for Blacks

This is one of the few arguments for low- and moderate-income housing in the suburbs which both proponents and opponents of such housing believe to have validity. The basis for the argument lies in the fact that blacks, on the average, have considerably lower incomes than whites. Thus while one-fourth of the population in the Baltimore Standard Metropolitan Statistical Area

(SMSA) is black, the proportion of blacks among families who would qualify for housing subsidies is much higher. Any particular subsidized project, therefore, might be as much as 50% nonwhite.

The argument fails because most eligible blacks currently live far away from where the suburban housing would be built, and because very few low-income blacks want to live in the suburbs (12). As a consequence, all but a handful of the subsidized units would be snapped up by whites, even if they were advertised, as they no doubt would be, in black newspapers. By contrast, subsidized projects built in or near the ghetto would become occupied almost entirely by blacks (13). For the nation as a whole, blacks would probably get half as many subsidized units annually in the suburbs than they would in the central cities.

It is true that public housing projects, which serve low- but not moderate-income families, would be more heavily black, but public housing currently accounts for only about one-seventh of all subsidized new construction. In brief, to increase housing opportunities for blacks there should be *less* low- and moderate-income housing built in the suburbs, with an equivalently larger amount in the city, and there should be much more effort directed at the discriminatory barriers which discourage the large number of blacks who can already afford to move to the suburbs from attempting to do so.

Eliminate the Spatial Mismatch of Jobs and Housing

Since World War II and especially since the early 1950's, most of the growth in employment opportunities in metropolitan areas has occurred in the suburbs. The number of jobs in central cities has increased only moderately and in some cases has actually declined. With low- and moderate-income families migrating to the cities at the same time that jobs are migrating to the suburbs, it is alleged that an increasing number of inner-city residents are finding themselves denied effective access to employment in the growth areas. And those who do find suburban jobs are forced to make excessively long commutes. Evidence of the serious consequences of mismatch between jobs and housing is said to be found in the high rates of unemployment in the inner city. Additional evidence is provided by the increase in reverse commuting (from the center city out rather than from the outer areas in), since most families who could afford to do so would rather live close to their jobs in the suburbs (14).

Conceptually, there are three possible solutions to the mismatch: (a) use subsidies to encourage more job growth in the cities; (b) improve public transportation for reverse commuters; and (c) construct large amounts of subsidized housing in the suburbs. Those who advocate (c) reject the notion of subsidies for business and industry on the grounds that such subsidies have been ineffective in the past and can be dismissed on theoretical grounds (15).

They dismiss transportation improvements on the basis of evidence from several cities where experimental systems have been tried and have not proved particularly successful. They push for housing partly because this approach would have the additional benefits of deconcentrating the poor in the cities and, at comparable public cost, of furnishing this group a better life in the suburbs.

Although the mismatch argument has a certain amount of merit, it is difficult to assign it the same importance as do its advocates. First of all, though it is true that central cities have experienced very little increase in employment, they have suffered actual losses in population. And these losses have been greater among households with working-age members than among households as a whole. As a consequence, the ratio of resident labor force to jobs has actually decreased in central cities over the last decade. In brief, aggregate data on employment trends in central cities and suburbs by no means indicate a growing mismatch (16). Indeed, since neither "match" nor "mismatch" has ever been operationally defined, it is not certain what the data do indicate in this regard.

Second, although it is claimed that the new suburban jobs are precisely those which are especially suitable for central-city residents while the jobs which have increased in the central cities are not, there is some evidence that only the first half of this assertion is correct. A major employer of low- and moderate-income persons in central cities, for example, is the public sector, which has expanded substantially.

Third, the central-city/suburb distinction is a statistical artifact which overstates whatever mismatch may indeed exist. In most metropolitan areas new suburban jobs are less than thirty minutes from central-city residences. It is only in large SMSA's where a significant distance barrier starts to emerge. But even in large SMSA's one must be careful about the significance that is assigned to distance. In the Philadelphia area, for example, low-income blacks in Camden are within minutes of one of the most rapidly growing job concentrations in the entire metropolitan area, but they experience the same high rates of unemployment as do Philadelphia blacks.

Fourth, as is suggested by the above observation, it is very doubtful that the jobs which are presumably being denied to central-city residents because of transportation barriers actually exist. Although every now and then one hears about jobs going begging in the suburbs, when surveys are conducted on this question and the number of such jobs totaled, the results are disappointingly low (17). But, it is argued, if the families were in the suburbs, they could compete on a more equal basis for the jobs that are there. They could, for example, replace some of the suburban housewives who are supplementing their husbands' income and who may not want the jobs that much anyway. The problem with this line of reasoning is that the suburbanites, both male and female, are generally better qualified for the jobs and would continue to get them. It is no doubt true that distance from the central city facilitates racial discrimination in hiring, but this problem can be handled much more effectively in the job market than in the housing market. Moreover, it is quite distinct from the question at hand. As one black leader in Baltimore remarked in private conversation, "If the suburban firms make jobs available, the blacks will get there."

Fifth, the transportation problems of lower-income reverse commuters will not be appreciably altered by suburbanizing housing opportunities. The argument is made that for central-city residents without a private automobile the suburban jobs are either too far away by public transportation or are completely inaccessible. This would be equally true, however, whether the families lived in the city or in the suburbs. Most persons who hold jobs in the suburbs have to have cars. A reverse commute by car might be somewhat longer than a local commute by car, but there are scarcely any metropolitan areas where reverse commutation by private automobile requires what could be deemed an excessive amount of time. For those who feel it is excessive, there is usually relatively inexpensive housing in the older suburbs that would enable them to live closer to their jobs. If there were a great demand by reverse commuters for these homes, the homes would be bid up in price. This does not seem to have happened.

It is argued by some that it is not so much the reverse commute per se that causes problems for low-income central-city residents, but the undue transportation difficulties imposed on them in their search for suburban jobs and in trying to hold their jobs until they have saved enough money to buy a car. It may take half a day to get from home to one job interview and back. And it may take two hours to commute by public transportation to the job, so the worker gets discouraged and quits before he ever gets the auto. But the same is true of the suburbanite. He is a long distance from most jobs. Indeed, the central-city resident is actually in closer proximity to the job market as a whole than is the suburbanite.

Sixth, the suburban housing solution seems out of scale with the size of the employment problem which it is supposed to correct. Subsidized moderate income housing goes almost entirely to persons who do not have an employment problem, except possibly a reverse commute which is of secondary importance. Low-income housing would go to many persons who do have an employment problem. But construction of low-income housing is not likely to greatly exceed 100,000 units a year nationally, a figure which seems miniscule beside the more than 11,000,000 subemployed and underemployed workers in the United States. Even if all the 100,000 units were placed in the suburbs, and even if all the occupants were placed in jobs, it would take decades before a dent was made in the employment problem via this route.

There is one partially compelling argument with respect to the housing/ jobs mismatch. It relates to employers who are having difficulty filling some of their job openings. Although, as suggested earlier, the number of hard-to-fill slots is usually not great, it may in some instances be sufficient to warrant public attention. If the cause of the problem is not inadequate wages or working conditions, then better transportation facilities or expanded housing opportunities might be a feasible solution. However, when the observation is made that jobs in the suburbs are going begging, the jobs in question are frequently entry-level positions which are beneath the skills of local residents and do not carry a high enough eage to attract workers from long distances. The solution to this problem may not necessarily lie in the housing arena.

Improve Central-City Finances

The argument here is that fair-share plans will reduce fiscal disparities between city and suburb. Even if this were true, it does not follow that fiscal imbalances need be corrected by altering housing patterns. It would be more efficient and certainly not more politically difficult to eliminate the disparities through legislation altering the tax base. But the argument itself is fallacious. If all of the families who moved into the subsidized suburban units came from the central cities and if they all had low incomes, then central cities would experience a modest reduction in the financial pressure which they now feel. However, because of the current thrust of federal programs, most of the families would have moderate, not low, incomes. And for a variety of reasons, most of them would come from the suburbs, unless strong steps were taken to prevent this from happening. In theory, the dwellings which the subsidized suburban families vacated could filter to low-income central-city households and to low-income in-migrants from outside the metropolitan area, but in the absence of a very large subsidy program, it seems doubtful that this would occur.

So to a degree, central cities are competing for housing dollars which fair-share efforts would channel into the suburbs. The number of dollars involved may not be very great. Nevertheless, the fact remains that, as presently structured, a suburban emphasis would leave city governments with virtually the same housing problems as now and fewer housing resources to solve them. The implicit assumption that the volume of subsidized housing could be increased in the suburbs without a corresponding reduction in central-city renewal is probably wishful thinking, as is the hope that by not providing low-income housing, cities will reduce the in-migration of poverty families (18).

Retard the Forces of Decay

Part of the explanation for the outward spread of blight in large communities appears to be the pressure which huge masses of low-income families exert on abutting areas. Unless neighborhood boundaries are wide and distinct and firm, the problems of these families spill across, adversely affecting investment and tenure horizons of those on the other side. Property owners close to the boundary know that as the low-income population expands or filters up in the housing stock, their entire neighborhood will undergo change, and they act accordingly. Mortgage lenders are similarly influenced.

Scattering the poor would eliminate the boundary problem, for almost by definition, if low-income families were evenly distributed throughout an urban area, there could be no *neighborhood* decay, only a thin sprinkling of shabby homes (19). It is important to recognize, however, that the market barriers to this level of deconcentration are formidable. Since families in the lower one-half of the income distribution typically must rely on filtering to obtain housing, and since dwellings usually obsolesce or deteriorate as they filter, and since the rate and extent of obsolescence and deterioration vary significantly across, but usually not within, neighborhoods, it is inevitable in the private market that locational choices of lower-income groups be largely confined to certain neighborhoods. To alter this situation requires much more drastic intervention in the housing market than either fair-share plans contemplate or the nation is yet willing to accept. Nevertheless, it might be possible, particularly in smaller SMSA's where all locational-choice problems are less severe, to expand the range of residential opportunities by an amount sufficient to keep existing low-income concentrations at their present size. Such a strategy would remove some of the threat to adjacent neighborhoods. It probably would not, however, arrest the gradual outward movement of families as their incomes rise relative to house prices and rents; hence this aspect of the boundary problem would still remain.

Promote a More Healthy, Open Society

This final argument is based on the value judgment that income mixing contributes to the "good" society whereas income segregation *on a large scale* leads us away from the American belief in loose rather than rigid class structures. The argument does not assume that greater spatial intermingling of different income groups will solve societal problems, only that it will make their solution somewhat easier and that it will mute class conflict, as different income groups are more likely to be on the same rather than opposite sides of community problems. The argument leans heavily, if implicitly, on the notion that in smaller self-contained communities where the rich and poor are never very far apart, there is a greater sense of responsibility on the part of individuals to the community as a whole. Everyone is in it together. Although there are many examples of the tyranny rather than the democracy of small towns, the notion is not wholly without merit.

Unlike the other arguments, this one does not confine itself to the benefits which would accrue to lower-income families, but emphasizes the positive gains to everyone, and especially to children who would be exposed at an earlier age to a much wider cross section of society (20). It does not allege that physical proximity would necessarily lead to greater intermingling of adults on a social basis but that it would promote more positive contacts across class lines. Finally, it assumes that although most Americans do like to be with their own kind, they also value the diversity of a heterogeneous community population, and that, indeed, when they move to the suburbs, they seek something of this small-town atmosphere. The fact that they do not get what they seek is due to zoning and subdivision controls and to the operation of the real estate market, not to their underlying preferences.

Attractive as the vision of diversity would seem to be, it cannot be supported by facts and figures. Studies of heterogeneity vs homogeneity at the neighborhood and community scale are sparse and inconclusive (21). They do not provide compelling arguments for using expensive housing subsidies to achieve only slightly more income mixing than already exists. If, however, such housing is to be constructed anyway to accomplish ends other than class integration, the value of dispersing it is still suggested.

ARGUMENTS AGAINST PROGRAMS TO EXPAND LOCATIONAL CHOICE

There is really only one compelling argument against an emphasis in housing policy on enlarging the geographic area within which low-income families can seek housing, and that is simply the huge cost of such a thrust. Given the high price of housing in newer neighborhoods and the limited funds available for housing subsidies, any attempt to significantly expand residential opportunities for the poor primarily through subsidized new construction (or its equivalent), whether in central cities or suburbs, would seriously deplete other antipoverty and urban renewal resources.

There might also be very adverse equity effects. Even a very large effort would leave most low- and moderate-income families untouched, and those who were helped would be provided better housing and living environments than many higher-income families can afford (22). Conversely, any program which spread existing subsidies evenly among low- and moderate-income families would give each family such a small amount that it would not materially expand locational choice. It has been suggested that the equity dilemma could be resolved by raffling off the subsidized dwellings (23). This approach presumes, however, that the purpose of the subsidy is simply to increase the aggregate level of new construction, not influence the spatial distribution of the population. With the latter as an objective, it becomes much more difficult to establish equitable rules for deciding which low-income families will be favored over others and what their fair share should be. This is a soluble problem but one which has not yet been properly addressed.

SOME CONCLUSIONS

The higher level goals which are being pursued through new-construction subsidies to expand locational choice for low-income central-city families are commendable. However, the subsidy programs themselves can be questioned on several grounds:

First, they are based on erroneous assumptions, are very costly, would take longer to implement than alternative approaches to many of the same goals, and raise serious questions with respect to horizontal and vertical equity.

Second, although the rhetoric for expanded choice and against concentration emphasizes "low-income" and "problem family," the programs which are being promoted in the name of dispersal and freedom of choice serve primarily moderate-income, nonproblem families, and will almost certainly continue to do so. Indeed, fair-share plans, unless they increase the aggregate volume of new construction, are likely to produce no more suburban housing opportunities for low-income families by the year 2000 than will ordinary filtering. Moreover, to the extent that they draw moderate-income families out of central cities, they will increase rather than reduce the geographic isolation of the poor.

Third, what constitutes "undue concentration" of low-income families has never been operationally defined, and the assumed benefits of varying amounts of deconcentration at various geographic scales have not been convincingly demonstrated. Although benefits would no doubt accrue, the assumption that diaspora of low-income families will substantially reduce poverty, or that it is a necessary precondition to such reduction, rises mostly from the heart. Equally, few inner-city neighborhoods appear to be beyond redemption if dispersal does not occur. It is the lack of concern of the haves, not the concentration of the have-nots, which make low-income sections of our cities appear to be unsalvageable.

Fourth, only a small proportion of central-city low-income families prefer to live in the suburbs. These are not necessarily the same families whom central cities would be most anxious to see leave or who would most benefit by doing so. Thus, expanded choice and deconcentration are not synonymous and in some instances may be antithetical.

Finally, if the goal is truly expanded choice, the means should not be confined to subsidized housing. Potential beneficiaries of the subsidies should be given the opportunity to decide whether they would prefer more health care, more education, or some other good or service. Given such a choice it is likely that a new home might have no special appeal to most of them.

In brief, our reservations regarding policies whose primary focus is expansion of low- and moderate-income housing in the suburbs do not reflect opposition to breaking up the ghetto or to increasing equality of opportunity across income and racial groups, but rather are based on simple skepticism as to whether these goals can be pursued most effectively in this fashion. While it is clearly desirable for lower-income families to have a wider array of housing choices, the costs and benefits of a substantially expanded array must be more carefully weighed. This is not to suggest that housing subsidies may not be needed in the suburbs at all. Certainly every minor civil division in a metropolitan area should at least attend to the needs of its own low-income residents. Equally, in the furthest extremities of large growing metropolitan areas and in new towns, residential opportunities might have to be created for low-income families if work journeys are to be kept at a reasonable length. Caution would have to be exercised in these two situations, however, not to use low-income housing subsidies to support an unconscionable wage structure. Beyond these few observations, we can offer no guidelines as to the proper distribution of housing subsidies between city and suburbs or among various parts of the city.

Throughout this chapter, the question of how much subsidized low- and moderate-income housing there should be has not been assumed to be in dispute, only its location. Much of the confusion surrounding the matter of locational choice, however, stems from a failure to make a policy distinction between the goal of expanded choice and the construction-subsidy programs that give rise to locational issues. How much subsidized construction is necessary to accommodate population growth and replace inventory losses, where subsidized construction should be located, and who should have the opportunity to live in newly built subsidized dwellings are three partially separable questions. Once a particular number of assisted housing starts is determined to be desirable, the matter of where to place the units can be resolved in part by reference to immediate needs of particular groups. Over the longer term, however, the spatial distribution of subsidized construction should not be tied directly to the desired spatial distribution of income groups. Rather, public efforts should be in the direction of reducing suburban barriers to less expensive construction in the unsubsidized sector, with the question of which families should be subsidized to live in new and used units in specific locations being decided on quite different grounds (income possibly being only one). This approach would produce the rotating public inventory advocated by Ernest Fisher 14 years ago (24). It would also clarify the issue of why particular families should receive housing subsidies of as much as $2,000 or more, while others receive nothing.

CHAPTER 8

The Need - Resources Gap

To this point in the study, an effort has been made to determine the scale of six of the twelve dimensions of housing need discussed in Chapter 3. In order to assess the magnitude of the low-income housing problem in Baltimore, it is necessary to translate these measures of need into resource requirements, and then to determine whether the required resources could be forthcoming in the short term without dramatic shifts in the allocation patterns of the public and private sectors. This chapter, therefore, examines the resource implications of attempting to eliminate low-income housing need in Baltimore within a single decade, and compares that scale of effort with the level of accomplishment of housing programs in the city during recent years. The main purpose of the analysis is to determine whether it seems reasonable to think in terms of *housing* interventions as the primary means of eliminating shelter-related deprivations. If the needed resources are so huge as to necessitate a substantial alteration of public and private spending, the nation should possibly turn to indirect approaches such as education and employment programs, whereas if the sums required are relatively small, the focus should be on devising more effective programs within the housing arena itself.

Many types of resources would be required in order to eliminate all dimensions of housing need. Mounting a comprehensive effort in housing which is commensurate with this objective is, obviously, more than a question of dollars alone, or even of dollars plus an available supply of construction labor for upgrading the stock. Additional types of resources would have to be mobilized, including political commitment as well as managerial and technical talent in both the public and private sectors.

By implication, all forms of resources which may reduce or eliminate a particular dimension of need are theoretically of interest in a comprehensive analysis of need-resource relationships. However, significant problems arise in attempting to explore simultaneously all dimensions of need and all potential forms of resources. In this study, therefore, it was felt necessary to simplify the analysis by limiting the number of dimensions and forms of resources to be considered. The examination of need-resource relationships is confined to three major goal areas—quality of dwelling unit, indoor space, and housing expense relative to income. Also, the analysis focuses upon just two types of resources — initial capital investments to upgrade the inventory and continuing subsidies to fill the gap between what low-income families can be expected to pay for housing and the economic cost of providing adequate shelter. The principal objective of the investigation, then, is to determine the extent to which *financial* resources pose a barrier to the elimination of three basic components of housing need. For the most part, the nine dimensions of need which have been excluded from consideration would not impose heavy financial burdens unless, of course, the neighborhood-environment dimension is defined to include many services and facilities which are beyond the scope of housing policy as presently formulated, or unless it implies suburbanization of the poor — an objective we view as not feasible. Consequently, the estimates which are described below do not greatly understate the total money cost of eliminating the entire problem.

RESOURCE REQUIREMENTS FOR THE ELIMINATION OF QUALITY, SPACE, AND EXPENSE NEEDS

In pursuing an estimate of the required expansion of effort in housing, three inputs must be provided: (1) the existing configuration of housing need with respect to dimensions of quality, interior space, and excessive housing expense, (2) a set of assumptions as to what types of actions are necessary for these needs to be met, and (3) a set of assumptions as to the capital costs and continuing outlays which are required for the various types of actions.

Findings presented in Chapter 4 provide the basic data for the first and third inputs. The second input, however, is largely a matter of policy rather than empirical investigation. In order to keep the calculations manageable, it is necessary to confine the analysis to one of the many possible policies which could be undertaken to eliminate the three dimensions of housing need. Hence, the particular actions which are assumed in the estimates of resource requirements have been selected with a view toward facilitating the calculations; they are not put forth as a strategy or plan of action. To further simplify the discussion, questions having to do with the dynamics of the housing market, especially those relating to residential and socioeconomic mobility, are initially ignored. Whenever possible, the selected set of policies assume a "static" solution to the problem, with family needs being met without a change of residence. This assumption is actually quite realistic, because for the vast majority of Baltimore's housing-deprived population, elimination of the three dimensions of housing need would not require displacement from present quarters. This potential for solving a large part of the problem without compulsory mobility stems mainly from the low level of overcrowding (22,000 households of whom about half are estimated to be either non-low-income or only temporarily cramped) and the small number of seriously substandard dwellings (8,000). Because a program that would eliminate housing need through massive relocation into new units is unlikely in the short run, it is reasonable to expect that families other than those in extreme situations will have their housing problem treated in their present location or in connection with a normal move.

Capital Costs of Upgrading the Stock

As described in Chapter 4, in 1969 there were 65,000 occupied substandard units in Baltimore which could be distributed according to the cost of upgrading to at least code level as follows: 8,000 units with major deficiencies requiring treatments ranging from rehabilitation costing at least $3,500, including overhead, to demolition and subsequent replacement at a cost exceeding $20,000; 13,000 units with intermediate deficiencies which would require an upgrading investment of $1,500 to $3,499 per dwelling; and 44,000 units with minor deficiencies needing treatment ranging in cost from $300 to $1,499 per dwelling (1).

Average capital investments were calculated to be $15,000 for units with major physical deficiencies, $2,500 for units with intermediate deficiencies, and $700 for units with minor deficiencies. The total cost of upgrading the entire substandard stock — both occupied and vacant — to a minimum level of adequacy would be $200 million in 1969 dollars (Table 8.1). These figures do not allow for the extra costs which would be incurred in a publicly assisted renewal effort. They also do not include any additional allowances for moderately substandard or standard units which might have to be razed because they are adjacent to seriously substandard units, or for demolitions due to highway construction or nonhousing renewal efforts. The former types of additional costs are likely to be marginal; the latter are difficult to predict but could be significant since the unit cost of replacement housing is high.

Fully two-thirds of the required $200 million is needed for treatment of the 8,000 seriously substandard units. The remaining one-third of the investment would be divided almost equally between minor and intermediate rehabilitation activities. If the assumed upgrading program were carried out over a ten-year period and no additional occupied units were to fall below the

Table 8.1. Capital Requirements for Upgrading the Substandard Housing Stock[1]
(Baltimore, Maryland, 1969)

Type of Treatment	Aggregate Investment
44,000 occupied units with minor deficiencies @ $700 per unit	$ 30,800,000
13,000 occupied units with intermediate deficiencies @ $2,500 per unit	32,500,000
8,000 occupied units with major deficiencies @ $15,000 per unit	120,000,000
Subtotal, requirements for upgrading the occupied substandard stock	$183,300,000
Allowance (10%) for upgrading vacant substandard stock	18,330,000
Total, estimated capital requirements for upgrading the entire substandard inventory	$201,630,000

[1] Source: Survey of Residential Structures.

minimum standard during that time, the average annual capital cost of eliminating the quality dimension of the housing problem would be only $20
million. While this may seem to be a large sum, it would be equivalent to less
than a 10% increase in residential construction for the Baltimore metropolitan area.

Having arrived at an estimate of required capital formation, we may turn
now to the question of what level of annual payments would be needed both
to amortize this investment and to eliminate overcrowding and excess housing
expense as well.

Annual Subsidy Requirements

. As noted in the discussion of multiple housing deprivations in Chapter 4,
162,000 households in Baltimore occupy sound dwellings which provide at
least one room per person at a cost to the family that is not burdensome
(Table 8.2). The shelter situations of an additional 20,000 households fail to
meet one or both of our space or quality standards, but these households
have incomes which are sufficient to enable them to correct these situations if
they wish (2). In all, therefore, 182,000 households are taken for the purposes
of this analysis as "not housing deprived" with respect to the three basic goals
under discussion. The remaining 94,000 households (including 9,000 families
with incomes just above our definition of low income) may be described as
the "housing-deprived" sector of the population.

Our initial approximation of the annual aggregate sum required to eliminate all three deprivations *instantaneously* is about $80 million, a large figure.

Table 8.2. Composite Need Profiles with Respect to Physical Quality, Indoor Space, and Excessive Housing Expense, by Number of Housing Problems Experienced and Requirement of Financial Assistance[1] (Baltimore, Maryland, 1969)

	Number of Households with Various Needs	Number of Households Requiring Subsidies to Eliminate Need
No Housing Problems (with respect to quality, space, and expense)	162,440	–
One Housing Problem	63,030	44,510
Excessive expense only	36,560	36,560
Inadequate space only	5,320	1,100
Minor physical deficiency only	17,640	3,450
Intermediate physical deficiency only	2,340	2,230
Major physical deficiency only	1,170	1,170
Two Housing Problems	43,700	42,460
Inadequate space – Excessive expense	7,100	7,100
Minor physical deficiency – Excessive expense	20,920	20,920
Minor physical deficiency – Inadequate space	1,760	770
Intermediate physical deficiency – Excessive expense	8,990	8,990
Intermediate physical deficiency – Inadequate space	260	10
Major physical deficiency – Excessive expense	4,670	4,670
Major physical deficiency – Inadequate space	–	–
Three Housing Problems	7,080	7,080
Minor physical deficiency – Inadequate space – Excessive expense	3,520	3,520
Intermediate physical deficiency – Inadequate space – Excessive expense	1,270	1,270
Major physical deficiency – Inadequate space – Excessive expense	2,290	2,290
One or More Housing Problems	113,810	94,050
Total Households	276,250	

[1] Sources: First Household Survey, and Survey of Residential Structures.

This figure is based on the following set of assumptions:

(1) The existing level of excessive housing expense is $50 million per year, or the average of the two estimates discussed in Chapter 4, after allowing for underreporting of income and overreporting of actual rental payments, and before considering the cost of upgrading the occupied accommodations to code level.

(2) The annual sum necessary to amortize the $200 million of capital investment is $26.5 million for the first five years and about $11 million for an

additional 20 years. These figures assume minor improvements and inter-mediate upgrading are financed over a period of five years, and maximum re-habilitation and new construction, 25 years, at interest rates averaging 7%. The figures also assume that operating costs do not change after units have been upgraded.

(3) The cost of eliminating permanent overcrowding is $3.5 million per year, using 1.5 additional rooms as the average need for the approximately 11,000 permanently overcrowded families, and $18 as the average monthly cost per room.

Of the $80 million, fully one-third ($26 million) would be allocated to 45,000 families who are already occupying standard units, but are either over-crowded or paying more for housing than they can afford. Another $38 million, or almost half of the total, would go toward improving the housing, relieving the overcrowding, and eliminating the expense burdens of 41,000 families who live in dwellings with minor or intermediate physical deficiencies and who need financial assistance to meet their shelter needs. The remaining $16 million is required to enable the 8,000 families living in seriously sub-standard units to occupy substantially rehabilitated or newly constructed accommodations, of adequate size, at a cost which is not burdensome for them (3).

In various ways, the estimate of $80 million both overstates and under-states the size of the problem from the standpoint of public policy. First of all, the estimate is based on what we described above as an "instantaneous" solution with all capital improvements being made in the first year. Since the upgrading activity would actually be phased over several years, the maximum cash requirement for amortization would not be reached until after 1980, by which time part of the subsidy required to reduce excess housing expense and overcrowding would hopefully have been eliminated by rising incomes (4). Even barring income effects, if upgrading occurred over, say, a ten-year period, the annual subsidy would average only $68 million. Second, not all of the expense of eliminating the three problems would have to be borne by taxpayers. We guess that minor repairs totalling approximately $20 million could be achieved through unassisted code enforcement, thus reducing the average burden on the public sector by about $1 million annually. Third, seriously substandard dwellings would not necessarily have to be upgraded. Families occupying these units could be relocated into the existing stock, a strategy which if implemented slowly would create only minor price inflation while indirectly triggering unsubsidized new construction. Assuming the dwellings in which the families were rehoused had an average market price of $5,000 which had to be amortized in 15 years, the annual subsidy requirement would drop by another $4 million. Fourth, if programs to reduce rent-income ratios and relieve overcrowding were actually implemented, a portion of eligible families, probably as many as 30% or more, would choose not to enroll (5). Assuming these families were not as disadvantaged, on the average, as actual recipients, it would seem reasonable to lower the estimated cost of these two programs by about 15%, or $8 million, to reflect less than 100% participation. Finally, in the absence of impossibly strict controls, it is likely that many families who were given money to reduce their rent-income ratios would use some of the funds received to improve their housing, thereby decreasing the amount of subsidy necessary for upgrading the stock while, of course, leaving part of their housing expense burden untouched. Assuming that families channelled one-fourth of their subsidy back into housing and that half of this amount was used to improve quality while the rest went for more space and better neighborhood, then a reduction of $5 million per year in the upgrading subsidy would be possible.

In brief, if it can be assumed that: (a) the housing objectives would not be fully attained, (b) that low-income families need not be rehoused in new or good-as-new structures, (c) that the private sector would bear part of the cost, and (d) that implementation would take several years, then the $80 million figure can be reduced to a more realistic $50 million, and even more if real incomes continue to rise and the absolute number of low-income families declines correspondingly.

On the other hand, the $50 million estimate does not reflect the desirability of upgrading rather than demolishing vacant substandard dwellings that are located on row-house blocks which are still salvageable. Nor does it allow for the likelihood that deterioration will continue in some parts of the stock even while remedial efforts are under way. Nor does it necessarily provide enough subsidy to assure that housing which has been upgraded can be adequately maintained (though it would seem to). Adjustments to account for these possibilities require more facts and theoretical analysis than it is possible to incorporate into the discussion until the dynamics of the housing market have been examined in later chapters. Arbitrarily, however, we should probably raise the $50 million figure by about one-third to $67 million to cover these omissions and to reflect additional costs associated with a public effort. If Baltimore's housing conditions are at all representative of those in central cities generally, then the corresponding national gap, just for central cities, is roughly $5 billion annually (1969 dollars). Huge as this gap may seem to be, it excludes nine dimensions of housing need, several of which are perceived by deprived families to be very important, and it ignores other expenditures which cities will have to incur in order to make their residential environments appealing to non-deprived sectors of the population.

Nevertheless, with this crude estimate of the aggregate financial resources required to eliminate the quality, space, and expense dimensions of housing need, we may now consider the likelihood that resources of this magnitude will be forthcoming. In order to reach a conclusion on this matter, it is necessary to examine the level of effort in housing which has been achieved in Baltimore over the past decade, a question to which we now turn.

THE HOUSING EFFORT IN BALTIMORE

In Baltimore, as in every major urban center, a large variety of steps are being taken to improve the housing opportunities of low-income families. The aggregation of measures which directly serve this end may be termed the city's low-income housing effort. To varying degrees the total effort is private as well as public, voluntary as well as compulsory, and federal as well as local. The modes of intervention and forms of subsidy employed in the effort are numerous. Some of them operate through the supply side of the housing market, others operate through the demand side. The actions do not always operate in concert. In all probability, certain types of action compete creatively so as to enhance the total effort, while other types conflict so as to reduce the favorable impact.

At the close of the last decade, an average of $37 million dollars was being spent annually to subsidize the low-income housing effort in Baltimore (6). In order to appreciate more fully the scope of ongoing activities and to place the $37 million in better perspective with the estimates just developed pertaining to resource requirements, this section presents a brief analysis of the overall effort. The analysis is divided into three parts. First, the achievements of publicly assisted upgrading activities during the period 1960-1969 are reviewed. Next, the contribution of demand-side interventions to the total effort is investigated. In the third part, the $37 million estimate is explained in greater detail. Then, having established the basic parameters of existing actions aimed at solving the low-income housing problem, the concluding section of the chapter attempts to assess the magnitude of the need-resource gap in housing and its implications for policy.

Publicly Assisted Upgrading Activities, 1960–1969

During the past decade, the range of publicly assisted housing programs has been broadened considerably. From the New Deal period to the early 1960's, the low-income housing effort in most cities consisted primarily of three types of activity: public housing, public assistance, and housing code enforcement (7). During these years, the public housing program was the prime source of additions to the stock of housing for low-income occupancy. Since 1959, however, a number of new federal housing programs have provided subsidies for a variety of supply-side activities. These programs include the Section 202 Housing for the Elderly Program (as amended in 1965), the

Section 221(d)(3) Program (as amended in 1965), the Section 117 Federally
Assisted Code Enforcement Program (1965), the Federal Rent Supplement
Program (1965), the Section 221(h) Low-Income Home Ownership Program
(1966), the Section 235 Low-Income Home Ownership Program (1968), and
the Section 236 Rental and Cooperative Housing Program (1968) (8). To close
any gaps which might persist despite this expanding array of federal housing
programs, localities have been able to utilize funds made available under the
more broadly conceived Community Action and Model Cities Programs, enacted in 1964 and 1966, respectively.

New Construction and Maximum Rehabilitation. From 1960 through
1969, approximately 5,000 units, equivalent to 2% of the occupied stock in
1960, were developed in Baltimore under several of the above programs that
promote new construction and maximum rehabilitation for low-income occupants (Table 8.3). Virtually all of the units were available on a rental basis,
and four-fifths of them were newly built.

This record of intensive upgrading activities is encouraging. Based on the
analysis of capital requirements for the elimination of housing need presented
in the previous section, a reasonable target for subsidized new construction
and maximum rehabilitation would be roughly 10,000 units by 1980, or an
annual rate of 1,000 per year. Figures reported for both upgrading that is
in process and commitments for development in the short run indicate that
this rate should be substantially exceeded through 1975. HUD's termination
of several supply-side subsidy programs in January 1973 will make a continuation of current levels of production past 1975 extremely difficult, however.

Although aggregate production rates have been higher than one might have
expected a few years ago, there appears to be something of a mismatch between the types of units currently being developed and those types most
urgently required. In part due to cost limitations and other restrictions govern-
ing the development of public housing (9), a significant proportion of the
total subsidized new construction effort of recent years has been directed
toward the provision of housing for the elderly. This pattern of allocation will
continue in the short run, as approximately three-fifths of the public housing
units projected for completion in the early 1970's are intended for senior
citizens.

While these units are undoubtedly superior in quality to the residences of
most low-income elderly persons, and while the projects are usually designed
to promote opportunities for efficient delivery of housing-related services,
there is a serious question as to whether housing of this type warrants the
level of priority which is implicit in the current pattern of development. According to the findings on physical quality of dwelling unit presented in
Chapter 4, the elderly rarely reside in seriously substandard housing. Further-

Table 8.3. Level of Effort in Housing: Number of Units Constructed Under Federal Subsidy Programs and Number of Units Receiving Maximum Rehabilitation Under Federal Subsidy Programs or Under Nonsubsidized Programs Operating in Low-Income Areas (Baltimore, Maryland, 1960–1969)

	1/1/60– 12/31/69	Under Development or Future Commitment as of 12/31/69
Rehabilitation		
Under subsidy programs	201	1,787
Used house		
public housing	191	1,449[1]
221(d)(3)		
BMIR	–	288
221H Low-income		
home ownership	10	–
235 Low-income		
home ownership	–	50[2]
Under nonsubsidized programs		
in low-income areas	780	–
Rental units in		
Harlem Park urban-		
renewal area financed		
with FHA 220 insured		
mortgages	780	–
Total	981	1,787
New Construction		
Public housing[3]	1,186	1,715
202 Housing for elderly	1,329	588
221 (d)(3) MIR[4]	225	–
221(d)(3)		
BMIR[3]	1,012	793
221(d)(3)		
MIR-RS[3]	92	425
236	–	790
Total	3,844	4,311

[1] This figure includes 14 units to be developed in conjunction with the city's vacant house program. Under this effort, 1,260 vacant shells suitable for single-family occupancy and 70 suitable for two-family occupancy are being rehabilitated and offered for sale under FHA 235 or Turnkey III. If the structures cannot be sold for owner occupancy, they will be transferred to the public housing stock as used house units.

[2] This figure represents the estimated short-run production of nonprofit developers such as HOPE, Inc., and Greater Baltimore Housing Development Corporation.

more, many private landlords whom we interviewed felt strongly that they were capable of housing the low-income elderly satisfactorily. Some of them voiced the complaint that the city was taking away their most desirable tenants — people who take good care of the property.

Conceivably, the development of new rental units for the elderly could be justified as a filtering mechanism if a significant number of those moving into the new units were former owner occupants who had found themselves over-housed and lacking either the desire or ability to maintain their homes. In these instances, the new units might serve the purpose of freeing up accom-modations for families with more pressing space deprivations. While the po-tential of this form of impact is not known, it is probably not sufficient to warrant the current concentration of resources on construction for elderly persons.

Modest Rehabilitation and Improved Maintenance. During the first half of the 1960's cities such as Baltimore faced a limited set of options in their efforts to achieve modest rehabilitation, remodeling, or maintenance of hous-ing units occupied by low-income families (10). At that time, federally assisted programs made no provision for subsidizing these types of activities. To achieve these ends, a locality had available only the following options: (a) fos-ter a favorable climate for investment by furnishing community facilities in low-income neighborhoods under the provisions of the Housing Act of 1954, (b) encourage property owners to avail themselves of FHA-insured home im-provement loans at market rates (which often required a parallel effort to cajole banks and the FHA into cooperating), (c) require improvements through the enforcement of local housing codes, and (d) set up its own programs using local funds to subsidize improvements. Given the generally unfavorable finan-cial position of local governments, few communities chose the last alternative, to our knowledge.

Beginning in 1964, however, the federal government began to develop pro-grams to subsidize modest rehabilitation of substandard units. Amendments to the Housing Act of 1949, enacted in 1964 and 1965, contained subsidy provisions for modest rehabilitation in federally assisted urban renewal and concentrated code of enforcement areas. Two types of subsidy mechanisms were

---

[3] Figures obtained from internal memo of Research Section, Baltimore Dept. of Housing and Community Development.

[4] Figures obtained from Regional Planning Council, Lower-Middle Income Housing in Baltimore City, February 1970. The 221 (d)(3) MIR-RS category includes projects wherein 100% of the occupants may qualify for rent supplements. Depending upon agreements with HUD, a given portion of the units (until recently up to 20%, now up to 40%) in other types of 202 and 221 (d)(3) projects could receive rent supplementa-tion. At the close of the period, less than one-fifth of all 202 and 221 (d)(3) tenants were receiving supplements.

provided: (a) Section 115 rehabilitation grants for low-income homeowners, and (b) Section 312 direct rehabilitation loans at 3% interest for owners and long-term leasees of residential properties located in designated areas.

These devices have been applied in Baltimore since 1966. By the end of the decade, a total of approximately 500 grants, loans, and grant-loan combinations had been approved and a similar number of applications were pending. Virtually all of the structures upgraded in this manner were single-family units. In the areas where these mechanisms have been utilized most intensively, rehabilitation grants averaged $1,200 per unit and direct loans averaged $2,600 per unit during 1968 (11).

The improvement of 500 units through the use of Section 115 grants and Section 312 loans represents the only subsidized modest rehabilitation activity of the entire period. Much additional modest upgrading has been accomplished in low-income areas without subsidy, however. Nonassisted code enforcement, for example, has covered thousands of units. Within urban renewal areas alone, over 7,000 units — only one-half of which are located in what could be described as low-income neighborhoods — were raised to officially sanctioned standards with the indirect support of environmental improvements (12). In the remainder of the inner city and in certain deteriorating sections of the outer city, regular code enforcement activities yielded limited improvements to a large number of additional units. Although the total amount of resultant investment can only be guessed, our data suggest that only in exceptional circumstances does nonassisted code enforcement produce significant upgrading.

Given even extremely optimistic assumptions regarding the achievements of nonassisted code enforcement and voluntary private investment over the past decade, there would still appear to be a huge gap between the existing modest rehabilitation and maintenance effort and that level which is required in order to eliminate this component of housing need. As pointed out initially in Chapter 4, there were approximately 57,000 occupied units with minor and intermediate physical deficiencies in 1969. Furthermore, in light of the current investment outlook in the inner city as well as the income levels of the families occupying the deteriorating sectors of the stock, and the escalating costs of labor, materials, and capital, it is clear that much, if not most, of the required modest upgrading cannot be achieved without direct subsidy. The present rate of subsidized modest rehabilitation must be expanded dramatically — perhaps 20-to-30-fold, if substandard housing is to be eliminated in the foreseeable future. This task may prove extremely difficult, since the achievement of a high volume of modest rehabilitation rests not only upon the availability of resources, which in itself appears manageable, but also upon the development of effective program mechanisms for bringing about the desired upgrading effort in the rental sector of the stock.

Demand-Side Housing Efforts, 1960—1969

A number of programs which furnish resources, other than shelter itself, to low-income families specifically for the purpose of preventing or remedying various dimensions of housing need may be classified somewhat loosely as the demand-side component of the housing effort. These interventions usually provide financial resources; however, housing programs which deliver market information, consumer education, or legal assistance may also be considered as elements of the effort (13).

The principal demand-side effort, both in terms of number of persons served and aggregate resources allocated, is public assistance which traditionally has not been viewed as a housing program. Paralleling the experience of virtually every major city, Baltimore's public assistance rolls increased dramatically over the past decade from an average caseload of 19,300 assistance units during calendar year 1960 to an average of 37,100 assistance units during fiscal year 1968—1969 (14). Fully three-quarters of the net caseload increase resulted from growth in the Aid to Families with Dependent Children category (AFDC), which, with respect to average number of cases handled at a point in time, more than tripled over the decade and, with respect to total grants disbursed per year, more than quadrupled in constant dollars (15).

During fiscal year 1968—1969, a total of $62,500,000 in cash payments was received under all forms of public assistance, including Foster Child Boarding Care, out of which an estimated $21,400,000 was expended for shelter and utilities (16). Despite periodic increases in shelter allowances, in the majority of cases the resources provided were not sufficient to enable recipients to acquire adequate accommodations (17). During 1969, the maximum monthly shelter allowance including heat and all utilities was $55 for a family of four and $66 for a family of seven or more. Since the monthly allowance for shelter is significantly below the current cost of standard housing on the private market, AFDC families who obtain adequate shelter either live in public housing (nearly half of the 11,000 households in public housing receive public assistance) or sacrifice monies budgeted for other commodities. Our data suggest that at least half of all AFDC families were spending more than their maximum shelter allowance for housing.

Since 1964, a number of demand-side interventions have been introduced which are intended to provide the supplementary resources required to close the gap between the cost of adequate housing and the price families can afford to pay; however, the level of effort which has been achieved is extremely small in relation to aggregate need. For renters, supplemental assistance has been made available through the following programs: the federal provisions for relocation adjustment payments (up to $1,500 distributed over two years, for families that are eligible for, but cannot be admitted to, public housing at time of displacement by public action); the public housing leasing program;

the federal rent-supplement program for families who cannot afford units constructed under the provisions of Sections 202, 221(d)(3) and 236; and a demonstration rent-supplement effort for large AFDC families sponsored by the Baltimore City Department of Social Services (DSS).

By the end of the decade, fewer than 2,000 renter families had benefited from the various supplemental efforts just mentioned, and at a given point in time no more than 1,000 were receiving these types of assistance. For most of the beneficiaries, unmet housing need was reduced rather than eliminated as a result of the given intervention. Whereas virtually all families obtained units which met minimum standards with respect to quality and space, burdensome housing expense was not unusual since the programs generally required a contribution of 20% or more of income toward monthly rent.

Another drawback associated with these efforts is lack of assurance that housing needs will be met on a long-term basis. Since the federal rent-supplement and public housing leasing programs in essence provide subsidies to dwelling units rather than to families, should the assisted occupants have to move, the supplemental assistance which they are receiving is transferred to the incoming residents. Relocation adjustment payments and DSS demonstration rent supplements, on the other hand, are extended directly to families, but there is no chance for continuous support.

Since 1964, two separate demand-side programs have been developed to provide supplemental assistance for low-income homeowners. The first program, involving property tax credits for elderly homeowners, was initiated by the Baltimore City Council in 1964 and three years later was modified slightly to conform with a similar enactment passed by the state legislature in 1967. The second program, involving special bonus payments to displaced homeowners for the purchase of replacement housing, was the result of an historic amendment to the state eminent domain law by the Maryland Legislature in early 1968 (18). This provision, which was the first of its kind enacted anywhere in the country, was incorporated subsequently at the federal level into both the Housing and Community Development Act of 1968 and the Highway Act of 1968.

The property tax relief for elderly homeowners has the broadest coverage of any of the current array of supplemental demand-side programs, but the amount of subsidy is small and relatively unrelated to the owner's actual need. In 1968, approximately 15,000 low-income and 7,500 non-low-income elderly owners benefited from property tax credits. The average credit amounted to $120 per year (19). Despite the wide coverage of the program, there are approximately 17,000 nonelderly, low-income homeowners whose need for supplemental resources is comparable and who, undoubtedly, would appreciate equal, albeit not munificent, treatment.

The impact of the provisions for special bonus payments to displaced homeowners appears to be the obverse of that for the tax relief effort. That is to say, whereas the tax credits help a large number of persons marginally, the bonus payments help a few persons significantly. During fiscal year 1968–1969, the first year of actual availability, 76 homeowners displaced due to urban renewal and code enforcement activities received bonuses averaging $4,950 for the purchase of standard quality replacement housing. The potential impact of this effort, of course, is a function of the level of future condemnation activity. Hopefully, the payments will serve to make the relocation process one of opportunity, as opposed to the baneful experience which, in general, it has been over the past two decades.

Annual Subsidy Level Associated with the Low-Income Housing Effort

In the last three years of the decade of the 1960's, the total annual subsidy associated with the various supply-side and demand-side interventions just described averaged $37 million (Table 8.4) (20). Over 90% of this amount involved actual outlays of funds; the rest was in the form of either tax credits or interest foregone through below-market-rate lending (Table 8.5). The major source of funds was the federal government, which contributed $19 million, or one-half the total amount. The State of Maryland furnished an additional $11 million through the public assistance program, and the City of Baltimore provided $6 million in miscellaneous outlays and tax reliefs. The remaining $1 million came from private sources.

On a program basis, the largest single contribution to the total housing effort, by far, was in the form of public-assistance payments. Housing expenditures from public assistance grants and related administrative costs accounted for $24 million, or two-thirds of the total annual housing subsidy. This figure is five times greater than the next largest program subsidy — public housing.

The non-public-assistance portion of the housing subsidy, which reflects the more traditional concept of the low-income housing effort, totaled $13 million annually. Within this segment of the effort, four programs accounted for four-fifths of the subsidy allocations. These programs and their corresponding subsidy figures were as follows: (a) public housing, $4.7 million; (b) housing code enforcement in low-income areas, $2.4 million; (c) the property tax credit program as it applies to low-income elderly homeowners, $1.8 million; and (d) the relocation program (both services and payments), $1.3 million. The remaining one-fifth of the $13 million was distributed among twelve programs, none of which involved a subsidy exceeding $0.5 million per year (Table 8.4).

Table 8.4. Average Annual Subsidy for Improvement of Housing Opportunities of Low-Income Households by Type of Subsidy and Operating Program, in Thousands of Dollars (Baltimore, Maryland, 1967–1969)

Type of Subsidy	Annual Average		
Direct Subsidies to Low-Income Households			$22,266
Section 115 rehabilitation grants[1]		$ 179	
Rent supplements		254	
Federal supplements to low-income occupants of Sections 202 and 221 (d)(3) units[2]	$ 117		
Department of Social Services (DDS) demonstration program[3]	137		
Shelter expenditures from welfare payments[4]		21,425	
Relocation payments[5]		408	
Indirect Subsidies to Low-Income Households			1,827
Property-tax credits granted to low-income homeowners[6]		1,820	
Interest foregone through Section 312 direct loans to low-income homeowners[7]		3	
Interest foregone through direct loans to finance sale of units rehabilitated under Section 221 (h)[8]		4	
Federal income taxes foregone[9]		not available	
Direct Subsidies to Suppliers of Low-Income Housing			4,372
Public housing program (including leased units)		4,237	
Federal contribution – Debt service[10]	3,793		
Federal contribution – Operating expenses[11]	444		
Federal support of administrative overhead of Home Ownership Plan Endeavor, Inc. (HOPE)[12]		75	
Private support of administrative overhead of Greater Baltimore Housing Development Corporation (GBHDC)[13]		60	
Indirect Subsidies to Suppliers of Low-Income Housing			839
Public housing program		477	
Local property taxes foregone[14]	477		
Federal and state income taxes foregone[15]	not available		
Interest foregone by federal government through direct below-market-rate lending[16]		362	
Section 202 program	220		
Section 221 (d)(3) BMIR program	142		

Type of Subsidy		Annual Average
Costs Associated with Administration and Operation of Miscellaneous Low-Income Housing Actions		7,824
Housing code enforcement in low-income areas[17]	2,381	
Relocation services[18]	910	
CAP self-help housing[19]	310	
CAP emergency services[20]	86	
DSS demonstration program[3]	136	
HCD field overhead in low-income residential renewal areas[21]	476	
Allocation to housing effort from cost of administration of public assistance program[22]	2,744	
Cost of administration of property-tax credit program for elderly homeowners[23]	31	
Allocation to housing effort, from cost of administration of CAP, Model Cities, Urban Renewal, City and Regional Planning Activities[24]	750	
Total, Average Annual Subsidy for the Improvement of Housing Opportunities of Low-Income Households, 1967-69		$37,128

[1] During fiscal year 1967-68 Section 115 rehabilitation grants were made to 149 low-income owner occupants who lived in either federally assisted code enforcement or urban renewal areas. Based on the experience in the Steuart Hill federally assisted code enforcement area, the average grant was assumed to be in the amount of $1,200.

[2] By mid-1968, a combined total of 1,299 units had been constructed under the Section 202 Housing for the Elderly Program and the Section 221 (d)(3) MIR and BMIR programs. The figure assumes that, at the close of the decade, 15% of the units were occupied by families receiving rent supplements. Since no data were available on the actual amount of supplementation received, a figure of $600 per unit was used for estimating purposes. This assumption was based on an exhibit presented by HUD in testimony before the Ribicoff Subcommittee on Executive Reorganization of the Committe on Government Operations, United States Senate, Eighty-ninth Congress, Second Session (August 15 and 16, Part I, Exhibit 17, pp. 197-199), which states that the agency reserves approximately $600 per year for each rent-supplement unit.

[3] On June 1, 1967, the Community Relations Division of the Baltimore City Department of Public Welfare began operating a demonstration project entitled Community Organization and Services to Improve Family Living. The program remained in operation until June 30, 1970, and was funded for the three-year period by the U.S. Department of Health, Education and Welfare. For fiscal year 1967-68, $273,000 was allocated by HEW for the total program. Arbitrarily, one-half of this amount has been assigned to direct payments to low-income households for housing-related expenditures, and the remaining half to cover the cost of administrative overhead and the provision of social services.

[4] During fiscal year 1968-69, AFDC assistance units received grants totaling $39.8 million and assistance units under other welfare categories (OAA, AB, APTD, GA, and Foster

Care) received grants totaling $22.7 million. The results of our initial field survey showed that the median gross-housing-expense/income ratio for households with persons in AFDC assistance units was 35%. The corresponding expense ratio for households with persons receiving assistance under other categories was 33%. These ratios were applied to the figures for aggregate grants received in order to arrive at an estimate of shelter expenditure from welfare payments for the period. The estimate of $21.4 million, therefore, reflects actual housing expenses incurred by recipients, rather than the aggregate amount of shelter allowances.

[5] The amount shown is the sum of (a) reimbursements for moving expenses and loss of personal property ($9,466) and relocation adjustment payments (53 households received a total of $22,582) during the period April 1967 to March 1968, and (b) bonus payments to displaced homeowners (75 households received a total of $376,025) during fiscal year 1968-69. The estimate covers only payments to families displaced by urban renewal and code enforcement activities; no comparable information was available for highway relocation or other public actions. Data on moving expenses, loss of personal property, and relocation adjustment payments were obtained from HUD Quarterly Reports on Relocation of Families and Individuals for Urban Renewal (Form HUD-666) which are on file at the HUD Regional Office in Philadelphia.

[6] The Baltimore City Department of Finance estimated that the total tax credit extended to elderly homeowners under the new state-mandated program was $2,730,000 for fiscal 1968. The eligibility requirements stipulate that the owner's gross income be no greater than $5,000, but no limits are placed upon either the assessed valuation of the home or the net assets (other than the home) of the household. These liberal eligibility criteria permit a number of persons to receive tax credits who would not be considered within the low-income population as defined herein. Since this number cannot be estimated with precision from the data at hand, we have assumed, somewhat arbitrarily, that one-third of the total tax credit accrues to non-low-income homeowners.

[7] During fiscal years 1967-68, 39 Section 312 direct loans were made for the improvement of residential properties in renewal and concentrated code enforcement areas of the city. Seventeen of this number were made in conjunction with Section 115 rehabilitation grants to low-income homeowners. Nearly all of the remaining 22 loans were used to finance the improvement of single-family structures; however, the incidence of owner occupancy among this group is not known. Three assumptions have been made in the calculation of the interest foregone by the federal government through the extension of Section 312 loans: (1) that all loans have been made to owner occupants, which enables us to classify the entire amount of the subsidy under indirect subsidies to low-income households (owner occupants are treated as households rather than suppliers for purposes herein), (2) that, based on the Steuart Hill experience, the average amount borrowed under the Section 312 program is $2,600 per loan, and (3) that the typical repayment period is the maximum 20 years permitted under the legislation. The annual aggregate interest foregone by the federal government through the operation of the Section 312 loan program during fiscal year 1967-68 was $2,570. This represents the difference in actual aggregate annual repayments under 3% 20-year financing, and the aggregate annual repayment which would have been necessary if the loans had been financed over a 20-year period at then current market rates 6¼% interest plus ½% for mortgage insurance premium).

[8] During the three-year period, approximately 10 dwellings were substantially rehabilitated and sold to low-income families under the Section 221 (h) program. The estimate reflects the difference in aggregate annual repayments under 3% 25-year financ-

ing, and the aggregate annual repayment which would have been necessary if the loans had been financed over a 25-year period at then current market rates (6¼% interest plus ½% for mortgage insurance premium). The amount of principal assumed is $15,000 per unit.

9 No attempt was made to estimate the amount of subsidy received indirectly by low-income families (or the much larger amount received by middle- and upper-income families) through either deductions for federal income tax purposes of interest on mortgages outstanding and selected payments to state and local governments or through forgiveness of imputed rentals on owner-occupied residential investments.

10 These contributions from the federal government cover the debt service on 40-year bonds which finance the development of public housing. The bonds are backed by the guarantee of the United States Government and are tax-exempt. Annual contributions may. be recoverable, to some extent, should the Housing Authority decide to transfer a portion of the public housing stock to private parties. Figure in table pertains to fiscal year 7/1/68 to 6/30/69, and was taken from "Annual Report 1969," of the Department of Housing and Community Development, City of Baltimore, p. 21.

11 For selected types of occupants who cannot afford regular public housing rentals, the Housing Authority receives additional subsidies to cover a portion of operating expense. The rents charged these families are reduced accordingly. The figure in table may also include special assistance for maintenance of older structures in the public housing stock. The amount pertains to fiscal year 7/1/68 to 6/30/69, and was taken from "Annual Report 1969," of the Department of Housing and Community Development, City of Baltimore, p. 21.

12 HOPE, Home Ownership Plan Endeavor, Inc., was organized in 1964. During its existence the organization acquired, rehabilitated, and resold homes to families referred by various church and community agencies. In September 1967, HOPE received a grant of $99,789 from the Office of Economic Opportunity, of which $74,789 was to be used to pay staff salaries and other administrative costs and the remaining $25,000 was to establish a revolving fund for acquisition, materials, and labor. The grant covered the fiscal year ending August 31, 1968, and was made in order to demonstrate (1) the feasibility of a financial formula and an approach to subsidizing home ownership for the poor as a basic alternative to the Rent Supplement Program, and (2) the feasibility of using a nonprofit development corporation as the principal delivery mechanism for developing and implementing a home-ownership program for the poor throughout Baltimore City. The principal financing mechanisms used during that year were (a) 4% five-year debenture notes for acquisition and construction, and (b) mortgages under Section 221 (h) of the National Housing Act as amended in 1966.

13 The Greater Baltimore Committee supplied approximately $60,000 to cover the operating expenses of the Greater Baltimore Housing Development Corporation (GBHDC) during the period 9/1/67 to 8/31/68. The GBHDC attempts to rehabilitate homes for sale to low-income families under federal subsidy programs.

14 The local Housing Authority makes an annual payment to the city, known as payment in lieu of taxes, which is intended to cover the cost of municipal services rendered to public housing dwellings. The amount paid is 10% of the shelter rent charged, which is rent minus utility costs. For the fiscal year ended June 30, 1969, this amount was $530,053. (Source: "Annual Report 1969," Department of Housing and Community Development, City of Baltimore, p. 21.)

For private rental units in the inner city, taxes on real property average about 16% of contract rents. Thus, the argument may be made that were there no public housing, the city would derive additional property tax revenues from the rentals of present public housing occupants. These revenues foregone may be conservatively estimated at the difference between 10% of shelter rent (paid in lieu of taxes) and 16% of the contract rent which public housing tenants would probably pay in the private market. This estimate is considered conservative because the contract rent for private rental units would often include the cost of utilities.

[15] Income taxes which would accrue to governments, if the interest which is received by private investors from Housing Authority bonds were not tax exempt. No attempt has been made to estimate this amount.

[16] This figure is the interest foregone annually by the federal government as a result of the direct financing (3%, 40 years, 100% loans) of rental units developed under the Sections 202 and 221(d)(3) programs. In Baltimore, the development costs of units constructed by mid-1968 under the Section 202 program were higher than those for units completed by that date under the Section 221(d)(3) program. This stems largely from two factors: (a) the 202 units were in elevator apartments, and (b) in general, the completed 221 units were developed earlier in the period than the 202 units, when construction costs were lower. In developing this estimate, based on actual rent levels in the various projects, we used the average development costs (site acquisition and construction) for units completed by mid-1968 under each program. The interest which the federal government was foregoing annually at that date as a result of financing development directly at 3% over a 40-year period averaged $220,000 per year for the 793 units which had been constructed by mid-1968 under the Section 202 program and $141,500 per year for the 506 units which had been constructed under the Section 221(d)(3) BMIR program. Some of these projects may have been refinanced under subsequent federal legislation.

[17] During fiscal year 1966-67, $2,976,000 was expended for housing code enforcement activities in Baltimore. [See Gordon Liechty, Housing Code Enforcement: The Baltimore Experience, Baltimore CAP Evaluation Project Working Paper No. 3 (August 1968) Table VI-1]. This amount includes all housing code enforcement activities of the Bureau of Building Inspection (BBI), related activities of the Health Department (environmental hygiene, rodent and insect control) and Fire Department (fire prevention), the assignment of rehabilitation estimators on the urban renewal program staff to the code enforcement effort, and the operation of the Baltimore Housing Court.

A precise breakdown of housing code enforcement by geographic subareas of the city was not available; however, it is felt that four-fifths of the total amount, or $2,381,000, is a reasonable estimate of the annual expenditure for housing code enforcement in predominantly low-income areas at the start of the period 1967-1969.

[18] This amount covers expenditures during fiscal year 1967-68 for salaries, fringe benefits, contractual services, and material which are associated with the operation of the central relocation office in Baltimore. Over 90% of the total cost is financed through a revolving fund administered by the Housing Authority, while the remainder is borne by the city from its operating budget.

[19] Actual appropriation for fiscal year 1966-67.

[20] Actual appropriation for fiscal year 1966-67. This amount was recommended by the Department of Finance for HCD field operations to be undertaken in the Harlem Park, Gay Street, Mt. Winans, and Upton urban renewal areas during fiscal year 1967-68.

The magnitude of the housing effort can be viewed in terms of number of families helped as well as number of dollars spent. Excluding unsubsidized code enforcement and miscellaneous overhead activities, $29 million of the $37 million annual housing subsidy was distributed in 1967-1968 among nearly 60,000 households, for an average of approximately $500 per household. Individual subsidies varied from around $5,000, for one-time relocation bonus payments to displaced owner occupants, to $1,100 per year to welfare families living in public housing, down to $120 per year for tax relief to elderly home owners (Table 8.6). About 25,000 low-income households received no assistance at all.

If taken over a longer time period, the range of amounts received by a

[21] During fiscal year 1968-69, the Department of Housing and Community Development spent $952,500 for field operations (including housing inspection, community organization, and rehabilitation and financial counseling) in residential renewal areas. Although precise breakdowns by geographic subareas is not available from published reports, an allocation of one-half of the total amount for field operations in predominantly low-income areas seems reasonable. Under administrative arrangements then existing in Baltimore, this allocation would not overlap the amounts taken for code enforcement activities under Footnote 17, above.

[22] For fiscal year 1968-69, the cost of administration of the public assistance program was approximately $8,000,000. An unknown but small portion of this amount covered the cost of certification for the medical assistance program which is done routinely as part of the application procedure for public assistance. Since expenditures for shelter from public assistance grants have been defined as a component of the low-income housing effort, it seems proper to allocate a portion of the cost of administration to the housing effort as well. The amount taken is 34.3% of $8,000,000, which reflects the ratio of estimated shelter expenditures from grant to total grants ($21.4 million/ $62.5 million).

[23] Prior to the adoption in 1967 of the state-mandated tax credit for the elderly, the administration of the city's own program was handled by one supervisor (at $7,300 per year) and four clerks (each at $3,200 per year). The Department of Finance estimated that conversion to operating procedures for the state-mandated program would necessitate a minimum additional expenditure of $21,400 during fiscal year 1967-68 (for notices, application forms, stationery, postage, overtime, additional filing and clerical equipment, printing the new ordinance, and computer operations). A portion of this amount, however, is properly allocated to subsequent years, since it involves initial expenditures for the setting up of new procedures to be implemented for an indefinite period. Thus, in arriving at the estimate for fiscal 1967-68, we have added one-half of the additional direct administrative costs to the city ($10,700) which are associated with the adoption of the state-mandated tax credit program to the total salaries for the personnel directly involved in the administration of the city's original program ($20,100).

[24] No data are readily available for a precise estimate of this amount. The figure shown is, at best, an educated guess.

Table 8.5. Average Annual Subsidy for Improvement of Housing Opportunities of Low-Income Households, by Type and Source of Subsidy (Baltimore, Maryland, 1967–1969)

Type of Subsidy[1]	Source and Amount (in Thousands of Dollars) of Subsidy				
	Total	Federal	State	City	Private
Subsidies involving actual outlays of funds	$34,462 (100.0%)	$18,916 (54.9%)	$11,133 (32.3%)	$ 3,582 (10.4%)	$831 (2.4%)
Direct subsidies to low-income households	22,266 (100.0)	10,799 (48.5)	9,632 (43.2)	1,064 (4.8)	771[2] (3.5)
Direct subsidies to suppliers of low-income housing	4,372 (100.0)	4,312 (98.6)	– (0.0)	– (0.0)	60 (1.4)
Costs associated with administration and operation of miscellaneous low-income housing actions	7,824 (100.0)	3,805 (48.6)	1,501 (19.2)	2,518 (32.2)	– (0.0)
Subsidies involving tax relief or below-market-rate lending	2,666 (100.0)	369 (13.8)	– (0.0)	2,297 (86.2)	– (0.0)
Indirect subsidies to low-income households	1,827 (100.0)	7 (0.4)	– (0.0)	1,820 (99.6)	– (0.0)
Indirect subsidies to suppliers of low-income housing	839 (100.0)	362 (43.1)	– (0.0)	477 (56.9)	– (0.0)
Total average annual subsidy, 1967–1969	37,128 (100.0)	19,285 (51.9)	11,133 (30.0)	5,879 (15.8)	831 (2.3)

[1] For operating programs under each subsidy type, see Table 8.4.

[2] Estimated contributions to housing portion of welfare grants from relatives of recipients and other private parties.

given family would obviously narrow. The annualized value of one-time and short-term payments is less than the payments themselves, and similarly, many families who occupy public housing or receive public assistance do so for relatively short periods of time. Equally, many of the 25,000 families who were not directly benefiting from any housing program may well have been helped subsequently. Given the above, it is impossible to make any firm judgments regarding the equity of the existing distribution of aid. It is apparent, however, that even among "equal need" categories, e.g., families who are eligible for public housing, some families benefit a great deal while others receive nothing.

THE NEED-RESOURCES GAP IN PERSPECTIVE

The $37 million in annual subsidies for low-income housing in Baltimore is equal to more than one-quarter of anti-poverty expenditures in the city (21). Housing ranks second (to the nonhousing component of public assistance) among the major anti-poverty sub-systems in terms of dollars expended annually. It exceeds the aggregate annual anti-poverty subsidy for (a) education by $24 million, (b) health services by $8 million, (c) employment programs by $13 million, and (d) family services and community development by $30 million per year. Clearly, a substantial portion of available anti-poverty resources is already being directed toward housing ends.

Ultimately, however, the significance of the housing effort must be measured in relation to the level of aggregate unmet need, that is, with respect to the capital and subsidy requirements which were estimated earlier in the chapter. These estimates placed the amount of capital investment needed to achieve a minimum standard of dwelling unit quality throughout the stock at $200 million, while the annual *additional* subsidy requirement for elimination of quality, space, and expense deprivations was calculated to be in the $67 million range. Because most of the substandard stock in Baltimore is still salvageable at modest cost, the capital investment gap appears manageable. The total subsidy gap, on the other hand, is huge, representing almost a tripling of present expenditures. Moreover, the expenditure of $67 million annually would not totally eliminate the three dimensions of need to which they are addressed, and it would leave the other nine dimensions relatively untouched.

The question which must be faced, therefore, is how likely is a large increase in housing subsidies in the coming years, and if the prospects are dim, what does this imply for housing policy? At first glance, the situation does not appear promising. If ten years were accepted as a reasonable length of time within which to reach target goals, then expansion of programs at a rate of about 10% a year would be necessary to achieve success, assuming rising

Table 8.6. Distribution of Housing Subsidies by Number of Families, and Size and Type of Subsidy (Baltimore, Maryland, 1967–1969)[1]

Housing Subsidy Situation	Number of Households	Average Annual Subsidy	Aggregate Annual Subsidy
Relocation bonus payment	80	$5,000	$ 400,000
Welfare family or individual in 202-221 (d)(3) unit with rent supplement[2,3]	100	1,440	144,000
115 grant and 312 loan	20	1,270	25,400
115 grant only	130	1,200	156,000
Welfare family or individual in public housing[2,3]	5,000	1,100	5,500,000
Welfare family or individual in private housing with DDS demonstration rent supplement[3]	300	1,000	300,000
Nonwelfare family or individual in 202-221 (d)(3) unit with rent supplement[2]	100	880	88,000
Welfare family or individual in private housing with no other subsidy[3]	31,700	560	17,752,000
Nonwelfare family or elderly individual in public housing[2]	6,000	440	2,640,000
Relocation adjustment payments	50	430	21,500
Purchaser of 221 (h) unit	10	400	4,000
Nonwelfare family or individual in 202-221 (d)(3) unit without rent supplement	1,100	280	308,000
Low-income, elderly homeowners receiving tax credits	15,000	120	1,820,000
312 loans only	20	70	1,400
Total, all subsidy situations	59,610	$490	$29,160,300

[1] Excludes overhead expenditures. For simplification, it was assumed that the only categories of overlapping housing subsidies were (a) 115 grants and 312 loans (actual overlap known), (b) public assistance and public housing (actual overlap known), (c) public assistance and 202-221 (d)(3) rent supplementation (actual overlap unknown, taken at one-half of total rent supplements), and (d) public assistance and DDS demonstration rent supplement (overlap 100% by definition).

[2] Average subsidies for 202-221 (d)(3) units exceed those for public housing because 202–221 (d)(3) figures reflect recent construction costs while public housing capital costs have been spread out over a 30-year period.

real incomes would close part of the gap. Although the 10% figure may seem modest, it would imply a sharply increasing share of housing dollars in federal, state, and local budgets; hence a much greater concern by legislators and voters for housing problems than is now the case.

Thus, barring a very clear political mandate to eliminate low-income housing problems, the need-resources gap would appear insurmountable in the coming decade. Nevertheless, it should be emphasized that since the bulk of the need-resources gap is accounted for simply by excessive rent-income ratios, it could be partially closed by income-maintenance, Medicare, and in fact any of a variety of programs that Congress is now considering in an attempt to relieve some of the expense burdens of low-income families. To this extent, housing goals are complementary to, not competitive with, other goals and will be furthered in direct proportion to the funding of related welfare programs.

On balance, then, one's optimism or pessimism must be based on a forecast of the attitude of Congress toward the problem of poverty generally in the coming years. If a reasonable forecast is that the present momentum will neither diminish nor be sharply accelerated, then a reasonable conclusion is that more than half the resource gap could be closed by 1985. Whether there would be a corresponding reduction in housing problems, however, depends on how the funds would be spent. Effective allocations will depend on a thorough understanding of the low-income housing market, a matter to which we now turn.

---

[3] Subsidy figures shown for welfare recipients are based on the average estimated expense per assistance unit for all welfare categories. Since, in fiscal year 1968-69, one-half of the total number of assistance units were AFDC families and the remaining half were virtually all individuals receiving other categorical assistance (OAA, AB, APTD, and GA), the average expense figure used probably differs significantly from the actual figure for each group taken separately.

CHAPTER 9
The Inner-City Housing Market

Previous chapters have reviewed the housing situation of Baltimore's low-income families primarily from a macro perspective. In order to understand more fully present conditions and trends and anticipate future changes in the housing environoment within a shifting policy framework, it is necessary to explore the dynamics of the low-income housing market at the micro-level and in particular to examine some of the institutional factors associated with the recent spiral of decay in this sector of the inventory. The purpose of this chapter, then, is to provide an understanding of the workings of the low-income market as one step toward the development of an analytical framework within which various housing policies can be evaluated.

In Baltimore (as in most large cities in the United States) the bulk of low-income households are concentrated in the older inner neighborhoods where they comprise approximately one-half of the population (Table 9.1). A dominant feature of the inner city is its black majority. Two-thirds of the households in the inner city are black. Substandard housing is even more an inner-city characteristic. Eighty-five percent of the substandard inventory — most of it rental — is located there. Almost three out of four low-income families in the inner city occupy substandard units, as compared with only one out of five in the outer city. Although not all neighborhoods in the inner city are low income or substandard or black, poor and near-poor black families do dominate most of the inner-city market and give it a special character and dynamic which would not exist if the neighborhoods had a broader income and racial mix. Real estate investment decisions both shape this character and are shaped by it. Hence, in order to understand how the low-income housing market in Baltimore functions, it is necessary to examine the inner-city

Table 9.1. Distribution of Households by Area of City, Income, and Quality of Dwelling Unit[1] (Baltimore, Maryland, 1969)

Dwelling Unit Quality	Inner City		Outer City		Total		
	Low Income	Non-Low Income	Low Income	Non-Low Income	Low Income	Non-Low Income	Total
Seriously sub-standard	5,100	1,000	2,000	–	7,100	1,000	8,100
Moderately sub-standard	10,000	2,200	700	–	10,700	2,200	12,900
Borderline	21,200	14,500	4,900	3,200	26,100	17,700	43,800
Standard	14,000	36,500	26,600	134,200	40,600	170,700	211,300
Total	50,300	54,200	34,200	137,400	84,500	191,600	276,100

[1] Source: First Household Survey.

market, and it is useful, in such an examination, to think of the low-income market and the inner-city market as being more or less the same thing (2).

HOUSING AND NEIGHBORHOOD

An Environment of Decay

As anyone who is familiar with Baltimore knows, both the better neighborhoods in the inner city and the poorer sections are typified by the traditional old, masonry row house. The similarity ends there, however. In the more middle-class neighborhoods, front and rear yards, while small, are usually well planted. Rear yards and alleyways are free from trash and debris. Although the streets in the majority of poorer neighborhoods in the inner city are also relatively clean, the alleys are frequently full of rubbish, broken glass, and junk. Many rear yards and vacant lots serve as the final resting place of abandoned automobiles, rusted bed-springs, mattresses, and other household leftovers. In place of the lawn in the rear, one sees either dirt or cemented yards, the latter being an indication of the city's continuing efforts to eliminate breeding places for rodents. In another context, these cement enclosures would be commonly referred to as patios.

The physical environment is affected by the social malaise found in the inner city in readily apparent ways. Thus, mounting threats to the lives and property of inner city residents have substantially increased the ownership of large watchdogs whose turf is the tiny rear patio. The patio has become a noisy smelly cage, as well as a feeding ground for rats, as the dogs tip over garbage cans and fail to eat all of the scraps offered them.

The quality of the physical environment in the poorer neighborhoods is additionally impaired by the interlarding of nonresidential uses and the added threats to physical safety posed by the large number of vacant and vandalized buildings. Interestingly, however, there are still high-quality houses even in very poor neighborhoods, with a wide variety of quality not only from block to block, but also within most blocks. While this is an encouraging sign, it cannot be simply considered reflective of better things to come without substantially more analysis.

Abandonments

A commonplace theme of several recent housing studies is the phenomenon of abandonments or walkaways as an owner response to the declining inner-city market. In New York, between 1965 and 1968, it has been estimated that sufficient units were abandoned to house more than 300,000 people (3). A similar if less extreme situation exists in most large eastern and midwestern cities. Even newer urban complexes such as Los Angeles have experienced abandonment to a minor degree (4). The phenomenon is not new. In several cities, the first signs of abandonment appeared as long ago as the late 1950's and were officially confirmed in the 1960 census.

In Baltimore, firm estimates of the current rate of abandonment are not available. Our data do, however, permit us to approximate a rate. As part of the total study, a random sample of households from throughout the city was interviewed in 1968. From this household sample a subsample of properties was inspected approximately 18 months after the interviews. Since the subsample of inspected units was weighted to be representative of the entire inventory, it was possible to convert the number of structures which were occupied at the beginning of the period but derelict or boarded-up at the end into a withdrawal rate for the period. According to our figures, 4.6% of all inner-city units were boarded-up between the winter and spring of 1968 and the summer and fall of 1969, for an average of almost 4,000 units a year. Roughly half of these board-ups can be traced directly to government action such as acquisition for renewal or highways. These do not represent part of the abandonment process. Other units, according to several informed persons, were abandoned because of the imminence of government action. The number of such units can only be guessed, however. During the years subsequent to 1969, abandonment has continued but, according to some observers, at a slightly diminished pace.

Although abandonments obviously reflect financial losses for private investors, they do not necessarily suggest a deteriorating situation for the city as a whole. It all depends on which units are withdrawn from the stock. If only the worst units are being boarded-up, then the trend would have to be regarded as encouraging. It could be inferred that generally rising incomes are permitting families to filter upward in the stock, and that the abandoned units represent an increasing real vacancy rate in the lowest quality sector of the stock prior to their ultimate demise.

Unfortunately, this is not what has occurred. A large portion of the abandoned structures are reasonably sound and located in blocks which are far from the worst in Baltimore. Investors walked away from the bulk of these buildings because they were vandalized while vacant, awaiting occupancy by new tenants. To a substantial but lesser degree, abandonments of sound structures resulted from the adverse effects of abutting public works and renewal projects or anticipation of same; tenants fled, vacancies increased, and vandalism followed. To a lesser degree still, a basic lack of demand for good-quality housing in undesirable neighborhoods appeared also to be a contributing factor to abandonment. In only a very few instances were there any indications that abandonments of basically sound structures followed directly the city's enforcement of the housing code. Neither, it might be added, did inability to get mortgage loans refinanced, or continuous periods of net operating losses, or the breakdown of costly components such as plumbing and wiring systems lead directly to a significant number of board-ups, though such problems are thought to be primary causes of abandonment in other cities. These observations must be regarded as tentative, however, because investors had to have an occupied structure at the time of our first household survey to fall into our sample. The universe of owners of abandoned structures may be quite different.

What is eminently clear is that much of the abandonment, far from measuring any sort of community gain, must be viewed as a problem of increasing seriousness. If the forces producing unnecessary boarding up are not arrested, "any achievable program of new construction will continue to be swamped by the hemorrhaging that is now bleeding our supply of existing housing. . . "(5) and efforts to renew the inner city will be overwhelmed, as they already have been in New York and Philadelphia. Abandonments are, however, but one indication, albeit a significant one, of the changing nature of housing market dynamics in the inner city and as such will be examined in more detail in Chapter 10.

THE HOUSING MARKET

The Market Environment

The social, economic, and political environments of the city are such that, for all intents and purposes, the nature of the institution of real property in the inner city has altered dramatically in the last few years. As often as not, the bundles of rights and privileges that have been traditionally associated with title to real property have become packages of burdens, and the assets have become liabilities. Rent losses have increased; operating costs have spiraled upward faster than rents can be raised; vandalism has become a serious problem; and many landlords fear for their personal safety when they visit their properties. As a consequence of these problems, the market has all but collapsed. Literally thousands of masonry row houses are available at prices that are close to or well below their assessed values which are supposed to be pegged at 60% of market value (6). Gross rent multipliers are extremely low, with the median falling between one and two. Hundreds of homes in the $1,000 to $2,500 price range are available for the taking, representing liabilities to their owners and draining resources which might be directed toward those parts of the inventory which can still be saved without public subsidy. With asset values eroded, there is little market activity and a widespread feeling among owners of being locked into the market; unable to earn sufficiently high returns on alternative investments to warrant converting such large paper losses into real ones. Although, at the present time (1974), there are signs that the market has bottomed out and is firming up in parts of the inner city, the underlying forces of decay and abandonment do not appear to have significantly diminished.

Such a state of affairs contributes directly to the decline in housing quality. First, it exhausts capital that would normally be used for renovation and major repairs. Second, it minimizes personal contact between landlord and tenant, as rents are increasingly collected by mail rather than in person. As a result, investors who traditionally prided themselves on their ability to develop a rapport with their tenants that was based upon mutual respect for each other are today no better off than those landlords who never made such efforts to understand or deal sensitively with their tenants. Third, since the landlord is absent from the neighborhood, he can no longer "police" his properties adequately and "secure" vacated units. Fourth, because the inner-city environment is fraught with dangers to life and limb, maintenance crews must usually travel in pairs, even if the job requires only a single man, further increasing already soaring maintenance costs.

Relationship of Rent to Housing Quality in the Inner City

In 1969, the median gross rent for minimum-code housing in the inner city was about $100 a month, while the lowest-quality units commanded a median rent of approximately $75 a month (7). According to our calculations the costs of upgrading most of the latter units to code level are not entirely out of line with potential post-rehabilitation rents and rates of profit that would ordinarily be required to induce investors to commit their capital to such ventures. Yet, no additional capital will be forthcoming until the investment climate is altered. The same deficiencies in the inner-city environment that are causing families, with any degree of choice, to move away are also causing private capital to flee and prices to decline. While values are down, however, rents are not. The costs of taxes, insurance, utilities and maintenance, when coupled with vacancies, arrears, and more than occasional acts of vandalism, keep the cost of housing to the city's low-income families sufficiently high to be comparable with better-quality accommodations located outside of the inner city.

Where neighborhood environment and housing quality permit, investors screen their potential tenantry, eliminating families who they feel might misuse the property or fall behind in their rent. Consequently one finds a three-track pricing policy in which the most desirable, long-term tenants receive discounts; average families pay market rents; and high-risk tenants pay premiums, frequently for the least desirable units. In part, because of these pricing policies, there exists a wide variation in quality at any rent level, with the result that the worst quality housing does not always command the lowest rents. More importantly, few families are paying rents which are too low to obtain decent units somewhere in the market. Most of them are spending more than they can afford, but because they are, low income per se does not explain the low quality of their housing.

Who Owns the Slums

Traditionally, the development of low-income housing policies in the United States has not been based upon an understanding of the institutional context and market dynamics of the low-rent sector. As a result, these policies have often been insensitive with respect to the class of individuals who now house poor families – the "slumlords." Their intimate knowledge of this sector of the market ordinarily has not been sought in setting policy directions. The possibility that they could play a positive role or contribute to a solution has commonly been rejected a priori. Many of those in government and academic circles reveal in both obvious and subtle ways their disdain for the inner-city landlord; categorically, he is regarded as a barrier to progress. Ironically, those who share these assumptions rarely know, in fact, who the inner-city landlord really is.

These unfriendly attitudes, even if justified, would be of no consequence if existing housing programs were making satisfactory progress. Since they are not and since investors in low-income housing will continue to be a major force in the foreseeable future, much more needs to be known about them, their investments, and their problems. How many of them are competent and responsible property managers who should be encouraged and assisted in their efforts? What proportion are simply speculators who would turn public programs into windfall profits? Under what circumstances, if any, would they improve their properties voluntarily? Should housing policy attempt to phase them out of the picture or enlarge their role? These questions can no longer be ignored; they never should have been. Insensitivity toward these investors has been expensive in other ways, for they, more than anyone else, can contribute to an understanding of the dynamics of the problem. From their particular position, submerged in day-to-day problems, they may not fully comprehend the dynamics themselves, but they can provide the detailed knowledge upon which understanding is based.

For some time now, and particularly since Sternlieb's study of tenement housing in Newark, the belief that the typical investor owns large quantities of poor quality housing has steadily been eroding (8). In Baltimore's inner city, however, there is a fair degree of concentration of ownership among professionals who hold a large number of units. According to our survey, over one-fourth of the private inner-city rental inventory is owned or controlled by about 50 professionals, with the largest having in excess of 1,500 low-rent units and the smallest about 100. At the other end of the scale are what might be termed casual investors, persons owning fewer than 5 units. In between are the small investors who have anywhere from 5 to 24 dwellings, and the medium-sized owners with holdings of from 25 to 100 units. It is our guess, based on very small samples, that medium-sized investors hold somewhere around 15% of the inventory, with the small and casual investors accounting for the remaining 60%.

Although these categories are, to some extent, arbitrary, they do help to distinguish salient characteristics that are associated with size of holdings. For example, casual investors are, almost without exception, amateurs who are difficult to reach through any potential program. Conversely, sophistication and permanence of operations increase with size of holdings. Another way of looking at the importance of scale is to identify that point at which an investor must cease being a part-time landlord and concentrate full-time on his holdings, lest he lose control of his operations. While the point is more realistically a range, one cannot very well manage more than 75 dwelling units on a part-time basis unless most of the units are in contiguous buildings. Similarly, market conditions are such that it would be extremely difficult to earn even a modest living through owning and managing less than 50 low-income units (9). Typically, then, so-called large investors have the equivalent of at least one full-time person in management. Some modest-sized owners do also, but have more difficulties because they are strapped for funds, cannot afford permanent crews for maintenance, and so forth.

The Large Investor. In all, 32 large investors, representing 90% of those sampled and with collective holdings in excess of 15,000 dwelling units, were contacted and interviewed. For the most part, these individuals spoke willingly and frankly, and provided useful financial and other information. Their willingness to submit themselves to our probing stemmed from the simple fact that someone wanted to listen to them. Almost to a man, they claimed there were no sympathetic ears to hear their plight, including city officials, the press, or any other person outside of their profession.

Virtually every one of them was a full-time professional in real estate investment and/or insurance, brokerage, management, or law. The majority of them inherited the bulk of their holdings or got into the business through their fathers or fathers-in-law. Many greatly expanded their inventories in the middle 1950's when liberal financing terms and the suburban explosion combined to produce very favorable market circumstances. Most of their properties are held free and clear and have been under the same ownership for many years. In fact, median length of ownership is just under 15 years, with one-quarter of the properties being held for more than 20 years.

Several of the large investors used to be traders rather than landlords and have only become the latter because of lack of a market for their holdings. Since the challenge, as they originally saw it, was acquisition at the right time and place and resale at a profit, and not maintenance and management in all of its dimensions, these investors never had an interest in or temperament for management, and as a result a few of them are in a great deal of trouble. The degree of dissatisfaction with the business is evidenced by the fact that most of the large investors would like to get out. Nevertheless, while they all but unanimously claim not to be buying inner-city residential properties anymore, three-fifths of them purchased at least one property in 1969 — but only because they considered the prices to be fantastic bargains.

Even though many large investors are either second or third generation professionals, there is an increasing unwillingness on their part to pass their "problems" on to their heirs and a similar unwillingness on the part of their children to enter the business. Consequently, there is the possibility that such inventories will be acquired by less knowledgeable and less well-capitalized holders, thus complicating the problem of encouraging sound maintenance.

As discussed later in the chapter, it does not appear that large-scale investors are "milking" (under maintaining) their properties. It is clear, though, that they are diversifying and putting any available capital into other housing and nonhousing investments. Few of them use accelerated depreciation, and straight-line rates are low, ranging between 2% and 5%. In a few cases, investors have arranged with the Internal Revenue Service to use 2% straight-line rates and to fully expense all capital items.

Cash flows for large investors, where positive, are generally not excessive, and as already mentioned, asset values against which large-scale investors once borrowed to expand operations or to send their children to college, or simply to build up an estate, are evaporating. Maintenance and management problems are increasing at a time when it is becoming more difficult for many investors to deal with them. Disillusionment is intensifying at the same time that pressures are growing for the city to bear down on the "slumlord." The large holders are right in the middle, because they know it is unrealistic to think about getting out altogether, not an unlikely alternative for small and casual investors. They continue to screen their potential tenantry more carefully than do other investors. They likewise take comfort in the fact that the vast majority of their inventories are held free and clear, unlike those of some of the younger, more eager investors who have entered the market more recently.

Because of the greater expertise of large investors, it seemed reasonable to hypothesize that the general condition of their properties would be better than that of smaller landlords. This did not turn out to be so. There are a few large investors whose holdings are concentrated in the worst neighborhoods in East Baltimore, as well as a few whose advanced age has made it impossible for them to supervise an efficient operation. According to our survey, however, while the median condition score for inventories held by large investors is virtually the same as that for all others, the range around the median is much less for large owners than it is for the smaller ones. In other words, the large investors own relatively few of the poorest quality units.

Equally important, they continue to have the financial capacity to recover from sporadic acts of vandalism and expensive code violation notices which can cause others to board-up. But this capacity and willingness to bail themselves out cannot be expected to continue indefinitely. In fact, a few of them are beginning to use delaying tactics to avoid having to comply with the housing code within the time specified by law.

Even though the large owners are generally among the most sophisticated investors, their participation in federal programs is nil. There are several reasons for this peculiar situation. A small number of investors simply know nothing about the programs. Others feel that the few subsidies which are available to them are not tailored to their needs. Still others have found that the costs of participation are not worth the benefits. In the words of one investor, "If there is a way for a program not to work, the administrators find it."

Medium, Small, and Casual Investors. If "troubled times" fairly summarizes the circumstances of most large investors, then the plight of the remaining holders of inner-city residential real estate must be viewed as much worse. Of the thousands of such owners in the city, only 60 were interviewed. Collectively, they owned 794 properties. Although our sample of these investors is too small to permit many generalizations to be made about them, a certain amount of reliable information was obtained. As a group, they represent a broad range of age, occupation, and ethnic categories. In other respects, however, they are quite similar. They are less willing to discuss openly their operations, feel more persecuted by the city and by others, and are more bitter about how things are going than are the large investors. They have less grasp of the state of the market as a whole. Also, they are more vulnerable to the whims of the market than are their larger counterparts, inasmuch as what happens in a particular block or neighborhood is of significance to most or all of their inventory. They cannot spread their risks, and are less likely to successfully average their losses.

In addition to being greatly confused and confounded by the city bureaucracy, which the larger investors learn to deal with, the smaller investors have much more limited management capacities (10). Frequently, such owners are widows, or are individuals in real estate related businesses who have found out too late that their properties are not returning the current income they had hoped for. Not only are their scale of operations and their resources insufficient to hire permanent work crews, they have few connections with firms providing such services and must pay retail prices for most maintenance work. Also, they are more frequently the victims of shoddy work for which they paid good money.

While a majority of the properties of large investors are held free and clear, most of those held by smaller investors are mortgaged. Because of the mortgage payments, these units seldom throw off any cash, as the hypothetical income-expense statement in Table 9.2 clearly illustrates. Several modest-sized investors who were interviewed were virtually completely mortgaged and were working full-time to try to stay afloat until their loans could be paid off. Meanwhile, they were minimizing maintenance outlays, delinquent in their taxes, and leaving vandalized units in their ravaged state.

Many dimensions of good management tend to go unrecognized by smaller and nonprofessional investors. They are less likely to appreciate the sunk nature of their initial capital investment, often putting more into their units than the market justifies. Many of them also appear to beat themselves through foolish rental policies, quickly evicting good tenants who fall a little behind in their rent, thus increasing vacancies, turnover, and the risk of vandalism.

Because of unfavorable cash-flow situations and perhaps a failure to appreciate the importance of good management practices as a way of working successfully within the present market context, smaller investors do not often contract with professional firms to manage their holdings. Moreover, according to one professional manager, contracts with small owners, where they do exist, are usually short term in nature. Thus, even when a management firm is called upon to bail some small owner out of trouble, its beneficial impact is only temporary.

The Economics of Low-Rent Housing

The notion that owners of low-rent inner-city properties earn exorbitant profits persists in the face of a large body of contrary evidence. If, it is argued, these excess profits could only be squeezed out of the slums and returned to the occupants in the form of more housing services, substandard housing could be significantly improved. The recent rapid spread of rent

Table 9.2. **Illustrative Cash Flow Statement, Inner-City Row House Held Free and Clear (Baltimore, Maryland, 1968)**

Gross Income − $76/month × 12	$912
Less: Vacancies and arrears (13%)	120
Effective Income	792
Less: Real estate taxes	125[1]
Ground rent	60
Liability insurance	15
Fire insurance	25
Total Fixed Expenses	225
Operating Income	567
Less: Maintenance and repair	240
Water and sewer charges	60
Miscellaneous	30
Total Operating Expenses	330
Net Income Before Management	237
Less: Management (10% of Collected rents)	79
Net Income From Operations	158
Less: Mortgage loan payments[2]	189
Net Cash Flow	$−31

[1] Assumes assessed value of land and building is $2,500.
[2] Assumes 10-year, 8%, level payment loan for $1,300.

escrow legislation gives witness to the durability of the belief that owners of substandard rental accommodations are salting away huge sums of money at the expense of their tenants. Declining inner-city property values and financial difficulties of public housing authorities should serve to dispel this myth, but it is helpful to go directly to profit-and-loss statements for additional proof. Analysis of these statements also reveals why ownership of low-rent residential property in the inner city is not profitable and what would have to happen for red ink to turn into black.

When this study began, several knowledgeable persons advised that it would be impossible to obtain adequate financial data on inner-city housing operations because many investors either would not reveal such information or keep such poor records that in effect they do not have the information themselves. In the course of the study, it was found that some investors indeed do not have good records, that others would not furnish specifics about properties, and that some of the furnished information was not accurate. These difficulties nowithstanding, we obtained 26 verifiable cash-flow statements, most of them from large investors. The statements were documented through examination of receipted bills. Items which seemed unreasonably large or small were checked with the owner. While the number of sampled properties for which acceptable data could be obtained is quite small, the properties themselves do not appear to be unrepresentative of the larger sample with respect to quality, rent, mortgage status, and type of structure.

To simplify the analysis for the reader, a composite hypothetical income statement has been constructed for a "typical" single-family row house (Table 9.2) and each of the individual items in the statement is explained. While the true median for any particular item or for the bottom-line figure may be slightly above or below those presented here, our experience suggests that the biases are small and that the magnitudes of the problems to be discussed are fairly represented by the data.

Contract Rent. In 1969, the median contract rent in the inner-city was approximately $76 a month, or $912 a year. This amount, or as much of it as is actually collected, must pay all fixed and operating expenses, including management and debt, before any income can be credited as a return on equity capital.

Uncollected Rents. According to our survey, 14% of the sampled units were vacant at least once during 1968 for periods ranging from less than one month to more than six months. In addition, virtually all investors experienced rent losses on occupied units. Combining vacancies and uncollected rents, the average inner-city investor appeared to lose about seven weeks' income a year, or more than 13% of gross income. Phrased differently, the landlord who charged $76 a month in rent could expect to receive only $66. Thus the $912 figure indicated above should be reduced by $120 to $792.

Taxes. Assuming that a property is owned free and clear, fixed expenses include real estate taxes, insurance, and most likely in Baltimore, a ground rent. Although the average effective tax rate in Baltimore is 3% of market value, nearly all inner-city property is overassessed, thereby increasing the effective rate in this sector of the stock. As in other cities, reassessments have not kept pace with declining values. A typical inner-city, single-family row house renting for $912 a year might be assessed, land and building, at around $2,500, even though current market values seldom exceed this figure. Thus, whereas the effective tax on most real property in the city is 3% of market value, the tax liability on inner-city properties is closer to 5% of actual value (11). For a $2,500 property this would come to $125, thereby reducing the hypothetical effective income from $792 to $667. It can be seen, from this example, that real estate taxes constitute about 16% of the rent which families actually pay.

Other Fixed Expenses. About one-fifth of the investors had no fire insurance on their inner-city properties at the time they were interviewed. Many of the remaining owners enjoyed only partial protection. Rates were high and many insurance companies were refusing to write policies in the inner city at all. Without insurance, mortgage funds were unobtainable. Since the recent creation of an assigned risk pool, the situation has much improved. A typical fire insurance policy for a single-family row house in good condition costs about $25, well below the previous $40 average. Liability coverage is also easier and cheaper to obtain than it once was, with the minimum premium averaging approximately $15. Only one-fifth of all investors have vandalism insurance, and such insurance is available only for occupied buildings. Fire and liability insurance together reduce income on our hypothetical property from $667 to $627.

As indicated above, ground rent is a peculiar component of housing cost associated with Baltimore, where many investors do not own the land under which their housing is situated and therefore must pay rents to the owners of record. Historically, the ground rent for a single-family dwelling has been 6% of the value of the land per year. It is not unusual to find investors buying properties in fee, creating a ground rent, and selling the land to independent investors. The primary reason for doing this is to recapture part of the acquisition price of the property while not reducing its depreciable base.

With the market in its presently depressed state, ground rents are no longer traded at 6%. Generally, capitalization rates are at least 12%, which represents a 50% decline in the value of the land under most inner-city real estate.

According to our survey, approximately three-quarters of all inner-city units are owned subject to ground rents, with the median being around $70. In the present example, assuming the land at time of purchase was valued at $1,000 and that the 6% figure was applied, ground rent would be $60 a year, thus reducing operating income from $627 to $567, with fixed expenses, exclusive of debt service, totaling $225.

Maintenance. Maintenance and repair expenses are the largest variable costs and thus play a key role in the whole cash-flow picture. According to our survey, the median cost of maintenance and repairs in 1968 was $240 a unit, with 20% of the investors claiming to have averaged $300, and another 30% between $100 and $200. While this particular cost item is difficult to verify precisely, we feel reasonably confident that minimum maintenance costs for a typical five- or six-room, single-family unit with a good tenant would be about $200 and accordingly higher for older, larger units as well as those in below-average condition and those in which more difficult tenants reside. As a matter of fact, the costs of such basic maintenance services as plumbing, carpentry, roofing, and heating are sufficiently high, when coupled with added costs of property abuse, and decoration and repair expenses associated with high turnover, to make the median expense of $240 seem quite conservative.

One way of assessing whether these cost estimates are in line is to compare them with maintenance and repair costs in the city's inventory of public housing. According to public housing officials, such costs average $28 per unit, per month, or $336 a unit annually. Non-routine expenditures, including extraordinary maintenance, replacement of equipment and appliances, and general improvement of the units, average $4 monthly, bringing the annual total to $384 per unit. In addition, annual turnover averages 18%, with typical turnover costs for cleaning, repairing, and redecorating vacated units being around $150, which when pro-rated, increases costs to $411 a year per unit.

Considering that these cost estimates include newer public housing units as well as those in the older projects and that most of the city's public housing is built with concrete floors and masonry block interior walls, which reduce maintenance needs, the outlays for the private sector would appear, if anything, inadequate. In any case, reduce net operating income on the hypothetical dwelling unit by $240, leaving $327.

Several investors indicated that, holding prices constant, maintenance outlays are increasing in the inner city rather than decreasing as is commonly believed, and several of them were able to document this statement. Although, as pointed out earlier, about one-half of the inner-city rental housing inventory is well below code, 80% of the investors interviewed claimed that their maintenance outlays were of sufficient magnitude to avoid further deterioration of their units. Only 8% said that they were deliberately undermaintaining any of their properties.

An important part of the financial picture, as it relates to quality and cash-flow, is the high maintenance expense in units in which less desirable tenants live. More than half of the investors interviewed said they spend excessive sums to keep such units in repair. In some cases, the underlying problem may relate as much to the landlord as to the tenant. Regardless of the reason, many landlords ultimately take the position that they will not put more money into the units while the problem persists. This attitude is of some importance inasmuch as the difference between adequate and inadequate maintenance can be as little as $100 a year per unit, or $2 a week.

Water and Other Charges. Additional operating expenses include water and sewer charges and related expenses of doing business in this sector of the stock. Water charges used to be quite minimal, averaging perhaps $30 a year before the city installed water meters and moved from flat-rate billing to user charges. Today, water bills are much higher, occasionally exceeding $100 per year in units where plumbing is faulty or where there is excessive use. Here, too, there is an inverse relationship between rental charges, housing quality, tenant character, and costs. In cheaper, poorer quality units which attract less careful tenants, water consumption is well above average, with water charges absorbing an excessive part of the rental dollar. While it might seem eminently reasonable for the tenant to be billed in accordance with water used, resistance to this idea among tenants coupled with the owner's legal liability for delinquent utility bills seems to minimize this possibility at least for the present.

The switchover to user charges has placed an additional premium on sound management. Many large investors, alerted by an atypically large quarterly water bill, automatically set into action a fairly elaborate system designed to uncover its cause. Initially, there is an extensive examination of all plumbing connections, including household systems as well as those below ground level. Concurrent with this inspection is a conversation about the problem with the tenant. As often as not, the problem lies in a leaky toilet, faulty washers, or general carelessness on the part of resident families. On occasion, landlords have found that overconsumption of water was due to such things as the tenant washing cars for pay, or continually running cold water over vegetables to keep them fresh on hot days. Good managers encourage their tenants to re-port plumbing problems to them, and many tenants respond accordingly. Some managers are unhappy that the city bills them only quarterly and that receipt of bills comes several weeks after meters are read, because potential problems can go for as long as 4 months before detection. Assuming reasonably good tenants and equipment, a moderate estimate for water and sewer charges is $60, shrinking net rental income to $267.

One other significant cost of doing business in the low-rent market is the extra expense associated with collecting rents. As indicated earlier, the nature of the market, along with the related sociopolitical climate of the inner city, has changed to such an extent as to seriously circumscribe some traditional landlord options. One of these options which is exercised increasingly less frequently, contrary to general opinion, is that of eviction. Almost 40% of the landlords who were interviewed suggested that, for a number of reasons, it is very difficult to evict a family in the inner city today. The barriers most frequently cited are not, as in some other cities, legal in nature. Instead, they are the expense involved in putting out the tenant's possessions, the potential for community retaliation, and the possibility of tenant retaliation on the property before the put-out occurs. Additionally, many landlords admitted to an aversion to evicting a family, preferring instead to encourage undesirable tenants to move through more subtle measures, such as reducing services, or in the case of one landlord, paying moving expenses. According to our survey, 55% of the investors did not evict a single tenant in 1968, while another 25% evicted fewer than three families each.

The above notwithstanding, investors issued large numbers of eviction notices for nonpayment of rent. These are different from actual put-outs. A notice, secured from the People's Court for $2.50, simply advises the tenant that he will be evicted for nonpayment if the rent due is not immediately forthcoming. Eviction notices require no court appearances, attorney fees, or the like, yet they have a certain "scare value" that encourages recalcitrant tenants to pay their rent. The median number of notices sent out in 1968 by large investors was 100, with one-fourth sending out more than 500, and 10%, more than 1,000. For the latter group, this represents a direct cost of over $2,500.

If 1,000 or more eviction notices seems unreasonably high, it is worth noting that, while actual put-outs in the city's public housing inventory are likewise few, the city mails out between 800 and 900 notices per month, or about 10,000 a year. In both the public and the private sector, most notices go repeatedly to a small proportion of tenants. Some families simply will not pay rent until they receive an eviction notice. In fact, one landlord informed us that one very good tenant of his lived in the same house for 10 years and received about five notices a year for each of his 10 years in residence. If we assume incidental costs, such as eviction notices, of only $30 a year, cash flow on the hypothetical unit drops to $237.

Management Fees. Whether a dwelling is looked after by the owner himself or by an employee or by a professional management company, a cost is involved. As indicated earlier, management firms usually charge a proportion of collected rents with an additional fee sometimes levied on the basis of the dollar value of maintenance expenditures. In either case, the percentage of rent that goes to management of low-rent properties is higher than it is in more expensive buildings because the task is more difficult and also because it costs just as much or more to collect a low rent as a higher one (12). Subtracting the typical fee of 10% of collected rents for management reduces net income to $158.

Net Income. If our hypothetical property were purchased for its assessed value of $2,500, the return free and clear would be only 6.3%. If the property were mortgaged, the cash-flow would very likely be negative. Any way one looks at it, the return is not attractive. And, it should be emphasized, we think this is the median experience; for reasons we will explore later, many investors did much worse. Of the 26 completed income statements that were obtained for 1968, 10 had negative cash-flows and only five showed earnings of as much as 10% before financing.

There are basically two ways in which these low rates of return could be raised to a more acceptable level. The first is by reducing several of the expense items to amounts that would be considered reasonable in the outer city. Thus, in our example, if the vacancy loss were cut to $45 (5%), and real estate taxes to $75 (3% of market value), net profit before financing would almost double to 11%. Even this larger return is quite inadequate if it is assumed that the remaining economic life of the structure in question is only ten or fifteen years, but much of the inner-city inventory could remain in service for a considerably longer period if neighborhood conditions were improved.

The second way in which a satisfactory return could be achieved is by a large recapitalization of values, i.e., additional losses by existing investors. And this is what has occurred. Unfortunately, the necessary losses are so great, they effectively dry up the market. In our example, the market value would have to drop by more than half, from an already depressed level, for the rate of return on a cash basis to approach a respectable figure. But at this price the present owner becomes reluctant to dispose of his property, because his rate of return when measured against *current* value is reasonably competitive with alternative investment opportunities. As his cash return dwindles further he may become more desperate to sell at any price, but by that time potential buyers have disappeared.

This picture is not favorably changed by income-tax considerations, since the amount by which depreciation allowances reduce income tax payments is low and the depreciation itself is all too real. The picture is improved, however, by only small shifts in our assumptions. If recapitalization of only 20 to 25% were coupled with reduction of several of the expense items (or a modest escalation of rents) inner-city rental structures would return to their former competitive position. The margin between happiness and despair is rather narrow.

Although the figures in Table 9.2 are presented primarily for the purpose of explaining the financial aspects of inner-city low-rent housing, they also serve to illustrate other aspects of the inner-city housing problem. For one, they suggest that low housing quality is perhaps as much a function of too much expenditure as of too little rent. Over 10% of cash inflow — an amount equal to about 80% of net income — is dissipated on expenditures which do not contribute directly to maintaining or improving resultant flows of housing services. This is why apparently high rent with respect to housing quality received can result in little or no profit to the investor. In part, this also explains why housing quality in the inner city is inferior to that obtainable elsewhere in the city at comparable or only slightly higher rents. Taxes, insurance, water charges, costs of high turnover and vandalism, and management expenses all absorb a smaller percentage of the rental dollar in better quality neighborhoods, with the result that a larger percentage of rent collections can be allocated to amenity-producing services.

The figures also demonstrate that although there is almost no floor on values, there is one on rents. As values drop, all of the components of rent, except real estate taxes, remain rigid or rise, and taxes do not adjust downward as fast or as far as they should. By inference, then, if taxes were lowered of if some other costs were brought into line, the benefits would not be passed on to the tenant. Instead, they would be absorbed by investors. Although this conclusion may not surprise anyone, it may also eliminate what little incentive there is to help the landlord. If so, this would be most unfortunate.

The Special Problem of Maintenance

Our analysis of median income and expense figures in Table 9.2 may leave the impression that the problems of the inner-city landlord are much less serious than suggested by the gloomy description in the opening pages of this chapter. Despite excessive real estate taxes, water bills, and vacancy losses, it is still possible for investors to obtain a positive, if modest, cash-flow. With a little cooperation from the public sector, they could enjoy an adequate return, and without cutting back on housing services. However, like the youngster who drowned while trying to wade across a lake having an average depth of two feet, many investors have not been able to keep their properties above water despite the averages.

The difference between landlords who earn a profit and those who experience substantial losses can often be explained by a single item — maintenance — the cost of which varies widely from owner to owner and structure to structure. Only a small absolute increase in maintenance expenditures is capable of eliminating cash-flow completely. And this is what so frequently happens in the inner city. The level of required maintenance expenditures is excessive when compared with what is normal in other sectors of the market.

The problem of excessive maintenance requirements has several origins. First, poor families often neglect or abuse their dwellings, either because they lack a sense of responsibility toward the property of others, or because they feel their landlord is unfair or not responsive to their needs, or because they are frustrated with life in general. Private owners and public housing managers sometimes unwittingly induce negative behavior, due to their insensitivity to the unique problems of the low-income population. Second, interruptions in earnings force many low-income families to move frequently. The moves themselves create extra costs for the landlord, and their frequency contributes to tenant neglect of the premises. Turnover expenses, excluding lost rent, can easily total about one year's net cash-flow, while it may cost as much as four years' cash-flow to repair a badly abused unit. Third, vandalism takes its toll of vacant units. Fourth, older structures are somewhat more expensive than newer ones to keep in good condition. Fifth, as mentioned earlier, when a repair becomes necessary, it often cannot be performed by a single individual as in times past. To prevent the theft of tools from their repair trucks and also for reasons of personal safety, maintenance personnel are forced to work in pairs in many inner-city neighborhoods. Some repairmen are reluctant to go into these neighborhoods at all. Finally, in the case of investors with small holdings, maintenance skills cannot be utilized effectively. These investors cannot find the skills when needed, or must pay retail prices for the services, or spend as much for the repairman's trip to the structure as for the repair itself. Owner occupants are faced with the same problem and to an even greater degree.

Whatever the reason in a particular case, the result is often a level of maintenance expenditures that is so high as to eliminate profits, but insufficient to prevent a decline in quality.

Although the problem of excessive maintenance requirements is widely recognized, the major portion of housing decay is generally ascribed either to "milking," which has already been mentioned, or to rents that are too low to support repairs that are normally necessary even if a unit is well cared for. Each of these alternate explanations merits closer scrutiny.

Milking. Because maintenance outlays have such a huge effect on net revenue and because they are deferrable, it might seem that slumlords and responsible investors alike would choose to scrimp on repairs rather than accept a cash-flow as low as that in Table 9.2. No doubt some do. Such behavior, however, is usually self-defeating, for it quickly reduces the desirability, hence rentability, of units which are so treated. Again referring to the table, while a 20% reduction in maintenance and repair expenditures would increase net cash-flow by $48, or 29%, this savings would be equivalent to less than three weeks' rent. If the probability were reasonably high that reductions in the quality of housing services would increase vacancies, turnover, and arrears, or would increase tenant apathy or turn apathy into hostility, the investor would quickly lose much more than he had temporarily gained by cutting back on upkeep. Thus, as long as cash-flow is positive, it is irrational for an investor not to pursue a policy of adequate maintenance, unless he desperately needs cash for other purposes or expects the property will soon stop producing income regardless of its condition (13). It seems reasonable to conclude, therefore, that deliberate undermaintenance is usually a last-ditch attempt to minimize losses, not maximize excess profits, and is at most a symptom of the inner-city maintenance problem.

Inadequate rent. The connection between low income, low rent, and low maintenance is so intuitively obvious that further elaboration hardly seems necessary. In Baltimore, however, the connection is a trifle confusing. At any given rent level, dwelling units in the outer city are much more likely to be of satisfactory quality than are dwelling units in the inner city, and at any given rent level, non-low-income families are much more likely to occupy standard housing than are low-income families (Table 9.3). These relationships obtain even if room size and family size are held constant. The inner-city/outer-city difference is explained in part by the presence of space heaters, inadequate wiring, etc., in many scrupulously maintained inner-city dwellings, and by structural defects which are relatively invisible to the potential renter. The difference between housing conditions of low- and non-low-income families at the same rent level is less easily accounted for. Standardizing for race helps a little, but the trail of explanation stops there.

Since the rental payments of most of Baltimore's low-income families

Table 9.3. Distribution of Standard Private Rental Housing by Location, Income of Occupants, and Rent Level,[1,2] (Baltimore, Maryland, 1969)

Gross Monthly Rent	Inner City				Outer City			
	Low Income		Non-Low Income		Low Income		Non-Low Income	
	Total Units	% Standard	Total Units	% Standard	Total Units	% Standard	Total Units	% Standard
Under $60	3,100	3	900	7	1,700	90	2,100	100
$60–$89	11,800	8	12,900	56	1,900	29	6,600	75
$90 +	13,100	17	13,600	67	7,400	100	24,200	98
Total	28,000	12	27,400	60	11,000	79	32,900	94

[1] Source: First Household Survey.
[2] Information on either gross rent or family income was not obtained for approximately 20% of the private rental dwellings in the sample.

appear to be sufficient to permit adequate maintenance in more equable
market environments, the problem of maintaining the inner-city inventory at
a given quality level, as opposed to upgrading it, would seem to require subsidy programs that address themselves to the behaviorial antecedents and
consequences of low-income, not just low-income per se.

INVESTORS AND THE CITY

Because of the peculiar nature of the commodity with which they deal,
members of the inner-city investment community would be expected to have
extensive relations with a number of local government institutions. Too, one
would expect that the city's low-rent housing and related community development policies and programs, as well as its day-to-day political ministrations,
would have both long-range and immediate impacts on the operations of
inner-city investors. Naturally, the socioeconomic characteristics of most of
the inner-city tenants, the ethical questions which are inevitably involved in
profit-seeking operations dealing with the poor, and the marginal condition of
so much of the housing, all contribute to the rather strained and unpleasant
relationships between the city and the investor. Of special interest and importance, therefore, is how the myriad of city policies either improve or impede efforts of the private sector to provide modest-quality housing to the
poor at reasonable cost. A number of issues involving local policy and its
execution are relevant to this problem.

Code Enforcement

Strange though it may seem to some observers, investors are favorably dis-
posed toward vigorous code-enforcement programs. Such programs are felt
to support the efforts of responsible owners. Investors generally favor area-
wide enforcement which stresses strict exterior inspections, with interior inspections aimed only at eliminating serious health and safety violations.
Given their tenuous economic circumstances, they object to inspections
in which so-called "laundry lists" of violations are compiled, where serious
structural, plumbing, wiring, and other similar violations are mixed with less
serious structural and cosmetic or decorative ones. Such lengthy violation
notices, according to investors, leave them little discretion in allocating
limited maintenance and repair resources and ignore the present state of
the market and the stark fact that much of the inner-city inventory is well
over 50 years old. Yet, if all elements of a violation notice are not complied
with, the notice is not withdrawn and the landlord is subject to criminal
penalties.

Another problem relates to violations that are tenant-induced. In many such cases, it is impossible to determine which tenant is responsible (e.g., when garbage is dumped in the rear yard of a multifamily unit), and the city, therefore, has no choice but to proceed against the owner. In other instances, tenant responsibility is clear, but the landlord is charged with the violation nevertheless. This is true not only in Baltimore but in other cities as well. From the landlord point of view, this practice encourages tenant carelessness. If tenants were brought into court, investors feel most of them would soon improve, as would landlord-tenant relations. The city does issue tenant-violation notices, but investors have suggested that the city adopt a two-party notice in which tenant violations would be listed separately from those which are the responsibility of the landlord. How much such a policy could improve things is difficult to say without speculating as to how the tenant component might be enforced.

In spite of investor support for code-enforcement efforts, owners could be expected to resist unsubsidized programs designed to upgrade all housing to code level since existing rents cannot support such expenditures. According to our data, the median expenditure required to bring the substandard inventory into compliance is in excess of $1,000, whereas actual expenditures which are incurred as a result of enforcement average only about $200 (14). If a policy of vigorous unsubsidized enforcement were pursued, widespread boarding-up would no doubt result.

Although code enforcement cannot be expected to improve the stock substantially, it can, in theory at least, hold the line against decay. In the inner city, however, the decline in quality since 1960 suggests that enforcement is not able to force as much investment into properties as vandalism, careless use of properties, and negative environmental factors (many of which are the city's responsibility) take out. Larger negative forces in the environment are overwhelming the positive contributions of the existing enforcement effort. Unless the city can arrest these forces, code enforcement can be considered, at best, a rear-guard action.

Vandalism

The serious problem of vandalism in the inner city has already been mentioned several times. It is not unusual to see vacant units being vandalized in broad daylight, the perpetrator proceeding with apparent impunity. According to our calculations, the median direct vandalism loss suffered by all investors in 1968 was $750, or around 2% of gross collections. Several investors estimated losses due to vandalism had been the primary determinant of their negative cash-flows during the preceding year.

There are four generic types of vandalism, although they are not mutually exclusive. The first involves those acts which frequently accompany civil disorder. According to our figures, almost one-fifth of the investors interviewed suffered vandalism losses during the riots following the assassination of Dr. King in April 1968. The second type of vandalism concerns what investors consider to be excessively abusive behavior by tenants during their period of residence, or extreme carelessness or disregard for the security of the property when the decision is made to vacate without notice. It is normally not vandalism in the usual sense of the word, though occasionally the behavior is deliberate in nature. The third and fourth types of vandalism both concern vacant units. The third can be characterized as acts of malicious mischief such as breaking windows, turning on water taps to flood interiors, splattering paint on walls and the like. Stemming largely from the hostility of unsupervised youths in the inner city, such acts of aggression against property are not normally viewed by the investment community as being as serious as the fourth type which is carried out by professional thieves. This latter type involves the systematic stripping of copper pipes and expensive fixtures, which are then sold for very little money at one of the three licensed junk yards in the city. An entire plumbing system may be cracked and destroyed for a few dollars worth of copper. The city has attempted to stop this form of vandalism by licensing those who transport junk, but this approach has been less successful than hoped.

Investors try a number of things to protect themselves against vandalism. Some are more successful than others. For a few very large investors, protective efforts are extensive, including removal and storage of plumbing facilities in warehouses until vacant units are ready for reoccupancy. Others board-up vacated units or secure windows and doors. Still others pay neighbors to keep an eye on empty units and to notify them when an occupied unit is vacated. Some send workmen to inspect their vacant units each day. In the past, a few kept police dogs in their empty units or hired watchmen, but these measures were too costly and are no longer used. Many investors simply do not use "For Rent" signs anymore, and keep curtains hung, shades drawn, and lights lit in empty buildings, hoping they will appear occupied. For owners of units in difficult neighborhoods, it is simply not practicable to keep the units vacant very long. Their protection against vandalism is to rent to less desirable tenants than they would like, thus increasing operating costs but saving their inventory in the short run. All of these measures are of some help. It seems clear, nevertheless, that the causes of vandalism go well beyond the context of housing policy alone and will probably have to be dealt with in other ways as well.

Unfortunately, the problem of vandalism is taken less seriously by policy-makers than it should be. The average loss incurred by investors is seen as modest; other problems in the inner city seem more pressing; and, in the opinion of some, many of the investors are getting what they deserve. The fact is, however, that vandalism appears to be the trigger which sets off waves of abandonment in stable, but marginal neighborhoods, and it is one of the primary reasons why competent investors have been withdrawing from the inner-city market. More will be said of this in Chapter 10.

Rent Escrow Law

In partial response to demands for reform of the common law of leases, a number of states have enacted statutes that allow some form of rent withholding when a building is in serious violation of state or local housing codes. In Baltimore, the law stipulates that only tenants who owe no back rent may avail themselves of its provisions. Since tenants who remain current are usually well served by their landlords, while the poorer, less desired tenants who live in the worst housing are frequently behind in their rents, the law is seldom used. To make it generally applicable to all tenants, regardless of rent-paying status, would surely aggravate the economic troubles of many investors and swell the abandonment rolls, as it already has in several other cities. Rent escrow is a program grounded on creditable intentions and discredited perceptions of market reality. Allowing a family to live rent-free in a structure that has been declared unfit for human habitation is analogous to permitting stores to give away food that is unfit for human consumption.

Public Housing

There are several dimensions along which private landlord problems and the low-rent public housing program relate. Two deserve special mention. First, the serious financial problems of local housing authorities across the country provide further indication, beyond the data which we have presented, that the problem of poor housing conditions is not caused by avaricious use of the low-income stock by landlords. Second, and perhaps most obvious, is the impact on the private sector of a large inventory of subsidized units — over one-fifth of the total low-rent stock in the case of Baltimore. While there is no unanimity among investors, many feel that public housing accepts only the more desirable tenants, leaving problem families for the private market to cope with. Housing officials argue that due to relaxation of admission requirements to public projects this is no longer true. It is true, however, that public housing, perhaps correctly, does exclude certain types of undesirable families. These families must live somewhere, so they are housed in the private market.

This situation raises the issue of who ought to be served by public housing. As mentioned in Chapter 8, the most desirable tenant from the investor viewpoint is the elderly family or individual. The reasons for this are quite obvious — the quiescent nature of old folks and the regularity with which they pay their rent. Many elderly households have not had their rents increased for a number of years and are excused from paying their rent when they face un-

usual personal crises. The record of elderly tenants clearly shows that regular
rental payments, when coupled with no unusual maintenance requirements
or water bills, permit investors to earn reasonable cash-flows even at minimum
rentals. Despite this fact, or perhaps because of it, many public housing
authorities across the country have greatly increased their focus on the elderly.
It is very questionable, though, whether authorities should continue to place
such great emphasis in their programs on groups who are heavily sought after
by responsible investors, while other sectors of the population cannot secure
decent housing at modest cost. Such a policy contributes little to social welfare and does nothing to shore up the investment climate in the inner city (15).

Public Assistance

By and large, landlords in Baltimore would prefer not to rent to families
on public assistance. While not being explicit about their attitudes, many
landlords simply equate public assistance with female-headed households receiving AFDC payments and indicate the problems they often experience in
renting to such families. Beneficiaries of Old Age Assistance, in the eyes of
these landlords, receive "retirement pensions" or "social security supplements"
rather than welfare.

The reluctance of investors to accept AFDC families stems from the extra
costs involved in renting to this group. Fatherless families are shied away from,
not simply because they are on welfare, but because it is felt that many of
them fail to adequately supervise their children, do not pay their rent promptly,
use excessive amounts of water and electricity, and cause more than average
plumbing and related maintenance problems.

Compounding the above problems is the fact that welfare families in
Baltimore receive a very low rent allowance. At the time the study was conducted, the maximum allowance was only $66 a month, including utilities,
and that amount was available only to families of seven or more persons. For
four-person households, the maximum monthly shelter allowance was $55.
These amounts were well below the median rent for minimum-quality standard
housing in the inner city.

Despite their feelings about families on public assistance, many investors
obtain a substantial portion of their revenues from welfare recipients. One-
sixth of the large investors whom we interviewed rented at least one-half their
units to AFDC households. Most of them, however, were able to shunt this
clientele onto the small landlord (16). Investors whose inventories are
supported to more than a minor degree by the public-assistance program
appear to have a symbiotic relationship with the city's Department of Social
Services and its welfare clients. The Department needs housing at very low
rents, and this group of landlords has quantities of such housing that cannot
be rented to families who can exercise a modicum of free choice. These in-

vestors do not necessarily specialize in such properties, but merely recognize the fact that environmental decline has necessitated changes in their rental policies. Rather than leave houses vacant, or partially so, thereby risking vandalism, they will rent to a welfare family for perhaps two-thirds of the rent that was charged the previous occupant.

As we mentioned in Chapter 8, the welfare program represents the largest single housing subsidy in the city, accounting for approximately 60% of the almost $40 million spent each year to improve the housing opportunities of low-income families. Yet, it supports more substandard housing then adequate shelter. Two-thirds of its clients occupy substandard units. Fully one-half of the seriously substandard stock is rented to welfare families. The results of a pilot project conducted by Baltimore's Department of Social Services suggest that many of these families can be significantly helped through higher housing allocations coupled with social services. In June 1967, the Department, under a federal grant from HEW, began a three-year demonstration program concerned with "rent deficiencies, housing that is not up to code standards, ineffective patterns of family behavior and needed social services" (17). Two hundred and eighty-one AFDC mothers (each with a minimum of four children) living in the most blighted areas in East Baltimore participated in the program and became eligible for: rent supplements up to a maximum of $54 a month above their existing rent allowance, a $5 monthly social participation allowance, one-time-only payments of up to $30 for utility turn-on, up to $125 for furniture, and up to $25 for moving expenses. In the middle of the program, they also became eligible for a utility supplement of up to $16 so long as the combined rent and utility supplement did not exceed $54 a month (18).

Family services were provided by teams composed of caseworkers, community organizers, and family aides who, in the course of the program, established a home-locator service, a pre-check system to determine whether prospective housing met code standards, a landlord-tenant council to improve communications, cooperation agreements between the program personnel and landlords whereby housing deficiencies would be removed without resort to filing official violation notices, a preventive dental program, a system of follow-ups on medical clinic appointments, assistance in money management matters, transportation aid, and other similar services. According to an official who was intimately connected with the program, approximately 70% of the participants did not want any services and did not receive anything except rent supplements which they desperately needed; another 15% not only benefited from improved housing conditions, but responded dramatically to the services offered, with measurable improvements in children's school

attendance, physical health, emotional stability and the like; and the final
15% were hard-core, multiproblem families who were not helped at all by
any facet of the program. While it is dangerous to generalize from the results
of a single demonstration effort of rather modest dimension, the experience
of this program is at least suggestive of the more positive role that local welfare departments could play in reducing housing problems of a large portion
of the low-income population.

Problem Tenants

A special dimension of the low-rent housing market, and perhaps a partial
explanation of inner-city decay, has to do with so-called problem tenan:s —
families and individuals who have lost the incentive to maintain their residential
environment and whose housing behavior ranges from disinterested to abusive.
Estimates vary as to the size and importance of this group of households and
how to deal with them. Up to now, what is meant by the term "problem
tenant" has not even been specified. According to investors, a problem tenant
is simply one who either intentionally or otherwise abuses the property, is not
a regular rent payer, or who disturbs other tenants in the structure. For our
purposes, it is necessary to break down this category more finely since families
who wantonly abuse or destroy property raise quite a different policy issue
than do those who are careless. Equally, those whose incomes are simply too
low to support a decent house present one set of problems while those who
are plagued by periodic interruptions in income present still another set.
Further, careless use of property stemming from a negative attitude toward
the landlord should be distinguished from carelessness resulting from domestic
or health disabilities. Finally, it is important to note that not all families who
exhibit deviant behavior create problems for the landlord or other tenants.

The demonstration program of the Department of Social Services, referred
to above, defined some of the characteristics of a class of families who most
likely contribute willfully or otherwise to the housing problem. "Moderate"
problem families were defined as "AFDC mothers having less than nine children; identified problems . . . primarily of an environmental nature; no more
than one major identified psychological or health problem" (19). "Severe"
problem families had nine or more children; two or more children out of wed-
lock fathered by two or more different men; unusual or severe health problems;
patterns of frequent hospitalization for physical or emotional reasons; school
problems with two or more children; problems which appear to be primarily
of an interpersonal nature" (20).

A quite different but popularly held image of the problem family pictures
a rural couple, just arrived from the South with their five children, and un-

familiar with indoor toilets, gas stoves, running water, and bathtubs. Landlords totally reject this image. Several of them said that recent in-migrants
were to be preferred over long-time Baltimore residents because of their more
positive and cooperative attitudes. Our household survey data indicate, moreover, that migrants from rural areas constitute only a tiny fraction of the city's
low-income population. The origins of the problem family lie in the urban,
not the rural, environment.

While many low-income families do create more than the average number
of problems for landlords, the true problem tenant is not representative of
the poverty population generally. Most low-income families who suffer housing deprivations make a reasonable attempt to cope with their situation. If
they create difficulties for the landlord, it is usually because their legitimate
requests have been ignored, or because of a situation beyond their control, such
as loss of income or physical disability. Inner-city investors themselves concur
in this observation. According to them, the bulk of their serious problems are
caused by only a few tenants, about 15% on the average. One-fifth of the investors indicated they had no bad tenants and another fifth claimed that
nearly one-third of their tenants were bad. Small investors had a greater
proportion of problem families than did the full-time professionals. These
estimates are, of course, those of the landlords. Allowing for the probability
that some landlords invite negative tenant behavior, the true figure for problem
tenants is probably closer to 10%. Not only does this estimate seem reasonable
in terms of our own data, but it crops up in other studies as well (21).

With respect to the kinds of difficulties which problem tenants cause, the
most common landlord complaint is careless misuse of housing. Whereas four-
fifths of the landlords indicated this to be their primary problem, less than
one-fifth attributed excessive wear and tear to deliberate tenant abuse of
the property. Also, while only a few landlords indicated that insufficient
tenant income was the most serious problem confronting them, one-half said
that rent delinquencies and "skip-outs" were the most serious problem for
which their tenants were responsible. The Department of Social Services
pilot program found that 6% of the AFDC participants "had to move within
the past six months because they could not pay the rent" (22). Considering
that the welfare program does not reach all who need assistance, the proportion of low-income families in the city who are involuntarily mobile might be
much larger (23).

Although it is risky to make any judgment as to the proportion of substandard dwelling units that can be directly attributed to the actions of
problem tenants, the probable figure would be something less than 10%. Included in this estimate are units which have been destroyed by vandalism as

a result of unannounced terminations of occupancy. Included also are units that are abused or partially destroyed by tenants who cannot cope with their individual and family responsibilities generally. One of the reasons why problem families are directly responsible for only a small fraction of poor quality housing in the inner city is that such families, by and large, are shunted to housing that is already in deteriorated condition. They are not generally the cause of original deterioration; they only accelerate it.

Since the proportion of tenants causing problems is so small and the probable proportion of the bad inventory for which they are directly responsible is, likewise, not very great, a question is raised as to why the average inner-city landlord is in such trouble. Part of the reason is that problem families represent difficulties well beyond their numbers and direct impact. Their actions raise the cost and lower the quality of housing for other poor families. Almost 60% of the landlords interviewed said that good tenants move as a result of the behavior of bad tenants, thus increasing turnover and vandalism while reducing further the already dwindling supply of funds for maintenance and improvement. Additionally, members of some problem families behave destructively in the neighborhood as well as in the home. They litter streets, vandalize properties, disrupt classrooms, and assault citizens.

Because the impact of problem families is a cumulative one and is contributing to the strong desire of responsible investors to get out of the business, the city ought to be concerned explicitly with this issue. Unfortunately, several existing policies exaggerate rather than lessen the problem. For example, the Baltimore Housing Authority has initiated and successfully implemented a policy which declares ineligible for future occupancy of public housing any family that leaves public housing while delinquent in rent. In a disaggregated private sector, such tight controls are clearly impossible. The net result of skip-outs and evictions for non-payment of rent is merely a reallocation of problem tenants among investors. And the individual tenant is not banished forever from a substantial sector of the stock.

Because of the negative effects which problem families have on the low-income market, it does not seem practicable to undertake any broad-based efforts to improve the investment climate and housing conditions without simultaneously addressing the needs of this group. Precisely how to deal with these families, however, remains a mystery. Some persons argue that the families must be dispersed into therapeutic environments, while others favor supportive services "on-site," and still others stress the need for a "comprehensive" anti-poverty effort. These approaches take time. They leave open the question of providing adequate housing for problem families and limiting their adverse effects on others while waiting for related programs to achieve perceptible results. We confess to having no answers. But certainly present policy, which simply forces these families on to private landlords, should not be allowed to continue.

MORTGAGE FINANCE AND HOME OWNERSHIP

In his study of the declining West Side of New York City, Chester Rapkin emphasized the fact that "every real estate market depends for its sustenance upon the flow and availability of mortgage credit" and that in so-called declining areas, the "flow of new money declines to a trickle, making the replacement of worn out equipment more difficult and/or rehabilitation virtually impossible" (24). He concluded that under such circumstances deterioration accelerates, thus "converting decline into galloping decay" (25).

In many cities, the dearth of mortgage capital is a critical factor in the declining inner-city market and in the middle ring as well. Both FHA and traditional lending institutions have been reluctant to insure or finance the sale of moderately priced housing for low-income families in older areas. As a consequence, existing homeowners who move from the inner city usually are forced to sell their homes to professional investors who have sufficient cash, ready access to non-institutional funds, or access to mortgage credit at the same lending institutions that will not finance home purchases by ordinary families.

This selective kind of credit squeeze produces a number of seriously unfavorable results. First, it forces out-migrating families to sell at depressed prices and, if outstanding mortgage balances exceed values, prevents some of them from moving at all.

Second, it denies home ownership opportunities to many families who could afford to make purchases if decent financing were available.

Third, it raises the cost of housing to many families, since their monthly out-of-pocket housing expenditures as owners would be less than their present gross rental payments. This is because as owners they would not be obliged to earn a profit, would have no vacancy losses, and could perform some of the maintenance themselves.

Fourth, it shifts the inventory to a class of owners who as a group do not nurture the inventory with the care exercised by owner occupants.

Fifth, it discourages and sometimes prevents investors from maintaining and upgrading their properties.

Finally, it forces lower-income families who fervently desire ownership to seek non-institutional loans which bear less attractive terms than do regular mortgage loans. For them the privilege of home ownership exacts a heavy price. This aspect of the problem is particularly severe in Baltimore. Because most of the older stock lends itself to home ownership, there has been, until quite recently, a large amount of non-institutional lending to families who could not obtain regular financing. Investors have purchased units from departing families and resold them to in-migrants on land installment contracts (LICs) or leases with options to buy. In effect, they have been non-institutional financial intermediaries who have enabled sellers to liquidate and potential buyers to realize their dreams. They have been most active at the edges of the inner city and among the near-poor and lower middle-income families.

At the time of our first household survey in 1968, about 9,000 families were buying under lease-purchase arrangements. All of their homes were either close to or well above housing code standards. We guess that another 5,000 owner occupants who now either have ordinary mortgages or own free and clear originally acquired their homes through lease purchase.

So far, so good. The investors who have engaged in this activity would appear to have provided a much needed service. Regrettably, the cost of the service is so great for the buyer that the entire practice has come under heavy criticism, and with increasing use of FHA Section 221-d-2 financing few LICs are being written. In order to clarify some of the issues concerning LICs, the following discussion describes the characteristics and use of this form of home financing by lower-income families.

The Land Installment Contract: Some Facts, Fictions, and Much Emotion

Despite the criticism which has been directed toward it, the land installment contract is inherently no more nefarious than is the more traditional mortgage. Nor, as some people think, is the term simply a catch-all used to describe a variety of individual, ad hoc arrangements between particular buyers and sellers of real property. It is in fact specifically defined in the Maryland Annotated Code, as follows:

> A legally binding executory agreement under which (a) the vendor agrees to sell an interest in property to the vendee and the vendee agrees to pay the purchase price in five or more subsequent payments exclusive of any down payment, and (b) the vendor retains title as security for the vendee's obligation (26).

In less formal and legalistic terms, a land installment contract provides the buyer with immediate possession of the premises in question, for which he will pay a particular sum each week or month, each payment contributing toward such costs as ground rent, taxes, insurance, interest, and principal. State law prohibits interest rates on LIC transactions from exceeding those of conventional mortgage loans; and, as in the case of the latter, interest on an LIC is paid only on the outstanding balance of the principal. As indicated above, title to property sold on an LIC remains vested in the seller until all principal has been paid, or until the buyer is able to secure a conventional

Table 9.4. Hypothetical Land Installment Transaction for a Baltimore Row House

Summary

Sold for		$13,000	(100%)
Price paid	$ 7,000		(54%0
Purchase commission	100		
Title and allied costs	100		
Prepaid items	150		
Mortgage loan closing,			
including points	250		
Renovation	800		
Sales commission	300		
Carrying costs: Taxes, interest,			
ground rent during renovation	100		
Overhead	600		
Total costs	$ 9,400	9,400	(72%)
Gross profit (deferred)		$ 3,600	(38%)[1]

Cash In and Out as of Date of Sale

Total Cash In:		
Down payment	$ 400	
Mortgage	9,000	
	$ 9,400	
Total Cash Out:		
Total direct costs	$ 8,800	
Total indirect costs (overhead)	600	
Deficit		$ 000[2]

Financing

Annual loan payments by buyer to investor	
($13,000 loan for 18 years at 6%)	$ 1,200
Annual loan payments by investor to	
lending institution ($9,400 loan	
for 18 years at 6%)	867
Gross proceeds per year	$ 333
Gross proceeds over 18 years	
(333 × 18)	$ 6,000
Cost of administrating the loan (10%)	600
Net proceeds over 18 years	--
(300 × 18)	$ 5,400
Present value of $300 annual income	
stream received over an 18-year	
period, assuming a 15%	
discount rate	$ 3,250
Present value of $300 annual income	
received over an 18-year period,	
assuming a 15% discount rate	$ 1,840 (continued)

Present value of $300 annual income
   stream received for 10 years, at which
   time loan to buyer is replaced by
   mortgage loan, and investor cashes
   out, assuming a 15% discount rate $ 2,095

---

[1] The 38% is based on a total cost of $9,400.
[2] Normally, Cash In will be slightly less than Cash Out. The two have been made equal here to facilitate explanation of the details of the contract.

mortgage after having accrued sufficient equity in the property. Foreclosure procedures, in the event of default, are regulated by state law, and are quite similar to those involving conventionally financed transactions, including disposal of the property at public auction.

There are also a number of differences between the typical LIC transaction and a conventionally financed purchase, most of which stem from the fact that the seller retains title to the property while providing permanent, long-term financing. First, although the transaction is recorded in the city or county where the property is located, there are no transfer taxes, title fees, prepaid items, or related settlement costs due at the time of sale because the title does not change hands. Also, no points are paid at time of closing since points and other costs are incorporated into the total price of the property. Because the seller finances the transaction, down payments are negotiable, commonly as low as $200 or $300, which is simply not possible today in a conventionally financed sale. Possession of the premises is rapid, usually a day or two after the contract is signed. Finally, the term of the contract is also negotiated by buyer and seller, with the typical contract specifying a 12-year to 18-year term. This term is a residual element in the contract inasmuch as the seller simply adds up all costs associated with a sale, and using his mortgage tables, looks for a term that will result in weekly or monthly costs that can be reasonably borne by the buyer. For some purchases, 12 years might be appropriate; for others, a longer period.

While the LIC was not originally created to finance the sale of homes to lower-income families, it is the primary means through which these families have purchased housing in many cities.

The details of a typical land installment transaction are presented in Table 9.4. To the base acquisition price of the house ($7,000) are added purchase commissions and allied costs such as financing charges to the investor and title search. Next, renovation and redecoration expenses are incurred and must be reflected in the ultimate sales price, along with sales commission and overhead costs. In the normal sale by an owner occupant about half of these costs would either be borne by the seller or not incurred at all. Finally, a gross profit margin is added.

In the present example, the $7,000 single-family row house is resold for $13,000. Gross profit is anticipated to be $3,600 or 38% earned over an 18-year period. To finance the transaction, the investor interposes his own credit rating between that of the buyer and the lending institution. He receives a mortgage loan for $9,400 from the institution and in turn lends the buyer $13,000. Here, an 18-year loan for $13,000 at 6% will cost the ultimate purchaser $100 a month, while the investor will pay out $72.30 (Table 9.4). The present value of the difference in the two income streams, less an allowance for administering the loan and any deficit at time of sale, is the investor's net profit, assuming the loan does not go sour.

Over the 18-year life of the contract, the aggregate difference between what the investor receives from the buyer and what he pays to the lender is $6,000. The present value of this income stream, discounted at the 6% mortgage interest rate is exactly equal to the investor's gross profit at time of sale — $3,600. After subtracting the cost of administering the loan, the total flow is $3,000. Given the higher risks in this sector of the market, however, a discount rate of 6% is unrealistically low. Without actuarial data, an appropriate discount rate cannot be determined, but 15% does not seem too far out of line to use for discussion purposes. Applying this rate, it may be seen that the present value of the $3,600-deferred profit is only $1,840. Assuming the loan is closed out after only 10 years, a not unlikely possibility, the present value of the profit is $2,095.

In other words, if the investor were able to buy and resell immediately, he should, if our assumptions are reasonable, be willing to accept a price somewhere in the neighborhood of $11,500, representing a profit of 22% on the transaction. He does not have this option, because the appraised value of the dwelling, for lending purposes, would fall well below this figure, and because in most cases the buyer or the property would not be accepted for a loan by any lending institution.

The above figures are viewed quite differently in various sectors of the Baltimore community. Blacks, who account for the bulk of the purchases under LICs, feel strongly that they have been exploited, while investors claim their returns are not excessive. Both arguments are substantially correct. Although the question of whether profits are excessive relative to the risks and expertise involved cannot be answered without more information, profits do not seem grossly unreasonable. Perhaps the $13,000 house should be sold for $12,000, but certainly not less. And yet, it is equally clear that when families who are good credit risks are forced by institutional lending practices to pay as much as $12,000 to $13,000 for an $8,000 home, something is very, very wrong. Several investors said their cumulative default rate on land installment contracts is around 25%–30%. If this experience is representative of investor experience generally, then a substantial number of low- and moderate income families participating in land installment transactions are successfully coping with higher monthly carrying charges than would be necessary under more traditional forms of mortgage financing. That is to say, an overestimation of mortgage risks, both borrower and property, have caused traditional lenders in the city to withdraw their support from the inner-city market. city market.

Our study was unable to determine how many LIC buyers had actually tried to obtain institutional financing and had been rejected, how many might have been rejected if they had tried, or how many who might have qualified for regular mortgage loans were unaware that such financing existed. And of those who were or would have been turned down, we obviously have no knowledge as to the number of situations in which the rejection related or would have related to the credit worthiness of the buyer as opposed to the condition of the structure being purchased or the neighborhood. The argument that LICs are exploitative is based largely on the premise that most LIC buyers are good credit risks who are forced to use LICs because they are denied institutional financing. It is the feeling of LIC sellers (investors), on the other hand, that exclusive of not having enough cash for down payment and closing costs, many LIC buyers do have certain characteristics, e.g., advanced age, previous difficulties in meeting financial obligations, and low or unstable income, which would be worrisome to the average mortgage-loan officer who must answer to directors, stockholders, and federal and state supervisory agencies. These investors argue that the default rate on LICs is satisfactory, not because of customized loan servicing which helps buyers avoid and cope with financial difficulties stemming from strikes, layoffs, sickness, domestic problems, etc. (27). Unfortunately, we cannot evaluate these arguments.

If investor experience is as satisfactory as it seems to be, the lower monthly carrying charges of institutional loans should reduce delinquencies even more, holding borrower characteristics and quality of loan servicing constant. It is clear that some kind of risk-insurance program similar to FHA's 221-d-2 program could considerably broaden the base of home ownership in the inner city, and largely within the existing private market context. Development of such a program would seem to merit top priority (28).

GOOD MANAGEMENT: THE KEY TO SUCCESS

It should be clear by now that the simple notion of slumlordism contributes little to an understanding of the dynamics of decay in the inner city, or to the development of remedial strategies. In the low-rent market, as in the rental market generally, investor income is ordinarily maximized by carefully screening tenants, maintaining full occupancy, losing no rent from existing tenants, minimizing turnover, satisfying reasonable tenant demands, and keeping maintenance and related operating expenses to a reasonable percentage of gross rents. "Milking" makes sense only if the owner anticipates that the economic life of the asset in question is about to terminate.

In the absence of the "bad guy" explanation of property deterioration, and with both poverty and racial discrimination possibly of less direct importance than generally realized, other variables must be found to help explain some of the fundamental problems rooted in the inner-city market. One variable which came through consistently in the course of our survey was *management,* broadly defined to include that collection of both public and private policies and practices which guide and characterize investor behavior with respect to property acquisition, rent schedules, tenant selection and eviction, maintenance and related services, tenant relations, and finally, general mode of organization and operation. While each of these components may be more finely disaggregated, management is, above all, an integrative function.

The successful manager of low-rent housing combines a number of highly specialized organizational, technical, and communicative skills that are not required to the same degree by the ordinary property manager. Since the population he serves has a larger than average number of families who can create problems for him, he must be adept at screening potential tenants and at explaining to them the provisions of the rental contract. Having accepted a family for a unit which, because of its age, requires frequent attention, he must strike a delicate balance between excessive heed to tenant complaints and failure to respond in a timely fashion to legitimate requests. And since he must frequently refuse requests, his manner cannot alienate, or his relationship with good tenants will deteriorate. Just as important, he must regularly make repairs and replacements on his own initiative, so the tenant will realize that he takes an interest in the property. Perhaps his most difficult role is that of policeman trying to enforce various rules for the general welfare of his tenants and neighbors in a firm yet diplomatic manner. As with the police, his efforts in this regard are more often resented than appreciated. In brief, he manages both real estate and people. Today, some investors do fine on the business side but fail miserably in their tenant relations, and as a result, they are in deep trouble.

Curiously, the importance of sound management of the existing stock of housing of marginal quality, until very recently, has not been even remotely recognized in deliberations of national housing policy. As part of the study, we attempted a rough evaluation of the quality of management in the inner city and its relationship to housing conditions. This exercise proved to be most difficult. Our interviews with landlords revealed the inexperience of many managers, but probably failed to identify those who could talk a good game. Checking landlord responses against the condition of their dwellings in our sample, as we did, was useful, but most investors vary their maintenance policies depending on the location and occupancy of the structure. As rational economic men, they may appear, therefore, to behave like slumlords in one situation and like long-term investors in another. Tenant opinions of landlords provided another useful measure of management quality. Seventy percent of low-income respondents thought their landlords were doing a good job and another 5% thought their landlords were at least trying. However, respondents' ratings of their dwelling units, presented in Chapter 4, strongly suggest that their housing horizons are rather limited. They expect little and that is what they get. Taking all our independent assessments into consideration, we concluded that about half the low-rent inventory in Baltimore is not well managed. On the other hand, the best managers with whom we spoke not only had exceptional business acumen but seemed much more sensitive to the needs and problems of low-income families than most public and nonprofit agencies that purport to serve these families. The following two sections of this chapter, based primarily on our interviews with these managers, will explain further the importance of management and detail some of its major components from the standpoint of both business and social relations.

Good Management: Some Business Considerations

A dimension of good management that is often overlooked is the ability to turn down what others might think is an attractive deal, to know the price to pay for properties actually acquired, and to know when to sell. The successful investor generally will only consider properties within close proximity of each other so that they can be properly supervised and reached quickly by maintenance crews. We were sometimes present when investors were solicited to buy properties. It was the good manager who recognized the importance of the maintenance and servicing aspects of the rental business, and who rejected a tempting offer that others, based on selling prices alone, might have accepted. As a matter of fact, not infrequently we had the intuitive feeling, as we interviewed investors throughout the inner city, that a reallocation of properties among existing investors would improve the collective maintenance and servicing abilities of the investment community as a whole.

Perhaps the most important business dimension of good management of inner-city properties is the ability to service housing at less than retail prices. Illustrative of this point are the arrangements used by one large-scale investor whose maintenance expenditures averaged only $220 per unit in 1969 even though his inventory was of high quality. To hold down plumbing repair costs, this investor had in his employ a master plumber and a plumber's assistant, both of whom held full-time jobs with the State of Maryland. The two plumbers had a contractual arrangement with the investor to work before and after their regular jobs, and on weekends, at an hourly rate that was only one-fourth of what plumbers charge retail. The investor was, however, aware of the need to keep his plumbers content with their arrangement, and in order to sweeten the pie, he had compiled a number of plumbing jobs, each of which averaged a particular number of man-hours of labor, for which he paid even if the jobs were done in less time. It was arrangements like these that made it lucrative to "moonlight" for him. Using similar arrangements with other trades-men and suppliers, he was able to have hot water heaters replaced, roofs re-paired, floors refinished, and painting done all at savings of 50% or more. Without the extensive relationships and contacts he had developed, he could not possibly afford to maintain his inventory at its currently high level of quality.

Another part of the business side of good management of inner-city real estate which seems to come only with extensive experience pertains to the ability to judge how much work a potential acquisition will require in order to make it attractive to good tenants, how much that work will cost, and the rents that the renovated units can command. Many successful investors, for example, believe that the kitchen is the most important room in the house, and allocate a good bit of their improvement budgets to such things as floor tile, new or rebuilt appliances, and built-in cabinets. Also, they are of the judgment that the time to put money into a house is at acquisition, so tenants can be convinced of the landlord's interest in providing them the best possible accommodations for their money.

Management and Social Relations

As already suggested, managing low-income housing is, in effect, managing people more than property. It requires a special personality, not just enlightened policies. The successful manager knows his tenants well. He has their respect and, not infrequently, their affection. But this is not enough. To make money he has to develop and effectively utilize competent maintenance personnel, make intelligent decisions about rent increases, and protect the neighborhood environment by persuading owners of nearby property to maintain their premises. As part businessman, part social worker, and part eleemosynary institution, the low-rent property manager is a unique community resource. That most managers cannot be expected to play all roles well should be more widely understood than it apparently is.

The human-relations side of the low-rent housing equation begins with the landlord's attempt to screen his potential tenantry thoroughly, renting where possible only to those who appear to be low-risk families. While all landlords screen tenants, this process is especially important in the low-rent sector. As indicated earlier, property abuse, rent delinquencies, and high turnover, can

destroy otherwise profitable operations. Consequently, not only do most of
the investors who were interviewed require potential renters to fill out applications, but many go beyond this, filing for a credit rating, talking with the
present employer and landlord, and paying a visit to the applicant's present
residence in order to observe housekeeping habits. If any of the findings are
disturbing, the rental application will be rejected. Many times landlords do not
advertise their vacancies, relying instead upon their trusted tenants to refer
potential occupants to them. As one might expect, the better the inventory,
the more selective the investor can be, and it is not unusual for more than 30
families to apply for a good unit in a good neighborhood.

In addition to careful screening, many investors devote a good deal of time
to discussing landlord-tenant responsibilities with potential renters, in the
conviction that poor communication and misunderstanding about who is responsible for what is at the root of many housing management problems. At
least one investor who was interviewed makes it very clear to his office staff
that no rental agreement is to be made with any family before there is complete agreement as to the division of responsibilities between the firm and the
family. As a precautionary measure, he requests that each member of his staff
who screens an accepted applicant file an internal form detailing what was discussed and identifying the person who showed the unit to the tenant.

As the general quality of a dwelling or neighborhood declines, opportunities
for the landlord to be selective shrink accordingly because there are fewer ap-
plicants for each vacant unit. At the same time, the risks of keeping a unit un-
occupied for any length of time are correspondingly greater, so even good
managers rent to marginal families rather than risk the chances of the unit
being vandalized. Also they accept occasional rent losses and delinquencies if
tenants are otherwise acceptable. This point is worthy of some elaboration.

A most sensitive aspect of landlord-tenant relations in the inner city, and
one which has evoked much controversy, is evictions. Low-income families
have periodic interruptions in income and an uneven pattern of expenses for
nonhousing necessities. As a result, landlords are faced with continual requests
for rent forgiveness. The common belief is that landlords ignore these requests
and evict unreasonably and unnecessarily. This may have been so in times past
when good tenants were easy to find, but today the competent investor evicts
only as a last resort. He would rather forego part of the rent than lose an otherwise good tenant. Evictions tend to be reserved for families who are abusive
of the property or for tenants who are no longer able to pay enough of the
face rent to cover the investor's cash outlay. It is not unusual, however, to find
inexperienced investors who are unwilling to tolerate rent delinquencies, and
who consequently evict families only to have their units stand unnecessarily
vacant and exposed to vandalism. The good manager becomes very familiar
with the paying habits of each family. In that way, he can sometimes uncover

problems before they become serious. For example, many tenants stop paying rent a few weeks before they are going to move. Managers who talk with these families when they become delinquent sometimes save not only a few weeks' rent, but their units as well.

Once their units are occupied, skilled managers devote most of their efforts to keeping them that way. They encourage their tenants to inform them of any problems not only because it makes sense to show tenants that they care about them, but more importantly because they can often save money if maintenance problems are caught early. Many investors complained that their tenants do not inform them early enough about problems. In order to keep track of the maintenance needs of their units, therefore, they do a good deal of spot-checking each day on their way to and from their offices. The importance of investor sensitivity to the periodic special needs of their tenants should not be underestimated. A friendly response to the request for repainting or papering the living room just prior to Thanksgiving or the Christmas holidays, even though the house is not due for a paint job, keeps relationships on a sound basis.

Many good managers are aware of nonhousing and housing-related needs of their tenants and, within their limited abilities, attempt to meet some of those needs. One of the most notable efforts in this regard was initiated in the early 1960's when an innovative landlord hired a social worker to perform personalized services for his low-income tenants. The landlord paid the salary of the social worker and donated a three-story row house for her to use as a base of operations. Over time, the house became known as Echo House and the operations were placed under the direction of the Echo House Foundation which, today, is privately financed. Now, Echo House is involved in assisting between 300 and 500 families and is engaged in services and activities ranging from intensive family counseling to recreation programs, tutoring, legal aid, and community organization.

Referring to the management function as one of the important explanatory variables in the dynamics of decay may seem an overstatement to some knowledgeable observers. While the collapse of core-city housing markets has not been due to poor management, it has become increasingly clear that the type and quality of management that would be satisfactory in most sectors of the existing stock is inappropriate and inadequate in the inner city. It is true that even excellent management cannot bridge the income gap, or cope with the serious problem family, or overcome the effects of a bad neighborhood environment. But it is equally true that programs directed at these other dilemmas will not be very successful unless the management problem is solved. The importance of good management has finally been recognized by HUD in its various subsidy programs. Over four-fifths of the low-income population, however, is privately housed.

CHAPTER 10
Images of the Housing Problem

A principal thesis of this study is that debate over housing policy arises in large part from purely political considerations which are beyond the realm of technical analysis: differences in opinion as to the relative importance of various housing and nonhousing goals; and related disagreement over what is an equitable distribution of national income and wealth. Also underlying most disputes, however, are conflicting assumptions regarding the social, economic, and market forces which produce blight and slums and which any remedial effort would have to alter. Unfortunately, these assumptions seem nearly always to be left either implicit or partially articulated, resulting in much unnecessary and misdirected controversy.

In the previous chapter we attempted to reduce such sources of conflict by examining inner-city market dynamics at the micro level. This chapter continues that effort at the macro level. Nine widely held notions about the origins of low-income housing problems in large cities are briefly explored. Because none of the nine has ever been presented as a completely reasoned theory, we have chosen to refer to them as "images" of the problem. Although the images overlap here and there, each has a dominant organizing theme. The nine themes are: the filtering process, inner-city obsolescence, spatial concentration of low-income families, low income itself, problem families, greedy investors, exploitative system, racial discrimination, and the deteriorating social fabric of inner-city neighborhoods. In the sections to follow, each image will be described and evaluated, and the special case of housing abandonment will be analyzed in an attempt to arrive at an image of the problem which accords with our own perception of reality.

FILTERING IMAGE

According to this traditional view of the problem, low-income families occupy unsatisfactory living accommodations primarily because of an inherent defect in the functioning of the housing market. Nearly all of them acquire homes through the filtering process, inheriting structures that no longer meet the needs of upper-income households. By itself, there is nothing necessarily wrong with this system of rationing shelter. Most of us live in used housing. However, because of the slow rate at which the residential inventory depreciates in value, by the time dwelling units come within the financial reach of poor families, most of the units, it is alleged, are in unsatisfactory condition. Although direct subsidies to the poor would be one way to solve this problem, a central assumption of the filtering image is that a cheaper and more politically acceptable alternative would be to make filtering "work" − to accelerate the process so as to free-up housing for low-income households much sooner than is now possible. According to the image, this could best be accomplished by subsidizing new construction for middle-income families. Such a strategy would be superior to direct subsidies to the poor, because at any given subsidy level it could induce a greater amount of new construction than could low-income subsidies, and thereby could serve, indirectly through the filtering process, more of the low-income population. If the same total subsidy were distributed to the same number of low-income families, it would not be sufficient to enable them to compete in the new construction market.

There are several problems with the filtering image, aside from the fact that it seems to be based on inadequate understanding of the filtering process. First, it looks at only one-half of the picture − low-income families improving themselves as they move upward in the stock. It does not examine what happens to the homes and neighborhoods these families leave behind. It ignores evidence suggesting that accelerated filtering, unaccompanied by market support mechanisms for the inner city, accelerates decay. Implicitly, it makes the incorrect assumption that these vacated neighborhoods are all bad, would be entirely vacated in short order, and could be quickly demolished. Second, it assumes that if low-income families did manage to obtain homes in good condition, they would have the necessary resources to keep them in adequate repair. Third, it fails to recognize that demand-side subsidies to the poor would, as have rising incomes for the population generally, precipitate an upward filtering of families which would ultimately play itself out in the form of increased demand for new homes and apartments by many of the same middle-income families whom filtering strategies seek to subsidize.

The filtering image does have validity in a more restricted context. Since the volume of new residential construction must be sufficient to accommodate total population growth and since at least half of the population cannot afford new homes, filtering is the only means by which low-income families can get any homes at all, good or bad. Yet it is theoretically possible that upper-income families would not always discard old homes and move into new units as fast as the increase of less affluent households required. To prevent this from happening, housing subsidies for the nonpoor may often be necessary. But when such subsidies are used to induce improvement in the stock rather than accommodate growth, they are open to question on both efficiency and equity grounds.

OBSOLESCENCE IMAGE

This image pictures the inner-city housing problem as stemming in large part from the market consequence of preferences for suburban living and the rise in incomes which permits these preferences to be satisfied. As families who can afford to do so move outward to new homes, they initiate a filtering process which initially makes better structures available to low-income families and ultimately results in the abandonment of the worst sectors of the inner-city stock. As values decline, however, home purchases become impossible, landlords' attitudes about upkeep shift, responsible ownership gradually disappears, institutional lenders withdraw from the market, the upgrading activities that occur on a regular basis in stable neighborhoods in order to combat obsolescence cease, and even the city reduces its level of services. Thus several forms of neighborhood abandonment occur even while the structures are occupied. In contrast to what is assumed in the filtering image, the filtering process is seen here as being partially perverse in its effects; the poor are in a real sense the victims as well as the beneficiaries of housing progress. They get less housing for their money than they would in a stable market. Demand-side subsidies do nothing to ameliorate the problem, because there is no way for individual owners to prevent site and locational obsolescence; they cannot alter either lot sizes or street patterns or surrounding land uses.

The key element of the image, though, concerns middle- and upper-income families. Since their desire for low density and for greenery is so widely held and deep-seated, and since inner-city row housing cannot readily be adapted to satisfy these preferences, residential rehabilitation, better city services, and related programs to prop up the inner city are incapable of stemming the outward flow. Only demolition and reconstruction can save the situation. Therefore, out-migration of low-income families should be encouraged so as to hasten the day when redevelopment can be launched. Within both city and suburb, the rebuilding process should be more cognizant of new societal values that began to emerge in the 1960's.

In its interpretation of both housing preferences and market dynamics this image seems essentially correct. As a description of what eventually should, and hopefully will, happen to the urban structure, it is quite appealing. It projects a picture of newness, cleanliness, beauty, and equality. Nevertheless, parts of the image are open to question. The fact that not only the worst housing in the city is being abandoned but also many fairly good structures as well would suggest that the explanation of market dynamics is incomplete. And the notion that the present row house pattern in the inner city is inherently obsolete and cannot be made attractive to middle- and upper-income families ignores neighborhoods such as Georgetown in Washington, D.C. and Bolton Hill in Baltimore as well as the rising volume of row house construction nationally. Its emphasis on out-migration and total renewal implicitly presumes a causal relationship between the physical and social environment which cannot be demonstrated; it suggests that deprived families who move to new neighborhoods will leave their personal problems and negative social relationships behind.

Most serious, the policy inferences drawn from the image lack a sense of immediacy. It will take a very long time even to begin to implement a suburban-migration/total-renewal strategy on a large enough scale to help significant numbers of inner-city families. The question arises, therefore, as to what is to be done in the meantime — the meantime being at least 20 to 30 years. An entire generation of families would have to be written off. Moreover, given the downward trends described earlier, many central cities do not have the luxury of looking only to the long-term. If decay is not arrested, it could swamp long-term programs.

LOW-INCOME IMAGE

This image, which is the most commonly held of all, emphasizes the lack of resources of the poor (1). As the outward movement of upper-income families occurs, the structures which are left behind for occupancy by low-income households are, contrary to what is assumed in the filtering image, in reasonably good condition. However, the costs of financing and operating these structures do not decline sufficiently to permit rents which the poor can afford unless adequate maintenance is sacrificed. Conversions to multifamily occupancy may raise rental incomes sufficiently to forestall decay for a time, but they also lead to increased wear and tear, so eventually deterioration wins the day anyway. The process is hastened by the competitive disadvantage of low-income families in dealing with a class of landlords who enjoy a partial monopoly in the market and who demonstrate less concern for the well-being of their tenants, structures, and neighborhoods than do landlords generally. It also is hastened by the powerlessness of the poor to prevent their neighborhoods from being inundated by bars, junkies, abandoned cars, and other unpleasant accoutrements. Thus, as long as there are poor families, so the reasoning goes, there will be substandard housing, overcrowding, and an unsuitable living environment. Housing preferences and market dynamics may also play a part, but they are secondary to low income. What is needed to correct the situation, therefore, are either employment and income-maintenance programs or, if these are not possible, some form of housing subsidy.

The low-income image accords very well with existing measures of the problem. As discussed earlier, in Baltimore almost 90% of the very worst structures — those which either must receive maximum-rehabilitation treatment or be demolished — are occupied by poor families, as are nearly two-thirds of the remaining substandard units. While it is true that almost half of the low-income population currently resides in adequate accommodations and that over 10% of non-low-income households can be found in unacceptable quarters, these figures probably understate the importance of income in determining housing quality. Many of the non-low-income families who reside in bad housing may only recently have moved out of a poverty status, having benefited by generally rising incomes during the 1960's. Similarly, many of the low-income households who own or rent good units may not have a history of inadequate earnings. If a family's average income over a five to ten-year period were correlated with housing quality, the relationship between the two should be more striking and the low-income image correspondingly strengthened (2). Further, it is likely that if adequacy of income were evaluated, not with respect to a standard based on average consumption patterns, but rather with reference to the particular needs of each family, the relationship of inadequate income to inadequate housing would become even more pronounced. Finally, it has been observed that many low-income families who pay rents which would normally be sufficient to obtain decent dwellings are poorly housed because their many other income-related problems have made them relatively oblivious to their physical environment.

There can be no question that significant improvements in housing quality for poor families will not occur without a corresponding rise in their incomes. This fact, however, does not validate the precise causal relationships that are assumed in the low-income image. There are, indeed, several flaws in the image. First, although it provides an obvious explanation as to why low-income families occupy the least desirable dwellings in the housing inventory, it offers no reason as to why so many of these units are of such inferior quality, nor why the poor are much better housed in some communities than in others, nor why decay has frequently infiltrated nonpoverty neighborhoods.

Second, in correctly assuming that rent is a function of income and that housing quality is a function of rent, the image overlooks the fairly broad range of rent-income ratios at any particular income level and the equally wide band of quality at each rent level. Differences in housing preferences among low-income families, and in the cost of providing housing services to various types of families, and in the way the market functions in the inner and outer city, significantly weaken the relationship between income and quality.

Third, the image is silent on the question of housing abandonment. Yet it is commonly argued that abandonment, one of whose root causes is *rising* income, may sometimes initiate its own cycles of decay (3).

Finally, the image is not entirely correct in its assumption that poor-quality structures occupied by low-income families have become substandard largely as a result of insufficient funds for maintenance. Some of the structures, though a rapidly declining number in most large cities, were either substandard when they were constructed or became so as housing code standards were raised over the years. More important, our data suggest that a minority of families pay rents that are so low as to preclude adequate maintenance in stable, well-functioning markets. Thus to the extent the low-income image suggests that income-maintenance programs or housing allowances would be an effective housing intervention, it requires a collateral assumption that the serious imperfections which obtain in many inner-city markets would be eliminated or circumvented in the process.

LOW-INCOME CONCENTRATION IMAGE

This view of the problem, elaborated in detail in Chapters 7 and 12, argues that although low income by itself may be less important in explaining blight and decay than is commonly alleged, the concentration of disadvantaged populations into separate geographic areas greatly aggravates housing and neighborhood problems, not only for these populations but also for those around them, and leads to other difficulties as well. In addition to the social dysfunctioning which is associated with large clusters of poor families, market failure, particularly in the area of housing, can be traced to these agglomerations. In growing urban areas, for example, low-income neighborhoods pose a constant threat to adjacent blocks and sometimes seem to precipitate withdrawal of investment funds from these blocks and their premature deterioration, just by being nearby. Although the precise way in which this happens is a matter of speculation, it is clear that the dynamics of decay in large metropolitan areas where the poor collect in massive numbers are quite different

from what obtains in smaller communities which have a similar proportion of
low-income families but few low-income neighborhoods. It does not necessarily follow from this observation, however, that the most cost-effective way
to alter negative market dynamics or to create decent neighborhoods or to
reduce poverty is to disperse the poor.

THE PROBLEM-FAMILY IMAGE

Attempts to explain why so many low-income families do *not* live in substandard housing have led many persons to this image. It presumes and stresses
a lack of middle-class norms of cleanliness and responsibility among the poor.
As filtering enables low-income families to move into better housing, many
of these families create the forces of decline, not because the rents which they
pay are too low to permit adequate maintenance, but because their behavior
raises the cost of maintenance and management. Investors, faced with vanish-
ing cash-flows and perceiving surrounding owners in the same situation,
eventually cease to try very hard to maintain their stock. So the ring of blight
spreads, not because of a collapse of market supports and investor greed, as in
several of the other images, but because of bad tenantry.

The problem-family image, insofar as it refers only to behavior toward
housing and not to social pathology generally, can probably be rejected on
factual grounds. As mentioned earlier, according to inner-city landlords themselves, problem families comprise a very small proportion of the tenantry, on
the average. Over a period of time, however, a bad tenant may abuse a number
of different dwellings and adversely affect entire structures. In some neighborhoods, moreover, such tenants, even though few in number, could conceivably
constitute a critical mass, and in both their housing and nonhousing behavior
reduce the attractiveness of the neighborhoods to the point where not all of
the dwelling units could be rented and would have to be abandoned. It is
equally possible, therefore, that identifying and concentrating on the small
minority of troublemakers would have a much more favorable impact on the
market than the numbers themselves would suggest. To ascribe a major part
of blight and decay to problem families, however, is to overlook too many
other variables.

GREEDY-INVESTOR IMAGE

Contrapuntal to the problem-family image is the belief that slums are
caused primarily by slumlords — owners who seek a quick dollar by crowding
their structures and charging monopoly rents to families who have nowhere

else to go. The image usually assumes as well that the slumlord, in order to extract even greater income from his inventory, pursues a deliberate policy of undermaintenance. The fact that his structures eventually become uninhabitable does not matter to him, because by then he has long since had his initial investment returned together with an exorbitant profit. It does matter to the community at large, however. Not only do neighborhoods which became accessible to poor households quickly deteriorate, but their decline weakens the market in adjacent areas, making it possible for the slumlord to extend his insidious practices into previously sound blocks. Thus, as he befouls one nest he moves on to another. Illustrative of the greedy-investor image is the frequently heard cry to "tax the profits out of slums," the hope being that this would force the avaricious speculator out of the slum business and replace him with more responsible entrepreneurs. Such persons would be in the business now, were it not for the stigma that the slumlord has brought to the ownership of low-rent property.

The image is relatively unweakened by data showing that inner-city investors currently earn little income from their holdings. The investors, it is argued, allowed their inventory to fall into disrepair *before* the profit picture turned gloomy. In fact, the low profits are the logical and inevitable results of a "milking" operation. Moreover, to continue the argument, since a majority of owners had already gotten their capital investment back several times over prior to the downturn in the market, their recent profit-and-loss statements are misleading if not meaningless. At most, the data indicate that some investors have justly been caught in a situation partially of their own making. Nothing in the figures suggests they were originally well motivated.

The policy implications of the image are more in the realm of what not to do rather than what should be done. Persons who hold the image resist any proposal which appears to either bail out the investor-owner or help improve his ability to continue operating. Better to drive him out of business by strict code enforcement and by various measures to eliminate his monopoly situation where it still exists. To help him liquidate his assets even at currently depressed market values is to pay him for socially valueless property and for property which has already been fully amortized. Moreover, if help were given, slumlords would simply use the proceeds to infect other neighborhoods.

There is a compelling logic to the greedy-investor image. The image fails, though, as a comprehensive explanation of inner-city decay. With respect to the charge of "milking," an investor would be foolish to undermaintain properties that can earn positive cash-flows with proper maintenance. This is true even if the cash-flow is inadequate by normal investment standards. To attempt to boost profits by deferring maintenance is to prematurely cut off the entire income stream. Most investors are more than aware that this is so. Our examination of both their books and their properties indicates that undermaintenance is the exception, not the rule, and in any case is not associated with high profits. As mentioned in Chapter 9, widespread lack of management competence appears to be a serious problem, but not greed.

Although the factual aspects of the image can be challenged on still other grounds, the policy portions are most worrisome. They contain a trace of vengeance, which is unfortunate in itself and which leads in addition to totally self-defeating programs. In some cities this has already happened, as the attempt to displace, not replace, the inner-city investor has resulted in unnecessary dislocation of tenants and abandonment of properties. Blaming the inner-city landlord may be convenient, but it is not an attitude that will lead to solution of housing problems.

EXPLOITATIVE-SYSTEM IMAGE

This image is perhaps best described as an extension of the previous one. It has two basic variations, with one centering on laws and customs which shape the housing market directly, and the other emphasizing larger societal forces. Both variations assert that social institutions create an environment within which exploitation of the poor by the suppliers of housing services is virtually inevitable. Those who hold to this view believe that it would do no good to drive existing exploiters out of business or to replace white investors with blacks, because in the absence of more fundamental changes, the new breed of landlord who would be attracted into the inner city would be as bad as the old.

Without accepting the exploitative-system image in its pure form, it is possible to embrace a less perjorative version. As already stated, housing-market mechanisms which collectively serve most of the population reasonably well do not function at all smoothly in the inner city, and the poor suffer as a result. Individual investors are, by and large, not exploitative, but serious imperfections in the system for delivering housing services do impose unnecessary hardship on low-income families. Restructuring of institutions in the low-income sector of the market should, therefore, be an important component of any proposed solution to housing problems.

RACIAL IMAGE

As formulated here, none of the above six images incorporates the element of race as an explanatory variable. Race, however, is frequently seen not only as an embellishment of all the images but also a separate theme. As an embellishment, it appears in the form of a belief, which is widely shared among blacks as well as whites, but for quite different reasons, that racial change generally triggers neighborhood deterioration. On one side, it is alleged that low-income black tenants behave less responsibly than do low-income white tenants, especially in failing to exercise control over their children; and in reverse, it is alleged that housing discrimination, which most observers agree is still widespread, explains more of the deterioration of housing in the inner city than do either low income or market forces generally. As neighborhoods change racially, landlords gouge tenants and milk properties, while the city not only ignores such practices as long as possible, but allows its own services in these areas to deteriorate. In a more benign context, race is also used as the variable to explain an apparent communication gap between reasonably responsible landlords and reasonably responsible tenants, a gap which adds to the basic difficulties. It is used, too, as a partial explanation of the exodus of white families to the suburbs.

Race becomes a separate seventh image in the argument that blacks basically reject the inner city, because the old decaying stock symbolizes their repression and even more particularly, because even if the inner city were a satisfactory place to live, it represents forced confinement. Any program to "gild the ghetto" cannot succeed as long as that attitude persists, and the attitude will persist until the housing market is genuinely open (4). Or so the argument goes.

The various racial images that serve to embellish the other images need not be evaluated, since they do not have any special policy significance by themselves. They emphasize the importance of exploring the racial implications of any program, but they do not either suggest or indict specific proposals of major importance. Not so in the case of the forced-confinement image. If solutions to the housing problems of the inner city are not possible until the residential market generally is desegregated, priorities must be reordered and the scale of existing desegregation efforts greatly expanded. Not only the barrier of discrimination, but also the reluctance of most blacks to attempt to exercise their rights must be overcome. This will take a number of years, even assuming acceleration in the current rate of progress. In the meantime, programs for the inner city are stalled or ineffective.

The image, then, is central to any discussion of housing policy. But how valid is it? Blacks themselves disagree on this point. Some scoff at the idea, arguing that it is the bad environment itself which is rejected. Others, however, feel that the effects of discrimination are more insidious than even the victims often realize, and that simply knowing that the game is fair could change a person's attitudes and behavior in ways that are immediately imperceptible but ultimately important. In addition, the comment is frequently heard that because blacks are forced to purchase homes which they might reject in a completely open market, many of them do not feel the same sense of attachment to their homes as they ordinarily would. As a consequence, even in some of the better inner-city neighborhoods there is said to be a lack of sense of community or feeling of identity with one's immediate surroundings. This situation could be due, of course, to a number of factors other than residential segregation.

The image, if broadly interpreted, is intuitively appealing. It would be unfortunate, however, if it led to policies which stressed desegregation at the expense of rebuilding the inner city, since the two thrusts are not aimed at the same clients. Efforts to create an open market would directly benefit only middle and upper-income blacks who can afford homes outside the ghetto. Low-income families, and many middle-income families as well, would remain behind. The knowledge that society was becoming more just might be of immense psychological value to them, but their economic circumstances would force them to face the day-to-day reality of unpleasant surroundings. Their plight cannot be waved aside with glib phrases. Nor need it be, for desegregation programs would not require such huge sums of money as to be competitive with the rebuilding process. Even if efforts in the inner city were likely to be less effective than they would be in an open-market environment, they must be pursued. The image does suggest, nevertheless, that renewal programs should give much more attention to creating social institutions and relationships which improve sense of self-worth, attitudes toward neighborhood, and related perceptions that discrimination and segregation have so badly warped.

SOCIAL-FABRIC IMAGE

All of the above images focus on housing. No matter which one is selected, the centerpiece is some aspect of either behavior toward housing or market forces. The ninth and final image explains the problem almost completely in nonhousing terms. It suggests that crime, poor schools, unemployment, family instability, and related social maladies turn inner-city neighborhoods into places to get out of (5). As families who can exercise this option do so, and as leadership in the city mentally makes a similar move, those who must remain behind are gradually overcome by a sense of impotence, and the deterioration of the social fabric becomes irreversible. With so many other concerns for families to worry about, much of the housing stock is badly neglected. The malaise is pervasive. It is not one of a few problem families, but of many families confronted by many problems. This image differs from the housing obsolescence concept in its emphasis on serious disabilities of inner-city areas, rather than on positive amenities of suburbia. It leads, however, to a similar conclusion that only drastic surgery — dispersal of the inner-city population and elimination of social ills — will solve the various dimensions of the housing problem. In some respects it is an even more disturbing view of the problem, because it implies that inner-city housing interventions deal only with symptoms and, consequently, are largely ineffective.

In assessing the image, it can be agreed that the fundamental barrier to improvement in the quality of the lives of inner-city residents is an oppressive social environment, i.e., patterns of behavior of individuals, groups, and organizations that degrade a segment of the population. It can also be agreed that, historically, physical renewal has not been successful in creating positive social relationships. This is not to say, however, that housing has no effect on the social environment. Indeed, the system of relationships which are directed toward the provision of shelter services are an integral element of the social environment. To equate housing with the physical environment is a mistake, or at least a common misunderstanding. Although setting the housing relationships straight is, by itself, not going to create a good social environment in the inner city, neither is any other single type of action. Each set of institutional relationships, of which housing is but one, must be changed if the income-related deprivations of inner-city populations are to be materially reduced. Whether the necessary changes can be achieved only if the poor are decon-centrated is the key unanswered question. The precise relationship between dispersal of the poor and dissolution of poverty has yet to be articulated.

THE SPECIAL CASE OF HOUSING ABANDONMENT

Only a few short years ago, city planners bemoaned the fact that older portions of the housing stock were being retired from use much too slowly. Old housing was often equated with bad housing, and descriptions of urban shelter problems were typically highlighted by reference to the increasing age of the residential inventory. Today, the concern of most planners appears to be just the opposite. The large-scale abandonment of inner-city residential structures commencing in the early 1960's is felt to have added a new dimension to the low-income housing problem.

Although abandonment is commonly described as but the tip of the iceberg of decay (not the most felicitous metaphor), it is actually an analytically distinct phenomenon. Decay often is not followed by abandonment, and conversely, abandonment frequently takes place without a prior period of neglect. In fact, concern over abandonment arises precisely because it appears in so many instances to precipitate rather than follow decay, striking solid structures in physically sound neighborhoods, not just those buildings and areas where deterioration has almost run its course (6). Were it confined to only the worst sectors of the housing inventory, there would be no need to examine it as a separate process. But, as George Sternlieb has pointed out, "Abandonment has a dynamic of its own" (7). Nevertheless, decay and abandonment do usually occur in the same neighborhoods, and for similar reasons. An understanding of abandonment thus helps to explain some of the negative forces which impinge on the inner city and make the solution to low-income housing problems so difficult.

Theories of abandonment bear a strong resemblance to the images of the housing problem just outlined. Depending on the particular analyst, abandonment is the consequence of:

(1)   Lack of demand for the units because of rising incomes, suburbanization of jobs, changing tastes, little or no growth in the number of low-income households, better alternatives in the subsidized market, etc. (obsolescence image).

(2)   Lack of demand for the units because the neighborhood is a bad place to live (social-fabric image).

(3)   Insufficient rents to support normal operating costs (low-income image).

(4)   Excessively high operating costs and vandalism (problem-tenant and social-fabric images).

(5)   Treatment of property as a wasting asset in expectation of the above problems, even though cash-flow is currently positive (greedy-investor image).

(6)   Withdrawal of debt capital that is needed to finance major repairs (exploitative-system image).

(7)   Market disorganization caused by racial transition (racial image).

(8)   Enforcement of the housing code without accompanying supply-side subsidies, rent-escrow, etc. (no counterpart housing problem image).

The first image stresses factors which pull families out of the inner city, while the second emphasizes conditions which push them out. Several of the others suggest that much abandonment may be due to mistaken judgments by either investors or public officials. Only one of the images stresses low income, and the literature on abandonment does not assign this image much importance. As a general rule, inheritance of structures by lower-income groups postpones rather than hastens abandonment.

It is virtually impossible to subject these images to rigorous analysis; however, a certain amount of insight into their relative merits can be gained by examining incipient abandonment in neighborhoods that are still reasonably stable and where the process has not yet begun to feed on itself. Two recent studies which pursued such an examination in Philadelphia found that first-generation abandonments were the result of a disparate variety of adverse events, such as a death in the family or an unexpected vacancy, which led directly or indirectly to fire or vandalism and the necessity for expensive repairs (8). In several instances, the chain of causation included urban renewal programs, racial transition, poor management, and other peculiarly inner-city phenomena. What all of the abandonments had in common was the fact that none of the units involved could be described as obsolete or, prior to being damaged, in poor condition. Their withdrawal from the inventory was not due to lack of demand. Rather, it was in response to a problem — serious property damage — which occurs with varying frequency throughout the entire real estate market. In higher income areas, however, damaged dwellings are soon repaired and reoccupied. And during their period of vacancy they seldom have to be boarded-up. In low-income neighborhoods, though, where less expensive assets are at stake and the risks associated with further investment are greater, the restoration of extensively damaged structures is not likely to be economically feasible from the standpoint of the individual investor. In the two Philadelphia neighborhoods, for example, post-repair market values would have seldom exceeded the cost of rehabilitation. And even in those cases where this was not true, owners chose to board-up rather than chance being vandalized again.

Although it would be easy to infer that the downfall of entire neighborhoods commences with "unnecessary" abandonment of the sort just described, we question whether this is usually so. In many lower-income neighborhoods, the open space created by demolishing abandoned structures should actually have a salutory effect (though this is less true in row house blocks, since the disappearance of several structures produces a jagged facade). Conceivably abandonment due to vandalism could continue to the point where it adversely affected investment and occupancy decisions throughout a neighborhood, thus kicking off its own cycle of withdrawals. But where abandonment continues unabated, there are almost certainly other problems besides vandalism affecting the market, and these problems probably confirm to varying degrees all of the images we have outlined. It is interesting, too, that if all of the images are at least partially correct, then two of the problems causing abandonment — inadequate household income and racial discrimination — are twin-faced. Their existence contributes to abandonment, but so too will their elimination. This fact suggests a point which should be obvious but which has been obscured by abandonment horror stories. Along with the many fine buildings that have been lost from the inventory, a large amount of junk has been discarded too. Indeed, most abandonment probably reflects economic and social progress and, as predicted more than a decade ago, can therefore be expected to continue in many parts of the inner city even if wanton destruction of property ceases (9). Whether public programs can control the process and contain it within the worst areas so as to prevent unnecessary boarding-up, financial losses, and disruption of stable neighborhoods is the critical unresolved question.

A COMPOSITE IMAGE

Since each of the nine images contains elements of both fact and fiction, it is likely that no person would identify totally with any one of them. Most people would accept varying proportions of all nine, constructing for themselves what might be described as a composite image. The overlap among these composites is probably much greater than the policy recommendations that emerge from them.

Our own composite differs from the individual images primarily in degree, and its major themes are revealed in the preceding critiques. It does, however, contain two additional assumptions of our own which should be mentioned. First, it is our feeling that indecent dwelling units are no longer the most troubling housing problem. The quality of accommodations occupied by low-income families in Baltimore is evidently improving even while decay is spreading (10). And we suspect that in many metropolitan areas, especially those which are smaller or newer, the situation is even better. The high cost of shelter, certain undesirable social relationships in housing, the element of "turf," and deleterious neighborhood environments are all much more important aspects of the housing dilemma than are the condition and quality of the stock, and they deserve greater emphasis in remedial programs. Moreover, physical improvement of the residential inventory does not strike at the basic causes of housing problems. Neither is such improvement likely to have substantially favorable effects on nonhousing deprivations of low-income and black families. Nevertheless, inadequate shelter *is* a problem for many families, and it is a serious problem for some. It cannot be entirely ignored while other housing objectives and more fundamental social reform are sought. This is especially so since decay is eating away at basically sound low-rent structures that potentially have many years of useful service ahead of them.

Second, it is our belief that none of the larger social and economic forces which some of the images use to explain the housing problems of deprived families are quite so overwhelming as they are made out to be. Their adverse effects on the residential environment can be counteracted to some degree by housing programs which are directed at the inner city, programs which modify rather than ignore existing market institutions, and which may not require impossibly large sums to implement. Moreover, most of the low-income housing inventory is not so deteriorated or so obsolete as to be unusable in satisfying the housing requirements of families with shelter problems. To this degree we are optimistic, not because things cannot get any worse, for they can get much worse, but because the problems seem manageable if there is a reasonable amount of interest in solving them. If the necessary resources are to be forthcoming, however, and if they are to be used effectively, programs for the low-income sector must be tied to and seen as an integral part of overall city renewal efforts for all income groups.

The one disturbing element in our image has to do with the question of whether the dynamics of neighborhood decay are well enough understood to enable anyone to state with confidence that a particular set of interventions will be effective in restoring deteriorated areas and preventing others from sliding downhill. In general, neighborhood stabilization efforts throughout the country have not been very successful, largely, we think, because of their implicit assumption that the forces of decay and abandonment are primarily endogenous to the neighborhood itself. There can be no disagreement that as long as a portion of the population suffers from inadequate income at least a corresponding portion of the housing inventory will be substandard. We can be equally certain, for reasons stated in Chapter 7, that most of this inventory will be clustered in older sections of the city. What is more in doubt is whether an expansion of housing resources that would be sufficient to both assure all families decent housing and halt physical obsolescence of older residential areas, but which would not be great enough to solve the social problems of the poor, could in fact stop further neighborhood disintegration.

The optimum mix of housing and nonhousing interventions, physical and social programs, and supply-side and demand-side subsidies will always be a matter of judgment. But regardless of the precise mix, it is inevitable that for a decade or so, the real incomes, both earned and subsidized, of low-income families will rise only modestly. As a consequence, these families will be forced to make housing choices from basically the same stock in the same neighborhoods where they now live. A suburban solution to their problem, however attractive, is simply impossible in the short run. It is too expensive; it would divert too much money from more basic needs in education and employment; and, in favoring low-income families over middle-income households in the new construction market, it contains an inherent political barrier to large-scale implementation. So housing policy must deal with what is and make it better. It cannot dream the impossible dream, while the poor endure the impossible life.

Our policy recommendations, which attempt to reflect, elaborate, and give specificity to this general image of the problem, follow.

CHAPTER 11

From Problems to Policy: Part I

In the preceding chapters, Baltimore's low-income housing problem has been analyzed from several different perspectives. Using the list of housing objectives presented in Chapter 3 as a framework, Chapters 4-8 examined the extent of housing need among particular low-income groups in the city and estimated the level of housing effort which is required in order to eliminate specified deprivations. Chapters 9 and 10 attempted to complement these findings by developing an understanding of the factors, other than inadequate resources alone, which have contributed to the shelter problems for many low-income families and promoted the spread of decay in portions of the inner-city stock. Taken together, the chapters describe: 1. the array of low-income housing objectives which housing advocates feel to be important; 2. the needs and preferences of deprived families with respect to a selected group of these objectives; 3. the size and focus of existing subsidy programs *vis à vis* these needs and objectives; and 4. the market environment and forces of change with which housing programs have to contend. With this foundation, the development of a set of policy and program proposals can now be attempted.

In this endeavor we recognize fully that the step from facts to policy is a huge one. Even the most complete understanding of housing problems will not lead directly to a set of viable policy prescriptions. Knowledge of the causes of the problems does not by itself suggest the cures. And in this case, there is the further difficulty of deciding which of several problems and whom among numerous deprived families should receive priority. While there are technical considerations in structuring such choices, the decisions themselves are inherently judgmental. In addition, even if there is a sense of which remedial paths might be most promising, political constraints may effectively prevent them from being seriously considered.

It would be well to emphasize also a point that was made in Chapter 1, that the policy focus is on what can be done for large numbers of families in the short and intermediate term, with amounts of resources that might reasonably be expected to be forthcoming during that period. Solutions requiring vast increases in existing subsidies or dramatic shifts in political behavior are taken as long term and, therefore, outside our purview. Equally, potential trade-offs between low-income housing programs and other housing and nonhousing programs, though obviously issues of some importance, are largely beyond the scope of this analysis.

THE CURRENT SITUATION SUMMARIZED

By constraining the universe of policy options so as to exclude those which would require a sharp rise in housing subsidies, it is at least theoretically possible to eliminate from consideration the only solutions that would be regarded favorably by the deprived families themselves. Fortunately, almost all U.S. cities appear not to be in that situation. Their housing problems are still manageable.

In Baltimore, for example, all but about 8,000 of the city's 65,000 occupied substandard dwellings are basically sound and could be upgraded to at least code level at an average cost of only $1,000 per unit (1969 dollars). The cost of upgrading the entire stock — all the way from inexpensive repairs for structures with only minor problems to demolition and replacement of dilapidated buildings — is estimated to be approximately $200 million, or about $3,000 per unit. More than half of this amount could be covered by a continuation of subsidized rehabilitation and new construction at their 1967-69 rate for a period of only eight years or so. Some of the cost could be borne by the private sector.

While it might be argued in the abstract that these estimates reflect standards which, if met, would not satisfy the perceived needs of the affected families, this does not appear to be the case. If the responses to our survey are valid, the number of low-income families who are seriously dissatisfied with their homes is even less than the number of dwellings that we rated as seriously substandard. There is considerably greater concern about neighborhood than about housing itself. Much of this concern, moreover, is over nonphysical aspects of the environment. The relative importance of physical vs nonphysical problems, as perceived by the residents, is of special significance, and merits greater attention than it has heretofore been given in federal policy.

Although the city's residential inventory is in better condition than most observers had until quite recently believed, it appears to have deteriorated, on balance, since 1960, and continues to deteriorate today. An especially disturbing aspect of this spreading decay is the boarding up of reasonably good houses in good blocks. Occurring as it has in the face of rising real income in the city, this trend implies that Baltimore's current housing effort is inadequate not simply in scale but also in scope. The decline can be observed in both the inner and middle rings, and downward trends in these two sections of the city are not unconnected. As lower income families have fled from the inner-city environment and sought homes in better neighborhoods in the middle ring, many homes in the latter area have shifted to rental occupancy, and some of them have been converted to multifamily use, thus planting the seeds of decay in once stable neighborhoods. By being unable to create suitable housing alternatives in the inner ring for families of modest means, the city is losing battles on two fronts simultaneously.

It is clear, however, that low income is only one factor in the process of decay. Fully half of the private dwelling units occupied by poor families are in conformance with the city's housing code, and about one-third (12,000) of the remainder are in noncompliance not because of failure of their owners to maintain them but rather because of inadequate original construction (1). Moreover, 30% of the substandard stock is in the hands of non-low-income households.

Some of this decay is inevitable. As obsolescent buildings in neighborhoods which are being vacated become increasingly difficult to rent, owners see the end in sight and treat them as wasting assets. Not a small part of the deterioration, though, is due to the fact that vandalism, careless tenants, high turnover, and rapidly rising costs of maintenance have made it impossible for many landlords to keep their buildings in good condition without incurring negative cash-flow. Perhaps more distressing is that it is a "Micawber" situation, i.e., the absolute dollar amounts of unattended needed repairs associated with the decline are quite small. An extra $100 or so a year allocated to maintenance, or an equivalent amount of extra care by tenants could turn a declining inventory into a gradually improving one.

Poor management has contributed to the problem. About 60% of the inner-city rental inventory is held by small investor-owners, many of whom do not have either the resources or the ability or the experience to cope with management problems. Living a considerable distance from their holdings, they seldom see their tenants and cannot respond to complaints quickly. Under these circumstances, financial losses are inevitable, and with the losses, declining quality. Even many good managers, however, are experiencing operating losses, and those who do earn a profit have watched the instability of the inner-city market erode the value of their properties.

Although values are declining and profits disappearing, rents are almost keeping pace with inflationary trends generally. This is because most of the rental dollar is consumed by operating costs, not amortization of capital investment. Nearly all of the categories of cost are actually higher for inner-city dwellings than they are for better quality apartments in more desirable neighborhoods. The result is that the poor pay very nearly as much for inferior accommodations as middle-income families spend for quite attractive homes.

Virtually all of the very bad housing in Baltimore is occupied by low-income black renters, approximately half of whom are in large households (six or more persons). Moderately substandard structures are more widely distributed among various demographic types, but blacks, the poor, and renters each continue to account for two-thirds or more of the problem. Most welfare clients are inadequately housed, and they comprise a fairly large portion (50%) of the families in seriously substandard accommodations.

In resource terms, and perhaps in other ways as well, the worst housing problem in the city is the very high proportion of income that low-income families spend for shelter, a fact which may partially explain why their housing is in better condition than might be expected. Because this problem is less visible than is the substandard inventory, its seriousness may not be fully appreciated. It translates itself into poor diet, inadequate medical care, ill health, and other deprivations that appear on the surface to be unrelated to housing. Just to reduce the rent-income ratios of low-income families to equal those of nonpoverty households (which would still leave the poor with higher housing costs than most of them can afford) would require grants totaling at least $40 million annually, assuming unrealistically that such a program would result in no escalation of rents. And this huge sum, which is greater than the aggregate of existing housing subsidies in the city, would not upgrade any of the stock, except indirectly to the extent that some of the assisted families chose to use the subsidy to obtain better housing rather than to lower their rent-income ratios.

From the standpoint of the families themselves one of the most widespread desires, expressed by a majority of those in rental quarters, is for home ownership. Baltimore's inventory lends itself to this form of tenure, but real estate financing practices do not. Lower-income families who seek to buy a home have been forced to use land installment contracts which place unnecessary and onerous housing costs on their already burdened shoulders. This situation, which is common in many other cities as well, was exposed nationally a number of years ago, but the federal response has been a source of controversy.

In attempting to solve its housing problems, the City of Baltimore has developed the same tools and programs that are found in other communities. It has a reasonably large public-housing inventory (4% of total units) as well as a good code-enforcement program, an abandoned-house program, and a housing development corporation. Its largest housing subsidy program, nevertheless, is the rent component of the welfare dollar which infuses almost twice as much money into the housing market each year as do all the other programs combined. If all housing subsidies from all sources are aggregated, the total annual figure for the city approximates $37 million. Although this is a significant sum, the current pattern of allocation produces results which are highly uneven. Some low-income families receive substantial benefits from these programs, while others receive very little, and still others (30%), nothing at all.

The reason Baltimore's housing programs are so similar on the surface to those elsewhere around the country is simple enough. Given the city's financial plight, allocation of resources to housing problems is tied closely to the development of federal subsidies. Baltimore does and prepares to do those things which Washington will pay for.

Historically, the city has used federal programs with considerable imagination. It has an enlightened and experienced group of public servants in its housing and planning agencies, and a large number of private individuals and groups who could be similarly described. Still, its efforts collectively represent more of a series of responses to Congressionally created largesse than a consciously determined housing strategy which is continuously sensitive to existing conditions.

Dependence on the federal arsenal dictates a rather limited range of possibilities for solving the various dimensions of the housing problem. The city's upgrading efforts place emphasis on the two ends of the housing-quality spectrum. At the upper end, there are programs of new construction and maximum rehabilitation which expend large amounts of subsidy on a small number of those in need. At the lower end, code enforcement deals with minor structural deficiencies. Except for the FACE upgrading program, there has been nothing in between. There is also very little actual attention, despite much concern, to other dimensions of the housing problem. Hence, collectively, all of Baltimore's housing programs (excluding the rent component of the welfare dollar) reach a minority (one-third) of the low-income population and are directed at only a few of the twelve housing goals presented in Chapter 3. This appraisal should not be interpreted as an indictment of either the city or the State of Maryland or the federal government. It does suggest, though, that legislators either do not perceive housing problems as especially important or do not regard housing interventions as a particularly effective way of dealing with these problems.

A PACKAGE OF POLICIES

Given the negative housing trends which absolutely must be reversed before the city can concentrate its attention on longer range residential goals and programs, and assuming that these trends cannot be appreciably altered without housing interventions, the very first priority would seem to be to turn the inner-city housing climate around for renters, for investors, and for owner occupants, and to set the stage, as it were, for the larger rebuilding programs which will become possible during the last quarter of the century as poverty and racial discrimination are gradually eliminated. Most of this rebuilding must be undertaken with private risk capital, but as long as income streams from inner city property are capitalized at 25% or more, it is certain very little unsubsidized renewal investment will take place. Associated with this priority and of equal importance is the need to bring the benefits of housing programs to the entire inner-city population, not just low-income families, and within a reasonable period of time.

These two objectives set the direction for and become the constraints on policy. They establish a program horizon of not more than ten years, and, because housing subsidies cannot be expected to be dramatically increased in so short a time, they fix the average subsidy per family at a relatively low level. Although it is not certain that the objectives can be achieved with the limited funds that are likely to become available, there are seven necessary, though possibly insufficient, steps which must be taken.

First, the substandard inventory must be upgraded to a level of quality that buyers and renters would find acceptable. Fortunately, this is not an inordinately expensive task. As discussed earlier in the chapter, it requires a large expansion of current modest rehabilitation efforts and a continuation of maximum rehabilitation/new construction programs at the production rates which were achieved in the late 1960's. In areas where little private or public open space is available, extensive physical redesigning must also be undertaken. These activities should be viewed as complementary, for in many neighborhoods, and even within the same blocks, a range of treatments is appropriate. The modest rehabilitation component is not just a holding action. Depending on original quality of construction and the city's long-range renewal plans, dwellings in this category may be expected to last for as long as 30 years without needing major additional investment.

Second, to insure that an upgraded inventory stays upgraded, a subsidy is required to close the gap between the cost of providing adequate housing and what low-income families are now able to pay. This subsidy could be given to either housing suppliers or consumers. For reasons to be detailed later, we recommend an increase in housing allowances to welfare recipients and selective expansion of the leased housing program to serve primarily large households now occupying seriously substandard structures.

Third, the physical and social environments of the inner city must be improved. Usable open space must be created, noxious uses removed, city services augmented, crime reduced, schools improved, and problem families helped.

Fourth, as one step toward a better social environment and also to improve the maintenance of the inventory, a large number of inner-city dwelling units, perhaps as many as 50,000, must be obtained from existing owners and placed in the hands of individuals and organizations who have the capability of managing residential real estate properly. It would be desirable for some of these units to pass into owner occupancy so as to contribute to other important housing objectives. The implementation of ownership transfer on a large scale is a most complex endeavor requiring several different financing plans and related programs to achieve the necessary sales volume.

Fifth, in order to expand demand for inner-city real estate among home buyers and responsible investors, and to encourage owners to improve their property, and to protect owners and lenders against capital losses resulting from events and trends which are beyond their control and against which society should properly provide protection, guarantees must be created to cover such contingencies as vandalism, neighborhood deterioration, and inability to make mortgage payments due to sickness or loss of job. In addition, the risks themselves must be substantially reduced.

Sixth, in connection with the ownership-transfer program the reservoir of maintenance and management skills must be enlarged. Emphasis must be placed on delivering housing services in a nonstigmatizing manner and on making special services available to many physically handicapped persons who now lack them.

Finally, both as a matter of simple equity and also in order to remove one apparent cause of neighborhood decay, vigorous efforts should be undertaken to eliminate totally all forms of racial discrimination in the housing market and to encourage blacks to exercise their legal rights in their search for suitable places to live.

In our judgment, these several steps should be viewed as a single, integrated package in the sense that all of them are required if each is to be effective. A healthy investment climate cannot develop without visible physical improvement, which in turn may depend on ownership transfer, and so on. The precise combination of interventions would, of course, vary among neighborhoods and over time, necessitating the development, integration, and continual adjustment of micro-strategies for each section of the city. The package as a whole leans heavily on the assumption that the housing situation overall for low-income families in Baltimore is not improving and that this is due in part to unstable market conditions. In cities where this may not be true, appropriate policy emphases would be quite different.

The package is not, as is readily apparent, comprehensive. It aims directly at only 9 of the 12 housing goals discussed in Chapter 2. It indirectly increases security of occupancy, helps only some of the families with excessive rent burdens, and barely touches locational choice. These partial omissions are not

accidental. Greatly expanded locational choice means, for all practical purposes, suburbanization of low-income families, an objective which would be
extremely expensive to achieve and one that the families themselves do not
value highly. Security of occupancy and lower rent-income ratios could be
most effectively achieved through income-maintenance and employment programs.

Although not comprehensive, the package is, unfortunately, expensive.
Assuming a 10-year capital improvement program, the average annual public-
sector cost of the seven proposals combined would initially lie in the vicinity
of $25 million (about $35 million in 1974 dollars), representing a two-thirds
expansion of existing programs (2). With the completion of upgrading at the
end of the decade, expenditures would drop approximately in half — more if
poverty were reduced appreciably in the meantime and less if a new round of
investment were needed.

The bulk of the funds ($18.5 million) would be consumed by inventory
improvement, housing allowances, and leased housing (Table 11.1). Largely
on the basis of guesswork, we estimate that not more than $1 million annually
would be required for investment guarantees; that ownership transfer, management-maintenance, and antidiscrimination programs would need only about
$500,000 each; and that upgrading the physical environment in lower-income
neighborhoods would cost an additional $4 million annually. Programs directed
at the social environment could properly be allocated to nonhousing budgets.

Table 11.1 Estimated Minimum Annual Cost of Additional Housing Programs That are
Needed to Solve the Housing Problems in the City of Baltimore by 1985 [1]

Program	Annual Cost
Modest rehabilitation	$5,700,000
Maximum rehabilitation and new construction	4,800,000
Neighborhood renewal	4,000,000
Housing allowances for welfare clients	6,200,000
Leased housing	1,800,000
Investment guarantees	1,000,000
Ownership transfer	500,000
Management-maintenance	500,000
Equal opportunity	500,000
Total	$25,000,000

[1] Estimates are in 1969 dollars.

Since these estimates come to less than half of the preliminary figures presented in Chapter 8, they merit brief elaboration. The major difference between the two sets of figures results from our exclusion here of any program designed specifically to reduce rent-income ratios and overcrowding, and our inclusion of programs to achieve other housing objectives. There are other important differences too, however. First, assuming a somewhat different renewal strategy than was presented in Chapter 8, we calculate that to bring the housing stock up to an acceptable level of quality would require an annual subsidy of only $11 million (1969 dollars). Of the 57,000 occupied dwellings that are only moderately substandard, we guess that a large number will either escape public attention or be demolished in connection with other programs. It is likely, though, that at least as many units will augment the substandard inventory before renewal efforts gain enough momentum to arrest decay. Therefore, we simply apply the mean rehabilitation figure of $1,000 per unit mentioned earlier in the chapter to the entire 57,000, and obtain an estimated yearly capital requirement of $5.7 million for this portion of the stock. Part of this cost would be absorbed by the private sector. Any savings to the taxpayer, however, are certain to be offset by administrative expenses and by the tendency of improvement standards to escalate above those originally specified. With respect to the 8,000 dwellings which must be either demolished or completely rehabilitated, we suggest that, both to minimize program costs and to maximize income mixing, these units or those which replace them should be sold wherever possible to non-low-income families and investors for whatever the traffic will bear. This figure would vary greatly throughout the city but would average about $6,000/unit under cost, necessitating an annual public contribution of $4.8 million. By implication, this approach precludes the construction of very much additional public housing.

Increased housing allowances for welfare recipients would cost about $6.2 million, assuming that approximately two-thirds of the 31,000 welfare households would qualify for an increase and that the amount of assistance could be varied according to individual needs (3). An extra $300 per year for these households may not seem sufficient to enable them to obtain decent accommodations, but it must be remembered that the additional revenue which landlords would receive is not meant to finance major upgrading, only operating expenses. The expanded leased-housing program would serve an additional 3,000 families at an average cost of $600 per family or $1.8 million per year. The higher average subsidy, relative to welfare clients, reflects the larger average family size of the leased-housing group.

The two programs combined would include only 24,000 low-income households, of whom 3,000 (most of whom are on welfare) already live in standard accommodations. It should not be inferred from these figures, however, that the bulk of the housing maintenance problem is therefore uncovered. Of the 65,000 currently substandard units in the city, about 20,000 are occupied by non-low-income families, hence susceptible to different treatment. Another 12,000, as pointed out earlier, are not substandard because of curtailed maintenance, but rather because of inadequate original construction. Still another 4,000 (not occupied by welfare families) are part of the public housing inventory. And a handful, perhaps 2,000 or so, could be satisfactorily maintained without a rent increase if pressure were placed on their owners to do so. Altogether, then, not more than 6,000 dwelling units, all moderately substandard, would remain at risk. More complete coverage is, practically speaking, impossible.

The $25 million estimate implicitly assumes population, income, and tastes will remain relatively constant throughout the ten-year period under consideration. Actually, as already suggested, all three of these variables are certain to change. The city's population is projected to decline while the number of households moves upward slightly (4). These two trends alone should raise real household income. Additional increases in income can be expected as a consequence of rising productivity in the economy generally, and possibly also as a result of reforms in health and welfare programs. Changing tastes are less predictable, but probably will not shift in the direction of the older, central-city stock, the energy crisis notwithstanding. It seems clear, therefore, that over the decade, poverty will decline, abandonment of substandard structures will continue, and a large number of dwellings which we have just included in our upgrading estimate – perhaps as many as 20,000 or so – will disappear from the stock by 1980. It does not follow from this fact, however, that our estimated program cost is too high. Until the dynamics of the inner-city market can be altered, deterioration of presently sound structures will offset favorable trends, and subsidized construction will be needed in marginal neighborhoods. Equally important, the types of families who would be eligible for our proposed housing-allowance and leased-housing programs do not appear to be diminishing in number.

Because of the changing social and economic environment within which housing programs must operate, the $25 million figure is perhaps best viewed only as an order of magnitude reflecting one set of perceptions as to the general size of the problem. The estimates for the individual program components should be interpreted in much the same way. Their precise size is less important than the reasoning behind them, namely, that any housing strategy cannot emphasize a single thrust or try to solve the bulk of the housing problem at a single scale. It must move on a number of fronts simultaneously: upgrading and maintenance, new construction and rehabilitation, supply and demand, race and class, and neighborhood and large geographic areas.

The form and mixture of programs will obviously vary from community to community, but the mixture must be there, and it must be carefully concocted and regularly adjusted.

PRELIMINARY EVALUATION OF THE POLICY PACKAGE

Collectively, the proposals demand such a large relative and absolute increase in current funding as to place housing in serious competition with other programs which may be more effective in dealing with basic causes of poverty and urban decay and which, as pointed out in Chapter 8, already have lower budgets than does housing. If the various parts of the package could be expected to finance themselves indirectly by reducing the necessary scope of other programs, their cost would be easier to justify. This is not the case, however. Except for possibly lowering the per-unit cost of code enforcement by making it possible for the city to increase the proportion of exterior inspections, the proposals would not ease any other budgets immediately. If they paid for themselves, it would be by increasing the effectiveness of existing programs and by obviating the need for even more expensive housing treatments in the future. But these potential benefits are difficult to demonstrate.

Given the above, it is clearly necessary to look at the proposals more closely. In this section, we briefly compare the general thrust of the package as a whole with three quite different and widely recommended approaches to the same set of urban housing problems. In the next chapter, each of the seven proposals is examined individually in more detail, and in Chapter 13, the feasibility of the most controversial of them — modest rehabilitation — is explored in depth. Unfortunately, the array of housing/non-housing, subsidy/non-subsidy, and supply-side/demand-side strategies that could be pursued at the federal, state, metropolitan, city, and neighborhood level is so broad that a systematic comparison of all alternatives is simply impossible here. We hope, however, that by touching on major characteristics of and differences among strategies and programs, we can materially reduce current areas of controversy over suitable directions for housing policy.

Housing Vs Nonhousing Strategies

The question here is whether the marginal benefits accruing from expanded housing programs would be greater or lesser than the benefits stemming from correspondingly larger efforts in employment, education, health, or ordinary income maintenance. Is it possible, for example, that an additional expenditure of $25 million a year to improve education and employment opportunities for the poor might lead indirectly, through higher earned income, to better housing for more families than would housing interventions themselves? Or could such an expenditure perhaps achieve not quite so many housing benefits, but in their stead, a number of other more valued objectives. These questions are essentially unanswerable without more knowledge as to the probable effectiveness of various nonhousing programs with respect to their own proximate goals. Nevertheless, a few superficial observations are possible.

With respect to housing vs employment programs, it is useful to look at the labor-force profile of Baltimore's low-income household heads. Of the 65,000 heads in our originally defined low-income group (5): (a) 19,000 (29%) were over 65; (b) 18,000 (28%) were under 65 but not in the labor force; (c) 23,000 (35%) were fully employed, but one-half of this group were classified as low income only because their household incomes were low with respect to the size of their households — over five persons; and (d) 5,000 (8%) were not employed or employed less than full-time. It can be seen that three-fourths of the household heads either were not in the labor force or did not have an employment problem as usually defined. In many of these households, of course, other members worked, and in a few, the heads had withdrawn from the labor force because of inability to find a job. But the fact remains, basic as is full employment to the elimination of poverty, it does not offer an immediate avenue of housing relief to most of those who are currently poor. In the short run, therefore, the trade-off — if one must be made — between housing and employment programs is a choice among partially overlapping client groups whose relative needs and potential for improvement must be assessed. Over the longer term, the choice is similar, but, hopefully, the competing client groups would be smaller.

Much the same comparisons as the above can be made between housing and education and between housing and health. The issues with respect to income maintenance vs housing, however, are quite different. All anti-poverty programs aim to redistribute income. Those which earmark funds, however, supply the low-income recipient with more of a particular good or service than he or she would normally purchase if given an equivalent amount of cash. By implication, the recipient would prefer the cash, so that purchases could be continually adjusted to match changing self-perceived needs. This being so, categorical assistance is the superior alternative only if it, more so than unencumbered cash grants, could do one of the following:

(a) alter expenditure and behavior patterns of recipients in such a way as to yield benefits for them which they would not recognize and value in advance

(b) confer socially desired benefits on nonrecipients

(c) place needed controls on the suppliers of the goods and services in question

(d) utilize inexpensive sources of supply

(e) overcome or reduce market inefficiencies.

The presumed superiority of housing aid in these respects may be real but is not well documented. When families are so poor they must spend nearly all of their income on bare necessities, it is not clear that the individual and societal benefits which would flow from housing assistance are greater than those which ordinary dollars would bring. On the other hand, it could be argued that $25 million a year divided evenly among 85,000 households would disappear almost without a trace, whereas if it were channelled into housing or health or education or employment it could make a material difference in the living conditions and opportunities of a substantial portion of the low-income population. We tend to agree. If much more than $25 million were at stake, the case for unrestricted grants would be much stronger. This is not meant to suggest, though, that just any housing thrust is superior to income maintenance. The social and institutional fabric of housing, not just physical improvement, must be emphasized, especially given the relatively good condition of most of the stock and the apparent dysfunctioning of the market.

Demand Vs Supply-Side Emphasis

The issue here is closely analogous to the previous one. Why not divide the $25 million equally among the 70,000 or so low-income households who are not already living in subsidized dwellings and let them all shop for housing like everyone else? Why allocate more than half of the funds to programs that would make specific improvements in specific places? The answer, which will be elaborated upon in the next chapter, is that in low-income neighborhoods such as those in Baltimore, housing allowances are incapable of doing the whole job. In the absence of complementary supply-side efforts which would improve the inner-city environment in pace with the increasing rent-paying ability of beneficiary families, the immediate effect of allowances would be to precipitate a centrifugal movement of families to better sections of the city, leaving many neighborhoods in even greater disarray than before (6). If only the worst areas were partially abandoned, this might actually be a blessing. It is almost certain, however, that many marginal neighborhoods would be adversely affected as well, as would also some of the places to which the families moved. Since, in Baltimore, eliminating housing deprivations and strengthening the inner city are almost synonymous objectives, neither one can be left to chance. Having said this, we should add that if the proposed $25 million budget had to be sharply cut, housing allowances for welfare families should possibly be given priority over rehabilitation programs.

City Vs Suburban Emphasis

We have already argued strongly against trying to suburbanize the housing problem, but now that we have the proposed $25 million annual budget as a firm constraint, the essence of the trade-off between city and suburb can be made much more clear. With this amount of money, approximately 10,000 low-income families could be dispersed to surrounding counties (7). Such a strategy would leave 60,000 privately housed low-income families in the city, and no funds to help them, beyond what current programs can now provide. Despite this fact, if it could be convincingly demonstrated either: (a) that the 10,000 families had a much greater chance of rising out of poverty in the suburbs than in the city; or (b) that their out-migration would materially improve conditions for those remaining behind without simultaneously worsening the living environment of their new suburban neighbors; or (c) that the loss of 10,000 low-income families would make it substantially easier for the city to retain middle- and upper-income households and renew decaying areas; then suburbanization would perhaps have to be recommended. Such a recommendation would imply, however, that the out-migrating families would be carefully screened with respect to precisely how suburbanization would alter their opportunities for improvement. It would also imply that the suburban housing subsidy of $2,500 per family per year would benefit the recipients and the city more than would, say, an unrestricted annual cash grant or some other form of assistance of equivalent amount. Even granting the efficacy of a suburban approach, however, the political barriers to relocating such a large number of families within a reasonable number of years seem insurmountable.

Finally, to repeat what was said in Chapter 7, if the present emphasis in housing subsidy program continues, the suburbanized families would be in the moderate-income category. Their departure would release housing for low-income families, but would not insure its proper upkeep and might further destabilize inner-city neighborhoods.

A SUMMARY OBSERVATION

As we tried to emphasize in Chapter 1, and as we will again in Chapter 14, many housing issues cannot be resolved by technical analysis. They arise in part out of differing perceptions concerning the importance of various housing objectives relative to each other and to nonhousing goals. Our recommendations reflect one set of perceptions. They may be properly challenged by those who have other priorities, who may feel, for example, that modest re-habilitation is not as necessary as is expansion of health programs, or that some neighborhoods should receive last rites in order for others to be improved well above the standards we set, or that the poor must be benignly neglected because of more urgent city problems.

Given this multiplicity of city and societal goals whose achievement is sought through the expenditure of public funds, the question arises as to the political feasibility of a housing strategy as expensive as the one which we have outlined. Although the cost of the seven proposals plus already existing programs is modest in comparison with many other housing proposals, being equivalent to a national program of only $10 billion (1974 dollars), it could not be financed locally, and it would put considerable additional pressure on a federal budget that is already under severe duress. "Indeed, for the next several years the growth in federal expenditures under existing programs and those proposed in the 1973 budget may exceed the growth in full employment revenues under current tax laws. By 1977, revenue increases may have equaled the growth in expenditures, but they are not likely to produce a surplus for use in launching major new governmental programs to meet emerging national priorities. This situation is in sharp contrast to earlier periods in the nation's economic history, during which peacetime economic growth tended to produce larger gains in federal revenues than were absorbed by ongoing federal expenditure programs. As a consequence – in the near future at least – major new federal programs will have to be financed either from higher taxes or from sharp reductions in current acitivites (8)." It seems to us, therefore, that a $10 billion national housing budget may be too much to expect, especially when there is pressure for large budget increases in health, education, employment, and other problem areas (9). Our feeling is supported by the Administration's housing and community development budget for fiscal year 1975, which totals only $5 billion. What this lower rate of expenditure will mean for the immediate future of urban areas is uncertain.

CHAPTER 12
From Problems to Policy: Part II

The preceding chapter attempted to move from a review of Baltimore's housing situation to a set of policy recommendations. The feasibility and desirability of these recommendations were subjected to superficial evaluation by comparing them briefly with several alternative strategies which have been widely discussed in the professional literature. Because of the nature of the examination, many detailed questions concerning the appropriateness and probable effectiveness of our proposals still remain to be answered. This chapter, therefore, treats each of the seven proposals in more depth, seeking to expose weaknesses as well as strengths. Following these individual analyses the chapter concludes with a short discussion of the relationship of a low-income housing strategy generally to larger market forces and broader central-city goals.

A thorough analysis of our recommendations and their possible substitutes would ordinarily have to address all of the following questions:

1. Probable cost-effectiveness with respect to the proximate objectives which are being sought. Can the proposed programs easily reach the target populations, produce the intended results, and be inexpensively administered?

2. Probable impact on the larger system for which change is desired. Can the programs facilitate achievement of higher level goals, or are there barriers in the system that would act to prevent favorable program effects from being sustained? What would be the favorable and unfavorable effects on non-target populations?

3. Probable costs and benefits and their distribution throughout the community. Given various assumptions about probable effectiveness and impact, do benefits as a whole exceed costs? For what groups is the reverse true?

4. Probable time required to mount the programs. Is the time reasonable relative to the immediacy of the problems being attacked?

5. Probable political feasibility. Do the programs employ methods which are in consonance with prevailing social values? Do they imply a large or small reallocation of rights and responsibilities among important interest groups? Do they impose a heavy burden on the public purse? Do they pursue objectives that are widely perceived to be important?

It is not possible here to cover all of these questions with respect to all of our proposals. Nor is it necessarily desirable. Other studies have already examined or are in the process of examining certain housing programs in some detail. So, for example, policy-makers already know a good bit about the cost-effectiveness of public housing, leased housing, and residential rehabilitation efforts, and they will soon have a much better understanding of the probable effectiveness and impact of housing allowances. Consequently, what we have tried to do in this chapter is confine our analysis to what we feel to be key issues concerning our proposals, each proposal being discussed separately. While this approach is not comprehensive, it is also not as unsystematic as may seem on the surface.

MODEST REHABILITATION

Some housing analysts and practitioners are skeptical of housing programs that emphasize residential rehabilitation, and they are particularly negative toward modest rehabilitation. Since such activity appears essential for Baltimore on a massive scale, it is important to examine the major reservations of its critics. The principal arguments which have been voiced against modest rehabilitation are summarized and evaluated below (1).

Modest rehabilitation programs do not yield sufficient visible improvements to satisfy recipient families and to change negative attitudes toward the inner city. As already suggested, any program to improve the residential inventory in the inner city will come to naught if the basic feelings of residents about home and environment are not altered. Some observers argue that modest rehabilitation would fail for this reason. Implicitly, they reject the housing code as an adequate standard of quality.

Two questions are involved here. The first is whether modest rehabilitation would indeed be less visible than maximum rehabilitation or new construction. Actually it is just the reverse. Holding aggregate investment constant, modest rehabilitation touches many more families, and thus is much *more* visible to inner-city residents than is new construction. Unfortunately, arguments against modest rehabilitation almost uniformly fail to include a realistic budget contraint. As a consequence, the visibility comparison is made while assuming erroneously that the same number of structures would be involved under either alternative.

The second question is what is key to consumer acceptance? Without denying the need for physical improvement of dwellings, we would argue that changes in the neighborhood environment and in ownership patterns are more pivotal. The question remains, however, as to whether modest rehabilitation, per se, could induce positive attitudes toward home and neighborhood. We feel the answer to this question is a qualified yes. What an upper-income observer might regard as a too modest or minimal improvement is not viewed as cosmetic by poverty-stricken families. In their eyes, $2,000 to $3,000 of improvements to a $2,000 structure constitute quite a significant change. And where the basic renovation budget is augmented by as little as a few hundred dollars in order to modernize a kitchen or bath, families sometimes become almost euphoric. Or so the experience of inner-city investors would suggest.

The most difficult argument to counter might seem on the surface to be the one associated with the social fabric image, i.e., that negative attitudes stem largely from high crime rates, poor schools, etc., and until these conditions improve, any substantial investment in housing in the inner city will be ineffective. In fact, however, modest rehabilitation, by tacitly supporting the view that significant physical changes cannot solve social problems, is in consonance with this image of the problem. It also reflects our finding that a majority of inner-city residents seem more concerned at the present moment about conditions in their neighborhood than about deficiencies in their homes.

Modest rehabilitation programs are wasteful because the total environment is not changed materially and the improvements are only temporary. There is some resistance to salvaging an old inventory, because the obsolete structures and land use patterns would remain, and could not permanently stem the outward flow of families. Modest rehabilitation might satisfy the population for a time, but over a period of 10 to 30 years, it would have to be followed by programs of "maximum" treatment. Thus, money spent on intermediate-term renovation would be wasted.

This line of reasoning seems to be based on what might be termed a bias toward newness. It does not flow out of an analysis of the economics of alternative treatments. Our own analysis, which is described in detail in Chapter 13, clearly indicates that modest rehabilitation of most of the inner-city stock *is* economically feasible in terms of the quality of housing which would be achieved and the life-expectancy of the renewed structures. On efficiency grounds, it is superior to either maximum rehabilitation or new construction, both of which provide many elements of luxury that the poor themselves would gladly trade for more necessary items if they had the opportunity.

Partial renewal, if it may be termed that, certainly cannot stem the outward tide permanently, but it can buy time for the city, and it can confine abandonments to the worst structures. In addition, it minimizes competition with nonhousing approaches to poverty problems that may have a greater long-term payoff, and it provides more flexibility for the city to implement complete renewal of the inner city with new techniques of housing production that are likely to be developed before the end of the century. Most important, on a large scale, it is the only program possible. Maximum rehabilitation and new construction could simply not muster the public resources and manpower required to create the same number of standard units.

Modest rehabilitation programs, because they operate in relatively good areas, are of little direct benefit to the lowest income families. In the early days of the federally assisted code enforcement program, HUD restricted modest upgrading to areas where "conservation" was deemed appropriate. There were few low-income families in these areas. Today these tools are being applied more broadly. They still, however, favor owner occupants and modestly deteriorated structures, whereas in many cities, the poor are renters and are concentrated in dwellings that are beyond repair. Baltimore is a fortunate exception. Modest rehabilitation is appropriate treatment for areas of the city and in structures where poor families already reside. It can directly benefit many of the families in greatest need. It is definitely not a "creaming" device that would only indirectly help the poor.

Therefore, modest rehabilitation constitutes a much more equitable distribution of resources than does either maximum rehabilitation or new construction for two reasons. First, assistance need not be limited to a lucky few, but can extend instead to most of those who are found to be in need. Second, the assistance which is given is not so bountiful as to enable the poor to enjoy accommodations that are better than those of lower-middle-income taxpayers and more luxurious than what subsidized families really need. It makes little sense to devote a large proportion of available funds to housing low-income families in newly constructed structures costing $20,000 a unit when, as in Baltimore, the median value of standard dwelling units in the private unsubsidized stock is half that amount. Congress has frequently been chastised for not authorizing more subsidized new construction for low-income families, but in this case it has probably been much more sensible than its critics in recognizing that attempting to solve the low-income housing problem in this fashion would result in a terrible mis-allocation of resources.

Modest rehabilitation means more recurrent maintenance problems, hence is not consistent with the ownership-transfer proposal. This reasoning is correct insofar as it applies to the owner-occupancy portion of the transfer proposal. Professional investors can easily handle maintenance problems which would pose serious difficulties for an ordinary homeowner. It would be unfortunate if families had the dream of a house of their own turn into a night-mare because they did not have the funds or skills to keep their homes in good repair. To prevent this real possibility from occurring, various forms of advice and assistance, several of which are discussed later under "Man-agement-maintenance," would surely have to be provided. In addition, a publicly underwritten warranty at time of purchase would be helpful. It might also be feasible to create professional maintenance companies which would service owners under contracts similar to those used by fuel oil com-panies. This approach to the maintenance problem has the potential advan-tage of being a partial substitute for code enforcement and at much less cost.

Modest rehabilitation programs are difficult and expensive to administer. This final argument is supported by the experience under the federally assisted code enforcement program (FACE) in Baltimore and other cities. Because of the customized nature of modest rehabilitation, processing of Section 312 loans and Section 115 grants under the program has proved to be a major bottleneck. The rehabilitation work itself has not gone smoothly, and adminis-trative overhead has been high relative to the value of work put in place.

There is the additional problem of constant pressure, usually successful, to raise standards well above what is absolutely necessary and what families can afford. There are countless examples of this, not only in Baltimore, but else-where as well. While not fatal to the program, it does sharply reduce the num-ber of families who can be helped with any given sum of money.

These problems are not inherently insoluble. To date, modest rehabilita-tion efforts have generally been viewed as low priority. If it is recognized that large portions of the inventory may be lost and that most of the low-income population may suffer without such activity, solutions to these problems should be possible. Also, coupling modest rehabilitation with an increase in various forms of owner occupancy should give some impetus to the develop-ment of administrative efficiency, since some of the administrative difficulties relate to ownership characteristics of the stock and not to the stock itself. On balance, however, one cannot be optimistic about implementing large scale modest rehabilitation under the direct supervision of a public agency. Mecha-nisms must be created which permit public control of some of the subsidies for inner-city rehabilitation to be indirectly exercised.

Conclusion

Modest rehabilitation does suffer from most of the limitations its critics ascribe to it. Since it focuses on structures which, for the most part, do not represent a serious threat to health and safety, it contributes little to these basic housing goals. And since it does not address the problem of obsoles-cence, it cannot prevent a *relative* decline in the quality of the city's housing stock; thus it cannot increase the city's ability to achieve income mixing while new construction adds modern dwellings to the suburban inventory. Nor, acting alone, can it arrest the forces that are causing absolute decline.

But these criticisms must be placed in perspective. Modest rehabilitation would not be the centerpiece of the low-income housing effort, except possibly in terms of the number of lives affected. It would consume few resources, and would operate in concert with other housing and nonhousing programs. Its potential contribution is in catching marginal structures before the expense of remedial treatment becomes exorbitant and before the condition of these structures adversely affects the investment decisions of nearby owners. In cities where deterioration is not spreading into stable neighborhoods and where the moderately substandard inventory is adequately maintained, the funds which might be allocated to modest rehabilitation could perhaps be better spent elsewhere. Generally speaking, though, it would seem negligent for cities not to attack decay in an important way until major surgery is needed.

The major barrier to modest rehabilitation has to do with the fact that most of the inventory needing such treatment is investor-owned. Effective politically acceptable devices for subsidizing rehabilitation by investors do not yet exist. FACE floundered partly for this reason. It could offer upgrading grants only to owner occupants, and its subsidized improvement loans were unappealing to landlords in declining neighborhoods. Housing allowances would obviously have some potential here, as would ownership-transfer and abatement of real estate taxes, but none of these alternatives could solve this problem by itself.

MAXIMUM REHABILITATION AND NEW CONSTRUCTION

As mentioned at the beginning of this chapter, at the time of our building survey 8,000 occupied dwelling units in Baltimore were found to be seriously substandard. Roughly another 5,000 vacant units, most of them boarded up or abandoned, were in the same condition. These 13,000 units and those which will join them in the future can be dealt with in either of two ways. They can all be permanently removed from the market and then demolished whenever appropriate, or they can be rehabilitated. If demolished, they can be replaced by new subsidized structures, or the sites on which they were located can remain vacant. Ignoring externalities, demolition without replacement would usually be the least expensive course of action. In the case of the 8,000 occupied substandard units, satisfactory homes for a majority of the displaced families could be found in the private inventory at an average price of around $5,000 (1969 dollars), whereas the cost of rehabilitation and new construction would be triple that amount. As for the 5,000 vacant substandard units, most of them are in neighborhoods where average market values are $6,000 or less per unit. If they were brought up to standard, they would have to be sold at a huge loss. Moreover, unless the rehabilitation activity were accompanied by an increase in the number of families desiring to live in the inner city, the upgraded units would simply draw occupants away from nearby buildings which would then lie vacant for lack of demand, leaving the overall situation not much better than before. In fact this has already happened. It is true that if renewal by musical chairs were continued, eventually entire neighborhoods would be upgraded, but at very heavy cost to the public sector, since the more "Cadillacs" that were given away, the more "Plymouths" that would be abandoned. Additionally, the strategy might solidify obsolete street and lot patterns.

It may seem from the above that if the volume of housing starts in a market area is adequate to take care of population growth and inventory losses, subsidized maximum rehabilitation or new construction in the inner city can rarely be justified, since low-income families can be provided with decent accommodations in less expensive fashion. There are three situations, however, in which a maximum-rehabilitation/new-construction approach may be appropriate. The first is where the physical environment of a neighborhood has been endangered by the abandonment of a few badly damaged buildings. Such structures could, of course, simply be razed; the newly created open space would often be most welcome. In Baltimore's row-house neighborhoods, though, demolition of other than corner properties would leave an unsightly facade which would be as grim a reminder of the decline of the area as would be a boarded-up unit.

The need for subsidized maximum rehabilitation and new construction is even greater in neighborhoods that are going downhill because of physical obsolescence. As mentioned in the previous section, upgrading efforts which do no more than bring deteriorating dwellings into conformance with code standards are powerless to prevent the *relative* decline of housing quality in the inner city, a trend which if not arrested is eventually likely to lead to absolute decline as well. Attacking the physical obsolescence of marginal neighborhoods through selective overimprovement of structures and redesign of block and lot patterns may often be effective in preventing more expensive wholesale redevelopment at a later date.

Finally, subsidized maximum rehabilitation and new construction can be instrumental in preserving a healthful social environment in the inner city if the dwellings in question are sold or rented at whatever the traffic will bear to non-low-income families, many of whom would otherwise migrate to newer neighborhoods (2). Subsidizing the nonpoor is already standard procedure in exclusive downtown redevelopment areas through the write-down of cleared land. If the same general principle were applied to Section 235 and 236 projects, just in the inner city, not only would the social and market environment be enhanced, but also the subsidies would travel further and the financial difficulties of most inner-city projects would be overcome. Needed subsidies to low-income families could be provided in other ways.

Although the potential role of subsidized maximum rehabilitation and new construction in stabilizing and improving inner-city neighborhoods is reasonably clear, the precise situations in which such expenditures would be justified remain to be identified. Suppose, for example, there are 50 row homes on a street front and one of them has been vandalized and boarded up. Suppose too that if the city were to acquire, upgrade, and resell the property, it would incur a net loss of $5,000; or similarly, that if the city upgraded the property but used it for public housing, the net loss relative to leasing a home in the private market would also be $5,000. Under what circumstances would taking a loss be warranted? A satisfactory answer to this question could in theory be obtained by applying a simple investment criterion. If the 50 surrounding properties each experienced a favorable price effect of $100 (either rising in value or ceasing to fall in value) then presumably the city could, if it wished, get back its investment through some combination of higher taxes, a longer stream of tax income, and special assessments. If the city could not recover its outlay, implying that despite the rehabilitation effort, the block continued to decline at the same or greater pace than before, then the money would probably have been better spent elsewhere.

Unfortunately, it is impossible to know in advance what effect the rehabilitation may have on surrounding properties, and we have very little experience to serve as a guide. A common observation is that if there are only one or two badly deteriorated structures in an otherwise "solid" block, then it would make sense for a city to invest more money in these structures than their post-rehabilitation market value might seem to warrant. Such blocks exist in fairly large numbers at the outer fringe of the inner city and in the middle ring. When this strategy has been pursued, however, the results have not always been as expected, indicating that the appearance of solidness had been deceptive and that the few spots of serious decay were not isolated phenomena but rather the spray from an oncoming wave of blight. Much more than spot rehabilitation was needed.

This experience suggests that to become candidates for subsidized maximum rehabilitation (or new construction), structures (or lots) should be in neighborhoods in which a comprehensive program of preservation and renewal is being actively pursued. Clearly, not all 8,000 of the occupied seriously substandard dwellings in Baltimore are located in such neighborhoods. It is assumed here, however, that those which should not be renovated or replaced will be matched over a decade or so by an equal number, including some of the 5,000 vacant substandard units for which such treatment is appropriate.

At the present time, programs which attempt to implement maximum-rehabilitation goals in neighborhoods where there is a high probability of success are seriously hampered by the frequent inability of sponsors to acquire deteriorated properties expeditiously and at a reasonable price. Owners either will not sell or cannot be found, and tax foreclosure takes several years. Meanwhile, neighboring properties suffer from the blighting effects of a nonconforming use. An equitable means must be found to force troublesome owners to fix up or give up. Also needed is an assist from the Federal Housing Administration which holds many properties requiring gut rehabilitation but which customarily is unwilling to incur the losses that attend such treatment. FHA further contributes to blight and decay by boarding up foreclosed properties that are in livable condition.

To encourage the rehabilitation of abandoned residential structures and simultaneously expand home ownership in declining neighborhoods, a number of cities throughout the country have recently launched urban homesteading programs. Under these programs, derelict properties which a municipality has acquired either through tax foreclosure or by gift are transferred to families at a nominal price in return for a written promise by the new owners to upgrade and occupy the properties within a stipulated period of time. Unfortunately, in the depressed inner-city market, the cost of rehabilitating abandoned structures (over $15,000 on the average) is much higher than the post-rehab market value of these structures (rarely over $10,000). So even if families paid nothing for their urban homestead, they would be making a bad investment.

Advocates of homesteading argue that the gap between post-rehab market values and the cost of improvements can be closed by the elimination of middle-man profits of developers and by donated labor of the homesteading families. The history of self-help housing, however, clearly demonstrates that this is impossible. Not more than a handful of families would have the requisite skills to enable them to make a substantial labor input. Moreover, even if they were able to do the work themselves, their loss would be no less real. Subsidies are obviously necessary to cover the losses which rehabilitation of abandoned structures in declining areas inevitably entails. These alone are not enough, however. Most of the neighborhoods in which cities own abandoned properties are simply not areas in which families should be encouraged to invest their financial resources, skills, and several years of their lives, unless collateral programs are developed to provide whatever additional resources are required to reverse downward market trends and upgrade the physical infrastructure and social environment. These programs do not now exist.

Urban homesteading has been described as a brightly wrapped package with nothing inside. This characterization may be too charitable. There *is* something inside—a badly conceived program that totally ignores a large body of housing theory and experience (3). As this fact has become recognized by those who are attempting to make homesteading work, the content of the program has been altered, so much so in fact that it is now beginning to resemble prior conservation and renewal efforts, with only the name remaining unchanged.

MANAGEMENT-MAINTENANCE

While the nation struggles to achieve a breakthrough in housing construction, it is experiencing a breakdown in housing management and maintenance stemming from a heavy loss of persons who have experience in the low-rent sector of the market and from a social climate which challenges the ability of even the most talented inner-city landlord to deliver adequate services to his tenants. The major victims of this situation are the tenants themselves who receive less for their housing dollar than they would in a more stable market environment. At present the only direct assault on mismanagement and undermaintenance, namely code enforcement, is the "second front" of housing policy. And given the present investment outlook, even federally assisted code enforcement does little to alter the fundamental underlying problems in the inner-city rental market.

Although it may be possible to restore the inner-city investment climate to the point where present landlords will enthusiastically participate in an effort to improve housing, widespread disenchantment with a business that has low prestige, coupled with the lack of competence and advancing age of many investor-owners, and the reluctance of heirs-apparent to carry on these businesses, all suggest strongly that the provision of adequate management and maintenance throughout the inventory will necessitate massive transfers of ownership from present holders. Any ownership change effort will fail, however, if the technical aspects of management-maintenance are not handled satisfactorily by and for the new owners. Many of the individuals and groups who would acquire properties neither possess nor have easy access to this sort of expertise. Unless appropriate housing service systems can be created, maintenance costs will still be excessive, and the change process will abort. Owner occupants will become overwhelmed by the costs of keeping their homes in good condition, and investors and nonprofit groups, after experiencing unsatisfactory returns, will stop acquiring properties.

What sorts of mechanisms and organizations must be developed to deliver housing services are a matter of some debate. One famous economist has stated that "for the most urgently needed services of the city dweller, private enterprise does not work and never will work. This is true especially of housing construction, housing repair, rehabilitation, maintenance and management . . ." (4) If this is so, it creates something of a dilemma, for all evidence on the subject would seem to indicate that public agencies are even less capable of managing and maintaining the inner-city housing inventory than are the present owners.

The nonprofit alternative, despite its many adherents, is equally impracticable on a large scale. It would require creation of neighborhood corporations, controlled by residents and other interests in the area, which could perform the task of acquisition, limited upgrading, management, and maintenance (5). But development of organizations of this type, in numbers commensurate with the overall objectives, would entail such significant departures from the existing pattern of housing operations as to raise serious questions about the entire approach. Interest in owning low-income housing is not widespread, even among nonprofit groups who are already active in the housing field. Already many church and other nonprofit sponsors of Section 236 and 221-d-3 housing projects have been so badly hurt by unexpected repair bills that they have discarded plans to undertake additional developments. This experience forces one to wonder whether such a delicate and involved task as management of low-rent housing can be satisfactorily executed by nonprofit groups, however well motivated. The empathy and social pressure which they bring to the landlord-tenant relationship, although helpful, are also a source of problems unless undergirded by basic management skills.

Neighborhood corporations would, however, appear to be a most appropriate form of organization for building the necessary positive relationships between occupants and suppliers of rental housing in the inner city. Grassroots groups can make housing an instrument for family and community development. Using community pressure, these groups, more easily than landlords, can obtain tenant cooperation in maintaining private and common areas and in controlling rodents and vermin (6). They also are in a position to help families with income or other problems that would normally result in an eviction. Further, they can monitor their areas daily, and thus reduce vandalism of vacant structures. Finally, they can deal effectively with city hall about neighborhood needs. Nevertheless, it is essential, somehow or other, to keep experienced owners and managers centrally involved in supervising the inventory, and to utilize their expertise in training others.

How this would be done is by no means clear. Successful models for integrating professional management with community participation are hard to find, except in public housing projects which tend to be atypical (7). Speaking generally, housing societies and tenant unions both offer opportunities for factoring the community into the delivery of housing services, but the decision-making powers, administrative tasks, operating functions, and ownership risks that would be appropriate and desirable for them to assume are not certain. Revision of rent schedules, rent collections, tenant selection, property maintenance, tenant education, and evictions are all matters on which they could offer useful advice and assistance. Most community groups, however, would be ill-equipped to accept responsibility for these activities. Whether they would agree with this assessment and be willing to work with skilled private management, and equally, whether owners would desire to enter into cooperative relationships with community groups is impossible to predict.

A partial solution might be the creation of inner-city management-maintenance corporations to serve all types of owners. Collective maintenance agreements are still another possibility. These have been tried, not always successfully, in many suburban housing developments (8). With the experience of these developments as a guide, it should not be difficult to construct workable maintenance formulas for the inner city. In view of the variety of neighborhood situations, a number of different arrangements would be possible. To make certain that owners did not suffer if a maintenance fund for any reason became exhausted, government would probably have to be given supervisory powers and also funds to use in emergency situations.

Concurrent with the above, programs could be sponsored by inner-city investors themselves to: put pressure on "problem" landlords to show a greater interest in their properties; assist owners who are having management difficulties to improve their operations; and create management agreements whereby professional organizations could take over properties from the marginal investor either for a fee or a share in the equity. A program aimed at prospective homeowners might also be helpful. Many lower-income home buyers need to be familiarized with the maintenance tasks which will arise and require assistance in their initial attempts at performing these tasks. The education of owners in simple repair skills has already been tried in several cities, but thus far with mixed results (9).

Finally, a program should be directed at so-called problem families for whom the public sector has to assume greater responsibility if their negative effects on the market are to be minimized. This group might actually prove not to be such a management dilemma if it were formally recognized to exist and dealt with as such.

These mechanisms will not be effective unless the manpower for both the management of maintenance and for maintenance itself is readily available at reasonable prices. In this connection, concern has been expressed that the necessary skills, which are already in short supply, will become even more scarce. The statistics of the situation suggest that these fears are exaggerated. The maintenance (not total management) of as many as 300 units can be supervised by a single individual, and the actual maintenance and repair work can be performed by as few as seven full-time persons or their equivalent.

Thus Baltimore's entire inner-city inventory could be professionally maintained by about 3,000 persons. In view of the fact that a good portion of the maintenance would be done by owners themselves, even this low figure overstates the manpower requirement. Moreover, most of the needed persons are already actively engaged in their trade. Whatever small deficit of skills exists should be relatively easy to eliminate.

This leaves only the problem of developing an environment within which competent management can flourish. Ownership-transfer, expanded programs of rehabilitation, training in management and maintenance, and various activities of neighborhood groups can all help to build positive relationships between owners and tenants, and between owners and the community. However, a frontal attack on other aspects of the environment is also needed. Some of the possible directions are discussed in the following sections.

OWNERSHIP-TRANSFER

Of the several steps that are necessary to reduce housing problems of Baltimore's low-income families within a reasonable period of time, the most critical (and also the most difficult) may be ownership-transfer. A major impediment to inner-city renewal is the prevalence of negative attitudes and behavior toward the stock, and while this situation cannot be reversed by a single thrust, any substantial alteration in behavior is incompatible with present ownership patterns.

This conclusion is not based on a belief that the inner city has been rotted by an infestation of slumlords. Our reservations concerning that widespread hypothesis were expressed in Chapter 9. It is true, however, that well over half of the rental stock is held by persons who cannot cope with the special problems of managing low-income property. Most of these individuals are nonprofessionals owning a few scattered structures and having neither special business acumen nor ability to work with people. A few of them are essentially speculators who became managers involuntarily when their acquisitions could not be resold. They too have no taste or stomach for management. In addition to having financial problems, they are the focus, along with more capable owners, of increasing pressures by individual tenants, tenant groups, and society in general to provide more services and housing of higher quality. Yet they are less and less able to cope with the severe problems of the new urban poor. Although they do perform an essential function, they feel overwhelmed. They want out of the business, and, unfortunately, so do many more competent investor-owners.

Cities, by a variety of actions which it must take anyway to improve the investment climate in the inner city, could ease the burden of these investors and perhaps make it possible for them to survive. This, however, is not enough. In attempts to nurture a group that will never be healthy, other programs, whether they are the ones which have been recommended here or others, will be effectively thwarted.

It would be possible, of course, to operate on the presumption that if the investment environment were revitalized, the incapable and unwilling investor-owners would gradually remove themselves from the scene via normal market processes. In time, this might very well happen. The difficulty with this reasoning is that ownership-transfer is an essential aspect of the revitalization process. For example, vandalism insurance without ownership-transfer would not reduce the costs of vandalism nor, therefore, the essential climate of investment. The same is true with respect to housing allowances. In the absence of specific programs to accelerate and direct transfers, the environment within which an allowance program would function cannot be materially improved in the short and intermediate term.

The importance of ownership-transfer to improvement of the investment environment is not solely, or possibly even most importantly, a function of the quality of present ownership. Even if the inventory were entirely in the hands of individuals and firms who ordinarily would be viewed as good managers, there would be reasons to recommend a substantial shift of ownership, though not on quite the same scale. For attitudes and behavior to change, for a sense of community to develop, for the neighborhood and home to be perceived as a haven which will always be there if necessary, for sense of powerlessness and its unfortunate consequences to be reduced, residents must feel that they have some stake in the game. Tenant unions are but a small step in that direction and not always the right one. They frequently do no more than pit the weak against the weak, and create a hostile environment when precisely the opposite is what is needed.

The primary focus of a transfer program, therefore, would be on ordinary families in all income categories and on community groups (through cooperatives, condominiums, and nonprofit corporations). A second group of considerable importance is the coterie of responsible investor-owners whose management skills are in scarce supply and who should not be allowed to disappear. In many little ways, some of these investors have already given their tenants a stake, and to the extent that tenant unions do develop, these investors are equipped to work with them in a positive way. Assuming that ownership-transfer could help to turn the overall investment climate around, and reduce some of the existing hostilities toward absentee owners generally, the large professional investor should be able to make a significant contribution to the revitalization of the inner city (10).

The most obvious transferee is the city itself. We feel, however, that public acquisitions should be confined largely to last resort situations — structures no one else wants or families no one else is willing to try to house adequately.

Our bias against a general expansion of public ownership is rooted primarily in our data, discussed in Chapter 9, showing that responsible investor-owners are able to provide adequate maintenance for much less than can the Housing Authority (11). Experience in several cities indicates that if the Authority were to acquire a large inventory of scattered-site housing, the relative advantage of the private sector would be even greater. If the per-unit difference in public and private maintenance costs is multiplied by the large number of dwellings which could conceivably come into public ownership, the aggregate difference totals several million dollars annually, a sum which cannot easily be ignored in setting policy.

Assuming programs of ownership-transfer were able to shift the pattern of holdings along the lines just described, they would directly or indirectly contribute to 10 of the 12 housing goals discussed in Chapter 3. Only lack of adequate furnishings and the need for special housing services for the sick and disabled appear to be problems that lie completely outside the scope of an ownership-transfer effort. Hardly a panacea, it does nevertheless have so much to offer to so many families, it must be assigned high priority.

The Negative Case

In spite of the benefits that would allegedly accrue from ownership-transfer, the portions of the idea having to do with home ownership for the poor (a modest part of the total proposal) have never been warmly received. In various quarters it is argued that lower-income families are not "ready" for ownership, would not benefit by it, and do not want it in the inner city. To the extent that ownership-transfer would be tied to modest rehabilitation, it is also felt by some that the task of maintaining a home which has been only partially renewed would be too burdensome for a household with limited resources. When transfer proposals are tied to the notion of nonprofit sponsorship, there is also resistance, this time on the grounds that such organizations are peculiarly ill equipped to undertake the management of low-income properties.

Some of these criticisms and reservations need not apply if the transfer program is properly structured. For example, the maintenance problem, which has been shown to be a serious one in the Section 235 and similar programs, could be handled, as outlined below, through a special repair fund. Similarly, nonprofit organizations could engage professional firms to perform most of the management functions.

As for whether home ownership would be beneficial for lower income families, this too depends on the nature of the program. The negative arguments here are that families might become locked into depreciating assets, or find it difficult to follow job opportunities, or lose their homes during an economic slump. It would indeed be unfortunate if families who are already deprived were given a stake in a no-win game; however, there are ample ways of protecting against this possibility. Land installment contracts, "walk-away" clauses in mortgages, and income-interruption insurance are examples of protective mechanisms that would add little to the cost of the program. A walk-away clause would permit an owner, without penalty, to return his property to the lender at a price equal to the outstanding balance of the loan. Such a clause would be unlikely to increase the number of properties that reverted to the mortgage guarantor, but it would protect the credit reputation of the family in the case of default (12). The income-interruption insurance would simply make sure that payments to the ill and unemployed were sufficient to prevent them from having to give up title to their homes. It would be surprising if the extra cost of the insurance program, which might well be greater than the premiums charged, exceeded the costs of foreclosure that would be incurred if the program did not exist. If, despite these and related protective mechanisms, many of the buyers decided later to return to a rental status, nothing would be lost and much would have been gained.

The assertion that low-income families are not ready for ownership lumps all the deprived population into an unstable, inexperienced category, when in fact these adjectives characterize only a fraction of the poor. A transfer program would without question carry with it a need for what might be termed ownership orientation. Many low-income renter families, accustomed all their lives to having someone else deliver their housing services and handle the maintenance, might not realize the constant attention which a home requires. To acquaint them with this fact would hardly seem a task of undue cost or complexity, however (13).

The potentially most devastating argument against expanded home ownership, though not against ownership-transfer generally, is that families really do not want to become owners in the inner city. Three pieces of evidence are advanced to support this view. The first has been most succinctly stated in the context of a rehabilitation program in another city: ". . . people who are able to buy do not want to own in South Providence, and the people who want to buy in South Providence are not able to own" (14). The second bit of evidence is the experience reported by inner-city investors in Baltimore that when they advertise homes either for sale or for rent at the same monthly terms, the number of interested renters exceeds potential buyers by ratios of as much as 30:1 or more. Even in good neighborhoods outside the inner city, such as Edmundson Village, they have detected this apparently strong preference for rental tenure. The final and most persuasive indication of preferences is from our own household survey which revealed that although almost three-quarters of low-income rental families would like to own a home, the vast majority of these families do not want to purchase in the inner city.

The Providence experience was the consequence of trying to market

$10,000 homes in run down areas where most of the houses were much less expensive. In Baltimore, by contrast, it would be possible with appropriate guarantees to offer homes in good condition for as little as $5,000 — and in spruced-up neighborhoods.

The experience reported by Baltimore investors can be traced only in part to the same underlying situation which exists in South Providence. Since the apparent dearth of buyers is not confined to poorer neighborhoods, there must be other reasons for the disinclination to purchase. One possibility has to do with financing. Prospective buyers might know they cannot obtain mortgage loans and may be unwilling to accept the burden of a land installment contract (LIC). Although this explanation seems weak on the surface, it is given some strength by the large number of families who do want ownership badly enough to have accepted LIC financing. If the desire for ownership were really so limited, LIC's would not have been so widely used. Under an owner-ship-transfer program, loans would be available on terms that are much more attractive than those which inner-city families can now obtain. These loans could make purchase of an inexpensive home not too uncomparable to buying a car.

As for our survey results, they indicate no more than what it is hoped has already been made eminently clear; that ownership-transfer without con-comitant programs of housing rehabilitation and neighborhood improvement would be both infeasible and undesirable. With these associated programs, though, large numbers of families should respond favorably to the opportunity, which thus far has been denied them by either economic circumstance or mortgage financing practices, of becoming homeowners in the inner city. Although the proportion who would seek to purchase cannot be precisely estimated, depending as it does on the quality of the end product, financing terms, and related imponderables, it would certainly be far greater than cur-rent expressions of preferences suggest.

Some Aspects of Implementation

Achieving the conveyance of a large number of parcels within a reasonably short period of time requires several different types of city intervention, in-cluding at least the following:

1. Traditional redevelopment of the worst neighborhoods.

2. Accelerated acquisition, rehabilitation (or demolition), and resale of properties which are located in marginal but viable neighborhoods and which owners will not upgrade to city standards.

3. Creation of a secondary market for properties which owners cannot dis-pose of in the private market.

4. Provision of financing assistance to facilitate transfers.

5. Encouragement, through appropriate legislation, of the creation of quasi-public or private instrumentalities which would undertake specific ownership and upgrading responsibilities in the inner city.

The first order of business is the creation of a special mortgage insurance fund plus underlying pools of capital to broaden ownership opportunities at the fringe of the inner city where mortgage loans are difficult to obtain but where the inventory is in reasonably good condition (15). As the demand for structures which do not require upgrading is satisfied, ownership-transfer can move downward in the stock and geographically inward to include structures which, in the hands of owner occupants, would qualify for Section 115 grants or their equivalent. Simultaneously, it could attempt to consolidate entire blocks for investors who have demonstrated their management capacity and for community groups trying to stabilize their neighborhoods. If this part of the program is to gain momentum, however, more and more resources must be allocated to neighborhood improvements as less and less desirable areas are penetrated by transfer efforts.

Generally speaking, the worst structures, the ones which cannot be made habitable without maximum rehabilitation, should remain in rental occupancy after they have been upgraded, unless a program can be created which transfers genuine title to such structures to recipient families. This has not been possible in most inner cities under the Section 235 home-ownership subsidy program because the subsidy which families receive is not appropriate to existing market conditions. Under Section 235, the selling price of a rehabilitated structure was set to cover the total cost of acquisition and upgrading, with the subsidy to the purchaser taking the form of a below market rate mortgage loan, rather than a capital grant of equivalent amount. Since in the depressed inner-city market, the cost of maximum rehabilitation is much higher than the post-rehabilitation market value of the renewed structure, families who bought structures which received this treatment assumed a mortgage loan obligation that was greater than the value of the property. In effect, they acquired negative equity and became nothing more than renters (albeit in better dwellings than they could otherwise afford) with ownership responsibilities. Ordinary write-down of upgraded structures, preferably without restrictions on the incomes of purchasers, would be a much superior, if slightly more expensive, approach.

NEIGHBORHOOD IMPROVEMENT

The Housing Act of 1949 established decent housing and a suitable living environment as national goals of presumably equal importance. Yet federal programs over the past two decades have stressed the former much more than the latter. If this emphasis is to be criticized, then our own study is equally at fault. For after having suggested in earlier chapters that environmental problems may be of greater concern to low-income families than is the quality of their housing, we do not have as much of substance to suggest in the way of neighborhood programs as the importance of the subject would seem to warrant. This is partly because the dimensions of the environment are so numerous that definition is difficult. It is also partly because many of the negative aspects of the environment are clearly beyond the realm of housing policy; they are, even more than is bad housing, merely symptoms of larger social ills. And it is due at least to some degree to the fact that individuals differ greatly in the extent to which they are sensitive toward various parts of their surroundings. What is said here, therefore, touches only a few pieces of the total problem.

In considering neighborhood goals and strategies, it is important to distinguish between the physical and social environment, deterioration and obsolescence, and the short and long run. The immediate objective, of course, is to stop deterioration of the environment and upgrade it to its previous level if possible. Over the longer term, however, this is not enough. With rising incomes and changing tastes, physical obsolescence must be contended with. Much of the inner-city housing inventory, compressed as it is into blocks where little private or public space is available, will appeal to a smaller and smaller sector of the population. In the absence of extensive physical redesigning of blocks and neighborhoods, the rehabilitation or new construction of individual homes will do nothing to retard declining demand for inner-city living; rather it will simply redistribute a shrinking population and an expanding inventory of abandoned structures (16).

Similarly, the favorable effects of remedial social programs will also be short-lived if basic elements of the social environment are not changed. As discussed in Chapter 7, one such element which is widely felt to be in need of alteration is the spatial concentration of low-income families. To provide these families with a suitable environment, it is alleged, requires moving them to higher income areas. If this is so, then many inner-city neighborhoods should not be saved; they should be eliminated. It must be remembered, however, that about half of the inner-city population is not poor. A prime objective of environmental upgrading, therefore, is to maintain this proportion and gradually increase it over time. Programs of inner-city improvement ought never to be just for the poor, but instead must speak as well to other population groups without whose presence the inner city cannot survive.

The first task in a city-wide program of neighborhood revival is the identification of areas in the community where viable neighborhood preservation groups exist or could readily be created. In the worst parts of the city, there may well be organizationless areas which, since the inner city will continue to thin out in any event, should be permitted to die gracefully, but under close city supervision and in a way that will not force private owners to suffer financial losses (17).

Once neighborhood groups have been identified, assistance should be provided in developing agendas for *limited* action involving residents, property owners, local organizations, and the city at a level of effort within the current dollar and manpower resources of each. At the same time, such studies as seem necessary for the development of longer term plans and strategies should be commenced. In order to avoid the failures of similar efforts which have occurred under the Community Action and Model Cities programs, examples of successful programs around the country merit careful study (18). Although program content will obviously vary from neighborhood to neighborhood, depending on current conditions and recent and expected trends, a few generalizations can perhaps be made concerning desirable short-term physical and social programs.

Some Remedial Physical Programs

Since most of the physical environment of housing is the residential inventory itself, structural improvements alone are a major component of any environmental effort and should be so recognized. This fact is not lost on inner-city residents. In our household survey, poor condition of housing was the fifth most frequently cited serious neighborhood problem, ranking just behind crime, noise, lack of play space for children, and dirty streets. Anything that could be done to upgrade exteriors of structures, reduce abandonments, and restore abandoned structures to residentially related uses would correspondingly reduce this source of discontent.

Moving beyond the dwelling unit to the immediate surroundings, according to our own ratings, alleys and backyards are the major eye- and nose-sore. The rear areas are used primarily for storage. They are too small and lacking in privacy to serve as patios, and the expense of furnishing them in this fashion would be prohibitive for low-income households with many more pressing needs. Further, unless most of the rear yards were improved, any one of them would be an unpleasant place to sit or cook out.

Yards and alleys adjoining rented structures are especially prone to the trash problem, even in relatively good neighborhoods and in blocks whose rear yards are of ample size (19). Renters in general are not interested in improving someone else's lawn, and in the case of structures with two or more dwelling units, they certainly are not willing to care for someone else's trash. If a maintenance man is not on the scene almost daily, debris will almost always be in evidence.

Bad as they are, most of the rear areas may be more sightly than they were several decades ago when outdoor toilets were prevalent and unpaved yards were a happy breeding ground for rodents. Over the years, the city has worked hard and in a number of different ways to solve the block-interior problem. Its most famous effort was an attempt to create 29 inner-block parks in conjunction with the Harlem Park urban renewal program. Due to various problems in implementation, however, most of the plans for small parks and formal recreation spaces were scrapped and instead block interiors were converted to hard-surface areas. Although the program has not been viewed by many as a great success, block interiors are better maintained in Harlem Park than in many comparable blocks located elsewhere in the inner city. This difference, however, may be primarily due to variations in the level of maintenance provided by the city rather than to variations in attitudes and patterns of behavior on the part of residents.

A second design effort of some magnitude, though still not in the implementation stage, is the block-strategy approach being developed by the Department of Planning. It attempts in various ways, depending on the particular situation, to redesign the block so as to eliminate its dysfunctional characteristics and restore abandoned open space to useable condition. In some cases, this may involve demolition of a few structures and creation of parking lots, public play areas, or extension of rear yards. In other instances, more radical surgery may be suggested. In general, a sense of openness, which many families find sadly lacking, is created without reducing population density per acre. It is an imaginative strategy. It is too early to say whether it can achieve a measure of success.

While the generally poor condition of block interiors in the inner city may not seem to be important enough to warrant the attention being given to it here, it is of special interest because it raises a fundamental point which extends across many other problems in the physical environment — ultimately, an improved environment will come about only if residents care. Relatively few resources are required to upgrade the environment initially. For example, a crash program heavily supported by volunteers and city, state, and federal equipment could clean junk out of the inner city of Baltimore in two or three days. Hundreds of similar efforts around the country attest to this fact. What happens after the clean-up is largely a function of attitudes on the part of those delivering and receiving maintenance services. Each individual must exert a little extra effort (20). More dollar resources are a relatively small part of the solution. A structure through which positive attitudes can be translated into behavior is obviously necessary, but whether anything is accomplished depends very much on the people themselves.

If attitudes are key, then the process by which the upgrading takes place is also critical to successful maintenance later on. The way in which residents and investors are involved, the amount of attention given to creating neighborhood identity, the system of rewards, the success of ownership-transfer efforts, the permanence or impermanence of neighborhood groups whose aid is solicited, the nature and frequency of follow-up actions, and the relative success of the city in solving other neighborhood problems, are all vital to the development of resident interest and to the triggering of independently initiated upgrading activities. This perhaps more than the precise results achieved is the lesson of the annual *Afro-American* Clean-Block Campaign in Baltimore.

Pursuing the emphasis on process, it would seem that a succession of small programs would permit maximum community involvement and at the same time gradually develop a sense of progress. The initial thrust might be the crash program of junk removel, just mentioned. Before the effects of that campaign had waned completely away, it could be followed by rodent eradication; then perhaps by minor paint-up/fix-up, using free paint and other materials. Still later could come painting of street furniture, tree planting, minor improvements to rear yards, and so on. Every few years the cycle could be repeated. Sandwiched between these special programs, continuing activities such as clean-block campaigns and, as in Baltimore, annual community fairs, could serve as additional vehicles for community organization and environmental improvement. Important also would be the creation of permanent neighborhood-based systems to watch-dog applications for zoning changes and liquor licenses, assist the city in code enforcement, trash collection, and other services, force immediate upgrading or demolition of abandoned structures, identify "problem" families whom public agencies or people in the neighborhood could help, and call attention of the city to other environmental problems of special local concern.

All of this is, superficially at least, cosmetic and it has been criticized as such. The criticisms fail to recognize that it is the process, not the immediate product, which is the important contribution to the environment; process and environment are overlapping sets. Noncosmetic approaches which ignore this fact are in their own way even more superficial, and for this reason frequently achieve disappointing results. The only valid test, therefore, is whether the intended beneficiaries respond favorably. If inner-city residents reject the effort, the worst that can be said is that an inexpensive test failed. If there is consumer acceptance, however, the basis is laid for more permanent improvement. Thus even though these proposals are perhaps best viewed as holding actions, not solutions, and even though their favorable effects would soon wear away, if they were not followed by more substantial changes, they would, nevertheless, serve as an inexpensive yet extremely valuable test of barriers to upgrading. In the process of succeeding with these ideas in some neighborhoods and failing in others, cities could develop much more sensitive micro-strategies than they now have.

Some Remedial Social Programs

In Philadelphia recently, after all of the apparently necessary physical improvements had been made to a number of neighborhoods under urban renewal programs, and after the programs had been "closed out," the processes of decay resumed. Since the families in these neighborhoods can afford adequate maintenance, it can be reasoned that something essential was still missing in the social environment. What? The city is like a ship. Because of its high population density, it offers the good life only if everyone shares certain values and exercises a high degree of self discipline. If even a small proportion of respondents do not respect the rules, things can easily go amuck because ferreting out wrong-doers is so difficult. Good fences may make good neighbors in the country, but in the city the only fences are the laws and customs which have general citizen acceptance. In our interviews with families and community leaders in Baltimore, a genuine affection for neighbors and neighborhoods frequently emerged. What discouraged respondents were the acts of a few individuals who had managed to inflict severe damage on both the physical and social environment. The antisocial behavior of these individuals had apparently not prompted stable families to take poor care of their homes. However, in contributing to a sense of impermanence among many residents, and in dissuading families from moving to the inner city, such behavior may be linked to overall neighborhood decline in an immediate and direct way. Thus, although ownership-transfer and related programs are bound to improve the social environment to a degree, we would place great emphasis on programs to protect life and property. As an extension of housing policy, such programs would address the neighborhood problem which, according to our survey, is ranked number one in seriousness by Baltimore's inner-city residents.

In particular, there should be a focus on youth. Most of the crimes in the city involve young people. Some youths are perpetrators; others are victims. They are also the major victims of poor schools, lack of jobs, and crowded conditions. Only if the social problems of youth can be ameliorated can the inner city become a desirable place for families to live and will it be able to attract stable households (21).

Just as physical decay is inevitable unless incomes are adequate to support maintenance, so too social deterioration is certain to occur in an environment of poverty. It is likely, therefore, that in some neighborhoods an emphasis on youth will be insufficient to prevent continued social and physical decline. In these areas, broader programs are needed to increase the sense of security, well being, and permanence of all residents. Building a community, in both the physical and social sense of the term, is largely an endeavour to order the future. This is virtually impossible in neighborhoods where a large proportion of the residents are engulfed by immediate personal problems, many of which may threaten their very survival.

The Proposal In Perspective

Neighborhood stabilization programs have a long history, most of it bad. Efforts to halt the outward flow of blight from inner-city slums by strengthening endangered neighborhoods have, more often than not, been overwhelmed by larger market and societal forces which preservation strategies have implicitly ignored by dealing with the problems of decline one-dimensionally and at a single scale. We should like to emphasize again, therefore, what we stressed at the outset of this discussion, that the proposals presented here are not intended to constitute a neighborhood stabilization strategy. They are aimed primarily at short-term environmental objectives; by themselves they could do little about the dynamics of decay. It is our entire package of programs which is designed to alter market trends. Whether it has a reasonable probability of doing so is discussed in the concluding section of the chapter.

IMPROVING THE INVESTMENT CLIMATE

The aggregate market value of Baltimore's inner-city residential inventory exceeds $500 million; its replacement cost would top $1.5 billion. To keep this inventory adequately maintained requires an investment of $30 million annually. To eliminate current substandard conditions and partially offset structural obsolescence will require additional capital outlays of at least $20 million per year for 10 years. Of the entire $50 million, the public sector must contribute, according to our estimates, about $14 million, and make extensive environmental improvements as well (22). Whether this infusion of funds will be sufficient to draw out the necessary $36 million in private capital depends on the ability of government to create a favorable investment climate in the inner city for homeowners, investors, and mortgage lenders. Without this climate the $14 million will be largely wasted; depreciation and deterioration of the $500 million in housing assets will continue; and replacement of a large portion of these assets at great expense to the taxpayer may become necessary.

Despite much discussion about the greater than average risks which owners and lenders face in inner-city areas, efforts to improve the situation have been few in number, narrow in scope, and, on the whole, less than satisfactory. Reliance has been placed almost exclusively on mortgage insurance programs of the Federal Housing Administration (FHA) (23). Owner occupants and equity investors have no protection at all against capital depreciation. And while the FHA has furnished critically needed support to parts of the inner city, it has never quite caught the rhythm of this sector of the market, alter-nating between unrealistically high property and credit standards and scandal-producing generosity.

A serious barrier to creation of a stable investment environment has to do with the fact that inherent in the filtering process is a situation of declining real prices in older neighborhoods. Inflation and expanding population mitigate some of the attendant investment risks in these neighborhoods, but government programs which artifically raise the rate of new construction may often have the opposite effect by accelerating housing abandonment. Only if the public sector finds a way to either place a floor under neighborhood quality in aging areas or otherwise insure potential homeowners and investors against rapid and unlimited filtering will an adequate flow of risk capital be forthcoming. Precisely how to do this, or even whether it can be done, is uncertain, though the recommendations elsewhere in this chapter for income supports and neighborhood development programs are seen by us as a large part of the answer. Until these approaches prove themselves, however, risks of inner-city investment will have to be underwritten directly.

Mortgage lenders have often been severely criticized for contributing to the poor investment climate in the inner city by prematurely red-lining still stable neighborhoods, thereby forcing down prices, diverting demand for long-term investment and owner occupancy to other areas, and further concentrating the poor. Their decisions to stop lending are alleged to seem rational only because they help to create the situation which has been prophesied. There are ample examples which seem to support this assertion, particularly in racially changing areas. The favorable foreclosure experience of land-installment contract investors in the very neighborhoods in which institutional lenders expect high rates of default is but one illustration of apparent excess caution.

Given present public policies, however, parts of most urban areas will continue to decline, and certain sections will ultimately experience almost complete rejection by the market. This being so, untimely withdrawal of lender support is understandable, and in many instances it may only hasten the inevitable. Joint action by local government and mortgage institutions is needed to prevent the conditions which give rise to lender concern in the first place. Development of better inner-city actuarial data for lenders and assistance to them in servicing loans to low-income families would likewise be helpful. Requiring lending institutions to allocate a certain portion of their assets to inner-city areas, as has been proposed in Massachusetts and Maryland, might also be desirable, but only if such assets are adequately protected by government guarantees.

It is useful to keep in mind, too, that although our discussion may convey the impression of a universal problem, the quality of the investment climate in older neighborhoods seems to vary considerably among metropolitan areas. If the existence of this apparent variation could be validated, and the reasons for it determined, programs to re-create stability in places such as Baltimore could be designed with greater sensitivity to all of the forces that might bring about the defeat of remedial efforts.

HOUSING ALLOWANCES

The collection of proposed policies just presented would do nothing to improve the financial ability of the low-income population to acquire better housing. The policies are concerned almost exclusively with the supply side of the market. Their purpose is to improve the quality of homes and neighborhoods at no expense to the consumer. For some consumers, primarily owner occupants, housing costs would be reduced, but not appreciably. Most low-income families would continue to pay about what they now spend for shelter. In many, but by no means most, cases these payments are insufficient to support adequate building maintenance. Hence, in the absence of some form of operating subsidy, portions of the upgraded inventory would soon deteriorate to their pretreatment condition. How can this situation be avoided?

There are several possibilities. On the supply side, perhaps the best approach from an administrative standpoint would be to attach a subsidy to the existing system of real estate taxation. Following the lead of a number of states, homestead tax exemptions could be granted to low-income owners and renters. Alternatively, tax exemption of up to, say, $150 a year could be granted to selected groups of property owners whose dwelling units were kept in good condition (24). For example, all owners of adequately maintained structures in designated conservation and renewal areas could be given an exemption regardless of the financial characteristics of the properties or their occupants. This procedure would avoid the cumbersome task of verifying income. Additionally, it would provide an equitable way of reducing the excessive tax burden that is often borne by inner-city real estate (25). It would obviously not be effective, however, in communities where much of the low-income population is highly scattered. In Baltimore, either strategy for dealing with the housing maintenance problem would cost about $8 million to $12 million annually, depending on the standards used and the number of owners receiving assistance.

On the demand side, adequate maintenance could probably be achieved through either housing allowances or broader forms of income supplementation. If the sole purpose of such subsidies were to keep the residential inventory in good repair, they could be characterized as overkill. Our minimum estimate of the annual cost of a program of allowances for Baltimore is $35 million (roughly $7 billion nationally in 1969 dollars), an amount which is about five times the annual maintenance deficit and equal to the sum of all current housing subsidies in the city (26). This fact argues strongly for the real estate tax subsidy as the preferred approach. It might be possible, though, to restrict the target population to just those low-income families who are most likely to occupy poorly maintained structures. Pursuing this notion, we centered our attention on the welfare population. In Baltimore, the overlap between public assistance rolls and bad housing is quite large. At the time of our household surveys, fully half of the seriously substandard units, as well as almost one-third of the moderately substandard dwellings were occupied by welfare recipients (Table 4.4). Among recipients not residing in public housing, only one-fourth had been able to find standard dwellings. These dismal figures appear to result directly from the very low benefit schedule for welfare clientele in Maryland (27). Liberalizing the rent component of this schedule to accord with individual family needs would immediately bring a large portion of the maintenance problem potentially under control. Newly enacted welfare, social security, and pension reforms will also be of some help. Much of the rest of the problem could be effectively attacked through a modest program of leased housing geared to a residuum of large, low-income, nonwelfare families (28).

This strategy would cost about the same amount of money as the real estate tax subsidy (29). Although less than comprehensive, it would channel money where the need is greatest, and unlike the tax subsidy, it would not carve away piecemeal at a revenue system which needs basic overhauling (30). As compared with a general program of housing allowances, it avoids the necessity of creating still another bureaucracy for dispensing aid to the poor. Nevertheless, a restricted program of allowances, as recommended here, may not be equally appropriate in all cities. It all depends on how the problem of substandard housing distributes itself throughout the local population. Furthermore, we cannot be certain that more liberal payments to welfare recipients would result in a corresponding improvement in their housing accommodations. If, because of racial discrimination or aversion of landlords to AFDC families, the low-income housing market in a particular city is highly segmented, increased allowances might simply drive up rents. Also if the allowance schedule permitted payments which were greatly in excess of the rents that welfare households would probably be able to pay after leaving public assistance, recipients might be reluctant to make a possibly temporary move to better quarters. The pilot allowance program of the Baltimore Department of Social Services, described in Chapter 9, provides some encouragement that higher allowances, coupled with certification of building quality, could be effective in forestalling deterioration of an improved housing inventory. But experience in other states where rental allowances for welfare families are much higher should be examined before seizing on this approach to better maintenance.

Housing Allowances And Societal Goals

The preceding examination of allowances concerned itself with a single objective — proper maintenance of the housing stock. In theory, however, a program of allowances should further, to varying degrees, all of the 12 housing goals described in Chapter 3, and a number of nonhousing objectives as well: Family stability, performance at work and in school, and health might all be favorably affected, not only as a result of better housing, but equally because of higher, more regular income. It is important, therefore, to examine allowances within a larger goals/means context in order to provide a broader foundation for policy formation. Present policy discussions of allowances fail to do so, concentrating instead on a single, increasingly amorphous objective — "standard" housing. For many cities, this goal may be of second-order importance. Either they have very few seriously substandard dwelling units or their other housing problems are much worse, or both. In these communities, improving the social environment of housing or reducing the financial pressures that lead to illness or to the break-up of families might make a far greater contribution to housing objectives than would forcing sagging porches back into plumb. Equally, if nicer housing were achieved by sacrificing healthful landlord/tenant relations or the financial independence of a large segment of the low-income population, the price might be too great. Unless it is demonstrated that allowances can do much more than improve the condition of the housing stock, they will probably enjoy the same popularity in Congress as public assistance, public housing, and other similar programs designed to raise the consumption levels of deprived sectors of the population.

Not only are the potential costs and benefits of allowances perceived too narrowly, they are generally misperceived. Perhaps the principal benefit which low-income families would receive from a general program of housing allowances is an easing of their rent burden. Among families participating in the Kansas City housing allowance experiment, for example, the proportion of family income (excluding the allowance itself) allocated to contract rent dropped from an average of about 17% before enrollment to only 6% after receipt of the allowance (31).

Some housing economists regard such a diversion of allowance payments to nonhousing uses as a measure of the inefficiency of allowances in achieving purely housing objectives. They argue that excessively high rent/income ratios are an income, not a housing, problem. Such a view presumes that the rents paid by individual low-income families are not artificially inflated by market imperfections or other factors. Chapter 9, however, has extensively documented the ways in which unstable inner-city markets fail to function efficiently. Moreover, as much as 10% to 20% of the rental dollar of low-income families does not pay for housing services at all; it goes to support public education and other community activities. Like households generally, poor families vary in their response to the high cost of shelter. Some of them allocate large portions of their income to housing in order to obtain accommodations of satisfactory quality, whereas others keep their rent payments low by accepting less desirable quarters. It is illogical to argue that only those who choose the latter alternative have a housing problem. And it would be an injudicious policy indeed that attempted to solve their problem by converting it to one of high rents (32).

Impact Of Allowances On The Housing Market

For the nearly four decades that the merits of housing allowances have been debated, concerns about market impact have dominated discussion. The particular question which has commanded most attention is whether a large infusion of housing dollars would produce a proportionate improvement in the quality of the standing stock or whether potentially favorable effects would be dissipated by inflation of rents (33). The worry over inflation is misplaced. Since the supply of housing is relatively elastic in the long run, any threat of increased rents could be eliminated by phasing in a program of allowances at whatever pace were necessary to avoid such an eventuality. There are, however, other possible market outcomes which are important to assess. These include:

1. Increase in the volume of new construction
2. Change in the spatial distribution of low-income families
3. Stabilization of inner-city neighborhoods

These outcomes not only bear on the ability of allowances to effect improvement of various parts of the inventory, they also influence efforts to achieve other urban objectives. Each of them, therefore, merits our attention.

1. New construction: The possible impact of housing allowances on the market for new homes can best be shown by using a simple numerical example. Imagine a metropolitan area of 100,000 households, with a normal vacancy rate of about 5% spread equally throughout the stock. One-fifth of the area's households have incomes which would qualify them to receive a housing allowance, and one-half of the qualified group (10,000) apply for assistance. To receive an allowance these enrollees must live in standard dwelling units. At the inception of the program, 8,000 enrollees occupy substandard accommodations. One-half of the 8,000 persuade their present landlords to make improvements while the other half (4,000) move to already standard structures. If the 4,000 moves were instantaneous, the immediate effect would be a zero vacancy rate in parts of the standard stock, escalation of rents, overcrowding, and the spill-over of nonrecipient households into substandard dwellings vacated by recipients. A slower and more orderly transition, however, would produce an upward filtering of recipients and nonrecipients alike. Lower-income families would appropriate some of the standard units which would otherwise have been occupied by middle-income families. Most of the latter could then be expected to settle for somewhat costlier quarters, in turn displacing upper-income families who could afford to compete in the new construction market but who otherwise would not have done so. Vacancy rates among standard units would return to 5%, and new home starts would rise in an amount almost equaling the initial number of moves, i.e., 4,000. If these starts occurred over a period of, say, 8 years, they would expand residential construction in this hypothetical metropolitan area by 15% to 25%, depending on the rate of growth in the area. Now in real life, participation in the allowance program might be less, and the proportion of moves fewer than assumed here, but even so, the impact on new construction would be substantial for an extended period of time. During that time, allowances would serve as an acceptable substitute for new construction subsidy programs that are intended to maintain housing production at a level adequate to accommodate population growth. In fact, they might be a superior substitute, for according to one study, while the size of the government's construction subsidy programs has been substantial, the impact on total housing starts has been minor (34). Allowances would not by themselves, however, be able to assure that very much of the increment to home building would occur in the central city where residential investment is vitally needed.

2. **Spatial distribution of the low-income population.** As outlined in earlier chapters, the question of where low-income families are able to live relates importantly to both housing and nonhousing goals. Depending on a number of factors, such as amount of subsidy per family, the characteristics of the stock, and the present spatial configuration of the population, allowances might promote scatter or concentration or creation of new low-income nodes of somewhat lesser size than now exist. In many communities dissatisfaction with the inner city is so great that, in the absence of companion programs to repair the social fabric of neighborhoods, allowances would precipitate wholesale flight to the middle and outer rings. The immediate effect, then, would be a scattering of families, but in such large numbers that inner-city problems might reassemble or be recreated a short distance away, with the intermingling of income and racial groups not appreciably different than before. By contrast, in cities such as Green Bay, Wisconsin, the site of one of the current housing allowance experiments where there are virtually no bad neighborhoods and very few seriously substandard structures, the incentive to move is not great. Nodes of low-income families are small and would remain so. In some southern metropolitan areas there is still a third possibility. In outlying sections of these areas the distribution of housing quality is not a smoothly shaped continuum. There are homes of recent vintage and there are shacks, but not much in between. In order to receive an allowance, many low-income

suburban families would have to move to the city. All in all, we feel that in most cities, allowance stipends would result in very little change in the present concentration of low-income families, and that whatever shifts occurred would not always be in the "right" direction.

3. **Neighborhood stabilization.** Perhaps the fondest hope for allowances is that they will be able to alter the dynamics of decay, stabilizing some neighborhoods at their present quality level and upgrading others. They would do this, presumably, by placing a floor under rents, changing investor attitudes toward the inner-city stock and toward low-income families, and improving the behavior of problem tenants. Over time, most or all of the market problems described in Chapter 9 would be resolved as the effects of income redistribution gradually took hold.

In some local markets, for example Green Bay, where deterioration stems almost solely from low income, and where race, vandalism, building obsolescence, and social disorganization are not intervening variables, such expectations may be reasonable. In some cities, however, to place such heavy responsibility for reform on allowances is to be severely disappointed. As suggested by our discussion of the impact of allowances on population movement, the immediate consequence of an allowance program might be to destabilize many inner-city neighborhoods, as families took their money and ran. Both standard and substandard dwellings would be vacated. Marginal neighborhoods tottering at preservation's edge might quickly topple. And more disturbing, many reception areas that are now in good health might lose their vitality, as has happened in connection with other housing subsidy programs. Even if allowances did not encourage flight from the inner city, they could not always successfully contend with certain other forces of decline. For example, in lower-income blocks where new construction or maximum rehabilitation of one or two structures would be appropriate, a subsidy much larger than even the most generous allowance would be necessary. In addition, since there is no way for individual owners to combat physical obsolescence of site and neighborhood, allowances by themselves could do nothing about this cause of declining demand, decay, and abandonment. In an analogous way obsolescence causes automobile abandonment, but abandoned cars can be removed. Boarded-up structures remain to remind owners of surrounding property that the end of their own investment may be near.

A Barrier To Implementation

Although housing allowance proposals differ in a number of respects, they all agree on one point. Entitlement to benefits should be contingent on occupancy of a standard dwelling unit, somehow defined. Under the currently most favored formula for assistance, each recipient would be given a certificate having a monetary value equal to the difference between the cost of minimally adequate housing and a specified proportion (usually 25%) of disposable household income. With the certificate, it is assumed, the recipient should be able to locate a unit that meets the standards of the program. For many families, however, this may be impossible.

The reason for this relates to the relatively weak correlation between housing cost and housing quality, holding the size of the dwelling unit constant. At each quality level there is a fairly wide range of rents (and at each rent level, a broad band of quality), reflecting differences in: pricing policies of landlords, length of tenure and quality of tenants, desirability of site and neighborhood, consumption of water and electricity, and number and seriousness of housing code violations that are not apparent to the consumer. In Baltimore, for example, one-sixth of the dwelling units that just met the minimum quality standards which were used in our building survey had gross rents of less than $70 per month, and an equal percentage commanded a figure in excess of $100. Because of this situation, for administrative purposes the cost of minimally adequate housing must be somehow fixed arbitrarily at a level consistent with the various requirements of the program. This requires a balancing act. The lower the cost is set, the fewer the number of standard units on the market at rents or prices which potential recipients can afford to pay; whereas the higher the cost is pegged, the more expensive the program and the greater the number and proportion of eligible families who are already satisfactorily housed. A figure must be arrived at which does not make the program too costly and wasteful but which also assures that standard units will be readily available to recipients. The most reasonable solution would seem to be to set the figure at a level at which a majority, but certainly not all, of the dwelling units meet program standards. Thus in Baltimore where the proportion of substandard units drops sharply from 55% to 30% as monthly rents rise from $90 to $100 (1969 dollars) and then declines gradually to about 20% at the $120 level, drawing the line at about $100 would seem reasonable. Raising it to even $110 would, according to our crude estimate, increase program outlays by almost one-third, and with it the potential for inflation of rents, without appreciably reducing the ratio of substandard to total units.

But herein lies a dilemma. If 30% of the families who are already paying $100 per month for shelter are, nevertheless, inadequately housed, why would allowance families with approximately the same rent paying ability fare any better, or even as well. The magnitude of the dilemma is suggested by the fact that at least one-fourth of the low-income families living in substandard units in Baltimore already pay rents which one would ordinarily think would be sufficient to acquire adequate housing (Table 12.1). The problem is not inherently insoluble, but it is one which may demand either much fine tuning

Table 12.1. Percentage Distribution of Low-Income Households, by Ratio of Housing Cost to Income, Housing Quality, and Amount of Housing Cost Relative to the Median Cost for Minimally Standard Accommodations (Baltimore, Maryland, 1969)

Quality and Cost of Housing	Cost/Income Ratio		
	Over 25%	25% or less	Total
Standard Housing			
Cost equals or exceeds median cost for min. std. dwelling	15	6	21
Cost is less than median cost for min. std. dwelling	16	11	27
Substandard Housing			
Cost equals or exceeds median cost for min. std. dwelling	11	2	13
Cost is less than median cost for min. std. dwelling	29	10	39
Total	71	29	100

or an equivalent amount of dissemblance about building quality. In the tradition of housing programs, the latter is more probable.

Some Conclusions

Although much about housing allowances remains to be learned, there are a few things which can be said with a fair degree of certainty concerning this approach to shelter problems.

First, used selectively, allowances represent a potentially valuable supplement to, but in most cities not a substitute for, existing housing programs. They are designed to encourage adequate maintenance and minor rehabilitation, not major upgrading. Since they would increase the rent paying ability of recipients only modestly and would typically be used in neighborhoods where gross rent multipliers are quite low, they cannot be expected by themselves to call forth the huge investment that is needed in many low-income areas to improve or replace structures requiring intermediate to maximum rehabilitation or replacement. Similarly, allowances are probably most effective where the market is functioning with acceptable efficiency and where the problem of low income is not aggravated by other difficulties. If market failure and social disorganization are widespread, subsidies that are welded directly to institutional reforms would also be necessary.

Second, in many cities a general program of allowances may not be the most cost-effective approach to adequate maintenance. A large portion of the substandard stock is either not occupied by low-income families or is not poorly maintained or is going downhill because of problem tenants who would have difficulty finding decent housing even with allowance assistance. In addition, a not insignificant percentage of eligible households already have decent shelter. Moreover, although allowances can place a floor under quality in a static economy, they are powerless to arrest decay stemming from the obsolescing forces of growth and change. Obsolescence is obviously much more extensive in some communities than in others.

Third, allowances may be a more effective way to expand the volume of construction than are existing low- and moderate-income housing programs. To the extent that they did stimulate home building, however, they might cancel some economically feasible upgrading that would otherwise have occurred in existing neighborhoods and might cause decline in still other neighborhoods. Supply-side subsidies in the inner city are necessary to avoid this possibility.

Fourth, allowances are nearly always advocated only as an equitable and efficient means to produce decent shelter. If this narrow focus is insisted upon, then the question must be raised as to whether the benefits which recipients would derive from standard housing are greater than those which would flow from an un-earmarked subsidy. Actually, it seems likely that substantial benefits other than good housing would in fact accrue to recipients, but then the additional question must be raised as to whether families should be asked to jump through the standard-housing hoop to obtain them. Also, is a program that promises to brighten the lives of recipients, and nothing more, likely to be politically acceptable? Ample opportunity exists for legislatures to help low-income families through expansion of present programs but there is no rush to do so.

Fifth, since a program of allowances must continuously monitor both family income and housing quality, it is bureaucratically more complex than most other poverty programs. Yet its average benefit level per family would, as indicated above, be quite modest. And it would add to the growing system of money substitutes — medicare cards, education vouchers, food stamps, transportation passes — for deprived sectors of the population. At a time when consolidation, simplification, and reform of welfare efforts seem to be needed, a comprehensive program of allowances might be a step in the wrong direction.

Sixth, allowances are aimed primarily at a dimension of the housing problem that is perceived to be of secondary and declining importance by the very sector of the population which is supposed to be helped. They would, however, contribute to the achievement of other important housing objectives.

Finally, despite the low benefit level per family, a comprehensive program of housing allowances would be very expensive. Nationally, it would cost

about twice as much as all of the present federally funded housing an
munity development programs combined without removing the need t
of these programs. However, by using allowances on a selective basis, as
mended here, cities could address several unmet housing needs without
jeopardizing the funding of other programs that would strengthen the inner
city and remove some of the underlying causes of poverty.

ELIMINATION OF RACIAL DISCRIMINATION

Although racial discrimination in housing has, with limited exceptions,
been prohibited by law for more than six years, blacks still do not receive
equal treatment in the market or enjoy complete market freedom. Discrimination's wall has been breached in many spots, but by no means removed completely. And, aware of the abuse, threats, and social isolation to which they
might be subjected if they attempted to exercise their legal rights, nearly all
blacks who change their place of residence move into already integrated or
predominantly black areas, thus perpetuating racial separation and insuring
the continued importance of race as a market variable (35).

Deplorable as this situation is by itself, it has equally undesirable side effects. One of these is discrimination against racially changing and already black
areas by mortgage lenders, who tend to view such areas as risky places for real
estate investment. A recent study in Baltimore, for example, discovered that,
holding income constant, availability of conventional home mortgage loans
in various neighborhoods throughout the city is inversely proportional to the
number of black residents in these neighborhoods (36). It is this sort of discrimination, replicated in other spheres of city life, that contributes importantly to neighborhood decline.

A second unfortunate side effect of residential discrimination is the current busing controversy which has polarized many communities. Court dictated busing plans to achieve racial balance in the public schools are the judici-
ary's response to the failure of the nation to achieve racial integration residentially. If, however, there were the same resolve to desegregate housing as
there has been in some jurisdictions to desegregate schools, busing might not
be necessary. The situation in Baltimore is illustrative in this regard. Over
25,000 black households in the metropolitan area make residential moves
each year. There is not a single census tract in the area which is beyond the
economic reach of at least some of these movers, and quite a large number of
blacks can afford to move into the vast majority of tracts. If the housing market were completely open and were so perceived by the black population, it
would take only four or five years to integrate nearly all of the white neighborhoods in the metropolitan area, even assuming that most black households

continued to prefer already mixed neighborhoods. Predominantly black and predominantly white neighborhoods (and schools) would still exist, but they would be the consequence of consumer preferences and of black/white income differentials, thus dictating a quite different educational response, one which might or might not include busing, depending on the particular local situation.

Most important from a housing standpoint, residential integration would alter market dynamics in significant ways. It would greatly retard the rate of racial change in transitional neighborhoods, since black demand would now be diffused over a much wider area. In so doing, it would radically change the image which buyers and lenders have of these areas. It would prevent confrontations, such as the unfortunate one in Oak Park, Ill., over racial quotas. For a period of time, it would accelerate the rate of new construction as blacks moved upward in the stock; and concomitantly, it would hasten the rate of housing abandonment in the worst sections of the inner city, thus laying the foundation for larger scale renewal projects.

Presently, many persons advocate using housing subsidies to enable low-income families, most of whom would be black, to move into middle- and upper-income neighborhoods in the central city and suburbs. This strategy would, it is argued, achieve racial and economic integration simultaneously. What is forgotten, however, is that the necessary subsidies are quite expensive and very limited. Thus, at most only a few thousand families could be served by such an approach. Neither the locational choices of blacks generally nor of low-income families generally would be very much affected. Moreover, as mentioned in Chapter 7, it is the low-income black family that expresses the least desire to leave familiar surroundings. In our judgment, the removal of racial barriers to locational choice is both more immediately necessary and less expensive than the removal of economic barriers.

The problem of desegregating the housing market is especially difficult when compared to civil rights problems in other sectors of the economy, for three reasons. First, the market is highly decentralized. Decisions affecting the residential choices of blacks are made by a multitude of individuals and organizations — homeowners, landlords, real estate brokers, mortgage lenders, and public agencies — not all of whom are regularly in the market. Monitoring behavior is, therefore, an expensive task. Second, acts of discrimination are becoming so subtle and sophisticated as to easily escape detection by the average home buyer or renter. Finally, blacks themselves do not push against housing discrimination as hard as they might. There are only two ways for them to establish their right to buy or rent where they please. They must either test all parts of the market on a regular basis, or they must actually move into presently all-white areas. The former course of action is helpful but by itself would do little to change perceptions among blacks as to what housing opportunities are open to them. The latter approach, integrating white neighborhoods, is something few blacks are willing to do. Even where their safety is assured and no unpleasantness is likely to occur, they know that they may lead a lonely existence, one which is particularly hard on their children. Their natural reluctance to be pioneers in a possibly hostile environment is frequently nourished by political and social pressures not to desert the black community. It is not surprising that when blacks do leave large central-city ghetto areas, they tend to move to smaller nonwhite nuclei elsewhere (37).

In time, all forms of racial discrimination in the housing market will disappear. However, progress toward this objective will gain momentum only if blacks are persuaded that elimination of housing discrimination should be a high priority item at this time and that it cannot be achieved unless enough white neighborhoods are integrated to verify the existence of an open market.

MARKET BARRIERS TO LOW-INCOME HOUSING GOALS

In Chapter 2 it was pointed out that for more than two decades median family income in Baltimore has steadily declined relative to the SMSA median. The city's proportion of the low-income population continues to rise while its share of more wealthy families declines. This situation, which is characteristic of many central cities, is almost exclusively attributable to the way in which the housing market operates: only households of above average income can afford to purchase or rent newly built dwelling units. Most of these units are constructed on vacant land, because sites having income producing assets on them are usually either too expensive, in terrible locations, or pose difficulties of land assembly (38). Since most vacant land is now in the suburbs, as the metropolitan area grows, the net increase of well-to-do families is accommodated there, while the corresponding expansion of the low-income population must be absorbed by the central city. Rising real income without population growth would produce a similar city/suburban split. If new housing were less expensive (as in Latin America's barrios) or if dwelling units in the central city could easily be enlarged and modernized (or replaced) to meet the demands of a growing affluent sector, the distribution of income groups between city and suburb would be quite different, though normal market dynamics would nearly always serve to keep high- and low-income families spatially separated.

The concentration of new construction in the suburbs does more than produce a gap between city and suburban family incomes with associated adverse effects on the central-city fisc. It complicates housing problems in the city by overlaying the usual difficulties associated with low income and racial discrimination with elements of market instability. The introduction of new

dwellings into the SMSA stock at prices which are well above the median
value of existing structures automatically forces a large percentage of the city
inventory to filter down on the scale of relative quality. This downward pressure is intensified by the obsolescing effect which new homes with new materials and new styles have on older units. Additional pressure is created by
the lower-income families themselves, for as filtering enables them to enter
better neighborhoods in large numbers, the attractiveness of these neighborhoods to higher income groups diminishes. At some point, even if the neighborhoods contained vacant land, they would not attract new construction
because the spread between the value of new and existing units would be too
great.

This basic market dynamic has important policy implications for central
cities. If they focus their housing efforts only on the low-income population
and if they are content just to bring substandard structures up to code level,
they will forever be fighting negative trends instead of altering them. Their
programs will operate in an environment of declining prices, decay, and abandonment as the upward, outward flow of families continues and as inner-city
investors, observing this trend, reduce their ownership horizons. This situation will persist even if poverty is eliminated. Although decline can perhaps
then be better managed, it cannot be stopped. It will not only retard the
efforts of cities to remain competitive with the suburbs, it will also nullify
the potential benefits to low-income families of ownership transfer.

Cities have sought to offset negative market forces and remain competitive
in several ways; first by urban renewal for upper-income families, then later
through neighborhood conservation, and more recently by supporting proposals designed to break up or prevent large concentrations of low-income
families. Casual observation suggests that the amount of favorable impact
which these approaches have had varies inversely with city size. The private
market forces which produce low-income ghettos, neighborhood obsolescence,
and moving blight seem to be an exponential function of size, while public
resources to oppose these forces are more readily available in small cities than
in large ones (39).

In the case of conservation efforts, however, something else is involved. In
trying to do little more than keep older marginal neighborhoods at their existing absolute level of quality, these efforts serve only to assure the inevitability
of further filtering as real incomes increase and new dwelling units are added
to the housing inventory. What is needed in many of these neighborhoods is
enough public and private investment to enable them to maintain their competitive position on the housing-quality scale in the face of rising incomes
and residential aspirations. Such a strategy would not, of course, be successful if the low-income population were expanding, for by retarding filtering in
selected neighborhoods the strategy would simply channel this expansion to

other neighborhoods or else force some families to double up. Where the low-income sector is stable or contracting, though, as is the case in most metropolitan areas, continuous neighborhood upgrading may be both appropriate and necessary.

Exactly what kinds and levels of improvement might be needed to stop the dynamics of decay and in which neighborhoods public improvements would be most effective in generating private investment is not at all certain. Much depends on trends in racial attitudes and on the rate at which rising incomes, improved technology, and changing tastes cause neighborhoods to obsolesce. Baltimore, with an already heavy burden of existing obsolescence, requires much larger investment than do many other cities. Given limited resources, this means a choice may have to be made between bringing the entire housing inventory up to minimum standards (as recommended earlier in the chapter) and ignoring portions of the deteriorated stock in order to permit more significant structural and neighborhood improvements elsewhere. Without further study, we are not prepared to suggest where the balance should be struck. Our proposed housing budget provides for 8,000 units of new construction and maximum rehabilitation plus a certain amount of neighborhood upgrading, but this may not be enough. Indeed, it may be that no reasonable amount of investment in neighborhood improvement can reverse present trends. If this is the case, Baltimore, and probably many other cities as well, must live with an irresolvable dilemma in the short run, because the only other alternatives — renewal for the rich and dispersal of the poor — cannot be substantially accelerated either. Political and financial barriers are too great. There will be no choice but to allow market forces to play themselves out and then pick up the pieces, as is now being done.

CHAPTER 13

A Closer Look at Modest Rehabilitation

A major conclusion of this study is that the preservation and renewal of the nation's older urban housing stock requires that much more attention be directed toward the portion of the inventory which is only moderately substandard. In Baltimore, dwellings in this category comprise one-half of the inner-city stock and almost 90% of all substandard units in the city as a whole. They are both growing in number and deteriorating in quality. While some of them are targets of concentrated code enforcement and urban renewal programs, most are not.

If it were not for the alarming downward trend in the quality of many of the structures, they could possibly be ignored in favor of buildings in more serious condition. But with negative forces enveloping such a large part of the inventory, the public response must be equally pervasive. Modest rehabilitation is one way of achieving widespread impact with limited public funds. Fortunately, most of the substandard structures in Baltimore and in other cities as well lend themselves to this form of treatment.

A program of modest rehabilitation could not, of course, function in isolation from other programs. It would have to support and be supported by efforts to expand home ownership, improve maintenance and management, broaden income maintenance, and restore the residential environment. And because of the wide range of housing quality within the inner city and even within individual blocks, it would have to be accompanied by ordinary code enforcement, maximum rehabilitation, and new construction.

In order to accomplish its own objectives as well as complement these other efforts, a program of modest upgrading in Baltimore would have to reach its target inventory of 50,000 dwelling units in not more than a decade. Most substandard structures which could not be upgraded within that period of time would probably become candidates for maximum rehabilitation or demolition. Such an ambitious goal — 5,000 units per year — may, like large scale ownership transfer, be impossible. The dollar resources do not appear to be a constraint, but the task of dealing with so many different structures and individual ownership situations is at the very least, formidable.

This chapter examines some general issues concerning the implementation of modest rehabilitation on a large scale, assuming that the city would continue with its present programs and that the other interventions mentioned above would also be brought to bear on the problem. An attempt is made first to define the universe of structures for which modest rehabilitation is economically feasible. Then the individuals, groups, and organizations who might be able to do various parts of the job are outlined, together with an analysis of their subsidy requirements. Finally, the possible role of limited partnerships in upgrading part of the inventory is outlined. Except inferentially, difficulties which seem to adhere to modest rehabilitation programs will not be explored; they have been alluded to earlier and are generally well known. Further, for the sake of simplicity, the empirical focus of the chapter is on the inner city, not the city as a whole.

MODEST REHABILITATION DEFINED

Before turning to the substance of the chapter, the term modest rehabilitation itself demands brief attention, since it is not always defined in quite the same way by various analysts. In general, modest rehabilitation covers the broad range of upgrading activities that lie between ordinary maintenance at one end of the quality spectrum and maximum rehabilitation at the other. The dividing lines at each end are not firmly established, however. At the upper end of the spectrum, maintenance and upgrading outlays are usually distinguished from each other according to the *purpose* of the expenditure. Painting, for example, would fall into the category of maintenance, while installation of central heating would be regarded as upgrading. At the lower end of the spectrum, the line between modest and maximum rehabilitation is usually drawn with reference to the nature of the two *processes*. Modest upgrading involves repair and selective replacement; maximum rehabilitation, the gutting and complete rebuilding of the inside of the structure.

Since none of these distinctions are suitable for quantitative analysis, modest rehabilitation is defined here exclusively in dollar terms. In Baltimore, what investors regard as ordinary maintenance seldom averages over $300 for a medium-sized dwelling unit, and maximum rehabilitation rarely can be accomplished for less than $7,500, including overhead. So modest rehabilitation, in this discussion, will include all expenditures falling between these two figures (1969 dollars). Because the range from $300 to $7,500 is so broad, it is subdivided for some parts of the analysis. Expenditures of less than $1,000 are termed "paint-up/fix-up"; outlays in the $1,000 to $2,499 category, "minor rehabilitation"; upgrading costing from $2,500 to $4,449, "low-intermediate rehabilitation"; and renewal in the $4,500 to $7,499 range, "high-intermediate rehabilitation" (1).

WHICH STRUCTURES QUALIFY FOR MODEST REHABILITATION

It will be recalled from Chapter 1 that, as part of the overall study, a random sample of approximately 600 structures throughout the city was inspected in order to determine the cost of bringing the substandard inventory into compliance with the housing code. In making this calculation, it was assumed that structures would be razed and replaced only if they were structurally unsound or if most of the other buildings on the block were either beyond repair or had already been demolished. The estimated cost of upgrading which resulted from these assumptions is not necessarily the preferred renewal approach; it is only a first approximation of the least costly solution in terms of total economic resources that would have to be brought to bear on the problem. Depending on the housing goals of the city and the contraints which it faces, there might be other strategies that would require more total resources but which would either absorb fewer public funds, or produce more than a proportionate improvement in housing quality, or have more favorable neighborhood effects, or enjoy greater consumer acceptance. Since it is our judgment, however, that the least-cost solution would also be the most desirable policy in many deteriorating sections of the city, the economic feasibility of rehabilitation must be scrutinized more carefully.

In particular, the time horizon of the original analysis must be extended. For, the fact that rehabilitation of a particular structure is initially less expensive than demolition and new construction does not necessarily mean that it would be the cheaper alternative over the life of the investment. A new building usually has a longer life expectancy and lower maintenance needs than does a rehabilitated one. As a consequence, in some cases it is cheaper in the long run to build anew rather than make modest improvements which soon have to be replaced or followed by additional investments. Additionally, new construction could, in theory, bring with it a very much higher level of amenity per dollar of investment than would modest upgrading. Thus, adjusted for differences in amenity, it might be the least-cost solution even if in all other respects it were the more expensive alternative.

The question of what is the least costly approach cannot be decided in the abstract, since it could vary with the quality and condition of the inventory. In the following section, therefore, the substandard structures in our sample are evaluated with respect to cost of upgrading, post-renewal life expectancy, amenity level, and maintenance requirements. Those structures which fail to pass this least-cost test should not be upgraded unless they meet other criteria which will be described later.

Calculating the Least-Cost Solution

The mathematical formula for this evaluation, as well as the underlying theoretical framework, has been developed by A. H. Schaaf (2). His formula and also our application of it, operates within prior decisions as to whether rehabilitation would provide an appropriate re-use at the site in question and whether more than one level of upgrading is in fact structurally possible. The formula deliberately does not attempt to deal with post-rehabilitation capital values, although these values are affected to a considerable degree by the four variables in the estimating equation.

The inputs for the calculations are presented in Table 13.1. The table postulates four renewal treatments that vary according to the initial condition of the structures as determined by our field inspections (column 1). Each treatment carries with it a typical renewal cost, also estimated from our inspection data (column 2) (3). All four treatments would raise the structures involved to *approximately* the same standard. Because of differences in basic quality of construction, however, the same expenditure could upgrade one building barely to code level and another to a somewhat higher standard. Therefore, as part of our inspection process, each dwelling was given a post-renewal quality rating that can be used as a reasonable proxy for the amenity variable. The highest and lowest post-renewal ratings that any structure actually received appear in column 3.

The four renewal treatments and two post-renewal quality levels combine to form eight renewal situations, each of which must be compared against a ninth possibility — new construction. To make this comparison, assumptions have to be made concerning the effect of the investment on the rent level, maintenance costs, and economic life of each structure. These assumptions are presented in columns 4, 5, and 6. The rent figures are equal to the median contract price (rounded to the nearest $100) for inner-city dwellings in our sample which were given the same quality scores as the ratings in column 3. The cost-of-maintenance estimates for rehabilitated units are higher than what investors experience in a normal year, but are not an unreasonable approximation of the average amount of capital that would have to be expended annually over the life of the investment to keep the structure competitive. Finally, the economic-life figures are more of a reflection of the ability of the structures to remain useable for the indicated period of years rather than an estimate of market conditions 7 to 30 years hence. While the reader may not agree with all of these assumptions, they represent a starting point, and can be altered if desired, once their effect on the final results is known.

Table 13.1. Characteristics of Five Hypothetical Renewal Situations[1] (Baltimore, Maryland)

1	2	3	4	5	6
Renewal Situation	Renewal Cost[2] ($)	Post-Renewal Quality Rating	Expected Post Renewal Average Annual Rental Value[3] ($)	Expected Post-Renewal Average Annual Maintenance Cost ($)	Post-Renewal Economic Life of Structure (years)
1. Paint-Up/Fix-Up	1,000	50	1,000	400	7-15
2. Paint-Up/Fix-Up	1,000	55	1,300	300	7-15
3. Minor Rehab	2,500	50	1,000	400	7-15
4. Minor Rehab	2,500	55	1,300	300	7-15
5. Low Intermediate Rehab	4,500	50	1,000	400	10-20
6. Low Intermediate Rehab	4,500	55	1,300	300	10-20
7. High Intermediate Rehab	7,500	50	1,000	400	20-30
8. High Intermediate Rehab	7,500	55	1,300	300	20-30
9. New Construction	20,000	75	2,000	200	40-50

[1] This table is patterned after Table 1, in A.H. Schaaf, Economic feasibility analysis for urban renewal housing rehabilitation. *Journal of the American Institute Of Planners*. November 1969, pg. 402.
[2] The figures are maximum costs, in 1969 prices, including overhead.
[3] Based on Baltimore Household Survey I, 1968.

Now to the calculation. Assuming for simplicity that at the expiration of the estimated economic life of the rehabilitated unit it would be demolished rather than upgraded once again, rehabilitation is preferred if:

$$C > [R + M \frac{1-(1+i)^{-n}}{i} + \frac{C(1-nr)}{(1+i)^n} + D \frac{1-(1+i)^{-n}}{i}]$$

where:

C = new construction cost,
R = rehabilitation cost,
M = difference between maintenance costs for a new and rehabilitated structure,
D = difference between annual rents of a new and a rehabilitated structure,
n = life of rehabilitated structure following upgrading, and
i = discount rate.

Expressed in nonmathematical language, rehabilitation is feasible if its net annual cost is less than that of new construction, after adjusting for differences in amenity achieved by the two alternative treatments.

Applying the formula to the data in Table 13.1, it was calculated that both paint-up/fix-up ($1,000) and minor rehabilitation ($2,500) are preferable on a cost basis to new construction, if the upgraded structure will last 15 years. If an economic life of only 7 years is assumed, paint-up/fix-up continues to come out on top as does minor rehabilitation of better quality units [55]. Minor upgrading of units which can be brought only to code level [50], however turns out to be more costly than new construction, and therefore, would probably be rejected except as part of a larger effort.

As we move into higher-cost treatments, the picture becomes even more mixed. Low-intermediate rehabilitation ($4,500) of basically good-quality [55] structures is preferable to new construction, while higher-intermediate rehabilitation ($7,500) of good-quality units barely breaks even. Low- and high-intermediate rehabilitation of structures that would be only marginal [50] after being treated run a poor second to demolition and replacement.

Reasonable changes in assumptions regarding economic life, maintenance costs, and rent levels do not alter the above conclusions. We can, therefore, summarize in general terms as follows: first, barring other considerations which will be examined in the following section, rehabilitation of structures that can be upgraded to a quality level somewhat above that prescribed in the housing code is economically feasible if the total expenditure does not exceed $7,500. Second, modest rehabilitation of structures that can be brought only to code level is also feasible if: (a) the total cost is not greater than $2,500 and; (b) the investment would last at least 15 years. Third, repairs and renovation costing up to $1,000 almost always will pass the least-cost test.

It is possible to be somewhat more precise insofar as Baltimore's inventory is concerned. Using the pre- and post-rehabilitation scores of each structure in the sample, the feasibility of upgrading each one can be calculated and blown up to give a city-wide estimate. When this was done, it was found that the least-cost solution, including overhead and profit, for approximately 3,000 dwelling units was not rehabilitation, as originally assumed, but rather demolition and replacement, requiring an additional investment of $33,000,000. This means that the least-cost estimate of $202,000,000 presented in Chapter 8 should be raised to $235,000,000, still a modest figure.

Some Additional Factors to Consider

It has already been suggested that the least-cost solution may not be the preferable one in some instances. It focuses on efficiency criteria whereas financial and equity considerations are also important. A few of these additional considerations should be reviewed since they may substantially alter the above estimates.

The first has to do with the question of externalities. An otherwise uneconomical expenditure may be valuable beyond its cost because of its contribution in preserving surrounding investments. A prime example of this is maximum rehabilitation. According to our calculations, based on extrapolation of the assumptions in Table 13.1, this treatment is usually uneconomical in its own right. Where there are only one or two or three structures in a block which require this much attention, however, it would be foolish to ignore them. Putting the matter more generally, rehabilitation should be confined to those blocks in which the necessary treatment for the block as a whole is economically feasible. It should also be emphasized, though, that at least in theory both modest and maximum rehabilitation could produce negative as well as positive externalities by siphoning demand away from previously stable blocks, thereby endangering rather than supporting existing investments. If rehabilitation programs start to achieve large volumes of production, this possibility will cease to be remote and will demand serious attention.

A second important consideration has to do with the question of what is politically and economically possible. New construction of the same number of units as might otherwise be rehabilitated requires a huge initial investment. Hence, even though the new construction approach could be shown to be cheaper in the long run, Congress would probably refuse to appropriate the necessary initial funds, and even if it did so, the resources to implement such a large program in a short period of time would almost certainly be impossible to obtain. Given this situation, the choice between modest rehabilitation and new construction would really be between a second best solution for many families and an optimum solution for a few.

Related to the above issue is the question of how to weigh amenity differences in deciding between rehabilitation and new construction (4). Schaaf's approach is to convert these differences directly into dollars which are then discounted at what might be termed a public-investment rate of interest (6%). While this procedure is valid within the frame of analysis which Schaaf has developed, it excludes consumer preferences from the equation. To illustrate, intermediate rehabilitation for structures of marginal original construction (nos. 5 and 7 in Table 13.1) fails Schaaf's economic feasibility test, because the post-renewal quality that is achieved, although adequate with respect to code standards, is substantially lower than what would be obtained in a newly built unit. If the quality variable were removed from Schaaf's formula, however, the various intermediate rehabilitation treatments would be only one-half to two-thirds as costly as new construction on a net annual cost basis. Assuming there was a fixed sum of money to spend, a decision to sacrifice extra quality would permit up to twice as many families to be helped. Such a decision would not be unlike that which is faced by the average consumer who is forced to purchase the cheap pair of shoes or the low-priced car even though he knows the more expensive model is a better buy. The public sector has limited resources too. If the superior choice on economic grounds is also substantially more expensive per family helped, it may not be within the range of possibility. Moreover, the price of *not* helping a large portion of the needy population may be greater than the aggregate benefits obtained by providing extra amenities, albeit at low cost, to those who do receive assistance.

Where to draw the line between quantity and quality (more decent dwelling units vs more quality per unit) should in theory be decided with reference to the needs of the beneficiaries themselves. It would be helpful also to know their time preferences. If families desired to trade quality for time, policies should be reflective of this wish. In this connection, it should be observed that the discount rate which Schaaf uses to calculate the present value of amenity differences may not accurately reflect the time preferences of the families involved. If the amenity variable were assigned a discount rate of 12% to 14%, which in our judgment would more accurately express the time orientation of low-income families, all the categories of rehabilitation which originally failed the least-cost test would become either superior to or reasonably competitive with the new construction alternative.

Still another consideration, if modest rehabilitation is pursued under public auspices, is the cost of program administration. The overhead expenses which an agency incurs in connection with renewal programs do not vary in proportion to the amount of private investment that is generated, but rather according to the number of owners and structures in the program and the nature of the controls required. Since modest rehabilitation is a low-cost, customized effort involving numerous owners, administrative overhead is disproportionately high when compared with supervisory expenses associated with new construction or maximum rehabilitation. This fact suggests not so much that our previous calculations should be revised but rather that less expensive control mechanisms must be created, as the volume of modest rehabilitation expands.

Finally, the feasibility of modest rehabilitation can not be determined without some attention to the capital values of the structures that need to be upgraded. Schaaf correctly excludes this aspect of the program from his analysis, since from the viewpoint of society as a whole, the standing stock of housing represents sunk capital which can be valued at zero for comparative purposes. Neither individual entrepreneurs nor public agencies can be so cavalier, however. As pointed out in Chapter 9, market prices in Baltimore's inner city have fallen to an extremely low level. Even fairly attractive dwellings in stable neighborhoods can be acquired for only a few thousand dollars. If the cost of acquiring and upgrading substandard structures to the same quality level as these dwellings requires a considerably larger outlay than would the purchase of an existing unit of satisfactory quality, then barring favorable externalities, it is doubtful whether rehabilitation is financially feasible.

Lumping all the caveats to Schaaf's formula together, it would seem that on balance modest rehabilitation is economically feasible across a broader spectrum of the inventory than the formula itself would suggest. Use of higher discount rates and a less weighty amenity adjustment would probably more than offset the counter effects of high administrative costs and, where applicable, distorted relationships of quality to capital values in the existing stock. In addition, if the formula is applied to entire blocks, as would be the most logical procedure, a greater number of structures are likely to fall in the "save" category than otherwise would be the case. For the remainder of the chapter, therefore, it will be presumed that most of the 3,000 dwellings which failed the least-cost test are actually suitable candidates for rehabilitation and that the original cost estimates still apply.

REHABILITATION BY WHOM?

As already suggested in Chapter 11, the proposed expansion of modest-rehabilitation activities would complement, not substitute for, current up-grading efforts by the city, nonprofit groups, private investors, and owner occupants. A most important question in this regard has to do with the dis-tribution of the total renewal effort among the various categories of investors mentioned above. Which types of structures should the city itself undertake to improve; which ones should nonprofit groups be encouraged to upgrade; and what sectors should be left to the private investment community and to owner occupants? To some extent the question may be answered in terms of what is already under way. The city and subsidized limited-profit groups and owner occupants should continue to focus on the few sectors of the stock which are in such bad condition that private entrepreneurs would have to by-pass them even in a more equable market climate. At the same time, limited partnerships, limited dividend corporations, ordinary investors, and also home-owners and nonprofit organizations, should be encouraged to take on the task of improving the vast number of less seriously deteriorated structures. While this division of labor may seem eminently reasonable, it is one which is im-portant to emphasize for two reasons: first, because the city has been criticized in some quarters for its maximum-rehabilitation thrust, when actually no profit-making organization could undertake this important assignment with-out subsidy (5); and second, because for reasons outlined earlier, public agen-cies, though not necessarily nonprofit groups, are currently incapable of effi-ciently administering customized modest rehabilitation on a large scale.

One possible way in which this general approach might be patterned in the inner city is described in Table 13.2. It can be seen from Table 13.2 that the total required upgrading expenditures of about $160,000,000 are divided among seven basic groups: existing investors, new investors, existing owner occupants, new owner occupants, the city, nonprofit corporations, and limited partnerships. Over one-half of this investment ($91,000,000) has been assigned

Table 13.2. Illustrative Distribution of Rehabilitation Activity, Dwelling Units that Are Now Privately Owned, by Type of Owner and Cost of Upgrading[1] (Baltimore Inner City, 1975-1984)

A. Number Of Dwelling Units

Type And Cost of Upgrading (Mean $)	Same Owner			Interim Owner				New Owner (Direct Transfer)						Grand Total
	Absentee Investors	Owner Occupants	Total	Limited Partner-ships, etc.	City	Non-profits	Total	Absentee Investors	Owner Occupants	Resident Investors	City	Non-profits	Total	
Ordinary maintenance	21,000	13,500	34,500	7,000	—	—	7,000	2,000	1,500	—	—	—	3,500	45,000
Paint-up/fix-up (500)	9,000	5,000	14,000	8,000	—	—	8,000	3,000	4,000	2,000	—	1,000	10,000	32,000
Minor rehab. (2000)	—	1,000	1,000	2,000	2,000	—	4,000	—	6,000	—	2,000	—	8,000	13,000
Low-intermediate rehab. (3,500)	—	500	500	—	1,500	500	2,000	—	500	—	—	—	500	3,000
High-intermediate rehab. (6,000)	—	—	—	—	1,000	—	1,000	—	—	—	—	—	—	1,000
Max.-rehab. and new construction (16,500)	—	—	—	—	2,500	500	3,000	—	—	—	3,000	—	3,000	6,000
Total	30,000	20,000	50,000	17,000	7,000	1,000	25,000	5,000	12,000	2,000	5,000	1,000	25,000	100,000

[1] Based on assumption that 50,000 dwelling units are sold as a consequence of ownership-transfer programs and ordinary market activity.

B. Dollar Value of Rehabilitation Activity (thousands)[2]

Type And Cost of Upgrading (Means $)	Same Owner				Interim Owner			New Owner (Direct Transfer)						Grand Total
	Absentee Investors	Owner Occupants	Total	Limited Partner-ships, etc.	City	Non-profits	Total	Absentee Investors	Owner Occupants	Resident Investors	City	Non-profits	Total	
Ordinary maintenance	—	—	—	—	—	—	—	—	—	—	—	—	—	—
Paint-up/fix-up (500)	4,500	2,500	7,000	4,000	—	—	4,000	1,500	2,000	1,000	—	500	5,000	16,000
Minor rehab. (2000)	—	2,000	2,000	4,000	4,000	—	8,000	—	12,000	—	4,000	—	16,000	26,000
Low-intermediate rehab. (3,500)	—	1,750	1,750	—	5,250	1,750	7,000	—	1,750	—	—	—	1,750	10,500
High-intermediate rehab. (6,000)	—	—	—	—	6,000	—	6,000	—	—	—	—	—	—	6,000
Max.-rehab. and new construction (16,500)	—	—	—	—	41,250	8,250	49,500	—	—	—	49,500	—	49,500	99,000
Total	4,500	6,250	10,750	8,000	56,500	10,000	74,500	1,500	15,750	1,000	53,500	500	72,250	157,500

[2] 1969 dollars. Figures include overhead.

A Closer Look at Modest Rehabilitation   277

to the city for the maximum rehabilitation or new construction of 5,500 units (6). Spread over a 10-year period, this assignment does little more than project the city's current rate of activity in this area. Only a small percentage of the maximum rehabilitation task (500 units) is designated in the table for nonprofit organizations, since both in Baltimore and nationally their rate of production has been quite low. At the other end of the quality scale, paint-up/ fix-up and minor rehabilitation (averaging $500 to $2,000 per unit) of 40,000 dwellings has been assigned to owner occupants and private investors, and to limited partnerships or similar entities. Five thousand units requiring this treatment are assigned to the city and nonprofit organizations, primarily to reflect the probability of gaps in the efforts of others.

Paint-up/fix-up and minor rehabilitation by the private sector would cost in the neighborhood of $34,000,000, or 22% of the total projected renewal expense. If market stability were restored in the inner city, the bulk of this sum could be provided without any public subsidy beyond loans at below-market rates of interest that are available under existing programs. Where attractive loans are insufficient to call forth private investment, however, grants under programs similar to the federally assisted code enforcement program (FACE) are a possibility, especially if transfers of properties to owner occupants can be properly coordinated with the rehabilitation process so as to enlarge the universe of potential grantees. Revenue sharing provides the potential for achieving this needed flexibility.

In between maximum and minimum rehabilitation are 4,000 dwellings which definitely require subsidy assistance under programs similar to FACE. These units have been assigned in the table to owner occupants, the city, and nonprofit groups, all of whom have access to subsidies for intermediate upgrading if they choose to embark upon this type of activity.

Although the assignments in Table 13.2 are hypothetical, they do help to reveal whether there are contradictory or unrealistic assumptions underlying the approach which the table is intended to illustrate. Thus, if the upgrading tasks that are assigned to the limited partnership category seem excessive, and if no other group is any better equipped to handle them, the validity of the general scheme is called somewhat into question. Looking at the table from this perspective, both strengths and weaknesses in the approach can be seen. On the favorable side, of the entire estimated inner-city rehabilitation investment of $160,000,000, over 90% would be undertaken by individuals and organizations that have been eligible for grants under previous programs. Only $6,000,000 must be produced by absentee investors, even though they now own two-thirds of the stock; and only $8,000,000 must be forthcoming from limited partnerships, even though they are shown to account for fully one-third of the units in the projected ownership-transfer program. Also encouraging is the fact that intermediate rehabilitation, which, according to our earlier analysis in this chapter, may frequently be of borderline feasibility, does not involve either many dwelling units or large sums of money. The most speculative assumptions in the table have to do with minor rehabilitation and paint-up/fix-up. The assignments to the city imply a large expansion of its direct participation in this area of housing activity. The same is true of the assignments to owner occupants; and, of course, the proposed limited partnerships do not even exist as yet.

The table is, of course, only one picture of what might happen. If the ownership-transfer program were to yield a different tenure pattern, the rehabilitation burden would be redistributed accordingly. Equally, even within the present ownership-transfer assumptions the city and nonprofit organizations could emphasize activities different from those shown in the table. Most important, though, is the question of what the limited partnerships and ordinary private investors might do. The extent of their activity and the amount of funds that they would be willing to put in any particular structure would depend to a considerable degree on the city's ability to re-establish an environment that can attract equity capital at relatively reasonable rates of return. Lacking such an environment, investors will resist expenditures of even as little as $500 per dwelling unless they feel certain that they can get their capital back in as few as two or three years, an unlikely possibility. If some of the risks of inner-city investment could be reduced and socialized, however, investors would be willing to make more extensive repairs, thus dipping much further into the substandard inventory and correspondingly diminishing the need for public subsidies and programs to administer them. In this same connection, it is important to recognize that the unsubsidized private sector will tend to avoid structures which, though not in especially bad condition, either do not have a ready market among desirable tenants, as is true for example of some of the large three-story row houses, or are not resistant to abuse, as is the case with many of the frame dwellings with cedar-shake siding. In order to maximize and complement the private contribution, a special effort has to be made to put these structures into the hands of owner occupants and nonprofit corporations.

THE ROLE OF LIMITED PARTNERSHIPS

Since modest rehabilitation is not an activity that lends itself to direct government supervision and control, various alternatives to government rehabilitation programs should be sought. Perhaps the best alternative is the creation of a healthful investment climate, but even if this objective were achieved, new private devices would be required to mobilize capital for upgrading. One such device is the limited partnership which can contribute as

well to programs of ownership transfer, improved management and maintenance, maximum rehabilitation, and new construction. Although revival of
the inner city does not depend on the creation of limited partnerships, it is important to outline in some detail the financial aspects of their proposed operations, as visualized here, so that the reader can evaluate the limits within which
they could be effective. It is especially important to go through this exercise,
because the projected contribution of limited partnerships in the revival of the
inner city rests on a key assumption which could be more broadly applicable
and which on the surface appears to be sheer nonsense — that private investors will forego a certain amount of profit to help restore Baltimore's housing
stock.

Basically, the argument is simply that any real estate company which invested wisely in income-producing real estate in the outer city and suburbs
could produce sufficiently attractive returns for its investors to enable it to
channel a small portion of its income into the inner city without inviting investor resistance; further that this lost income, although of small consequence
to the investor, could be stretched across a large number of units if it were
used to improve the modestly substandard stock.

The limited partnership device is particularly suited to this approach because it can bring to its investors all of the tax benefits of real estate investment trusts, but is not burdened by many of the regulations which restrict
trust activities.

To see how the idea might work in practice, let us construct a hypothetical
situation. Assume that a limited partnership or several limited partnerships are
able to acquire $50,000,000 of equity capital over a six-year period; that four-
fifths of these funds are invested in real property; that the real property investments are divided between the inner city and elsewhere on a 20/80 basis (Table
13.3); and that 80% financing can be obtained for the outer-city purchases, and
virtually 100% (purchase money) financing is possible for much of the inner-
city acquisitions (7). Using these assumptions, the partnership(s) could acquire
real assets with a total value of $234,000,000, about 30% of which would be
in the inner city (Table 13.3). The inner-city investments would be spread
among 17,000 dwelling units (Table 13.2) at an average of $3,800 per unit,
including administrative and related costs of acquisition (Table 13.3).

With our hypothetical portfolio established, the next step is to estimate
what the portfolio might earn, hence what potential there is for diluting returns in order to upgrade the inner-city holdings. There are three possible
types of return that could be used for this calculation: net cash-flow; net cash-
flow plus loan amortization; and net cash-flow plus loan amortization plus
capital gains or losses. There are also important tax adjustments that could be

Table 13.3. Hypothetical Investment Portfolio for One or More Limited Partnerships that Invest 20% of Their Funds in the Inner City (Thousands of Dollars)

A. Inner-City Portfolio

	1975	1976	1977	1978	1979	1980	Total
Annual investment in fund[1]	$200	$400	$1,000	$2,000	$3,000	$3,400	$10,000
Down payment for real estate[2]	160	320	800	1,600	2,400	2,720	8,000
Total real estate assets	1,280	2,560	6,400	12,800	19,200	21,760	64,000
Liquid assets	40	80	200	400	600	680	2,000
Total assets added to fund during year	1,320	2,640	6,600	13,200	19,800	22,440	66,000
Total assets in fund	1,320	3,960	10,560	23,760	43,560	66,000	—

B. Outer-City Portfolio

	1975	1976	1977	1978	1979	1980	Total
Annual investment in fund[1]	$800	$1,600	$4,000	$8,000	$12,000	$13,600	$40,000
Down payment for real estate[2]	640	1,280	3,200	6,400	9,600	10,880	32,000
Total real estate assets	3,200	6,400	16,000	32,000	48,000	54,400	160,000
Liquid assets	160	320	800	1,600	2,400	2,720	8,000
Total assets added to fund during year	3,360	6,720	16,800	33,600	50,400	57,120	168,000
Total assets in fund	3,360	10,080	26,880	60,480	110,880	168,000	—

[1] After sales commissions.
[2] Includes administrative and related costs of acquisition.

included in the calculation, especially if some of the rehabilitation expenditures are likely to qualify for special accelerated-depreciation treatment by the Internal Revenue Service. For our purposes it is sufficient initially to calculate net cash-flow. Then, assuming a diversion of some of this flow to rehabilitation, the effect on the real rate of return of the portfolio, after incorporating loan amortization and capital gains or losses into the equation, can be computed.

Depending on the financing that can be obtained and the judiciousness of the investments, it should not be too difficult for the partnerships to generate a net cash-flow equal to about 10% of initial equities. Assuming this were the case and assuming also, for simplicity, that all properties acquired in any year are purchased on January 1st, then cash-flow for the six-year acquisition period and for an additional four years of continued renewal effort would total $31,300,000 (Table 13.4). If 25% of this sum could be diverted to rehabilitation, 10,000 dwelling units (the number assigned to limited partnerships for upgrading in Table 13.2) could receive an average improvement expenditure of almost $800 (Table 13.5). While this may not seem like a large sum, it is equivalent to a figure of at least $1,200 in any public program utilizing independent contractors. All in all, the potential contribution is not insignificant.

Table 13.4. Cash Generated for Rehabilitation by Hypothetical Investment Portfolio in Table 13.3 (Thousands of Dollars)

Year	Annual Investment In Fund	Total Equity Investment	Net Cash-Flow[1]	Diversion to Rehabilitation[2]
1975	$ 1,000	$ 1,000	$ 100	$ 25
1976	2,000	3,000	300	75
1977	5,000	8,000	800	200
1978	10,000	18,000	1,800	450
1979	15,000	33,000	3,300	825
1980	17,000	50,000	5,000	1,250
1981	–	50,000	5,000	1,250
1982	–	50,000	5,000	1,250
1983	–	50,000	5,000	1,250
1984	–	50,000	5,000	1,250
Total	$50,000	–	$31,300	$7,825

[1] Assumed to be 10%.
[2] Average diversion is assumed to be 25%.

Table 13.5. Allocation of Rehabilitation Funds to Hypothetical Inner-City Investment Portfolio in Table 13.3

Year	Inner-City Dwellings Acquired Annually[1]	Inner-City Dwellings in Portfolio	Dwellings Acquired To Be Re-habbed[2]	Dwellings in col. #3 Rehabbed Annually[3]	Cumulative Rehab. Effort (Dwell's)	Value of Rehabili-tation[4] (000's $)	Average Rehab. Investment/ Dwelling ($)
1975	340	340	200	40	40	25	625
1976	680	1,020	400	80	120	75	625
1977	1,700	2,720	1,000	200	320	200	625
1978	3,400	6,120	2,000	400	720	450	625
1979	5,100	11,220	3,000	600	1,320	825	625
1980	5,460	16,680	3,500	700	1,980	1,250	630
1981	-680	16,000	–	–	1,900	1,250	660
1982	−1,700	14,300	–	–	1,700	1,250	735
1983	−3,400	10,900	–	–	1,300	1,250	960
1984	−5,100	5,800	–	–	700	1,250	1,790
Total	–	–	10,100	–	10,100	7,825	780

[1] An average value per dwelling unit of approximately $3,000 is assumed (Table 13.1). See Table 13.3 for estimate of total value of acquisitions. A five-year holding period is also assumed. At the end of the six-year acquisition period, no more dwellings are purchased, and the inner-city inventory is phased out of the portfolio. In 1980, 5,800 units are purchased and 340 are sold.
[2] Assumed to be about 60% of annual acquisitions.
[3] It is assumed that one-fifth of the dwellings in column 3 are rehabilitated each year. This rate of improvement could be associated with a shorter holding period if sufficient demand were present.
[4] From Table 13.4

This brings us to the final question, whether a diversion of as much as 25% of net cash-flow could be expected to occur. This figure is actually an average of what primarily profit-motivated enterprises might be willing to set aside and what limited-dividend organizations would consider reasonable. Assuming a diversion figure of only 20% for the former category of investor, net cash-flow would be reduced from 10% to 8% of initial equity. Eight percent is not an unattractive cash return. Most real estate investment trusts have not ex-ceeded this figure, and a majority of the trusts do not produce tax-sheltered income.

Before ending on such an optimistic note, however, it is necessary to look at the effects of the diversion on *total* return. A sophisticated real estate firm should be able to earn at least 15% on its property investments after loan-amortization payments and capital gains are included. If one-fifth of its equity capital were placed in liquid assets (Table 13.3) that yielded only a 10% return, the average return for the portfolio would drop only slightly to 14%. In our hypothetical portfolio, though, an additional one-sixth of total equity funds are invested in inner-city property which, like the liquid assets, would probably earn little other than the 10% cash return. Certainly, there would be no capital appreciation, since that is not the objective of the acquisitions. And transfer costs associated with purchase and resale, if allocated over such a short period as five years, would cancel out the amortization payments. Thus even before any allocations for rehabilitation, 36% of the portfolio would earn only 10%, and the return of the total portfolio would be only 13.2%. (64% × 15% plus 36% × 10%). Diverting 20% of the cash-flow to rehabilitation would reduce this figure to 11.2%. Although this rate of return is much better than what most real estate investment trusts earn, it may be a trifle too low to keep the average limited partner happy, since he is less liquid and is exposed to greater risks than an individual who invests in a trust. At least 12% might be necessary to keep equity capital flowing into the partnerships.

If the partnerships could qualify for federal low interest rate rehabilitation loans, the dollar value of which do not appear anywhere in these calculations, this would raise the return to about 11.6%, but would also add to administrative headaches. If in addition, special legislation could extend accelerated depreciation to the partnerships, the gap between 11.2% and 12% would be closed. Without these aids, the limited partnerships could still engage in inner-city rehabilitation but would have to cut their participation approximately in half in order to earn an adequate return for their investors.

It must be emphasized that all of the above calculations assume that the limited partnerships would be able to manage their properties competently while holding them for resale and also that they and the city could together reduce neighborhood problems which adversely affect management costs and resale potential. To accomplish these ends would require, at minimum, a close working relationship with neighborhood groups and attention to residents' expressed preferences. The calculations also assume some attention by the city to inequities in the real estate tax. Only with these inputs can profitable income statements become a reality. And without this reality, limited partnerships would quickly lose interest in the inner city.

SOME RANDOM OBSERVATIONS

. Deliberately, this chapter has tried to avoid exploring the details involved in mounting a modest rehabilitation effort. It was felt to be more important to describe the basic outline of one possible approach, particularly as it would relate to a companion program of ownership-transfer. There are, however, several important points having to do with implementing rehabilitation that deserve special mention, since they bear directly on what is already either being done or being considered in this area. Most of the points are not connected with each other, so will simply be listed in no special order.

First, while major plans are being formulated, there are a number of small steps which can be taken to retard present negative trends. One important step is to create mechanisms to return vacant, partially vandalized structures to the habitable inventory before renovation becomes unduly expensive and before the surrounding environment is permanently damaged. These mechanisms include systems to monitor the inventory almost daily; loans or grants for owners of vandalized structures; better condemnation procedures where owners are unwilling to upgrade even if loans or grants are made available to them; and a write-down/resale device to move the structures quickly back into the hands of responsible investors or owner occupants.

Second, the 1969 amendment to the Internal Revenue Code permitting accelerated depreciation to be taken by owners of low-income rental housing for rehabilitation expenditures in excess of $3,000 per unit, while reflective of actual risks inherent in inner-city investments and therefore a step in the right direction, does not touch owners of most of the substandard dwellings in Baltimore and probably does not in many other cities as well. To accomplish its purpose, the limit would have to be lowered to about $1,000.

Third, with a greatly expanded modest rehabilitation effort, ordinary code enforcement should probably assume a quite different role than it has in the recent past. Ordinary enforcement programs have never been an effective device for significantly improving the standing stock of housing, and they have been a rather expensive undertaking relative to the small amount of private investment that they have induced. If most of the inner city were blanketed by modest rehabilitation, regular enforcement activities could be confined largely to halting incipient decay in the middle ring and outer city and, through annual inspections, preventing catastrophies in multifamily structures. Evidence from Baltimore, where this shift in emphasis is already occurring, suggests that such efforts have widespread public acceptance and are quite effective. In addition, because most of the inspections can be restricted to building exteriors and common spaces, the programs can cover large portions of the inventory relatively inexpensively.

Fourth, the most appropriate roles for nonprofit corporations in the overall renewal endeavor need to be thoroughly re-examined. In many cities they have been enticed by government programs into an activity — maximum rehabilitation — which they are not particularly well equipped to perform, which is not entirely consistent with their primary objectives, and which does not adequately leverage their limited resources. Assuming suitable vehicles to undertake maximum rehabilitation could be created, it may be that nonprofit organizations could make a more significant contribution by guaranteeing loans, processing loan applications, or providing services for mortgage departments, property managers, homeowners, and tenants.

Fifth, it would seem desirable to pursue modest rehabilitation in such a

way as to connect it with a strategy that contemplates a higher level of upgrading over the long term. One approach might be to set aside a certain sum
of money for each block, depending on its general physical condition and on
the ultimate renewal plan that had been designed for it, but allow owners and
residents a voice in allocating the funds and programming expenditures. This
procedure might result in deviation from the housing code but might also
produce greater consumer satisfaction and more private investment than
would be possible if there were strict adherence to existing renewal standards.

Sixth, unlike maximum rehabilitation, modest upgrading offers little potential for refinancing on substantially more favorable terms than now prevail.
Ten-year mortgage loans can be replaced by loans with 15-year maturities, but
this will frequently not be sufficient to permit the required improvements to
be undertaken without either a rent increase or a subsidy. Moreover, a large
proportion of modest rehabilitation, even in stable sectors of the market where
institutional funds are readily available, is financed internally. For these reasons, no attempt was made in the chapter to adjust the subsidy estimates downward to reflect the possible contribution which refinancing at market rates of
interest might make in reducing cash contributions by government.

Seventh, the employment opportunities for low-income ghetto residents
that are frequently cited as a major benefit of inner-city renewal do not appear to be very large in the case of modest rehabilitation. Assuming that the
total required capital expenditures, excluding overhead and profit, of about
$70,000,000 were spread over a 10-year period and that half of this amount
was for on-site labor and that half of this labor would come from existing
skill pools, only $1,750,000 of new employment would be generated each
year. At an average full-time wage of around $8,500, only 200 on-site jobs
would be created. Even if the entire $70,000,000 could be channeled so as
to benefit inner-city residents, which is most improbable, only 800 jobs would
be created. Associated renewal programs could conceivably double this figure,
but neither construction nor any other single industry can be looked upon to
reduce underemployment to a significant degree.

Finally, even though modest rehabilitation programs will not create a large
number of jobs, they will exacerbate the shortage of skills which already exists,
unless immediate steps are taken to recruit workers and subcontractors and
train them in the special requirements of building renovation. The private sector cannot be expected to mobilize these resources unassisted. One specific
way in which the needed manpower might be obtained is through the use of
the MESBIC (Minority Enterprise Small Business Investment Corporation)
program to create organizations that would not only train workers using Department of Labor grants, but also rehabilitate, manage, and maintain inner-
city properties.

CHAPTER 14

The Constituency of Housing Interests: Toward an Understanding of Program Feasibility *

No strategy for eliminating a social problem, however appealing in the abstract, is worth more than passing attention unless it has some likelihood of being implemented. A determination of the constraints upon implementation must go beyond usual questions of economic and technical feasibility and into issues having to do with possible effects on various interest groups, the distribution of power within the political system, and so on. To assess feasibility of a given policy or set of programs is to ask, first, whether they have realistically some chance of being adopted, and second, whether the organizations exist or can be created to develop, administer, and sustain them.

These observations apply with particular force to low-income housing policy. The fact that a particular strategy for dealing with the shelter problems of poor families can be demonstrated theoretically to be both efficient and equitable by no means assures its political acceptance. Most of the groups who shape domestic policy in the United States do not appear to attach high priority to the housing needs of the low-income population. Central-city governments, fighting for their fiscal survival, are forced to be especially callous in this regard, while suburban municipalities and their constituencies simply don't care. Even among those whose lives are dedicated to fighting poverty and injustice, housing problems must compete with many other deprivations for attention. And there are differences of opinion among informed and dedicated persons as to which housing objectives should be stressed and just how effective various proposed interventions would actually be. Thus, it is virtually impossible for even the most sophisticated, carefully reasoned, completely

*This chapter was written by James Taylor

documented housing analysis (which ours is not) to lead directly to a corresponding set of policies and programs. Other societal goals, other problems, other clients, and other values must also be considered. Moreover, contrary to an implicit assumption underlying much policy-related research, better understanding of the consequences of particular interventions may inhibit rather than facilitate proper action. As Marcuse, for example, points out, "interest groups may enter into various compromise arrangements because of insufficient information or doubt as to the future results of present actions. Such compromises may be socially very desirable; more complete information may render them less likely" (1).

The final portion of our research, therefore, attempted to bridge part of the gap between analysis and policy by taking a first step into the politics of housing. This concluding chapter describes our efforts, and offers a preliminary assessment of the feasibility, in a political/administrative sense, of the program proposals presented earlier.

ROLE OF INTEREST GROUPS IN PROGRAM ADOPTION AND IMPLEMENTATION

To the extent that proposed housing policies are in fact innovative, they imply, as one by-product, a reallocation of values within the community of housing interests, and also within the community as a whole. This is so for two reasons. First, when a housing policy is implemented — when it becomes a reality and not just an idea — it leads to the growth of organizations responsible for its administration. A national mortgage-loan program requires banking institutions; a federal policy to expand home building needs a building industry; an urban renewal policy demands a government bureaucracy capable of the necessary administration. Second, for every policy in housing, existing or proposed, there is some consumer clientele of relevant interest, either real or potential. It follows, therefore, that innovations in policy must result in a rearrangement of existing institutions and in a new distribution of burdens and benefits. Existing interest groups, as a result, scan each policy proposal to assess its implication for them as opportunity or threat. These assessments become, in turn, important determinants of whether a given program will ever be adopted, and effectively implemented.

Broadly speaking, everyone who occupies shelter is engaged in making and executing housing policy, in the sense that his behavior has some effect on the outcome of the housing system as a whole. However, the roles and relative influence of individuals, groups, and classes of interest differ greatly. To determine the probability of instituting changes in housing policy, the relative decision-making weight of federal and local governments, financial and business organizations, political groups, and citizen-action groups has to be considered, and the stage in the overall process at which their influence becomes effective must be understood.

From the beginning of the study, therefore, it was envisaged that when the results of our research had become clear, the findings would be presented to groups most directly concerned with the development and administration of housing policy in the city, in order to evaluate as fully as possible the feasibility of our programmatic proposals. We reasoned that if: (1) *a consensus* could be found among these groups as to the nature of the problem and how to deal with it; (2) the groups appeared willing to make a *commitment* themselves to furnish financial resources, managerial capability, executive authority, or political support; and (3) *cooperation* between groups prepared to commit resources could be achieved; then the proposals could be said to be feasible. Such a combination of interests would constitute a *critical coalition.*

Near the end of the study, a number of informal meetings to discuss our findings were arranged with organizations who have clearly defined housing interests in Baltimore. In the selection of groups to talk with, six general categories of interest were identified: the federal government, the city government, the business and financial community, property owners and managers, community groups, and tenants and homeowners.

For five of the six categories, at least one meeting was held with one or more representative organizations, as follows:

1. Federal government
    Department of Housing and Urban Development (Regional Staff)
2. City government
    Department of Housing and Community Development
    City Planning Commission
    Department of Planning
    Model Cities Agency
3. Business and financial community
    Greater Baltimore Committee (housing task force)
    American City Corporation
4. Property owners and managers
    Property Owners Association of Baltimore City
5. Community groups
    Urban Coalition
    Baltimore Neighborhoods Inc.
    Citizens Planning and Housing Association
    Model Cities Steering Committee

The sixth category, the otherwise unrepresented tenants and homeowners, was covered through our survey of inner-city residents. In addition, individual meetings were held with persons in most of the organizations listed. It can readily be seen that not all of the five interests were adequately covered. Equally, most of the organizations in each group do not constitute a single interest. Nevertheless, collectively, the organizations and the persons in them are broadly representative of power, influence, and opinion in the community.

From the meetings, it was hoped to obtain answers to three questions relating to the three elements of a critical coalition mentioned above.

First, whether there exists a reasonable degree of consensus among interests as to the various dimensions of the present housing problem — its causes, the nature of existing conditions, the urgency of the situation in relation to other problems, and what can be done to alleviate it; and whether these perceptions lead to policy conclusions similar to our own, or, failing that, to some set of conclusions which are at least not incompatible with the type of programs proposed in this report.

Second, assuming that out of the meetings would emerge a reasonable amount of agreement as to conditions and possible courses of action, whether there is willingness on the part of groups to commit their own resources to remedial efforts, either along the lines we propose or to other programs.

Finally, whether the groups are likely to be willing to cooperate with each other in translating the programs into action.

The structure of the meetings was simple: at the outset some time was spent describing the study, its background assumptions, the research design, and whatever results were available *at the time of the meeting.* The latter half of the meetings were devoted to a two-way discussion, questions, and criticisms of points in the initial presentation. The remainder of the chapter reports on the general results of the meetings and on what these results seem to imply for our recommended innovations in housing policy in the city.

THE QUESTION OF CONSENSUS

Perceptions of the housing problem could vary with respect to at least five general areas of concern: size and characteristics of the problem, apparent causes, urgency of the situation, salience, and possible courses of remedial action. Each of these is discussed in turn.

Size and Characteristics

Although our study attempted to cover twelve different types of housing deprivation, most persons still perceive shelter problems principally in physical terms. Not surprisingly, therefore, throughout the series of meetings much of the discussion surrounded our estimates of the state of deterioration of the city's housing stock. In some meetings reactions to our modest figures varied from mild skepticism to outright scorn. Not everyone took issue, but many did. It seemed that each person brought to the discussions his own private estimate, based either on personal experience in the city or on other surveys. City officials had a perspective based on their experience in managing a large block of inner-city housing and in conducting code enforcement and rehabilitation programs. Inner-city property owners, community groups, and residents evaluated the seriousness of deterioration in terms of specific facets of the problem — vandalism, decline of neighborhood morale, overcrowding, and neglect by owners and tenants — in specific neighborhoods.

When differences in estimating procedures had been taken into account, it turned out that most estimates compared quite well with those of the study. Apart from the encouragement which we were able to take from this confirmation, the responses suggested that there might be in the city a general acceptance that housing has become a problem which demands new kinds of initiatives. On the negative side, however, there was still a predominant concern with the physical dimensions of the overall problem, an emphasis which does not provide an especially congenial atmosphere for several of the innovations which we have suggested.

Causes of the Problem

The theories or images which groups employed to explain the causes of the housing problem have already been discussed in Chapter 10. There was, as has been noted, a great diversity of opinion, and by no means all of the views represented explanations that match up well with our own analysis of the situation. Rather than rehearse again the range of opinions, we will instead offer here an assessment of the implications of the differences as they relate to possible acceptance or rejection of our recommendations.

It seems useful to distinguish between images which are mostly ideological and those which are primarily pragmatic. The distinction can be illustrated as follows. During one discussion a government official expressed an almost apocalyptic view of the decline of the city. He argued that the dynamics of the situation were such that the only reasonable strategy is, in effect, to hasten abandonment of the inner city. In this sense, he appeared to refute our analysis. When the discussion turned to practical choices of policy, however, his reasoning reflected both a well-developed awareness of trends within the city and a disposition to work within conventional frameworks to deal with existing problems which he recognized. Similarly, a leader in the black community, while stressing an explanation of the situation which implied the need for very deep-seated social change, also recognized the necessity to work toward more limited immediate goals which were consistent with our own proposals. We were led to conclude from these discussions that differences in images of the problem, while very important, often do not represent a barrier to action. In addition, it appears that the images themselves change, usually in the direction of a common image, as new evidence and argument are discussed.

On another dimension, however, divergence of images appeared to have more disturbing implications. Some groups explained the problem largely in terms of the actions of other groups, e.g., landlords blaming tenants and vice versa. These explanations obviously make it difficult for the groups concerned to cooperate with each other around any program. In certain instances, this inability to work together might continue even after both sides have gained a common perspective. In the controversy over land installment contracts, for example, the opposing interests have offered almost identical analyses of the cause of the situation, but seemingly because of underlying animosities, have been unable to reach agreement as to how to solve the problem. Unfortunately, the extent to which these conflicting images of the problem could be a barrier to program innovations is difficult to assess.

Urgency of the Problem

There is a large body of opinion that problems in the United States must reach crisis proportions before legislatures can be mobilized to take action. Recognizing this fact, pressure groups describe nearly every problem as a crisis, and the word is now almost totally debased. Consequently, although the notion of a housing crisis in Baltimore has, on the surface, almost universal acceptance, it seemed necessary to determine where on the hierarchy of local crises housing actually ranks. Is the problem truly perceived to be urgent enough to elicit support for programs that would reallocate resources in its direction?

Initially, as expected, everyone in the meetings accepted the notion that the city is in the midst of a housing crisis. Soon, however, we began to discern differences in the use which individuals made of the term "crisis." It some-times was employed simply to mean that conditions are very bad. We found ourselves trying to introduce a different connotation, one which would incorporate the idea that when the patient is dead, the crisis has passed. Our use of the term grew out of the finding that, on the one hand, the state of the housing stock in Baltimore is fairly good and could be upgraded at a surprisingly low cost, while on the other hand, there is continuing deterioration and abandonment. This combination of opportunity and danger provided our definition of crisis.

By contrast, many persons who discussed the "urgency" of the problem seemed to have already mentally abandoned the city and were no longer thinking of solutions which would utilize what appeared to us to represent the considerable resources which Baltimore possesses in its existing stock and real estate management skills. In their view the patient was indeed dead. For others, there were so many urgent problems, that concern over housing was widely diffused and unfocused. They could seriously cope with only one or two crises at a time.

The interpretation which might be given to this finding would seem to be that the widely felt sense of urgency is not likely in many cases to lead groups to take significant remedial steps.

Salience of the Problem

For many individuals, housing problems either cannot easily be separated from larger societal problems, or are not viewed as being as crisis laden. We therefore sought, as an extension of our inquiry into the question of urgency, to determine what importance is given by various groups to housing as against other concerns with which they are preoccupied.

Often in our discussions, persons talked only superficially about housing: they saw it as symptom, or symbol, or index of some other negative phenomenon which was of greater moment to them. City officials, with their eyes on the wealthier suburbs, tended to see housing issues within the framework of the declining-resource/increasing-responsibility bind into which most older cities have been forced. They felt that housing problems like those of education, transportation, urban blight, welfare, and so on, can only be resolved when a more realistic adjustment of public resources and responsibility within the region has been achieved. To them, housing problems are important but necessarily secondary to resolving this more basic fiscal issue.

The black community has a similar concern. It sees itself increasingly the prisoner of the inner city, but simultaneously the potential custodian of a still influential city government. Housing problems are viewed in the perspective of the *realpolitik* of race relations in the region, the state, and the nation as a whole. In addition, the exclusionary policies of the counties around Baltimore make almost any outside suggestion for an inner-city oriented housing program immediately suspect.

A few individuals put housing problems into a framework of concern about the deterioration of the overall "quality of life" along with environmental pollution, the decay of democratic institutions, and similarly broad problems. It was argued, for example, that existing laws and institutions make irresponsible, exploitative behavior in housing profitable, and that this behavior beats down the poor. Mortgage-loan policies frustrate pride of ownership among those with lower incomes; urban renewal destroys their community spirit; and so on. Thus, housing problems are viewed as subsidiary to inequities in a larger decision-making structure.

What should we conclude from this finding? The fact that housing problems were not seen as the most salient problem to several of the interest groups who are directly concerned with housing is neither surprising, nor particularly discouraging. For several groups, however, there is the less optimistic implication that while the low priority accorded to housing would not mean our proposals would be opposed, it also means that they would not be strongly advocated.

Courses of Action

The general views described above can perhaps be better understood if they are related directly to several of the major courses of action which we have suggested as candidates for effectively dealing with the housing problem (2).

1. **Ownership-Transfer.** Some skepticism was expressed as to whether individuals could be found who would want to buy in inner-city neighborhoods, or if they could be found, whether they would be a great improvement over present ownership. Some observers felt that because of crime, neighborhood decline, poor schools, weakening property values, and inadequate city services, only properties outside the inner city are now attractive to buyers. Other evidence was advanced to show that existing opportunities for purchase are not being taken up. The prevailing opinion, however, was that expansion of home ownership opportunities is an important objective. Support for this view was expressed, often strongly, in almost every meeting.

2. **Neighborhood Improvement.** The declining state of inner-city neighborhoods and its unfortunate effects on housing was universally commented on. In principle there is widespread support for policies to upgrade the quality of the housing environment. However, many persons doubted whether programs to achieve these improvements could be funded at the necessary levels.

3. **Housing Rehabilitation.** The concept of modest rehabilitation seemed to find strongest support among those most closely associated with day-to-day management of the stock. Some other groups felt its scope to be unduly limited relative to the need. Part of the negative attitude may have been due to difficulty in understanding what operations, precisely, would be involved in modest rehabilitation programs. Modest rehabilitation was seen as a stopgap that would not get at fundamental problems.

4. **Maintenance-Management.** While the importance of maintenance of the stock was generally accepted, on the whole there was not great interest evidenced in programs to improve upkeep. Like soil erosion, the gradual effects of lack of maintenance tend to underplay its importance.

THE QUESTION OF COMMITMENT

What does the pattern of response indicate about the possibility of establishing a basis of general support for either the proposals discussed or others which might be advanced?

First, despite the reservations noted above, the study appeared to receive a sympathetic hearing from all groups. Interest was expressed in the findings and conclusions of the study. Some groups pressed hard to clarify questions arising out of substantive points. Often these were groups closest to the housing situation, best informed, and most apparently interested in using the findings. One or two individuals manifested a measure of hostility, calling into question the motives of the study itself. This response, which came from persons who had a clear grasp of many dimensions of the housing problem, did not seem general enough, however, to become a powerful determinant in policy-making processes of the city.

As for the possibility of active pursuit of the proposals in the study, we are still uncertain. Although it would appear that serious opposition to the recommendations need not be expected, neither, as already mentioned, is there likely to be a strong spontaneous move in those directions. This judgment is elaborated upon in the next section as part of our discussion of the probability of effective collaboration.

THE CHANCES FOR COLLABORATION

While a positive response to the findings of the study and a reasonable measure of commitment to the suggested courses of action is encouraging, widespread support is not in itself adequate. Two additional ingredients are required:

First is the willingness of certain strategic interest groups to collaborate. Without financial backing, entrepreneurship, political support, and consumer acceptability, programs such as management-maintenance and ownership-transfer can not function. Unless the various interests which provide these inputs can work together, the potential for improvement remains unrealized.

Second is a process by which to develop the necessary level of collaboration among interests. Any considerable change of direction in housing policy can normally be achieved only by overcoming the forces of inertia which support the status quo. Policy innovation may be best thought of in many cases as a step-by-step incremental process in which the several parts of a critical coalition for promoting and sustaining new programs are gradually assembled. For each organization, the adjustments which have to be made to meet the challenges of new policies require the replanning of activities and this takes time.

In this section, the prospects for collaboration are assessed, both in terms of the role of key interests in making policy and in relationship to their perceived level of commitment.

A Nucleus of Support
The early meetings seemed to indicate the existence of at least one con-

gruence of interest between two groups who are of strategic importance to
the proposed programs but who would normally not think of themselves as
allies. These are the leaders of the black community and inner-city property
owners. They both wish to re-introduce a measure of stability into the housing market. The reason for their individual concerns are clear: they suffer most
directly from the existing downward trends. As potential collaborators, they
do not constitute the most likely combination, since each party has a tendency
to think of the other as a principal author of its own present discomfort, and
has very little inclination to see the other as common victim of the same disas-
ter. Nevertheless, we explored with each group at some length one particular
area of potentially common interest – ownership-transfer. This program would
simultaneously provide the means for (a) partially satisfying home ownership
desires in the black community and (b) creating the opportunity for owners
of inner-city properties to rid themselves of investments which they can no
longer manage profitably. The response from property owners was encouraging; we were told that this group would probably be willing to commit resources to make such a program feasible. Response from the black community
was more difficult to gauge. Several leaders expressed skepticism based on
their feeling that the envisaged program was too limited in scope. Some were
concerned that new owners would be loaded with undesirable properties. At
the same time, however, our surveys indicated a measure of unsatisfied consumer demand for homes. In addition, black leaders by no means rejected the
proposed program entirely, and some indicated that, if there were some guarantees that home buyers would not be victimized, they would be supporters.

The Role of the Black Community

The reaction of blacks to the ownership-transfer proposal raises the larger
question of their role in housing policy generally. In Baltimore, as in many
other cities, a fact of life of tremendous importance in understanding the
policy-making process is the existence of a large black community which does
not have fully effective representation in the policy-making arena. Although
almost half of the city's present population is black, the business of making
major housing decisions in and for the city, in both public and private spheres
of activity, is dominated by whites. As a result, the interests of a huge proportion of the city's citizens are not vigorously pushed, even by those sympathetic
to their particular problems.

There are, of course, many divergent points of view within the black community paralleling these within the white, but circumstances have also brought
about the existence of a uniquely black perspective. The absence of this perspective in policy-making may sometimes lead to errors of judgment, based
on poor or inaccurate information. An equally serious problem is that many
programs directed toward the inner city, no matter what their intrinsic merit,

are understandably viewed with distrust and hostility. An instance was pointed out to us where vandalism in a housing construction project fell spectacularly when local residents fully understood that the project was intended to and indeed would help their neighborhood. Similarly, one of the best managed private rental complexes in the inner city is in a block where there is a high measure of citizen participation in management decisions. Authority is a two-way relationship: it exists in reality only if it is granted by those over whom it presumably is exercised. Unfortunately, in Baltimore, those whose personal fates are intimately associated with the future of the inner city often seem to have least to say about policies which affect them most directly.

This deficiency in the policy-making process is especially unfortunate because the black community itself would benefit most from an evolution in housing programs toward interventions designed to arrest deterioration. Certainly without collaboration of blacks, programs of housing rehabilitation, ownership-transfer, neighborhood improvement, and maintenance-management would be greatly hindered. At the present, however, the way in which policies are made does not contribute to such collaboration.

The Role of the Business and Financial Community

While the support of property owners and the black community represents a necessary element in a critical coalition, these two interests are not sufficient by themselves to form such a coalition. Neither singly nor together do they add up to a combination with access to capital to support the recommended programs. Nor do they command the necessary political strength to manage the adoption of such programs and their subsequent sustenance. For this kind of support, there would have to be assistance from the business community and from government. Some of what was discovered concerning the prospects for developing the support of the business and financial community has already been covered in the discussion of limited partnerships (Chapter 13). Here we attempt to summarize only by offering one additional comment.

In general, it seems easiest to attract large capital investments to the kind of venture represented in Baltimore by Charles Center and the Inner-Harbour Project — something which is new, striking, and monumental, which has the kind of definition that allows the investor to see the results of his investment in a more or less immediate way, merging civic pride and a sense of having accomplished something of major proportions, forward-looking and progressive. Programs to arrest housing decay and save obsolescing stock from rapid deterioration, whatever volume such programs might reach and however successful they might be, lack the same kind of flair. As against this, there is some evidence of increasing concern by businessmen over the fate of the inner city. There are increasing attempts — through housing task forces, development corporations, and the like — to develop appropriate housing policy. There is, there-

fore, every reason to expect cooperation from the business and financial community in the development of new programs. The potential size of the inputs,
though, is problematic. Despite its huge resources, business is highly constrained in a variety of ways in what it can do to solve social problems.

The Role of Government

All but one of the government agencies with whom we met are part of the
city administration. The meetings were valuable as exchanges of information
and interpretation. They also elicited some measure of support. Most of all,
they served to emphasize the dominance of the federal government in shaping
local housing destinies. Direct and indirect acknowledgment of the importance
of federal policy formed a consistent theme in the meetings. This fact is of
special importance here, because federal policy is currently not moving in
quite the same direction as our proposed thrusts.

Federal policy pervades thinking at every level. An early meeting with
officials of a nonprofit development corporation, for example, led to the discovery that the policy of the corporation was oriented toward maximum rehabilitation, following the lead of the federal government, even though its
efforts tended to duplicate those of the city. At another meeting, the problem of Baltimore's housing was stated in terms of number of new units which
have to be built in order to close the existing gap and meet shelter needs, again
a federal definition of the problem.

Still another tribute to the influence of federal policy appeared indirectly.
The institutional organization most immediately concerned with the maintenance and upkeep of the present stock (apart from owner occupants) is the
Property Owners Association. From members of the association came the observation that federal programs which were available to them were set up in
such a way as to be of little benefit to their inventory. In a sense, the pessimism of the investors testified to the strength of the prevailing federal program structure. For the individual owner or potential buyer, much the same
can be said. Widespread use of land installment contracts stemmed directly
from the way in which federal mortgage-loan programs have operated.

Thus, the federal government, in one respect or another, has to be factored
into nearly every successful policy change in the housing field. Its power to
influence other key interests is immense. In the past its policies have not worked
well to improve the "middle range" of substandard housing or to stabilize
inner-city housing conditions. These weaknesses are likely to continue unless
there is substantial prodding from the outside.

CAN A CRITICAL COALITION BE FORMED?

What can be concluded about the willingness of strategic interest groups
to collaborate? On the whole we are uncertain. Since inner-city decay and

declining property values undermine the shaky financial base of the city, local government could be expected to support federally financed programs to arrest housing deterioration. The black community stands to be a potential gainer from programs of neighborhood renewal and ownership-transfer, and therefore would probably cooperate providing it is convinced these interventions are not simply devices to turn them away from other goals. Property owners would be a prime source of political support. Once the programs were adopted, owners would not, however, be soft bargainers should the occasion to get out of the market appear. Nevertheless, they are not in an advantageous position at present, and could and probably would make a useful and positive contribution to all of the programs. Progressive elements in the business community have manifested a positive interest in reevaluating their traditional position and could be counted on for assistance. Community groups could also be expected to support reasonable programs and help make them effective. The ultimate key to a large part of the proposed effort is the federal government (both the legislative and executive branches) which would have to be convinced not only to spend more money for housing but also, as just noted, to spend it quite differently than it has in the past.

Whether Washington would today lead a coalition seems extremely unlikely. There is disenchantment in the Administration with the performance of housing subsidy programs and honest doubt as to the extent and seriousness of the specific housing problems which these programs address. Given this attitude and the budget squeeze discussed in Chapter 11, a large increase in federal housing dollars is just not in the cards. The trend toward revenue sharing increases our pessimism. While this form of decentralization has favorable attributes, it may realign power structures to the disadvantage of the poor. Historically, cities have not found arguments for allocating a large amount of their own resources to low-income housing problems to be compelling, nor the strategies for doing so, persuasive. Currently, they cling to the conviction that the poor should be suburbanized, and they are beleagured by more politically urgent matters. Given some latitude, as they well might be under revenue sharing, most local governments would reduce their emphasis on low-income housing programs, drawing their intellectual support from Forrester's untenable argument that such efforts are self-defeating (3). Unless the housing situation of the poor gets much worse, the commitment to make it much better will not be forthcoming. Only if low-income housing programs become viewed as an integral part of broader efforts that are essential to improve the quality of the urban environment for all citizens will they receive broad support. Without that support, most dimensions of housing need will, nevertheless, continue to decline in severity as rising incomes and expanding federal social welfare programs gradually erode away the foundations of poverty and discrimination. The nation is not likely in these circumstances, however, to meet its housing goals as rapidly as seemed possible several years ago.

APPENDIX A
First Household Survey

The first household survey had two objectives: first, to define a universe of low-income families for subsequent interviewing in depth; and second, to determine in general terms the distribution of various poverty-related problems across income and racial groups throughout the city. Both of these objectives dictated a city-wide sample rather than one which was confined exclusively to predefined "poverty" areas. The first objective also dictated, however, that the sampling rate be much higher in those areas where low-income families were known to be concentrated. Since most of Baltimore's low-income population resides in a contiguous group of census tracts which could be said to comprise an inner city and since for planning purposes it is useful to distinguish this inner sector from the rest of the city, it was decided to vary the sampling rate by these two areas rather than try to pinpoint possible concentrations of low-income families more precisely in advance of actual interviewing. Thus, of approximately 9,000 interviews that were ultimately conducted, 7,250 (80%) were in the inner city, as we defined it using 1960 census-tract data on income and rent (Figure 2.1). The sampling rate for the inner city was about 7% and for the outer city, 1%.

The sample may be described as a two-stage area probability sample, with the sampling unit defined as two clusters of ten contiguous households in each of 560 randomly selected inner-city blocks and single clusters of 10 contiguous households in each of 280 outer-city blocks. The probability of a block being selected was proportionate to the number of dwelling units in the block in 1960. Within blocks, interviewers were instructed first to count the number of dwelling units, and then, depending on the number, to select the starting point for the 10 contiguous households on the basis of a set of random numbers which had been supplied to them.

Interviewers were originally directed to make as many as four calls per household to complete an interview. Late in the survey when it was discovered that the yields on the third and fourth calls were very low, the procedure was changed to require two calls. In most cases, the interviewers were of the same race as the respondent.

The survey encountered a number of difficulties, and we would be less than candid if we did not mention these, since they may have affected our results in ways that are not yet apparent to us.

First of all, the response rate was very low, barely reaching 55% in the outer city and 67% in the inner city. The lower rate of response in the outer city may reflect in part the perceived lack of relevance of the questions to the respondents' situation. In both areas, the respondents resented some of the nosy questions, and a number of persons terminated interviews for this reason. These questions were ultimately moved toward the end of the survey instrument, but this change improved the response rate only slightly. Midway in the survey, gifts were offered to potential respondents, but this gesture was not very helpful either.

In retrospect, most of the problem of high nonresponse seems to have been associated with the inability of the interviewing firm to train and keep on its payroll a crew of competent interviewers. Turnover of personnel was very high, with a total of over 250 interviewers eventually being used. This meant that the time which had to be devoted to training was much more than originally anticipated, and probably as a result, that the training itself was less than adequate. With insufficient preparation, interviewers may have experienced more than the usual amount of difficulty in getting inside the door and, once inside, in completing the interview. And discouraged by their low rate of success, they quit. If this reasoning is correct, some of the nonresponse problem was in the nature of a vicious circle.

Unfortunately, our problems did not end here. When the interviews had been completed, weights applied, and the data blown up to provide city-wide totals, it became apparent that the sample was badly biased. The household-population estimate for the city exceeded 1,000,000, an error of over 10% as compared with an expected sampling error of not over 3.8%. The discrepancy for school-age population was, proportionately, even greater. The estimated number of large apartment structures (10 or more units) was only 20% of the known true figure. The black population had been overestimated, and so on. In reviewing the sample design and the interviewing procedures, five basic reasons for these discrepancies emerged.

(1) The interviewing firm had failed to adjust the 1960 housing data for new construction, conversions, and demolitions which occurred subsequent to the decennial count. As a consequence, the estimated number of households in the outer city was much too low, and the reverse was true for the

inner city. It was possible to correct this mistake through the use of building-permit data maintained by the Baltimore Department of Housing and Community Development.

(2) The interviewing firm had failed to sample apartment houses as a separate universe and had experienced an extraordinarily high nonresponse rate in the structures which were sampled. The result was an undercount of small, white, upper-income households. To correct this mistake, a listing of all apartments was made with the assistance of the Department of Housing and Community Development; an abbreviated questionnaire was constructed; and, using the reverse telephone directory, 200 additional families were interviewed over the phone.

(3) Interviewers had grossly miscounted the number of dwelling units in a large number of blocks. Some of the interviewers had counted structures rather than dwellings, others apparently enumerated only the dwelling units on one of the four sides of the block, and still others may simply have been careless. To correct this mistake, all blocks in which the interviewer count differed from the 1960 Census count by more than 10% were re-enumerated.

(4) There were systematic differences between respondents who were contacted on the first and second call and those who were contacted on the third and fourth call. Hence, by extrapolation, there were probably systematic differences between respondents and nonrespondents. The most pronounced difference related to family size and employment status. Small households with at least one employed member frequently, as would be expected, had no one at home when the interviewer called. This particular bias was exaggerated by the decision, referred to earlier, to eliminate third and fourth calls because of their low yield. It obviously would have been better to continue these calls, but to attempt to contact the household at a different time of day. In any event, to compensate for the bias, higher weights were applied to households who were contacted on the third or fourth call. Because of the small size of the sample in the outer city, the amount by which the weights could be adjusted upward without reducing reliability to an intolerable level was quite limited.

(5) Interviewers failed to record vacancies and abandonments correctly and frequently not at all. Because vacancy rates are much higher in the inner city than elsewhere, this error biased our inner-city population estimate upward. To correct this mistake, the vacancy data were simply thrown out and arbitrary figures for the inner and outer city applied. This adjustment helped to give us more accurate estimates of total households in each of the two areas, but nothing at all can now be said about the characteristics of the vacant stock.

Collectively, these corrections did not eliminate all of the obvious discrepancies in the data. In particular, total population and school-age population still exceeded true figures by an unacceptable amount. In addition, the number of female-headed households seemed much too large. At this point in the clean-up process, therefore, we sampled completed questionnaires for possible systematic errors in coding or punching. This effort uncovered the fact that the head of household had been incorrectly recorded in a large number of cases, but it revealed nothing which would suggest why the other errors persisted. It was decided, therefore, to reduce the weights of the school-age population and their families downward until the resulting figures were consistent with school enrollment data. In effect, this adjustment was simply a more selective approach to the high nonresponse rate among small households. It solved all of the remaining discrepancies except for a few irregularities in the age/sex/race profile stemming, we believe, from difficulties encountered in trying to find black males in the 20-39 year age group.

With all of the mistakes in sampling and some of the mistakes in coding, the validity of the recorded responses is also called into question. To allay (or confirm) our fears on this score, we subsampled a small group of families and re-interviewed them. We also compared first- and second-survey responses to several questions which appeared in both surveys. Although a few peculiar differences were noted, the overall correspondence among answers gave us confidence that the interviews had been properly conducted in nearly all cases. This fact does not mean that invalid responses might not have been obtained for other reasons. It does, nevertheless, eliminate the major source of concern.

This short account of our survey procedures and out attempts to salvage the data may understate the amount of work that was required to make the data useable, and yet at the same time leave the reader in doubt as to whether all of the problems were indeed satisfactorily solved. It is worth noting, therefore, that our figures are substantially confirmed by the 1970 Census.

APPENDIX B

Second Household Survey

In order to determine in detail the housing, employment, education, and health deprivations of low-income families, as well as something about their attitudes toward and participation in anti-poverty programs, a subsample of families who were interviewed in the first household survey was contacted and interviewed again. The second interview also served as an opportunity to verify some of the information obtained initially and, in the case of families who had moved between the two surveys, to learn something about mobility patterns.

The subsample was stratified by age, sex, and race of head; by participation in employment programs; and by self-perceived upward or downward mobility as revealed from answers to an attitudinal question on this subject in the first survey. The universe of potential respondents consisted not only of families whose incomes fell below our poverty line (see Chapter 2) but also of a borderline group, since it was felt that unless "low income" was defined quite liberally a priori, important segments of the deprived population might be missed.

The sample of intended respondents consisted of one adult plus all (other) employable adults in approximately 1,400 families. Three attempts were made to reach each eligible respondent. A gift having a retail value of about $7.00 was given to each respondent in return for his time and cooperation in completing the interview. Interviews lasted from 1½ to 2½ hours. In nearly all cases the interviewer was of the same race as the respondent.

Although less than a year had elapsed since the 1,400 families had been first interviewed, about 15% of them could not be found. Either their original address was incorrect and no one at or near the recorded address had heard of them, or they had moved and could not be traced, or they were never at home when the interviewer called. Another 15% declined to be interviewed again, so in all, the response rate was very close to 70%. To see whether the families who were interviewed differed in any important way from those who were not, the answers of the two groups to questions on the first household survey were compared. While the differences have not been tested statistically, they appear in nearly all cases to be insignificant.

When the interviews were finished, weights were applied so that the sample would blow up to city-wide totals for the low-income population, *as defined by us.* Since, as already mentioned, our definition is a liberal one, the composition of our low-income population may be different from, and the rates of various deprivations less than, what is reported for low-income populations in other studies.

APPENDIX C
Survey of Inner-City Investors

The sample of investors who were interviewed in conjunction with our study of the inner-city housing market (Chapter 9) was drawn from the list of 320 inner-city rental properties that were inspected as part of the survey of residential structures (Appendix D). For 50% of these properties, the owners of record were identified. With the assistance of the Property Owners Association those owners who were thought to have major investments in the inner city (100 or more dwelling units) were listed, and a special effort, again with the assistance of the Association, was made to interview all of them. Thirty-five were reached in this fashion. For the remaining 125, the initial effort to arrange a meeting was just as great, but the difficulties in doing so were even greater. Some of the smaller owners did not live in Baltimore; several did not have a listed phone; a few were never home; and a number, in one way or another, simply refused to be interviewed. Many of those who did consent to see us did not provide very much useful information. As a consequence, our diligence in seeking the small owner gradually waned, and whereas all but 3 of the 35 large investors were interviewed, less than half (60) of the remaining ones were.

The interview itself was semistructured. A primarily closed-end questionnaire provided the general format for the interview, but the order in which the questions were asked depended very much on the respondent. If in the process of answering one question, he mentioned something which we would not ordinarily have brought up until later in the discussion we pursued the matter at that point. Since only three persons did all of the interviewing, they soon were able to jump back and forth in this fashion and still not become confused. At the same time, this procedure permitted a much more free flowing exchange than would have otherwise been possible.

The questionnaire covered three basic areas: the property in the sample; the investor's holdings throughout the inner city; and the investor's attitudes about the inner-city investment climate. The quality of the responses varied greatly from respondent to respondent and, on the average, was less than had been hoped for, though much better than had been expected. Many owners, particularly the smaller ones, did not keep good records and had to speak largely from memory. Many of our questions, therefore, were answered by too few respondents to be tabulated.

In the beginning, it was our intention to produce a representative sample, so that we could present a statistical profile of the inner-city investor. With respect to the large investor, we were successful. On the basis of conversations with knowledgeable persons, we were able to determine that about two-thirds of the city's large investors were in our sample, and the names and general characteristics of nearly all of those who were not in the sample are now known to us. Unfortunately, almost the opposite is true in the case of the smaller investor. So few were interviewed (60 out of at least 5,000); they differed so widely, and their responses were so incomplete that few generalizations can be made. When it became apparent to us in the course of our survey that this result could not be avoided, our interviews turned into an attempt to fit together pieces of a puzzle, and in the process they probably became more focused than they had been. We feel reasonably confident that the pieces are all in place, and that the interviews have enabled us to describe the dynamics of the inner-city housing market accurately with respect to those characteristics which are most important to public policy.

APPENDIX D
Survey of Residential Structures

The primary purpose of this survey was to determine the cost of upgrading the *occupied* residential inventory in Baltimore City to an acceptable standard. From the sample of households who were interviewed in the first household survey, a subsample of 625 addresses was drawn, 475 in the inner city and 150 in the outer city. The sample was stratified by income and tenure of occupant, by dwelling units per structure, and by first survey condition rating. Within these cells preference was given in drawing the sample to addresses at which an interview had also been conducted in the second household survey.

Once the sample had been drawn, each address was visited initially by relatively untrained observers. If the structure appeared on external examination to be in any way marginal or substandard, it was revisited by a person experienced in rehabilitation who estimated the cost of upgrading. In one-third of the cases, the estimate had to be made without benefit of interior inspection. If the structure was unsound, the cost of replacing it with a newly constructed unit of comparable size was recorded. The cost of removing lead-based paint was not calculated.

Although the primary purpose of the inspections was to determine the seriousness of Baltimore's substandard housing problem, the survey provided the opportunity to rank the standard as well as the substandard inventory, (and also the physical quality of the neighborhoods) for later comparison with price and rent data for the same units. In brief, structures could receive a score anywhere from zero to 100, with the lowest figure identifying buildings which should be demolished, and the highest, a luxurious home or apartment. A rating of 50 was given to dwellings which barely met code requirements and were minimal in all other respects (1). Ratings from two to 49 measured the amount of money, as determined by our inspections, required to upgrade dwellings to a quality level ranging anywhere from code standard (50) to somewhat above code (55), depending on the original quality of construction. Ratings of 51 to 54 signified basic compliance with the code, sound construction, but few amenities, and usually the need for minor repairs or a few modest improvements to make the unit attractive to stable, low-income tenants. Many of these structures originally had outdoor toilets, and the move inside often was not accomplished satisfactorily by today's standards. Scores of 55 or more were based on a different rating system which ranked dwellings according to our best guess as to what their market value would be if neighborhood factors were ignored. Very few of these structures needed any remedial attention other than normal maintenance. Those which did require attention had their scores adjusted accordingly, but in no case did this bring a structure below 55.

It can be seen that the rating system lays end to end two different scales, one based on repair costs and the other on market values. The benchmark housing-quality objective is set at the end of one scale and the beginning of the other. Although the system is encumbered by squeezing more than one variable into a single scale, it also accomplishes its several purposes: it is easily replicable, regionally if not nationally; it is reliable; it permits much more finely grained analysis than do many rating systems; it can be translated almost automatically into resource requirements; and most important, although it specifies certain quality benchmarks, as reference points, it allows the analyst to select any minimum standard that meets his fancy.

The standard which was used as a referent in establishing rehabilitation costs was, in effect, slightly above housing code specifications for the city. The individual who made the inspections was asked to include in his calculations all items which represented violations of the code plus whatever else a prudent investor might spend to make the unit attractive to a stable, low-income tenant. Because of the subjective nature of this standard, a few of the structures were inspected by a second experienced rehabilitator whose estimates proved to be very close to the original ones. As an added check, our estimator also inspected several of the structures in the FACE program and compared his figures with those of the FACE inspectors. These structures required modest rehabilitation costing anywhere from $2,000 to $4,000. As expected, the FACE standards resulted in estimated costs that were somewhat higher (about one-third) than our own (2). However, for structures requiring either much more or much less upgrading, we feel that the difference in the standards would be much less, and, therefore, that our cost estimate for the city as a whole is not appreciably less than what would have been produced using FACE standards throughout.

As mentioned at the outset, inspections and cost estimates were made for the occupied inventory only. Using the 1960 Census of Housing to determine the relative proportion of substandard dwellings in the occupied and vacant inventory, a guesstimate was made of the cost of upgrading the vacant inventory. This figure included, however, only 1,000 of the abandoned units in the city, since it was assumed that the remaining ones should be demolished and would not have to be replaced.

Notes and References

Chapter 1

1. See the article City housing, Municipal Performance Report, Council On Municipal Performance, N.Y., N.Y., Vol. 1, November, 1973, p. 4. According to our own calculations, the proportion of families who can afford new construction is slightly smaller in 1974 than it was even as long ago as 1960.

2. This is not to suggest that urban conditions generally are deteriorating. Whether most cities offer better or worse living environments for most citizens than they did in the recent past is difficult to say because so many different dimensions of environment must be measured and weighted according to their presumed relative importance. Our feeling is that urban problems which directly affect most of the population in the United States ultimately seem to get at least partially solved, because the nation has the technology, resources, and will to solve them. The problems must get worse for a time before any action is taken, but eventually they are made manageable. This view is similar to one of the themes in Edward Banfield's controversial book, "The Unheavenly City," (1968). Boston: Little, Brown and Co.

3. Recent attempts to close this gap in our knowledge include: Martin Rein, Welfare and housing, Working Paper No. 4, Joint Center For Urban Studies, Cambridge, Mass., 1972. Also George Sternlieb and Bernard P. Indik, "The Ecology Of Welfare," (1973). Center For Urban Policy Research, Rutgers University, New Brunswick, N.J.

4. "Building the American City," (1968). Report of the National Commission on Urban Problems to the Congress and to the President of the United States, U. S. Government Printing Office, Washington, D.C.; "A Decent Home," (1968). U. S. President's Committee on Urban Housing, U. S. Government Printing Office, Washington; Anthony Downs, Moving toward realistic housing goals, (1968).

"Agenda for the Nation," Kermit Gordon, ed., The Brookings Institution, Washington, pp. 141-178; and Henry J. Aaron, "Shelter And Subsidies," (1972). Brookings Institution, Washington, D.C.

5. James S. Coleman, Ernest Q. Campbell, Carol J. Hobson, James McPartland, Alexander M. Mood, Frederic D. Weinfield, and Robert L. York, (1966). "Equality of Educational Opportunity," U.S. Government Printing Office, Washington; John F. Kain and Joseph J. Persky, (Winter, 1969). Alternatives to the gilded ghetto, The Public Interest, pp. 74-87; National Committee Against Discrimination in Housing, (1968). "The Impact of Housing Patterns on Job Opportunities," New York.

6. Lewis Mumford, "The City In History," (1961). New York: Harcourt, Brace, and World, Inc., p. 5.

7. It is not certain that the few families who do obtain a new home experience an improvement in living conditions that is proportional to the subsidy involved, since their prior housing situation is not known.

8. To illustrate, assuming not unreasonably that: 20% of the population is ill housed; one-half of the standard stock (40% of the total inventory) is appropriate for re-housing this group; one-fifth of the 40% comes on the market each year; and interception of more than 10% of this market supply would disrupt the market; then the rehousing program would require a quarter of a century.

    The amount of market supply of standard units which the government could siphon off for low-income families without disrupting the market is, of course, a guess. However, since the effect of the government program would be to reduce the vacancy rate, the reasonableness of the guess can be evaluated by comparing the number of intercepted units with the current vacancy level. Even assuming a vacancy rate of as high as 6 or 7%, a diversion of 10% of the appropriate market supply can be seen to be potentially even disruptive.

9. Preferences of the low-income population in this regard will, nevertheless, be examined.

10. This statement does not necessarily imply a supply-side approach to upgrading the stock. Analysis of the relative merits of supply-and-demand-side approaches is undertaken in the body of the study.

11. The sample design and questionnaire are described in Appendix A.

12. The sample design and questionnaire are described in Appendix B.

13. The sample design and rating procedures are described in Appendix D.

14. The sample design and questionnaire are described in Appendix C.

Chapter 2

1. House and Home, October 1967, p. 90.
2. Except in the case of our discussion of the inner city, all population and housing data in this chapter are taken from the decennial counts by the U.S. Bureau of the Census rather than from our own household survey. As compared with the 1970

census, our household survey estimated total population approximately correctly, and also came quite close on all other variables except white, female-headed, renter households which were substantially undercounted (see Appendix A).

The National Urban League has estimated that census takers failed to find 41,000 Baltimoreans, 32,000 of them black ("Estimating the 1970 Census Undercount for State and Local Areas," National Urban League, Washington, D.C., July, 1973). Our own calculations suggest that the undercount is much less.

3. Baltimore Department of Planning, "Baltimore Plans," January, 1970; and Baltimore Department of Planning, "Population and Housing," March, 1964.

4. Mollie Orshansky (March, 1968). The shape of poverty in 1966, Social Security Bulletin, pp. 3-32.

5. Anthony Downs (1968). Moving toward realistic housing goals. In: "Agenda for the Nation," Kermit Gordon, ed., Washington, D.C.: Brookings Institution, p. 147.

6. This figure includes 11,000 households for whom no income data were reported. The assignment of these households to the low-income population was based upon their status with respect to selected variables which were taken as surrogates for income deprivation such as receipt of public assistance, residence in public housing, occupancy of seriously dilapidated private housing, absence of employed household member, etc. The 20,000 additional families who became classified as low income when we shifted to the more liberal low income include a much higher proportion of households with an employed head and a much lower proportion of large households (6 persons or more) than do the more deprived 65,000. Given these differences and also the fact that we did not make adjustments for under-reporting of income or for wealth holdings, it could perhaps be argued that we should have divided the population, for analytical purposes, into three groups — low income (65,000), near low income (20,000), and non-low income (191,000). We tested this possibility, but except in our consideration of subsidies to relieve excess housing expense, the refinement altered the results very little.

7. Mollie Orshansky, The shape of poverty in 1966, op cit.

8. For this calculation the Consumer Price Index was used as a deflator. According to Social Security Administration standards, the total number of poor and near-poor households in the U.S. declined between 1959 and 1966 from 18 million, or 32% of all households, to 15 million, or 25% of all households. Figures for 1959 were taken from Orshansky, Recounting the poor — A five-year review, Social Security Bulletin, April 1966, Table 2, p. 24. Figures for 1966 were taken from Orshansky, The shape of poverty in 1966, Social Security Bulletin, March 1968, Table 2, p. 5.

9. Residential building permits issued from 1960 through 1969 averaged only 3,100 units annually, with the figure for 1969 being scarcely half this amount. If the rate for the decade were maintained and if each new dwelling were matched by the demolition of an old unit, the inventory would replace itself in one century. Approximately 90% of the new construction was in multifamily units with that figure rising to 97% in 1968 and 1969.

10. Daniel U. Levine (August, 1970). Threshold phenomena in inner-city schools and society, Education and Urban Society, pp. 347-358.

11. A technique similar to that developed by the Bureau of the Census (for the Office of Economic Opportunity) for classifying "poverty areas" within major cities was employed in defining a contiguous group of inner-city census tracts. (See U.S. Bureau of the Census, "Characteristics of Families Residing in Poverty Areas,"

March 1966, Series P-23, No. 19.) The defined area is somewhat more extensive than that which is ordinarily perceived by Baltimoreans as the inner city (i.e., the most severely blighted areas situated immediately adjacent to the central business district). Also included under our definition, for example, are outlying areas to the south and southeast which contain substantial numbers of public housing units.

12.   In Philadelphia, the Philadelphia Housing Development Corporation has had great difficulty in selling rehabilitated two-bedroom houses in the inner city.

Chapter 3

1.   For an elaboration of this concept, see Morton S. Baratz and William G. Grigsby (1966). "Meaning and Measurement of Poverty," Institute for Environmental Studies, University of Pennsylvania. Also, Peter Marcuse (December, 1971). Social indicators and housing policy, Urban Affairs Quarterly, 27:210.

2.   Strictly speaking, for each of the objectives to be completely measurable, target dates for achievement would have to be suggested and precise measures given. This has not been done.

3.   In nearly all cases the objectives describe a so-called end state, e.g., decent housing for everyone, rather than a process, i.e., a system allowing greater freedom of choice, which, if implemented, might lead to the desired end state. Process-type objectives are appropriate either when a clearly defined end state, e.g., a desegregated housing market, cannot be visualized in measurable terms, or as a lower level means to an end state that has already been defined.

4.   In this discussion, the term "quality" will be used to mean both quality and condition.

5.   This conclusion is based on conversations with housing officials and residents in Stockholm, but has not, as of this writing, been exposed to their critical review.

6.   The rating system is described in more detail in Appendix D.

7.   In this connection, see Lee Rainwater (January, 1966). Fear and the house-as-haven in the lower class, Journal of the American Institute of Planners, pp. 23–30. Rainwater's observations are also relevant to the discussions of neighborhood environment and stigma.

8.   The dividing line between shelter and furnishings has become blurred in recent years. For example, carpeting may be a substitute for hardwood floors; stoves are now regarded as fixtures of the dwelling, etc.

9.   As a consequence of which very few husbands in the United States sit in ugly chairs, but a rather large number of widows sip coffee in elegantly furnished surroundings.

10.   For example, see Robert C. Schmitt (January, 1966). Density, health, and social disorganization, Journal of the American Institute of Planners, pp. 38–39.

11.   A conceptually valid but practically impossible alternative would be to give each neighborhood a budget and allow residents to set their own standards.

12.   In Baltimore, this problem evidently is compounded by the fact that inner-city lots and parks have become dumping grounds for private junkmen who have no other place to dispose of their worthless accumulations inexpensively. For a most interesting account of this situation, see Edgar L. Jones (May 22, 1970). Dirty Baltimore custom, Baltimore Sun.

13. See Robert Schmitt, *op. cit.*, for a description of one attempt to relate neighborhood densities to health and social-disorganization indicators.

14. James S. Coleman, Ernest Q. Campbell, Carol J. Hobson, James McPartland, Alexander M. Mood, Frederic D. Weinfield, and Robert L. York (1966). "Equality of Educational Opportunity." U.S. Government Printing Office: Washington, D.C.

15. A more subtle measure might be the perception of individuals as to the geographic radius within which they would search for a job if they became unemployed.

16. The most scholarly rethinking has been by Peter Marcuse who finds the arguments favoring home ownership by low-income families less than compelling. See his "The Legal Attributes Of Home Ownership For Low- and Moderate-Income Families," Working Paper: 209-1-1, The Urban Institute, Washington, D.C., April 1970. Also, "The Financial Attributes of Home Ownership for Low and Moderate Income Families," Working Paper: 209-1-2, April 1972. Also, "Home Ownership for the Poor: Economic Implications for the Owner-Occupant," Working Paper: 112-26, March 10, 1971.

17. Robert Merton distinguishes racial discrimination by prejudiced persons from that practiced by individuals who are not themselves bigoted but who willingly go along with the discriminatory practices of society at large. In our terms, both of these forms would be direct and nonbenign. See Robert K. Merton (1949). Discrimination and the American creed, in R. M. MacIver, (ed.) "Discrimination and the National Welfare," New York: Institute for Religious and Social Studies.

18. This change in thinking is not universal. See Shannon v. U.S. Dept. of Housing and Urban Development, U.S. Court of Appeals, Third Circuit, 1970, 436 F. 2d 809, p. 67. It is interesting, too, since residential patterns tend to determine the racial configuration of schools, that uniform mixing in the classroom is still widely sought.

19. Chester Rapkin and William G. Grigsby (1960). "The Demand for Housing in Racially Mixed Areas," Berkeley: University of California Press.

20. A widely discussed but relatively minor villain is the family-income limit for continued occupancy in public housing.

21. Relocation adjustment payments are required under federal law, but many families move without receiving them.

22. Except to the extent that lack of security of occupancy is the independent variable leading to negative behavior.

23. See Chapters 7 and 11 for discussions of these two strategies.

24. Enunciated by Congress in the Housing and Urban Development Act of 1968.

Chapter 4

1. See in particular, "Building the American City," Report of the National Commission on Urban Problems to the Congress and to the President of the United States, U.S. Government Printing Office, Washington, D.C., 1968; and "A Decent Home, U.S. President's Committee on Urban Housing," U.S. Government Printing Office, Washington, D.C., 1968.

2. The minimum standards used in rating the inventory were actually somewhat higher than those in the city code even though the code had been enacted only a few years earlier and was widely regarded as adequate. For a description of our rating system, see Appendix D.

3.   Actually, the census-type ratings produced a slightly larger estimate of the number of substandard units than did the inspections of the 600 structures, with all of the difference being in the "Deteriorating" category. Thus our estimates of the decline in quality since 1960, since they are based on the inspections, may be viewed as conservative.

4.   Virtually all of this increase is accounted for by the particularly unfavorable experience of black renters.

5.   In 1960, there were 10,639 nonwhite families reported in Anne Arundel, Baltimore, Carroll, and Howard counties, of whom 5,701 were living in substandard dwellings. In 1970, the number of nonwhite families reported for these counties was 14,663.

6.   Obviously, the findings relating the proportion of substandard units that were occupied by low-income families is conditional upon our definition of low income. If it were reduced by $1,000, so that the cutoff point for a family of four was $4,000, three-fifths of the 65,000 households in need of a standard-quality unit would have been classified as low income. Similarly, if the income criteria had been set at $1,000 higher, on the average, fully three-fourths of the occupants of substandard housing would have been classified as low income.

7.   The figures shown in subsequent tables for number of AFDC households is 3,000 to 5,000 lower than the actual average caseload in Baltimore during 1968. Since the reported number of low-income, female-headed households does not appear low, we feel the undercount of AFDC recipients is due to reluctance on the part of the respondents to state that they were receiving public assistance, rather than to a systematic sampling error.

8.   If households living in public housing units are excluded, the risk factor for privately housed AFDC families increases to only 26%.

9.   During the second household survey, respondents were asked whether any of the following items were "big" problems: receiving enough hot water; unreliable heating system; receiving enough fuel; drafts; a leaking or clogged bathroom sink, shower, or tub; basement flooding; leaks in plumbing; poorly operating kitchen sink, stove, or refrigerator; lack of kitchen cabinet space; fuses; fires from bad wiring; leaking doors, windows, or ceilings; broken windows or lack of screens; weak or broken floors; bad stairs or railings; loose or falling plaster and paint; weak or broken porch; too hot in summer; rats and roaches.

10.   Since the 1960 Census did not subdivide the 1.01-or-more persons-per-room category for the city as a whole, it is not possible to state whether the problem of severe overcrowding improved or worsened over the decade. However, since the proportion of households with less than 1 room per person has declined somewhat since 1960, it seems reasonable to assume that the level of severe overcrowding has also diminished during the period.

11.   These figures, as well as others cited in the remainder of the section, are based upon the cases for which it was actually possible to compute the ratio of gross annual housing expense to total household income before taxes. Due to nonreporting of either income, rent, or value, the computation could be made for only 210,000 households out of a total population of 276,000 households. Although the number of households for whom these data are missing is large, with the exception of the elderly, the error does appear to be distributed more or less randomly throughout the population. Consequently, the decision was made to treat the findings for the 210,000 households as generally representative of the total population.

Also, because owner occupants were not asked in the field surveys to state their housing expenses explicitly, it was necessary to estimate this amount in order to analyze expenditure patterns for the entire population and to compare the relative positions of homeowners vs. renters. Estimates of the gross housing expenses of owner occupants were based upon both the respondent's assessment of the market value of the house and whether or not the home was mortgaged.

12. Traditionally, housing has been viewed as a necessity for which the quantity of demand changes less than proportionally in response to changes in price or income. Over the years, many analysts have used cross-sectional data to show that the percentage of current income spent for housing decreased markedly as income increases (Schwabe's Law of Rents). From this, it was generally assumed that the income elasticity of demand for housing is less than unity.

During the mid-1950's, the research of Friedman, Modigliani, and others, on the theory of the consumption function suggested that in relating income to consumption the most relevant concept of income is permanent rather than current income. This is because the income a consumer receives in a given year may differ from his expectations about his normal income level, and it is the latter that is the more important determinant of consumption patterns. Since housing consumption is particularly likely to be affected by the long-term prospect of income rather than the level for any given year, a number of analysts set out to determine the income elasticity of demand for housing using the permanent-income concept.

The initial efforts in this direction generated a considerable degree of controversy in the literature. At the start of the last decade, Maisel and Winnick analysed the results of BLS's 1950 Survey of Consumer Expenditures and found that similar elasticities were obtained regardless of whether the computation was based upon permanent or current income (Sherman J. Maisel and Louis Winnick, 1966). Family housing expenditures: Elusive laws and intrusive variances. In "Urban Housing," William L. C. Wheaton, Grace Milgram, and Margy Ellen Meyerson, (eds.). New York: The Free Press, pp. 139-153). Therefore, they concluded, the traditional view of housing consumption should be allowed to stand.

At about the same point in time, Muth performed an analysis which suggested that when permanent income is considered, the resulting elasticity is about unity (Richard F. Muth, 1960). The demand for non-farm housing. In "The Demand for Durable Goods," Arnold C. Harberger, (ed.). Chicago: University of Chicago Press, pp. 29-96). Soon thereafter, Reid put forth a position which deviated even more sharply from previous theory. Upon conducting an extensive cross-sectional study using primarily tract data from the 1950 Census of Housing, she maintained that the permanent income elasticity of housing was substantially greater than one, and in fact ranged from 1.5 to 2.0 (Margaret G. Reid, (1962). "Housing and Income," Chicago: University of Chicago Press). More recently, additional research has concluded that income elasticities are at least 1.0. See Frank de Lęeuw, (Feb. 1971). "The Demand For Housing: A Review Of Cross-Section Evidence," "The Review of Economics and Statistics," pp. 1-10. Also Richard F. Muth, (1971). "Cities and Housing," Chicago: The University of Chicago Press, pp. 199-200. Also Gunnar Du Rietz and Goran Eriksson, (1969). "Factors Determining the Demand for Housing," Translation from the IUI report, "Bostadsefterfragana bestamningsfaktorer," Stockholm, Ch. 7 and 8.

It would appear that during the past five years, several investigators have successfully refuted the dissenting claims of Muth and Reid, mainly by employing improved analytical techniques and more refined data. In 1968, Lee analyzed the 1960-1961-1962 reinterviews of the Survey of Consumer Finances and found that although the estimates of permanent income elasticity which were obtained were consistently higher than those based on current income (thus contradicting the earlier work of Maisel and Winnick), the maximum estimates of permanent income elasticity were always less than 0.9 (Tong Hun Lee, 1968). Housing and permanent income: Tests based on a three-year reinterview survey. Review of Economics and Statistics, 50:480–490. From these results, he concluded that the permanent income elasticity of housing is clearly less than unity, and that, as tradition held, the ratio of housing expense to income is lower for the rich than for the poor. Also, using data from the 1966 and 1967 Surveys of Economic Opportunity, Ohls made an extremely thorough investigation which suggested that the permanent income elasticity is 0.7, or even lower than the estimate of Lee (James C. Ohls, 1971). A Cross Section Study of Demand Functions for Housing and Policy Implications of the Results, unpublished Ph.D. dissertation, University of Pennsylvania. Also Henry J. Aaron ("Shelter and Subsidies – Who Benefits From Federal Housing Policies?," Washington, D.C.: Brookings Institution, 1972, Appendix C), using data from the BLS 1960-1961 Survey of Consumer Expenditures, and using housing expenditures rather than current measured income as an explanatory variable "because household expenditures are a better guide to permanent income than is current measured income," has calculated that "high- and low-income households on the average devote the same fraction of total outlays to housing after the influence of family size and age have been removed." Since the proportion of income that households save varies directly with permanent income, Aaron's calculation implies an income elasticity significantly less than 1.0.

The Baltimore results provide little or no evidence to support the contentions of Muth and Reid that the income elasticity of demand is unity or above. When life cycle position and household size are held constant, the pattern of expense-income ratios within cells still shows substantial decreases in the proportion of income spent on housing as income rises. It is extremely unlikely that the observed disparities could be accounted for by temporary fluctuations in income alone. Similarly, although the disparities across income groups would diminish somewhat if expense-income ratios were based on disposable rather than total household income, they would neither disappear completely nor be reversed.

It should also be pointed out that in all of the studies of income elasticity of demand for housing which have been mentioned, the investigators used a traditional definition of housing costs which did *not* include outlays for furnishings, appliances, transportation, etc. If the definition of housing expense were broadened to include these items, the patterns of allocation for upper- and lower-income families might show greater similarity since the most affluent households probably spend a larger proportion of income on such residentially related items.

13.   For a more complete discussion of this standard, see Jean C. Brackett, (April, 1969). New BLS budgets. Monthly Labor Review, 92:3-16; and Mary H. Hawes, (November, 1969). Measuring retired couples' living costs. Monthly Labor Review, 92:3-16.

14.   Some low-income families reported face rents, rather than rents actually paid, which are less. Even the lower rents, however, are usually excessive for them, so they do not distort the figures seriously. In addition to this group, many families show excessive rent-income ratios due to a temporary decline in income, but they

are probably offset in aggregate by those showing temporary increases. These fluctuations in income do suggest, however, that for families so affected, present housing subsidies may not be an appropriate remedial mechanism.

15.   The following median gross housing expense-income ratios for non-low-income households were derived empirically and were used to determine the amount which low-income families should allocate to housing: 1 person, 22%; 2 persons, 18%; 3 to 5 persons, 17%; 6-7 persons, 16%; 8 persons, 14%; 9 persons, 13%; and 10 persons or more, 12%.

16.   The 21,000 positive replies were divided more or less equally among families who considered high housing expense to be a serious problem and those who felt it was only a minor problem.

17.   There appears to be little variation in housing allocation patterns with respect to race, once differences in income are taken into account. In 1968, at any given income level, the median gross rent-income ratios for both blacks and whites fall into the same class interval. This relationship also held in 1960, although the class intervals which pertained for a given money income level were systematically lower.

18.   The three independent standards are the inspectors' ratings of dwelling unit quality, the one-room-per-person criterion for crowding, and the initial ("priority to nonhousing needs") method for measuring excessive housing expense relative to income received. With respect to the standard for the expense dimension, it is assumed that, despite some underreporting of income and overreporting of actual rental outlays, the initial method of estimation does not seriously overstate the *aggregate number* of families in need. See the qualifications in the preceding section in this regard.

Chapter 5

1.   Suzanne Keller (1968). "The Urban Neighborhood." Random House: New York. J. B. Lansing, R. W. Marans, and R. B. Zehner (1970). "Planned Residential Environments." Institute for Social Research, University of Michigan.

2.   During the course of second-survey interviews, nearly 1,000 respondents were asked whether various neighborhood services and other aspects of the residential environment were a *big* problem. Specific comments were elicited with regard to the following items: schools, public transportation, street cleaning, police protection, fire protection, condition of other housing on block, abandoned housing, littered lots, street lighting, traffic, abandoned cars, parking spaces, play areas for small children, neighborhood shopping, bars and taverns, neighbors, and robberies and other crimes. After opinions about each of these items were obtained, respondents were then asked if anything else was a big problem in the neighborhood, and if so, to describe the nature of the problem(s).

3.   Even for respondents with school-age children, the figure was not very large. It is possible that families who were most concerned about the quality of the schools had already moved to better neighborhoods.

4.   Health and Welfare Council of the Baltimore Area, Survey of Action Area Residents: Baltimore, Maryland, January, 1965. The portion of the survey which dealt with neighborhood problems was based upon a sample of 250 adults who were

living in the CAP Action Areas on blocks where in 1960 at least 30% of the families occupied dwelling units that provided less than one room per person. Among this group, six aspects of neighborhood environment were perceived as "big" problems by roughly one-half of the respondents – dirty streets and alleys (56%), no safe place for children to play (55%), rats (47%), substandard housing (45%), juvenile delinquency (44%), and too noisy to sleep (43%). In terms of types of problems identified, with the exception of rats which for our purposes were considered a dwelling unit rather than a neighborhood problem, the Health and Welfare Council Study findings correspond very closely with the results obtained from the second household survey. The higher percentage of the Health and Welfare Council Study respondents who mentioned each problem is due to the fact that their sample was drawn from the worst blocks within the area we have defined as the inner city. Taking this into account, the difference in the proportion of respondents who expressed negative attitudes is, in our view, about the level that would be expected.

5. These perceptions were not shared by the three professionals who performed the inspections of physical quality of dwelling unit and immediate residential environment. They considered streets and alleys throughout the outer city to be generally clean and parking space ample.

6. Respondents to the neighborhood-safety question included non-low-income families.

7. Peter H. Rossi (1955). "Why Families Move." The Free Press: Glencoe, Illinois, pp. 138-142.

Ronald J. McAllister, Edward J. Kaiser, and Edgar W. Butler (1971). Residential mobility of blacks and whites: A national longitudinal survey. American Journal of Sociology, 77:445-456. Figures deduced from table on p. 454.

Theodore Droettboom, Jr., Ronald J. McAllister, Edward J. Kaiser, and Edgar W. Butler (1971). Urban violence and residential mobility. Journal of the American Institute of Planners, 37:319-325.

Stanislav V. Kasl and Ernest Harburg (1972). Perceptions of the neighborhood and the desire to move out. Journal of the American Institute of Planners, 38: 318-324.

8. Similar preferences have been found to exist in at least one other city. See Nina Jaffe Gruen and Claude Gruen (1972). "Low and Moderate Income Housing in the Suburbs: An Analysis for the Dayton Ohio Region." Praeger Publishers: New York.

9. Suburban subsidies for the less affluent, non-low-income families who can afford decent housing but not new homes raise a different set of policy issues. At present, middle-income families, too, are priced out of many suburban neighborhoods. Accommodating this potential demand, however, is primarily a matter of breaking down exclusionary zoning so that single-family homes may be constructed at higher densities, and secondarily a matter of providing subsidization.

Chapter 6

1. John F. Kain and John M. Quigley (1972). Housing Market Discrimination, Home Ownership, and Savings Behavior. American Economic Review, 62:263-277.

2. Peter Marcuse (1972). The Legal Attributes of Homeownership for Low- and

Moderate-Income Families. Working Paper: 209-1-1, The Urban Institute, Washington, D.C.

3. See Chapter 9 for a discussion of this form of home financing.

Chapter 7

1. James S. Coleman, Ernest Q. Campbell, Carol J. Hobson, James McPartland, Alexander M. Mood, Frederic D. Weinfield, and Robert L. York (1966). "Equality of Educational Opportunity." U.S. Government Printing Office: Washington, D.C.

2. The most widely known fair-share plans are those in Dayton, Ohio, Washington, D.C., Minneapolis-St. Paul, and San Bernardino County, Calif., but several other metropolitan areas also have similar plans, and the number is growing. See Trends In Housing, National Committee Against Discrimination In Housing, Inc., Vol. XVI, No. 3, Fall 1972.

3. For more complete, and in places somewhat different, arguments see: Anthony Downs (Summer-Fall 1968). Alternative futures for the American ghetto, Daedalus, 97:1331-1378. Anthony Downs (1973). "Opening Up the Suburbs," Yale Univ. Press: New Haven. John F. Kain and Joseph J. Persky (Winter 1969). Alternatives to the gilded ghetto. The Public Interest, pp. 74-87.

4. Coleman, op. cit. Also Daniel U. Levine (December 1973). Racial and socioeconomic balance in the public schools. Unpublished paper, University of Missouri, Kansas City.

5. Bureau of Census, Undergraduate Enrollment in Two-Year and Four-Year Colleges, October 1970, P-20, No. 231, February 1972. U.S. Government Printing Office: Washington, 1972.

6. Life, January 21, 1972, p. 10.

7. Though the situations in which busing has produced measurable improvement merit much closer scrutiny before giving up on this approach.

8. A specific long-term plan that would have significant housing market effects is outlined in Duane L. Bay (June 1973). How schools can attack segregation at the roots. The Urban Review, 6:12-14.

9. For an elaboration of this thesis, see Daniel U. Levine (August 1970). Threshold phenomena in inner-city schools and society. Education and Urban Society, 2:347-358.

10. An additional argument has been made that certain physical illnesses to which the poor are especially susceptible, for example, tuberculosis, would be less prevalent if low-income families were dispersed, because the likelihood of communication of disease would be less. This is a public health question with which we do not feel competent to deal, though it would seem that even if the argument is correct, dispersion is not the only solution, nor necessarily the best one.

11. We also note that affluent groups have a fair amount of antisocial behavior, but it frequently isn't publicized.

12. Our survey of low-income black families in Baltimore revealed that only 7% would want to move out of the city if they had the opportunity. The corresponding figure for low-income white families is 25%.

13.   This, of course, is the very result which the recent Shannon decision (cited in Chapter 3) and subsequent HUD guidelines with respect to low- and moderate-income housing seek to avoid. The explicit assumption in the Shannon decision that "racial concentration is prima facie likely to lead to urban blight" reflects racist thinking among jurists who could hardly be classified as racists in the ordinary sense of the word, but who should know better.

14.   National Committee Against Discrimination In Housing, "Jobs And Housing," New York: 1970.
Neil N. Gold (1972). The mismatch of jobs and low-income people in metropolitan areas and its implications for the central-city poor. Population Distribution And Policy, No. 5, Part III, Ch. 4, The Commission On Population Growth And The American Future, U.S. Government Printing Office: Washington.

15.   See Sammis White (1971). The Potential of Subsidized Job Creation to Reduce Employment Deprivations at a Time of Full Aggregate Employment, unpublished doctoral dissertation, University of Pennsylvania, pp. 172-174.

16.   Persuasive evidence on this point is presented by Alexander Ganz and Thomas O'Brien, (Winter 1973). The city: Sandbox, reservation, or dynamo? Public Policy, 21:107-124. Ganz and O'Brien show that of 11 large cities (Boston, Baltimore, Denver, Minneapolis, Newark, New Orleans, New York, Philadelphia, San Francisco, St. Louis, and Washington, D.C.), all but two of which have been losing population since 1950, only Boston, Philadelphia, and St. Louis had less employment in 1967 than in any prior year, and both Boston and St. Louis appeared to be regaining their previous highs. Moreover, all cities were experiencing growing employment/population ratios.
Using Census Bureau place-of-work data for 1960 and 1970, several analysts have painted a more gloomy picture of central-city employment trends (for example, see New York Times, Oct. 15, 1972, p. 1). All other data, however, including: Bureau of Labor Statistics monthly report, Employment and Earnings, Table B-7; unpublished data of the Office of Business Economics, Dept. of Commerce; and unpublished data of the Center for Urban Policy Research, Rutgers University, contradict the Census figures.

17.   Sammis White, op. cit.

18.   J. Forrester (1969). "Urban Dynamics." MIT Press: Cambridge.

19.   More generally, the more scattered the low-income population is, the less threat its expansion poses to any one neighborhood.

20.   A. Miel (1969). The Shortchanged Children of Suburbia, Pamphlet Series #8, Institute of Human Relations Press.

21.   David W. Stroh (June 1972). "The Balanced Community: Issues and an Outline for a Research Design." Fels Center of Government, University of Pennsylvania.
"Freedom Of Choice In Housing" (1972). National Academy Of Sciences, National Academy Of Engineering, Washington, D.C.
Bruce W. Hamilton (October 1972). Zoning and property taxation in a system of local governments. Working Paper: 1207-14. The Urban Institute: Washington, D.C.

22.   In the Baltimore area, the minimum cost for a new Section 235 owner-occupied unit is over $6,000 higher than the median value of all owner-occupied, single-family dwellings in the SMSA in 1970. Moreover, the owner of such a unit continues to receive a subsidy until his income rises to the upper-quartile of the income distribution.

23.   Irving H. Welfeld (Spring 1970). Toward a new housing policy. The Public Interest, No. 19, p. 41.

24.   Ernest M. Fisher (January 1960). "A Study of Housing Programs and Policies." Housing And Home Finance Agency, Washington, D.C. Mimeo.

Chapter 8

1.   The expression "at least code level" is used because major and intermediate treatment would automatically bring the affected units well above minimal code standards.

2.   Some of these households no doubt are experiencing only a temporary rise in income, but they are at least partially offset by similarly housed families who have underreported their incomes and by poorly housed families who have suffered a temporary drop in income.

3.   The distribution of payments within the housing-deprived population would probably be altered if an effort of this type were actually implemented. Although the average of $800 per recipient might not change much, the amount received by a given family would obviously vary significantly depending upon both the amount of income which it has available for housing and the cost of the unit which it would occupy under the program. Because of ordinary mobility and normal operations of public programs, the pattern of occupancy could be quite different from that which is assumed under our "instantaneous" solution. Although the actual number of instances might be few, the largest individual payment would still be in the $3,500-$4,000 range. This would occur when a large family which can afford little or nothing for housing were placed in a newly constructed unit.

4.   A small amount of overcrowding will also be eliminated as a consequence of the declining birth rate.

5.   In designing the Housing Allowance Supply Experiment for the Department of HUD, Rand Corporation has estimated that a 60–70% participation rate seems reasonable to expect. See Barbara M. Woodfill, Tiina Repnau, and Ira S. Lowry (September 1973). Estimates Of Eligibility, Enrollment, And Allowance Payments In Green Bay And Saginaw: 1974-1979. WN-8439-HUD, Rand.

6.   This figure does *not* include housing subsidies which are received by non-low-income families. Schorr and Aaron, among others, have argued that tax advantages granted to homeowners result in substantial subsidies to middle- and upper-income families and may be viewed as the federal government's largest direct subsidy for housing. Whether, strictly speaking, these privileges should be considered housing subsidies is a matter of debate. A detailed analysis of either the level of subsidization for housing of non-low-income families in the Baltimore region or the distributional effects of housing subsidy pattern across income groups is beyond the scope of this study. For discussions of these issues at the national level, see Alvin L. Schorr, National community and housing policy, in "Urban Planning and Social Policy." Edited by Bernard J. Frieden and Robert Morris. Basic Books: New York, 1968, pp. 107-118; and Henry J. Aaron, "Shelter and Subsidies." Brookings Institution: Washington, 1972.
A very crude estimate based on Aaron's figures for national averages of per family tax savings of homeowners by income class suggests that, in the Baltimore metropolitan area, federal income tax deductions for interest on home mortgages and payments for real estate taxes result in aggregate savings of $40 million annually. Allowance for the fact that imputed rent of owner-occupied dwellings does not

have to be reported for federal income tax purposes results in an additional savings of approximately $60 million per year. Of the total estimated savings of $100 million for the Baltimore area, less than 5% would accrue to families with incomes under $5,000 per year.

7.   The inclusion of housing code enforcement is problematic. Prior to the enactment of the Workable Program requirements in the Housing Act of 1954, the vast majority of cities either did not have codes or did not enforce them. Also, in instances where codes were enforced, the net effect was often reduction, rather than upgrading, of the existing inventory.

8.   The Federal Rent Supplement Program provides funds which enable households with incomes below public housing admissions limits to occupy units developed under the Section 202, 221 (d)(3), 231, and 236 programs. Also, rent supplements are now available to public housing occupants whose gross rental expense exceeds 25% of income (minus allowances). Section 235 and 236 superseded Section 221 (d)(3) and 221 (h).

9.   Primarily an administrative regulation prohibiting the development of high rise apartment projects for occupancy by families with children.

10.   For purposes herein, modest rehabilitation is defined as improvements costing up to $3,500 per unit including overhead, in 1969 dollars.

11.   For a more detailed description of Baltimore's experience under the federally assisted code enforcement program, see Gordon Liechty (August 1968). Housing Code Enforcement: The Baltimore Experience. Baltimore CAP Evaluation Project, Working Paper No. 3, Institute For Environmental Studies, University of Pennsylvania.

12.   Baltimore City Department of Housing and Community Development, "1969 Annual Report," pp. 24-25.

13.   In their "purest" forms, demand-side interventions provide resources which are not tied directly to specific dwelling units in the stock. Characteristics of demand-side interventions which have relevance for policy analysis include: (a) type of resources provided (e.g., financial, informational, educational, etc.), (b) method providing the resources (e.g., direct payment to households, indirect payment via tax credits, etc.), (c) degree of choice afforded the household in expending the resources and selecting a dwelling unit, (d) relationship of the resources provided to household income (i.e., whether the resources supplement income or are part of the household's regular source of income), and (e) extent to which the household is guaranteed a standard unit as a result of the assistance.

14.   These figures exclude the average annual number of children receiving foster care, which increased over the period from 3,450 to 4,850.

15.   Data obtained from Department of Social Services, City of Baltimore, Statements of Expenditures and Case Statistics, Calendar Year 1960 and Fiscal Year 1968-69. In the AFDC category, average grant per case per month increased in real dollars by only 15% (no account taken of changes in average family size).

16.   Data on actual housing expenditures (as opposed to shelter grants) are not recorded by the Department of Social Services (DSS). For a description of the procedure used to arrive at this estimate, see Table 8.4, Ref. 4.

17.   For details on the quality of housing occupied by public-assistance families, see Chapter 4.

18.   The "bonus payment" is not to exceed $5,000, and may be made to owner occupants displaced from one- and two-family dwellings when the acquisition price is less than the average price required for a decent, safe, and sanitary dwelling of modest standards and adequate in size and location for the displaced household.

19. An income limit of $5,000 is used to determine eligibility.

20. Ideally, in arriving at an estimate of the current annual level of subsidy associated with the low-income housing effort in Baltimore, data would be gathered on actual costs incurred during a given one-year period. Unfortunately, this proved impossible due to the variation in budgeting procedures and funding periods of the many public and private organizations that are engaged in the low-income housing effort. As a compromise solution, an estimate has been derived from a collection of data covering various one-year intervals during the three-year period 1967-1969 (in a few instances figures for fiscal year 1966-67 are used). Table 8.4, therefore, sets forth an estimate of the *average* annual subsidy for improving the housing opportunities of low-income families during the period 1967-1969, rather than the amount for a specific calendar year. For a detailed description of data source and estimating procedures, see footnotes to Table 8.4.

21. For the conceptual definition of the larger anti-poverty effort employed in this comparison, see Pao-Yu-Chou (1968). The Level of Effort in the Anti-Poverty System in Baltimore, Baltimore CAP Evaluation Project Working Paper No. 6, Institute For Environmental Studies, University Of Pennsylvania. The discussion of the relationship between the housing and anti-poverty efforts is based upon earlier estimates covering the period 1966-67. During these years, the annual aggregate housing subsidy was $33 million and the subsidy for the total anti-poverty effort was $127 million.

Chapter 9

1. Much of the data for this chapter came from our survey of investor-owners. See Appendix C for a description of the survey.

2. For the purposes of this portion of the study, the inner city of Baltimore was re-defined. It may be remembered from Chapter 2 that the inner city was originally delineated as a contiguous group of census tracts that were characterized in 1960 by low family incomes and poor housing. Such a procedure is inappropriate for a study of market dynamics because it fails to consider the perceptions of either investors or families seeking housing. Therefore, rather than simply drawing in the boundaries of the so-called least desirable neighborhoods in the city, an attempt was made, with the help of investors, to identify those areas in which the problems of housing decay and neighborhood deterioration were of most concern, and to envelop those areas in an inner city. This approach resulted in an inner-city area somewhat larger than our original one.

3. Frank S. Kristof (1970). Housing: The economic facets of New York City's problems, in "Agenda for a City," L. Fitch and A. Walsh, editors, Institute of Public Administration. Sage Publications: New York.

4. Ibid.

5. Jason R. Nathan, former New York City Administrator of Housing and Development, quoted in Associated Press story by Terri Shaw, Durham Morning Herald, December 1, 1969.

6. Of a random sample of 85 inner-city residential properties drawn from "Lusk's Baltimore City Real Estate Directory: 1969 Property Transfers" (Rufus S. Lusk and Sons, 1970), 60% were sold for prices below their assessed value.

7. "Minimum code" was defined in this study to include central heating and new

interior paint and floor covering where appropriate. The present code is somewhat equivocal with respect to these items.

8.   George Sternlieb (1966). "The Tenement Landlord," Urban Studies Center, Rutgers, New Brunswick, New Jersey.

9.   At various points along the size scale, investors start to resemble managers of any other business organization rather than property managers. The quality of landlord-tenant relations in these situations depends on the attitudes and behavior of subordinates which in turn are a function of staffing and training by top management.

10.   The Property Owners Association, the professional organization to which most of the major inner-city investors belong, co-sponsors with the city's Department of Housing and Community Development a management clinic, the purpose of which is to upgrade the management skills of smaller investors.

11.   Another study has concluded that effective tax rate is even higher than 5% and that a similar situation prevails in other cities as well. See Arthur D. Little, Inc., A Study of Property Taxes and Urban Blight. Report to the U.S. Department of Housing And Urban Development, January 1973.

12.   Facts which HUD, to its great misfortune, failed to recognize in connection with its Section 236 subsidized rental projects.

13.   In Philadelphia, for example, where entire blocks have been observed to become abandoned in as little as two or three years, some institutional lenders who have acquired properties by foreclosure in bad neighborhoods are said to be pursuing policies of undermaintenance in an effort to get some of their capital back before the neighborhoods are abandoned. They do not attempt to lengthen their income stream through adequate maintenance, because they expect that, regardless of their actions, the end of the neighborhoods is at hand.

14.   Some of which investors claim would have soon been spent anyway in the absence of any inspection.

15.   Frank de Leeuw (1970). "Operating Costs in Public Housing: A Financial Crisis," The Urban Institute: Washington, D.C.

16.   A similar situation has been found to exist in New York City where "most buildings which house a great many welfare tenants are in the hands of small-scale owners who have, at most, one or two additional parcels." George S. Sternlieb and Bernard P. Indik (1973). "The Ecology of Welfare: Housing and the Welfare Crisis in New York City," Transaction Books: New Brunswick, New Jersey.

17.   Harris Chaiklin, Richard Sterne, and Paul H. Ephross (1969). "Community Organization and Services to Improve Family Living–II." University of Maryland School of Social Work Research Center, p. 5.

18.   Ibid.

19.   "Community Organization and Services to Improve Family Living." Community Relations Division of the Baltimore City Department of Social Services, March 1968, p. 16.

20.   Ibid., p. 17.

21.   See our discussion of poor housekeeping in Chapter 4. Also Melvin R. Levin (editor) (1969). "Innovations in Housing Rehabilitation." Boston University Urban Institute, Monograph 2, p. 14.

22.   Chaiklin, H., et al., op. cit., p. 36.

23.   Other studies have found that the proportion of involuntary moves for all reasons is much higher. See: Lenora E. Berson (December 1967). "The Dispossessed: A Study of Involuntary Mobility Among Philadelphia's Low-Income Families,"

Philadelphia Housing Association, pp. 2–3. Also Louis S. Rosenberg (1973). New Perspectives on Housing Need: A Case Study of the Low-Income Housing Problem in Baltimore, Maryland, unpublished Ph.D. dissertation, University of Pennsylvania. Peter H. Rossi (1955). "Why Families Move," The Free Press: Glencoe, Ill., pp. 134-136.

Ronald J. McAllister, Edward J. Kaiser, and Edgar W. Butler (1971). Residential mobility of blacks and whites: A national longitudinal survey, American Journal of Sociology, 77:452.

24. Chester Rapkin (1959). "The Real Estate Market in an Urban Renewal Area," New York City Planning Commission: New York, p. 44.

25. Ibid.

26. Annotated Code of Maryland, Article 21, Section 110.

27. The same argument has been made by others. See Frederick E. Case (editor) (1972). "Inner-City Housing and Private Enterprise: Based on Studies in Nine Cities," Praeger: New York, p. 1.

28. The Maryland legislature has created such a program, but it is not yet fully operative. Somewhat similar programs exist in Fresno, Pittsburgh, and New York City.

Chapter 10

1. William G. Grigsby (1963). "Housing Markets and Public Policy," University of Pennsylvania Press: Philadelphia, p. 277.

Richard F. Muth (1970). "Cities and Housing," The University Of Chicago Press: Chicago and London, p. 126.

Jerome Rothenberg (1967). "Economic Evaluation of Urban Renewal," The Brookings Institution: Washington, D.C., p. 37.

Wallace F. Smith (1970). "Housing," University of California Press: Berkeley and Los Angeles, California, p. 85.

None of these authors allege that low income is the only cause of bad housing conditions.

2. Indeed, occupancy of poor housing may constitute a better measure of poverty than low income at a point in time.

3. We return to this point later in the chapter.

4. A related racial image, one which is not in the realm of housing but which has important implications for housing policy, is that *de facto* segregation in the schools leads to inferior education, primarily because it has the effect of separating children by socioeconomic class. Children from the lower socioeconomic groups, in this case primarily blacks, are said to do better if they are mixed in with children from upper-class homes than if they are concentrated together. James S. Coleman, Ernest Q. Campbell, Carol J. Hobson, James McPartland, Alexander M. Mood, Frederic D. Weinfield, and Robert L. York, (1966). "Equality of Educational Opportunity," U.S. Government Printing Office, Washington, D.C. This image would demand more than simply an open housing market; heterogeneity within neighborhoods would be the goal.

5. George Sternlieb. The city as sandbox; and Norton E. Long, (Fall, 1971). The city as reservation. The Public Interest, No. 25, pp. 14-38.

Anthony Downs (1973). "Opening Up the Suburbs," Yale University Press: New Haven and London, pp. 115-130.

Daniel U. Levine (August 1970). Threshold phenomena in inner-city schools and society, Education And Urban Society, 2:347-359.

6. Ingram and Kain carry this distinction further by suggesting that structures which have deteriorated to the point where they are no longer useable and must be withdrawn from the inventory are "scrapped" not "abandoned." Gregory K. Ingram and John F. Kain, A Simple Model of Housing Production and the Abandonment Problem. Paper presented at a Joint Session of the American Economic Association and the American Real Estate and Urban Economics Association, Toronto, Canada, December 30, 1972.

7. George Sternlieb (March 1972). Abandoned housing, Urban Land, 31:4.

8. One study looked at a working-class neighborhood with homes in the $5,000-$9,000 range (as compared with a city median of $10,700), and the other at a middle-class area with dwellings valued from $7,000 to $16,000. Both study areas had a very high rate of owner occupancy (over 70%), had recently experienced rapid racial transition, and had abandonment rates of under 2%. Sandra Featherman, A Profile Of Early Abandonment, unpublished paper, Institute For Environmental Studies, University of Pennsylvania, 1973. The Allegheny West Community Development Project, A Report Prepared for the Department Of Housing And Urban Development, Institute for Environmental Studies, University of Pennsylvania, 1973.

9. Grigsby, op. cit., pp. 247-248. Also Chester Rapkin and William G. Grigsby (1960). "The Demand For Housing In Eastwick," Institute For Urban Studies, University of Pennsylvania, pp. 38-39.

10. Chapter 4.

Chapter 11

1. A small number are in renewal areas awaiting demolition by the city.

2. The equivalent national figure today (1974) is roughly $7 billion, assuming Baltimore's housing problems are not appreciably more or less serious than those in the country as a whole. One study, however, concludes that the housing situation in Baltimore is better than that in all but one central city in the 30 largest urban areas in the United States. See City housing, Municipal Performance Report, Vol. 1, No. 2., November 1973, Table 2, page 7. We feel that Baltimore's ranking may reflect serious imperfections in published housing data.

3. Over 4,000 welfare families in public housing would not qualify, and probably an equal number of households in which only one member is a welfare recipient would be excluded.

4. Unpublished data, Department of Planning, City of Baltimore.

5. Before we liberalized our low-income definition to include 20,000 additional households. See Chapter 2.

6. See Chapter 5.

7. Assuming an average dwelling-unit value of $20,000, an average gross rent multiplier of 6:1, and an average family contribution of $800 per year.

8. Charles L. Schultze, Edward R. Fried, Alice M. Rivlin, Nancy H. Teeter (1972). "Setting National Priorities, The 1973 Budget," The Brookings Institution, Washington, D.C.

9.   A number of persons have argued that most housing subsidies go to the nonpoor in the form of favorable tax treatment of owner-occupied housing. In their view a large increase in low-income housing programs would simply equalize subsidies across income groups. Such reasoning fails to recognize that if the tax benefits to homeowners were removed, there would almost certainly be a concomitant adjustment in basic tax schedules, leaving the relative tax situation of the poor and nonpoor virtually unchanged.

Chapter 12

1.   To our knowledge the first extended argument *for* modest rehabilitation appears in Charles Abrams (December 1966). The Negro Housing Problem: A Program For Philadelphia. CRP Technical Report No. 18, City of Philadelphia. Several of Abrams' other recommendations in that report parallel those in this volume.
2.   This approach is being taken in a maximum-rehabilitation program launched by the City of Philadelphia in the Fall of 1973.
3.   For a more optimistic view of a special form of urban homesteading, see Robert Kolodny (September 1973). Self Help in the Inner City, United Neighborhood Houses of New York, Inc., New York City.
4.   John Kenneth Galbraith (1970). "Who Needs the Democrats." New York: Signet.
5.   See, for example, bill (S.4181) introduced in the 91st Congress (2nd session) by Senators Goodell and Brooke to establish "community oriented and sponsored non-profit organizations" to provide housing management services in declining neighborhoods.
6.   As one example which was reported to us, a tenant organization in the Bronx, after several of its warnings to a family not to place garbage in the hallway went unheeded, put a large pile of garbage in the family's apartment. That ended the problem. Obviously this type of action could not be taken by a municipal agency or a landlord.
7.   One apparently successful public housing model is the Bromley-Heath Tenant Management Corporation in Boston.
8.   A failure which merits close examination has occurred in the otherwise successful Roland Park subdivision in northwest Baltimore. The maintenance clause in the deed does not have an escalation provision to allow for inflation, is cumbersome to enforce, and does not protect owners adequately against possible mismanagement. A better arrangement would be to specify the services to be performed and a procedure for contracting out the work on a low-bid basis. For a detailed treatment of how maintenance responsibilities might be organized and managed by a neighborhood corporation, see Jan Krasnowiecki, Model State Housing Societies Law, U.S. Dept. of HEW, Public Health Service Publication No. 2025, U.S. Government Printing Office, 1970.
9.   See "The Allegheny West Community Development Project," Institute for Environmental Studies, University of Pennsylvania, April 1973.
10. In this respect we differ sharply from those who feel that "the legal relationship between landlords and tenants is an outmoded, unworkable, and mischievous anachronism that is dangerously maladjusted to the social, economic, and political needs of an urban democracy . . ." Jerome G. Rose (1973). "Landlords and

Tenants," New Brunswick: Transaction Books; distributed by E. P. Dutton and Co., p. 2. See also Emily Jane Goodman (1973). "The Tenant Survival Book" New York: Bobbs-Merrill.

11.   This has been found to be the case in other cities as well. See M. Isler, M. Drury, and C. Wellborn, "Housing Management: A Progress Report," Working Paper 112-27. The Urban Institute, Washington, D.C., 1970.

12.   Statistics on interurban migration of low-income families suggest moreover that there would be very few walk-aways as a result of moves from one community to another in pursuit of job opportunities.

13.   For a discussion of other forms of counseling which lower-income families might require as well as a description of all aspects of an experimental home-ownership program, see Elizabeth Eudey (December 1970). "A Move To Home Ownership," San Francisco Development Fund.

14.   John Kenower (September 1969). A Case Study in Housing Rehabilitation Through Non-Profit Sponsorship. MICAH, State of Rhode Island, Department of Community Affairs, Providence, p. 7.

15.   Such a fund has been created in Maryland, but exactly how it will be administered is still uncertain.

16.   The results of the vacant-house maximum-rehabilitation programs in several cities are witness to this fact.

17.   See Alex Henney (February 1973). Managing older housing areas. Journal of the Royal Town Planning Institute, pp. 73-77.

18.   For a description of one better than average program see, The Allegheny West Community Development Project, op. cit.

19.   For an interesting example, see Baltimore Evening Sun, April 22, 1970, p. F-1.

20.   This may sound platitudinous, but in many blocks we observed this extra effort being exerted — residents sweeping sidewalks and streets, cleaning alleys, etc. In areas where both parents in many of the families are employed, few persons may have the extra free time needed to help maintain the environment.

21.   Some favorable effects of a quite modest youth employment program are reported in The Allegheny West Community Development Project, op. cit.

22.   This figure is the inner-city share of the estimates, presented earlier, of $10.5 million for upgrading and $8 million for housing allowances and leased housing. It is arbitrarily assumed that about one-quarter of the public expenditures for housing allowances and leased housing are diverted away from housing by recipients and landlords.

23.   Maryland, New York City, Pittsburgh, Fresno, and possibly, by now, several other cities and states have their own such programs, but FHA still dwarfs them all.

24.   The figure of $150 follows from our finding, discussed in Chapter 9, that the shortfall between actual and adequate maintenance expenditures is usually not more than $100 per year.

25.   See Chapter 9.

26.   The figure of $35 million is based on the $40 million estimate presented in Chapter 4, but assumes a 70% participation rate among eligible families, with the rate of participation varying inversely with family income. Approximately the same figure was obtained using assumptions similar to those used by the RAND Corporation in its design of the Housing Allowance Supply Experiment for the Department of Housing And Urban Development. See Tiina Repnau and Barbara M. Woodfill (March 1973). Additional Estimates Of Enrollment And Allowance

Payments Under A National Housing Allowance Program. WN-8167-HUD, Rand, Santa Monica, Calif. Also Frank de Leeuw (1971). The Housing Allowance Approach, Papers submitted to Subcommittee On Housing Panels On Housing Production, Housing Demand, and Developing a Suitable Living Environment, Part 2, Committee On Banking And Currency, House Of Representatives, 92nd Congress, First Session, USGPO, Washington, 1971, pp. 546-547.

Enrollment rates in several of the housing allowance experiments suggest that our assumed 70% participation rate may be too high and that a 60% rate may be more likely. Again, however, if participation rates vary inversely with income, the cost of the program would be reduced less than proportionately, so would be unlikely to drop below $30 million, or $6 billion nationally.

27. See Chapter 9.

28. See Chapters 4 and 9. Also, Walter Smart, Walter Rybeck, and Howard E. Shuman (1968). The Large Poor Family – A Housing Gap. Research Report No. 4, The National Commission On Urban Problems, Washington, D.C. Also Frank de Leeuw and Sam H. Leaman (November 24, 1971). The Section 23 Leasing Program. Working Paper 716-1, The Urban Institute, Washington, D.C.

29. Unless it made welfare so attractive as to cause a substantial increase in the number of recipients, a doubtful possibility.

30. Homestead exemptions, abatements for the elderly, and abatements for rehabilitation and new construction have already altered the real estate tax structure in several states and localities.

31. Unpublished data supplied by Arthur Solomon, Joint Center For Urban Studies Of The Massachusetts Institute Of Technology And Harvard University. The Kansas City experience will probably prove to be fairly typical. In cases where housing is not in very bad condition (and especially where most of the defects are on the exterior and thus of no great concern to rental occupants) and where the neighborhoods in which the housing is located are reasonably satisfactory, the only incentive for families to enroll in a housing-allowance program may be the opportunity to ease their rent burden.

32. In this connection, it should be noted that to participate in a program of housing allowances, some low-income families would have to increase the proportion of their own income spent for shelter and thus might have their total welfare position worsened even though their housing situation had improved.

33. Curiously, similar concern has seldom been expressed over the potential inflationary effects of supply-side interventions. A detailed discussion of these effects appears in Henry B. Schechter (October 15, 1971). Federally Subsidized Housing. Congressional Research Service, Library of Congress. See also D. Belsley, R. Kuh, and L. Thurow (August 1970). Macro-Economic Study Prepared for the Urban Coalition Housing Task Force, Urban Coalition, Washington, D.C. James R. Cooper (1971). Can the 1968-78 National Housing Goals Be Achieved. Committee On Housing Research And Development, University Of Illinois At Urbana-Champaign.

34. ". . . changes in nonsubsidized starts work to offset just over 85% of changes in subsidized starts." Craig Swan (1973). Housing subsidies and housing starts. American Real Estate And Urban Economics Journal, 1:134.

35. The Civil Rights Act of 1968 does not prohibit discrimination in the sale or rental of housing by owners of three or fewer dwelling units if the units are not offered · on the open market through the use of newspaper advertising, for-sale signs,

brokers, etc. The Act also does not prohibit discrimination in the rental of housing by owner occupants of multifamily structures containing four or fewer dwelling units.

36. Home Ownership and the Baltimore Mortgage Market, Department of Housing and Community Development, City of Baltimore, Oct. 1973. See also John F. McDonald (March 1974). Housing market discrimination, homeownership and savings behavior: Comment and reply by John F. Kain and John M. Quigley. American Economic Review, 64:225-231.

37. Raymond Skinner (June 1972). The Growth of the Black Suburban Population in the Philadelphia Metropolitan Area, Fels Center Of Government, University Of Pennsylvania, June 1972.
Mark Keintz, "Black Residential Patterns In The Philadelphia SMSA /And Urbanized Area, 1970," Fels Center Of Government, University Of Pennsylvania, September 1972.

38. An acre of land with 20 $6,000 row homes on it, for example, could only be superceded by new housing that would bid at least $120,000 for a parcel of this size. Typically, nothing but luxury town houses or high-rise apartments would compete for such expensive acreage, and then only if it were very well situated and could be easily acquired.

39. See Exhibit 3, Myths/realities of urban renewal. Journal of Housing, No. 5, May 1973, page 171. The Exhibit, from Table 38 of the 1971 Statistical Yearbook of the Department of Housing and Urban Development, indicates that aggregate federal grants for urban renewal through December 1971 vary from over $200 per capita for communities with populations of less than 25,000 down to about $50 for cities of 1 million or more.

Chapter 13

1. It will be observed that the definition of modest rehabilitation which is used here differs from the one used in earlier chapters. The change was made only to facilitate the present analysis, and in no way does it have the effect of altering or contradicting any of the findings or conclusions which have already been presented.

2. A. H. Schaaf (November 1969). Economic feasibility analysis for urban renewal housing rehabilitation. Journal of the American Institute of Planners, pp. 399-404.

3. The illustrative cost figures are actually the maxima for each category, including overhead. Using the maximum limits somewhat understates the potential of rehabilitation in each category.

4. Or in choosing which structures should receive priority and which of several post-renewal quality standards are most appropriate for a given unit. In our study, resources did not permit analysis of the relative economic feasibility of various possible levels of upgrading for each structure.

5. Some of the criticism has been of the choices of which structures to include in the maximum-rehabilitation effort, not of maximum rehabilitation itself, but as in most controversies, the issues have become blurred. For reasons already discussed, maximum-rehabilitation should commence first in the better blocks, usually at the fringe of the inner city where only one or two bad structures threaten otherwise stable environments. This approach has generally not been emphasized because of the relatively greater ease with which structures in poor neighborhoods can be acquired.

6. The paint-up/fix-up and minor rehabilitation figures, except those for the city and for nonprofit corporations, assume that the activity would be undertaken by force-account labor without government subsidy. Use of independent contractors would increase costs by 15%; however, wherever a public program provides assistance, total costs can be expected to rise by up to 50%.
7. In many cases, shares in the partnership could be used as payment. Administrative and related costs of acquisition in the inner city are equivalent to a 10% down payment and are capitalized in this illustration.

Chapter 14

1. P. Marcuse (December 1971). Social indicators and housing policy. Urban Affairs Quarterly, 7:214.
2. In our discussions, neighborhood environment and the investment climate were handled as a single topic as were modest rehabilitation, maximum rehabilitation, and new construction. Housing allowances were not explored separately. Instead, the conversations proceeded on the prior assumption that an expansion of subsidies in some form would be necessary to close the low-income gap. Views regarding the size of the gap were not solicited, and our specific estimates, though presented, were not part of the deliberations.
3. Jay W. Forrester (1969). "Urban Dynamics." Cambridge: The MIT Press.

Index

333